**international
review of
social history**

Special Issue 23

Migration and Ethnicity in Coalfield History: Global Perspectives

Edited by Ad Knotter and David Mayer

Shaftesbury Road, Cambridge CB2 8EA, United Kingdom

One Liberty Plaza, 20th Floor, New York, NY 10006, USA

477 Williamstown Road, Port Melbourne, VIC 3207, Australia

314–321, 3rd Floor, Plot 3, Splendor Forum, Jasola District Centre, New Delhi – 110025, India

103 Penang Road, #05–06/07, Visioncrest Commercial, Singapore 238467

Cambridge University Press is part of Cambridge University Press & Assessment, a department of the University of Cambridge.

We share the University's mission to contribute to society through the pursuit of education, learning and research at the highest international levels of excellence.

www.cambridge.org
Information on this title: www.cambridge.org/9781316601303

A catalogue record for this publication is available from the British Library

ISBN   978-1-316-60130-3   Paperback

Cambridge University Press & Assessment has no responsibility for the persistence or accuracy of URLs for external or third-party internet websites referred to in this publication and does not guarantee that any content on such websites is, or will remain, accurate or appropriate.

SUBSCRIPTIONS
International Review of Social History (ISSN 0020–8590) is published in three parts in April, August and December plus one special issue in December. Three parts plus one special issue form a volume. The subscription price (excluding VAT) of volume 60 (2015) which includes electronic access and delivery by air where appropriate is £199 net (US$338 in the USA, Canada and Mexico) for institutions; £53 net (US$85 in the USA, Canada and Mexico) for individuals ordering direct from the publisher and certifying that the journal is for their own personal use. Single parts and the special issue are £54 (US$91 in the USA, Canada and Mexico) plus postage. An electronic only price available to institutional subscribers is £160 (US$276 in USA, Canada and Mexico). EU subscribers (outside the UK) who are not registered for VAT should add VAT at their country's rate. VAT registered subscribers should provide their VAT registration number. Japanese prices for institutions are available from Kinokuniya Company Ltd, P.O. Box 55, Chitose, Tokyo 156, Japan.

Orders, which must be accompanied by payment, may be sent to a bookseller, subscription agent or direct to the publisher: Cambridge University Press, Journals Fulfillment Department, UPH, Shaftesbury Road, Cambridge CB2 8BS, UK; or in the USA, Canada and Mexico: Cambridge University Press, Journals Fulfillment Department, 100 Brook Hill Drive, West Nyack, New York 10994–2133. Periodicals postage paid at New York, NY and at additional mailing offices. Postmaster: send address changes in USA, Canada and Mexico to International Review of Social History, Cambridge University Press, 100 Brook Hill Drive, West Nyack, New York 10994–2133.

Information on International Review of Social History and all other Cambridge journals can be accessed via journals.cambridge.org

COPYING

GUIDELINES FOR CONTRIBUTORS

Submission of an article is taken to imply that it has not previously been published and is not being considered for publication elsewhere. Authors are also asked to provide brief details of any book they are publishing which includes all or part of a submitted article. Articles should be submitted in two paginated versions as soft copy (preferably by e-mail), one version containing the author's details, the other anonymized as far as possible, in order to facilitate "blind" refereeing. Authors should also include an abstract not exceeding 150 words, specifying the principal conclusion and methods in the context of currently accepted views on the subject. The files should be saved either in a recent version of MSWord for Windows, or in an MSWord compatible format, or as a PDF file. In case of doubt, please contact the editorial staff at: irsh@iisg.nl. Footnote commands should be used to create footnotes. Notes should be confined, as far as possible, to necessary references.

Manuscripts should be in British English (or American English for American authors). In cases where no English text can be provided, authors should *always* contact the executive editor before submitting an article.

Sample citation forms

Book: E.P. Thompson, *The Making of the English Working Class* (London, 1963), pp. 320–322.
Journal: Walter Galenson, "The Unionization of the American Steel Industry", *International Review of Social History*, 1 (1956), pp. 8–40.
Detailed instructions for contributors are available from http://socialhistory.org/en/irsh-instructions-contributors. It is essential that contributors observe the journal's stylistic conventions closely. If not, their articles may be returned for amendment.

DISCLAIMER

The Internationaal Instituut voor Sociale Geschiedenis (IISG) has used its best endeavours to ensure that the URLs for external websites referred to in this journal are correct and active at the time of going to press. However, the IISG has no responsibility for the websites and can make no guarantee that a site will remain live or that the content is or will remain appropriate.

Every effort has been made to trace all copyright holders, but if any have been inadvertently overlooked the Internationaal Instituut voor Sociale Geschiedenis (IISG) will be pleased to include any necessary credits in any subsequent issue.

CONTENTS

Migration and Ethnicity in Coalfield History:
Global Perspectives

Edited by
Ad Knotter and David Mayer

IRSH 60 (2015), Special Issue, pp. 1–11 doi:10.1017/S0020859015000450
© 2015 Internationaal Instituut voor Sociale Geschiedenis

Introduction

AD KNOTTER

Sociaal Historisch Centrum voor Limburg at Maastricht University
Sint-Pieterstraat 7, 6211 JM Maastricht, The Netherlands

E-mail: a.knotter@maastrichtuniversity.nl

DAVID MAYER

International Institute of Social History
Cruquiusweg 31, 1019 AT Amsterdam, The Netherlands

E-mail: david.mayer@iisg.nl

ABSTRACT: This introduction presents the main topics and analytical concerns of the contributions to this Special Issue about ethnicity and migration in coalfield history in a global perspective. From the nineteenth century the development of industrial and transport technologies required the supply of coal-based energy in every part of the world. Nineteenth- and early twentieth-century globalization, including colonialism, would not have been possible without coal. Coalmining operations were launched in all world regions, and to enable exploitation mine operators had to find, mobilize, and direct workers to the mining sites. This quest for labour triggered a series of migration processes (both from nearby and far away) and resulted in a broad array of labour relations (both free and unfree). This introduction points to the variety of constellations analysed in the different contributions to this Special Issue. These cover cases from Africa (Nigeria, Zimbabwe), Asia (China, Japan), the Americas (USA, Brazil), Turkey, the Soviet Union, and western Europe (France, Germany), and a broad range of topics, from segregation, forced labour, and subcontracting to labour struggles, discrimination, ethnic paternalism, and sport.

Between the Spitsbergen (Svalbard) islands (Norway) in the far north, South Island (New Zealand) in the far south, Vancouver Island (Canada) in the far west, and the island of Hokkaidō (Japan) in the far east, coalmining has been (and in fact still is) a truly global industry.[1] From the nineteenth

---

1. Cameron C. Hartnell, "Arctic Network Builders: The Arctic Coal Company's Operations on Spitsbergen and Its Relationship with the Environment" (Ph.D. dissertation, Michigan Technological University 2009), available at: http://digitalcommons.mtu.edu/cgi/viewcontent.cgi?article=1288&context=etds, last accessed 6 August 2015; Louwrens Hacquebord (ed.),

century the development of industrial and transport technologies required the supply of coal-based energy in every part of the world, and to provide this energy coalmining expanded globally. In several of the grand interpretations of the emergence of modern industrial capitalism and the rise of the West, coal is thus a decisive factor.[2]

Nineteenth- and early twentieth-century globalization, including colonialism, depended to a great extent on a transport and industrial revolution, based on coal as a supplier of energy. The Suez Canal, for instance, both instrument and symbol of colonialism, is scarcely imaginable without steamships, and of course there were no steamships without coal. The same holds for railways all over the world, which, together with steamships, formed the infrastructure of colonialism. The exploitation of coalmines expanded with rising energy needs in transport and industry. Wherever in the world coal was found, even in the most desolate and remote areas, mines were opened, and to enable exploitation mine operators had to find, mobilize, and direct workers to these sites. The urgent quest for labour to work in a hostile and "alien" environment characterizes the history of coalmining everywhere and drove varying constellations of labour relations, migration, and ethnicity.

These salient features of coalmining have generated a great deal of research, especially in labour history. For a considerable time, these histories have helped to perpetuate rather than question the myths around coalmining. It was only after the decline of the industry in the countries of the Global North and after a series of conceptual commotions within the historical sciences that more critical assessments and new approaches began to appear. One of the myths to be deconstructed was the common saying that "everybody was black down there".[3] In histories of coalmining communities and

Lashipa: History of Large Scale Resource Exploration in Polar Areas (Groningen, 2012); Len Richardson, *Coal, Class and Community: The United Mineworkers of New Zealand, 1880–1960* (Auckland, 1995); John Douglas Belshaw, *Colonization and Community: The Vancouver Island Coalfield and the Making of the British Columbian Working Class* (Montreal, 2002); Suzanne Culter, *Managing Decline: Japan's Coal Industry Restructuring and Community Response* (Honolulu, 1999); Ann B. Irish, *Hokkaido: A History of Ethnic Transition and Development on Japan's Northern Island* (Jefferson, NC, 2009). For an overview of current coal exploitation worldwide, see Ulrike Stottrop (ed.), *Kohle. Global – eine Reise in die Reviere der anderen. Katalog zur Ausstellung im Ruhr-Museum vom 15. April bis 24. November 2013* (Essen, 2013).

2. Edward A. Wrigley, *Continuity, Chance and Change: The Character of the Industrial Revolution in England* (Cambridge, 1988); idem, *Energy and the English Industrial Revolution* (Cambridge, 2010); Kenneth Pomeranz, *The Great Divergence: China, Europe, and the Making of the Modern World Economy* (Princeton, NJ, 2000).

3. Robert H. Woodrum, *Everybody Was Black Down There: Race and Industrial Change in the Alabama Coalfields* (Athens, GA, 2007); Leen Beyers, *Iedereen zwart: het samenleven van nieuwkomers en gevestigden in de mijncité Zwartberg, 1930–1990* (Amsterdam, 2010); see also Leen Beyers, "Everyone Black? Ethnic, Class and Gender Identities at Street Level in a Belgian Mining Town, 1930–50", in Stefan Berger, Andy Croll, and Norman LaPorte (eds), *Towards a*

mining labour, issues of ethnicity and culture have become major topics, for instance in studies on Polish migrant workers in Europe, on African-American miners in the United States, and on the migration of different ethnic groups in coalmining in Asia and Africa.[4] Most of these studies concerned separate companies, mining areas, or nations only, however. A volume edited in 2005 by Stefan Berger, Andy Croll, and Norman LaPorte, *Towards a Comparative History of Coalfield Societies*, offered a preliminary attempt to overcome the national focus and contained several (comparative) studies on migration and ethnicity.[5]

At the same time, as the editors and many contributors to the above volume made clear, comparative research in this field had only just started, and many cases and places were still to be covered. Besides, the debate about global history, which has burgeoned internationally over the last decade, has emphasized that comparisons – while still fundamental and useful – should be complemented by approaches that focus on connections and the embeddedness of the local in processes of grander scope (from the local to the global). Coalfields, both the situation in the mines themselves and in the mining communities, are perfect candidates for studies that privilege the contextualization of local events in global constellations and that emphasize the connections of mining locations to other regions. One of these connections spanning both shorter and longer distances – apart from the flow of coal as both a commodity and a bearer of energy – is evidently labour migration and its repercussions on ethnic identifications, interracial relations, and class formation.

The present Special Issue not only reflects a wish to continue and enhance previous attempts at analysing coalfields in a global historical perspective, it also specifically emphasizes two analytical concerns: migration and ethnicity. One of our main conceptual reference points in this endeavour is the Global Labour History approach that has been co-developed at the International Institute of Social History in Amsterdam, and that has one of its most important publication venues in the *International Review of Social History*. The major tenet of this approach is that in the modern period a broad array of labour relations has existed next to "free" wage labour, often in the same location. Unfree labour and forms of non-economic coercion were perfectly compatible with market development and capitalism. Even if

---

Comparative History of Coalfield Societies (Aldershot, 2005), pp. 146–163; Marcel Deprez, Anne Morelli, Jean-François Potelle *et al.*, *"Siamo tutti neri!": des hommes contre du charbon. Etudes et témoignages sur l'immigration italienne en Wallonie* (Seraing, 1998); Marie Cegarra, Olivier Chovaux, Rudy Damiani, Gérard Dumont, Jean-René Genty, and Janine Ponty, *Tous gueules noires. Histoire de l'immigration dans le bassin minier du Nord-Pas-de-Calais* (Lewarde, 2004).
4. Ian Phimister, "Global Labour History in the Twenty-First Century: Coal Mining and Its Recent Pasts", in Jan Lucassen (ed.), *Global Labour History: A State of the Art* (Bern [etc.], 2006), pp. 573–589.
5. Berger *et al.*, *Towards a Comparative History of Coalfield Societies*.

we can recognize a secular trend towards "free wage labour", slaves and other forms of unfree labourers (like indentured labourers, debt peons, and convict workers) made up an important part of the world's labour force. Coalmining in different parts of the world was historically associated with the full panoply of these labour relations. One of the aims of this Special Issue is to highlight the relationships between the diversity of labour relations, migration, and ethnic mobilization in the coalfields.

The worldwide response to our call for papers enabled us to organize a two-day workshop in November 2014 at the Netherlands Institute for Advanced Studies in the Humanities and Social Sciences (NIAS) in Wassenaar,[6] where we discussed the papers that we are now able to publish in this Special Issue. We thank the authors again for their participation and the lively debates. We are confident that this process of exchange and mutual debate, which we consider an important preliminary of any global historical endeavour that aims to go beyond juxtaposing single cases, is reflected positively in the present Special Issue. While Ad Knotter offers a general survey of the research on and themes in the history of coalfields worldwide, the individual contributions to this Special Issue cover topics as diverse as segregation, forced labour, subcontracting, labour struggles, discrimination, ethnic paternalism, gender, and sport. All of them, however, gravitate around the interlocked processes of migration and ethnic identity formation.

Being place-bound by geology, often originating in isolated places, and always labour-intensive, coalmining was dependent on migrant labour in almost every district.[7] At the start, experienced miners were often recruited from other mining areas. Migration trajectories, return and circular migration, resulting in ethnic diasporas of skilled miners, can be traced in many coalmining districts. British miners and engineers were the expert workers of the coal-based energy revolution in the nineteenth century, transferring their knowledge to develop coal industries in the British Empire, in the United States, and in other parts of the world.

Early migration of skilled groups of workers to introduce mining skills was supplemented by waves of inexperienced migrants from the surrounding countryside, and soon also from more distant places, regions, and countries. Workers had to be found who could be coerced or motivated to move hundreds of kilometres from their places of birth, not only

6. The workshop was supported financially by the NIAS and by the N.W. Posthumus Institute, Nederlandsch Economisch Historisch Archief, the Limburg University Fund Maastricht, and the Research Stimulation Fund of the Faculty of Arts and Social Sciences at Maastricht University. We would like to thank Stefano Bellucci for his help in the preparation of the workshop, and our anonymous referee for reviewing the whole pack of papers and for making many valuable comments.
7. For the European coalfields, see René Leboutte, *Vie et mort des bassins industriels en Europe 1750–2000* (Paris, 1997), ch. 9: "Croissance démographique et migrations".

changing places, but also their entire way of life. Cross-border migratory labour connected coalfields, regions, and countries, and mobilized new groups of workers of a variety of national and ethnic descents.

Labour migration for the coalmining industry was often closely linked to the transition from agriculture to industry, the creation of a wage-labour market, and the formation of an ethnically stratified coalmining proletariat. These processes were not easy or straightforward. In areas where labour markets were underdeveloped, mining labour was often combined with subsistence agriculture and could be employed only seasonally. Special recruitment mechanisms, such as subcontracting, were employed to bridge the gap between agriculture and industry. In other cases force was used to recruit ethnic groups with a perceived inferior status to work in the mines. In these cases forced labour and ethnic or racial discrimination could be closely related. Also, when miners worked for wages, mining labour markets were systematically structured and institutionalized by means of wage discrimination and ethnic stratification. As in any labour market, there was no such thing as a free, homogeneous market for mine labour.[8]

A salient and perhaps prototypical example of the interconnection of mining labour with subsistence agriculture can be found in the Zonguldak coalfield on Turkey's western Black Sea coast, which is the topic of Erol Kahveci's contribution to this Special Issue. Coal had been mined there since the 1840s to satisfy the demands of the Ottoman government for supplies to its navy, transport, government installations, and utilities. To provide for the labour needed, it obliged peasants from surrounding villages to work in the mines on a rotational basis (from 1867). Peasants continued to work part-time in the mines after the end of this forced labour regime in 1921, and after its reinstatement between 1940 and 1947. In this system there was a clear division of labour. Underground work was performed by rotational peasant miners, while migrants, most of them of *Laz* origin (from the eastern Black Sea coast), were employed full-time as skilled surface workers.

Rural, often part-time seasonal migrants, also formed a large part of the highly mobile workforce in coalmining in Manchuria (north-east China). Limin Teh analyses how recruitment and control of migrant labour was reorganized after Japanese owners had taken over the Fushun Coalmine in Manchuria in 1905. During the years 1907–1932, Japanese mine management transformed labour contractors from independent third-party contractors to salaried pit foremen with clearly defined responsibilities in labour recruitment and supervision. Because labour contractors interfaced between the Fushun Coalmine and Chinese migration, mine management assumed that control over contractors would grant it control over migration too. In the end,

8. See, among others, Jamie Peck, *Work-Place: The Social Regulation of Labor Markets* (New York [etc.], 1996). Peck ignores the impact of migration on labour markets however.

however, Teh concludes, these bureaucratic measures failed. Chinese workers stuck to their mobility patterns, in spite of all Japanese investments in recruitment procedures and administrative control. Her analysis, based on managerial sources, makes clear how important the role of mining operators was in labour intermediation and migration processes.

The history of coalmining witnessed a broad array of types of force used to press workers into the mines. In many cases, this was realized by a combination of physical and economic coercion through indenturing, debt, and other bonds. Examples can be found in Ian Phimister and Alfred Tembo's contribution on Wankie Colliery in colonial Zimbabwe, Limin Teh's on Fushun in Manchuria, Carolyn Brown's on Enugu, Nigeria, and Erol Kahveci's on Zonguldak, Turkey. Outright force was used in the case of convict workers, deportees, prisoners of war, and internees of labour camps. At one time or another convicts were part of the mining labour force in the US South (Trotter), Japan (Arents and Tsuneishi), and Turkey (Kahveci).

The interrelation of different groups of "politically" forced labourers is highlighted by Julia Landau in her analysis of coalmining in the Kuzbass region in Siberia. This coalfield was developed within the framework of Soviet industrialization in the 1920s and 1930s. In this harsh and isolated place, first migrants of all kind were mobilized to work in the mines (new workers from the countryside, foreign experts), but from the late 1920s onward the workforce was dominated by forced settlers, deported convicts, and prisoners of war. Landau describes the complex mechanisms of social segregation in this frontier society. She analyses how the specific conditions of developing heavy industry on the one hand and policies of repression on the other created social tensions that affected everyday life in local society.

In many cases, labourers who came to the coalfields, or who were forced to go there, were part of a specific ethnic (minority) group. These were mobilized from outside, but also from within, national states and empires. Telling examples in the nineteenth and early twentieth centuries are: Flemish workers to the Walloon coalfields in Belgium, the Irish to Scotland in the United Kingdom (before Irish independence), Poles to the Ruhr in the German Empire (before Polish independence), African Americans from the South to Virginia and Alabama in the United States, migrants from the French colonies in the Maghreb (Algeria and Morocco) to France, and Koreans to the Hokkaidō and Kyushū coalfields in Japan (Korea then being part of the Japanese Empire). It is certainly no coincidence that at that time these ethnic minorities were all considered and treated as people of a lower status than the dominant ethnic groups in these countries. Their mobilization as miners reflected the low status of work in the mines, and also the position of migrants as second-rate workers within the mines.

Timothy Mitchell has labelled societies based on coal and related technologies "machines for democracy", i.e. as enablers of claims towards a more equal participation. The transformation of energy flows through the exploiting of carbon fuels (first coal, then oil), he argues, has translated into political constellations that made democratic claims ever more difficult to hold off.[9] From a global labour history point of view, however, coalmining developed no tendency towards "equalization" and "homogenization", but an innate, countervailing need for a fragmented labour force, backed up by ideologies to justify the unequal treatment of specific groups along lines of gender, class, race, ethnicity, or age.

The contributions in this Special Issue bear witness to the ways in which "race" and "ethnicity" were not static categories or forms of identification, but a constant process in which certain groups were discursively produced, both by being addressed by others and by defining and identifying themselves.[10] In the case of coalmining, the proclivity to attract and/or mobilize migrant workers from a distinct ethnic background was closely related to racialized distinctions – although "race" and "ethnicity" were by no means the same.

This is pointed out by Joe Trotter in his overview of race and ethnic relations in coalmining in the United States. While recognizing the ethnic fragmentation of the immigrant and American-born white coalmining workforce, both from the British Isles and from southern, central, and eastern Europe, his article identifies the colour line as the most enduring and pronounced division among coalminers in industrial America. The entrenched racial hostility of white workers, employers, and the state did not obliterate the influence of black miners over their own lives, however. African-American miners forged a variety of strategies for shaping their own communities. While emphasizing the deep racial divide in both the coalmining workforce and the United Mine Workers of America (UMWA), Trotter also draws attention to the attempts of this union to galvanize interracial unity.

Although slaves were used in some antebellum coalmines in the US South, classical chattel slavery was relatively rare in the history of coalmining. At the same time, slavery, the slave trade, and their repercussions in post-abolition times were major constituents of labour relations in several coalfields. In different world regions slavery and the slave trade had created a specific sector of the population, which was racially or ethnically oppressed and socially marginalized.

---

9. Timothy Mitchell, *Carbon Democracy: Political Power in the Age of Oil* (London [etc.], 2011), pp. 12–31.

10. On "identification" as an alternative to "identity", see Frederick Cooper and Roger Brubaker, "Identity", in Frederick Cooper, *Colonialism in Question: Theory, Knowledge, History* (Berkeley, CA [etc.], 2005), pp. 59–90. On "race" as process, see, among many possible interventions, Laura Gotkowitz, "Introduction: Racisms of the Present and the Past in Latin America", in *idem*, *Histories of Race and Racism: The Andes and Mesoamerica from Colonial Times to the Present* (Durham, NC, 2011), pp. 1–55. See also Eileen Boris and Angélique Janssens (eds), *Complicating Categories: Gender, Class, Race and Ethnicity* (Cambridge, 1999).

Carolyn Brown relates the background of the differences between "locals" and "foreigners" in the mining town of Enegu (Nigeria) to the history of the slave trade and the role British colonizers assigned to former local slave traders as "tribal chiefs" and labour recruiters for the mine. Her analysis highlights the fluidity of ethno-linguistic identifications. Once the mine had opened and certain ethnically marginalized groups from the surrounding region had been pressed into minework, the established attributions began to shift as these miners started to interact with other groups, especially more skilled migrants from further away (seen as "foreigners"), thereby adopting an identity of modern and urban "coal men". Subsequently, this enabled these workers to claim a new status in their village communities and to question old hierarchies both of age/seniority and local ethnic privilege of one group over another.

A similar intermingling of "race" and "ethnicity" is described by Clarice Speranza in her contribution on the coalmining towns of Arroio dos Ratos, Butiá, and others, near Porto Alegre in Rio Grande do Sul, the southernmost Brazilian state. From the start, in the 1850s, European workers were recruited, many of them experienced miners. Among the various nationalities coming to the Brazilian coalfields, Spaniards were the most numerous. European newcomers were valued as promoters of the "whitening" of Brazilian society and were always considered superior to the local population, many of them descendants of former slaves. The prevalent cultural perspective of that time placed the "white" (equated to European) above the native mixed population. Although they worked side by side in the mines, were members of the same union, and stood alongside each other in strikes and protest movements, descendants of Europeans and "nationals" did not mix socially.

The recruitment of specific ethnic groups did not follow the clear-cut logics of supply and demand, and could differ considerably even within the same region. As Tom Arents and Norihiko Tsuneishi show in their investigation of a number of coalmines in the Chikuhō and Miike districts in Japan on the southern island of Kyūshū, migrants from Korea, then a Japanese colony, were unevenly distributed among these mines in the first few decades of the twentieth century. While some mining companies brought Korean workers into coal production as a cheap and disposable workforce, others did not. Arents and Tsuneishi argue that the distribution of Koreans was a consequence of uneven capital accumulation among different mining companies. Companies that in an earlier phase had relied on other groups of cheap labourers, such as convict workers, had been able to accumulate enough capital to pay higher wages afterwards, and to recruit a stable Japanese workforce, which they also privileged because of racial prejudice. Others had accumulated less capital and had to rely on Korean immigrants, who were cheaper but, from the management's point of view, only the second-best option.

Three articles in this Special Issue focus on the highly ethnicized dynamics of migrant labour in continental western European coalfields.

Philip Slaby and Marion Fontaine write on different aspects of the history of the Nord-Pas-de-Calais coalfields, Diethelm Blecking on the Ruhr. In the case of the Nord-Pas-de-Calais coalfield in northern France, labour scarcity after World War I triggered the recruitment of tens of thousands of immigrants, mainly Poles. Philip Slaby uses the very apt term "ethnic paternalism" to describe the strategies of French mining companies to attract, retain, and control foreigners. By creating Polish neighbourhoods, by fostering Polish clubs and associations, by supporting Polish clergy and religious institutions, and by cooperating with Polish officials, coal firms contributed to the segregation of the immigrant community. Ethnic paternalism accentuated the ethnic and cultural dissimilarities between Poles and Frenchmen in the coalfields and reinforced the foreigners' isolation from the local working-class society and its institutions. It also influenced the relationship with the French state. Members of the Polish community were strictly policed by local officials, who considered their separate collective organizations as a menace to the republican conception of citizenship.

In the French republican vision, sport is considered an integrative power in society, especially for migrants. In her article on immigration and football as a miners' sport in the northern French coalfield, Marion Fontaine deconstructs this idea by exploring how football could both strengthen and weaken the boundaries inside the mining communities. In the 1920s, migrants played football in separate Polish sports associations, sustaining a sense of Polish identity in accordance with the ethnic particularism described by Slaby. In the 1930s, however, Polish and French children started to play together in street football and in French clubs. After World War II many descendants of Polish immigrants were able to penetrate the world of professional football. Managers of Racing Club de Lens, a football team closely connected to the mines, started to recruit players from non-professional mining clubs in the region. Its professional team became a reflection of the coalfield population, including the children of Polish migrants. In this respect there were huge differences with the migrants of Moroccan and Algerian descent, who arrived after World War II. These were not able to participate in the social life of the mining communities, which had already begun to disintegrate shortly after their arrival as a consequence of the industry's decline.

In his article on Polish miners in the German Ruhr, Diethelm Blecking also addresses the idea that sport can overcome problems of ethnic heterogeneity. Before World War I the so-called Ruhr Poles were completely segregated in their social activities and widely participated in the *Sokół* gymnastics movement. The *Sokół* clubs were part of an array of organizational structures that offered migrants opportunities to take on a new, Polish identity and were aimed at preventing the "integration" of Polish migrants into German society. After World War I the situation of the

Polish inhabitants in the Ruhr changed dramatically, however. In 1918 a Polish state had finally been re-established, and many of the Ruhr Poles had moved to coalmines in northern France and other countries. Football became very popular as a miners' sport, also for those of Polish descent remaining in the Ruhr. In the 1920s, as in northern France, segregation in sports clubs began to give way to integration. Players with a Polish migrant background now became particularly active in top-class football in the Ruhr. These histories of football as a miners' sport both in France and in Germany point to the ambivalent role of sport in inter-ethnic relations, ranging from the construction of ethnic identities to intercultural integration.

Beyond the two analytical concerns "migration" and "ethnicity", the contributions to this Special Issue potentially offer pathways to many other issues. All of these would merit further exploration in a comparative and global historical perspective. One of these issues is social struggles. Most of the contributions to this Special Issue mention and analyse struggles by miners and their communities. In several instances these struggles saw miners overcome cleavages of race and ethnicity. The mobilization of miners could also be part of broader political struggles.

As Ian Phimister and Alfred Tembo show in their contribution about a strike that broke out in March 1964 among the African workforce at Wankie Colliery in Zimbabwe (then Southern Rhodesia), this mobilization was deeply connected to the national liberation struggle in Zambia (then Northern Rhodesia). The core of the black workers were migrants from Northern Rhodesia, a British protectorate that, at the time, was engaged in an independence struggle organized by Kenneth Kaunda's United National Independence Party (UNIP), while Southern Rhodesia was ruled by an exclusionary white government. While originating in grievances, primarily of women demanding full money wages instead of food rations, the strike evolved in a highly charged political atmosphere. UNIP members were heavily involved: slogans were sung and UNIP badges prominently displayed. Phimister and Tembo conclude that there was a close association between labour and militant nationalist politics in this strike, and suggest that greater weight should be given to the leading roles of women activists in the politicization of African mining communities.

As the example of Wankie Colliery shows, gender aspects are fundamental to understanding the dynamics of mining communities. Miners and mining companies depended on women, both for their unpaid reproductive labour and for their wage earnings, sometimes even for working in the mines themselves.[11]

---

11. For a recent assessment of the role of women in mining and fishing communities in Britain, see Valerie G. Hall, *Women at Work, 1860–1939: How Different Industries Shaped Women's Experiences* (Woodbridge, 2013).

As Tom Arents and Norihiko Tsuneishi highlight, female labourers for a while replaced convict workers (whose deployment had been prohibited by law). They went down the pits together with their husbands in work teams. Coalmining could also entail new ways of constructing masculinity and acquiring the status of full male adult in an community, as Carolyn Brown analyses in her contribution on the Enugu Government Colliery (Nigeria). The work in the mines (into which young men with a marginalized status had been pressed) opened new pathways to attributes of manhood. The self-confidence and improved position enabled these men to challenge imposed "chiefs" and other authorities in their villages.

Coal as a fossil rock is compressed and stored solar energy. This image of density can justly be transferred to the social level. As the contributions to this Special Issue show, coalmining is associated with a compact intensity of experiences in labour and communities. Coalmining regularly upset and reshaped local constellations, and reached out to places further, often very far, away. Thus, although coalmining developed mostly in locations of relatively small size, it compressed in these communities some of the far-reaching and fundamental experiences of modern societies, among them the grand and contested processes of industrial labour, migration, and identity formation.

IRSH 60 (2015), Special Issue, pp. 13–39 doi:10.1017/S0020859015000413
© 2015 Internationaal Instituut voor Sociale Geschiedenis

Migration and Ethnicity in Coalfield History: Global Perspectives

AD KNOTTER

*Sociaal Historisch Centrum voor Limburg at Maastricht University
Sint-Pieterstraat 7, 6211 JM Maastricht, The Netherlands*

E-mail: a.knotter@maastrichtuniversity.nl

ABSTRACT: This article provides a general background to the case studies in this Special Issue by highlighting some general themes in the history of migration to coalfields worldwide. All over the world, mining companies have struggled with labour shortages and had to find ways to recruit sufficient numbers of mineworkers. The solutions adopted ranged from the involvement of part-time peasant miners, organized mediation by labour contractors, and systems of forced labour, to state regulation of national and international migration. The importance of these kinds of "intervening institution" in mobilizing labour for the coalmines is illustrated by examples from different parts of the world. Efforts to find new workers for the mines often resulted in the recruitment of ethnic groups of a lower social status, not only because they were rural and unskilled, but also because they were considered inferior from a cultural or ethnic viewpoint. In this respect there was a huge difference from the migration and settlement of skilled miners, like those from Britain and other countries. Ethnic differences were often closely related to differences in skill and social status. Although there are many instances of inter-ethnic solidarity and cooperation, depending on the time-frame and circumstances, these differences could have a profound effect on social relations in mining communities.

In this article I give an overview of the most relevant issues in the history of migration and ethnicity in coalmining from a global perspective. I will refer to articles in this Special Issue where possible, but also to the very rich literature on coalfields elsewhere in the world. The article is roughly divided into four parts. The first part deals with the recruitment of migrants and ethnic minorities in upcoming coalfields in the nineteenth century and the first few decades of the twentieth century in areas where wage labour markets were underdeveloped. This was the case in colonies of the British Empire, such as India, South Africa, and Nigeria, but also in countries that at that time were less developed, such as Japan, China, and Ukraine. In these cases mining companies had to rely on temporary migrants, peasant miners from the land; on special recruitment systems, mainly subcontracting; or on systems of coercion, such as convict labour, indentured/contract labour, or blunt force and violence.

The second part of the article deals with diasporas of specific groups, such as skilled British workers, who migrated all over the world to introduce mining skills and often took a position of privilege vis-à-vis unskilled workers from other ethnic groups, including African Americans or eastern European migrants in the United States. British migrants were particularly important in the coalmines in the white settler colonies of South Africa, Canada, Australia, and New Zealand, and also in the emerging coal industry of the United States. Another mobile group were Polish miners, both in Europe and in the United States. At first, Polish miners were often skilled migrants from Silesia or the German Ruhr (one of their first migration destinations), but most subsequent Polish migrants were peasants or landless rural labourers, migrating to coalfields as unskilled workers.

The third part deals with state-regulated migration to the coalfields of western Europe (Britain excepted), which started after World War I and became fully developed after World War II. This was the so-called "guestworker" system, which brought migrants at first from eastern Europe and later from the Mediterranean periphery to Germany, France, Belgium, and the Netherlands. I pay special attention to Turkish migrants in Germany, Italian migrants in France and Belgium, and Moroccan migrants in France, Belgium, and the Netherlands, but at different phases migrants from several other countries were involved, both from eastern Europe (Czechoslovakia and Hungary, for instance) and from the Mediterranean (Yugoslavia, Spain, and Greece being examples).

The fourth part of this article looks at the social relationship of migrants and established workers in the mining communities. How did different ethnic groups live together? How did they cope with racial discrimination and ethnic segregation? To what extent could new groups of workers and their families integrate in the mining community?

PEASANT MINERS AND OSCILLATING MIGRATION

In emerging coalfields, large parts of the labour force were recruited seasonally as peasant migrants from the land. In this way labour supply and the agrarian seasons were interconnected, coal extraction proceeding in reverse tandem with agrarian seasons. Seasonal peasant workers were recruited both locally and as temporary migrants. A striking example of the local recruiting of peasant miners is the labour system in the Zonguldak coalfield in Turkey, as described by Erol Kahveci in this Special Issue, where an intricate system of rotational work was installed in the nineteenth century (since the 1860s), forcing peasants from villages in the region to work underground during several weeks of the year.[1] In 1965 rotational workers were still drawn from some 377 villages located throughout the province of Zonguldak. Force was no longer used, however, as working in the mines had become a family tradition, handed down from father to son.[2]

In the large Jahria coalfield in India (opened in the 1890s), "recruited" or seasonal workers comprised 50 to 75 per cent of the workforce by the 1920s, compared with "settled" migrants who made up 15 to 25 per cent and "local" workers amounting to only 5 to 10 per cent. Peasants and landless labourers, who were seasonally unemployed, and often indebted, came to work in the coalfields to keep the village households functioning. The mining workforce, male and female working together in family teams, was mainly "low caste" and "tribal" (so-called Adivasi, or "aboriginals"); "upper caste" were to be found only in the supervisory grades.[3]

Seasonal peasant workers, mainly from Russia, were also recruited on a massive scale for the Donbass coalmines in Ukraine. The first mineworkers in Juzovka (renamed Stalino at the end of the 1920s, today's Donetsk) were winter migrants, who returned to their villages for the planting, fieldwork, and the harvest. In the mid-1880s, 60 to 70 per cent of Donbass workers were migratory, and in 1904 31.7 per cent of the coal cutters were away from the mines in the summer.[4] The seasonal pendulum of village to mine was mixed with other types of wandering. For a long time, employers were unable to consolidate the workforce, and a more stable working class emerged only relatively late. The local population being persistently reluctant to enter the mines, Russian migrants and migratory workers formed the rank and file of the mining labour force. In 1889 only 5 per cent of miners were of local origin.[5] The seasonal migration of peasant miners in the Donbass persisted well into the early Soviet period (1920s). Again, most

1. On the early history of the Zonguldak coalfield see also Donald Quataert, *Miners and the State in the Ottoman Empire: The Zonguldak Coalfield, 1822–1920* (New York [etc.], 2006).
2. Delwin A. Roy, "Labour and Trade Unionism in Turkey: The Eregli Coalminers", *Middle Eastern Studies*, 12:3 (1976), pp. 125–172, 126–134.
3. Dilip Simeon, *The Politics of Labour under Late Colonialism: Workers, Unions and the State in Chota Nagpur 1928–1939* (New Delhi, 1995), p. 28; *idem*, "Coal and Colonialism: Production Relations in an Indian Coalfield, c.1895–1947", *International Review of Social History*, 41 (1996), pp. 83–108, 93–94; C.P. Simmons, "Recruiting and Organizing an Industrial Labour Force in Colonial India: The Case of the Coal Mining Industry, c.1880–1939", *The Indian Economic and Social History Review*, 13 (1976), pp. 455–585, 458–460. On the seasonality of migrant labour in the Jahria coalfield, also leading to ethnic specialization, see Prabhu Prasad Mohapatra, "Coolies and Colliers: A Study of the Agrarian Context of Labour Migration from Chotanagpur, 1880–1920", *Studies in History*, 1 (1985), pp. 247–303, 283–297.
4. Theodore H. Friedgut, *Iuzovka and Revolution*, I: *Life and Work in Russia's Donbass, 1869–1924* (Princeton, NJ, 1989), pp. 209, 215 n. 80, 217, and 221.
5. *Ibid.*, pp. 211–212.

of them (about 75 per cent) were Russians. Seasonal migration greatly diminished after forced collectivization and so-called dekulakization.[6]

The importance of oscillating migrants working in the South African gold mines has been established in numerous studies;[7] in Witbank's coalmines, too, by 1925 about 75 per cent of the miners were migratory workers from rural areas of Mozambique. These collieries produced coal mainly for the gold industry, and were often owned by goldmining companies. Mozambicans were recruited by the Witwatersrand Native Labour Association (WNLA, or "Wenela"), which had established a kind of monopoly to obtain mine and colliery labour from the Portuguese territory of Mozambique. The association had been created by the Chamber of Mines to provide the goldmines with cheap labour, but it also supported the Transvaal coal industry. In 1920s over 80 per cent of African workers in the Witbank coalmining district were recorded as "Portuguese". They often had to be compelled to work in the collieries, especially in the years before World War I, as migrants favoured work in the goldmines. Although since 1907 there had been a tendency among "detribalized" families to settle around the collieries, the proportion of "permanent" miners, permitted to live with their wives, was officially restricted in 1926 to 15 per cent. It seemed unlikely, however, that this percentage could be maintained.[8]

Also, in the Appalachian coalfields in West Virginia (United States), the great wave of black migrants from the South before and during World War I initially consisted of small peasants or sharecroppers. A significant percentage either owned farms in Virginia and North Carolina or had relatives who did. When work became irregular or wages declined substantially, they returned to these homes until work in West Virginia improved, often in a seasonal pattern. It was not until the 1920s that they started to settle in coal towns, where semi-rural life was often maintained by miners' families, who cultivated gardens and raised livestock.[9]

6. Tanja Penter, *Kohle für Stalin und Hitler. Arbeiten und Leben im Donbass 1929–1953* (Essen, 2010), pp. 39–42.

7. T. Dunbar Moodie (with Vivienne Ndatshe), *Going for Gold: Men, Mines, and Migration* (Berkeley, CA, 1994); Ruth First, *Black Gold: The Mozambican Miner, Proletarian and Peasant* (Manchester, 1983); Alan Jeeves, *Migrant Labour in South Africa's Mining Economy: The Struggle for the Gold Mines' Labour Supply 1890–1920* (Kingston, 1985); Jonathan Crush, "Migrations Past: An Historical Overview of Cross-Border Movement in Southern Africa", in David A. McDonald (ed.), *On Borders: Perspectives on International Migration in Southern Africa* (Kingston [etc.], 2000), pp. 12–24.

8. Peter Alexander, "Oscillating Migrants, 'Detribalised Families' and Militancy: Mozambicans on Witbank Collieries, 1918–1927", *Journal of Southern African Studies*, 27 (2001), pp. 505–525, 507, 509, 517; *idem*, "Challenging Cheap-Labour Theory: Natal and Transvaal Coal Miners, ca.1890–1950", *Labor History*, 49 (2008), pp. 47–70, 53–54.

9. Ronald L. Lewis, "From Peasant to Proletarian: The Migration of Southern Blacks to the Central Appalachian Coalfields", *The Journal of Southern History*, 55 (1989), pp. 77–102, 87–88.

MIGRATION AND LABOUR CONTRACTORS

Where the distance between mine owners, managers, and migrant miners was large, systems of intermediation emerged, with a major role for labour contractors. They shaped both the recruitment and deployment of labour, and the systems of control inside and often outside the mines. Recruiting migrants using subcontractors seems to have been a common device in countries with underdeveloped labour markets and a rural population reluctant to enter the mines. During early industrialization, it was often difficult for large-scale enterprises to recruit sufficient numbers of miners, because labour markets were either non-existent or highly fragmented. The contractors had closer ties to the rural population than owners and managers did, and this made it easier for them to recruit labour from their home villages.

Subcontracting had been known in the British coal industry since the eighteenth century. It was associated with "controlling and maintaining an increasingly turbulent body of workmen", and described as "a form of organization peculiar to the adolescence of industrial society and destined to disappear as the British economy grew to maturity".[10] Elsewhere in the world, the system was widely used to recruit and control both local and migrant labour. In Chinese coalmining, until the 1920s the largest part of the labour force, up to between 60 and 80 per cent, was recruited by contractors, to work the coalface as well as to haul and tunnel underground. Apart from supplying labour, many contractors also had to provide most of the materials to work the mine.[11] As Limin Teh makes clear in her article in this Special Issue, the large Japanese-owned Manchurian mines, however, incorporated labour contractors in their system of management and met severe shortages of labour in the 1920s by sending their own agents to the Hebei and Shandong regions south of Manchuria, which formed an important reservoir of labour for these mines.

After 1907–1908 the use of labour contractors became widespread in South African goldmining for recruitment in South Africa itself (the supply of Mozambican labour was monopolized by WNLA). In many cases the labour contractor not only recruited, but also arranged transport, and fed and housed the worker after his arrival.[12] In her article in this Special Issue on the Enugu Colliery in Nigeria, Carolyn Brown shows how African

---

10. Arthur J. Taylor, "The Sub-Contract System in the British Coal Industry", in Leslie S. Pressnell (ed.), *Studies in the Industrial Revolution Presented to T.S. Ashton* (London, 1960), pp. 215–235, 229 and 234; for empirical qualifications, see James A. Jaffe, *The Struggle for Market Power: Industrial Relations in the British Coal Industry, 1800–1840* (Cambridge, 1991), pp. 54–56.
11. Tim Wright, "'A Method of Evading Management': Contract Labor in Chinese Coal Mines before 1937", *Comparative Studies in Society and History*, 23 (1981), pp. 656–678, 659, 663–665, 669.
12. Jeeves, *Migrant Labour in South Africa's Mining Economy*, pp. 97 and 153–183.

"boss boys" were responsible for recruitment and discipline also beyond the workplace, in the labour camps where recruits from the villages were housed. Discipline was enforced by physical violence, extortion, and fines.[13]

In Indian coalmining large groups of migrant labour were recruited by labour contractors, engaged for the entire labour process, from the hiring of the labour force to the supervision of the cutting and loading of coal. At its lowest end, the system relied on gangmasters (so called *sardars*), who led groups of fifteen to forty miners, supervising work and receiving and distributing wages. The system was closely related to seasonal migration, as it enabled a stable but flexible connection between demand in the coalfields and supply in more or less remote villages. A contractor recruited relatives and personal friends from his home village or thereabouts, and made every effort to ensure that his "gang" would return to a particular mine next year. He advanced train fares, food, and money to his co-villagers, later to be deducted from wages earned, obliging workers to stay with him and to work at a particular colliery.[14] In this way mining companies were able to get a hold over the migratory labour force.

A similar recruiting system existed for the Russian seasonal miners in the Ukrainian Donbass. Agents (*verbovshchiki*) went to the villages to persuade peasants to work in the mines, paying their travel and living expenses. These advances were later deducted from wages, keeping the worker in debt from the beginning. Mostly, these recruiters also acted as *artel'schick*, the leader of a team (or *artel'*) of up to thirty peasant miners, often friends and relatives from one village, who negotiated with the employers on behalf of the team, coordinated the work, and organized living arrangements. Much like his Indian counterpart, the contractor took responsibility for arranging for sufficient numbers of miners, and might provide horses for transport, and foremen and gang bosses to supervise daily work. He received the sum negotiated for piecework and in turn paid his workers by the shift.[15] This kind of contracting ran counter to the aim of settling a permanent workforce, but it was the only way for the mining companies to recruit migratory workers from the land in sufficient numbers.

In Japan, too, a system of recruitment by labour contractors was generally used in coal and other mines. A contractor (known as *hamba-gashira* in the Hokkaido coalfields in the north and *naya-gashira* in Kyūshū coalfields in the south) hired several groups of between ten and twenty mineworkers from farming backgrounds, provided lodging, and supervised

13. See also Carolyn A. Brown, *"We Were All Slaves": African Miners, Culture, and Resistance at the Enugu Government Colliery* (Portsmouth, NH, 2003), pp. 119–121.
14. Simeon, *The Politics of Labour under Late Colonialism*, pp. 27 and 149; Simmons, "Recruiting and Organizing an Industrial Labour Force", pp. 471–482.
15. Friedgut, *Iuzovka and Revolution*, I, pp. 234, 260–263, and 269–271.

labour underground. On behalf of the mine owners the contractors had complete authority over the workforce, both at work and in daily life. They recruited the miners, supervised them at the production site, and controlled their life at their lodges.[16] The system was a means to secure a regular supply of workers. In the southern Kyūshū coalfield the contracting system was also used to recruit families, to include females to work as haulers underground, but also at the surface. The system declined there only with the demise of female work in the underground teams after longwall mining had replaced pillar mining in the 1920s. This in turn was made possible by the massive recruitment of Koreans, who were initially also recruited by Korean *naya-gashira*.[17] Many of these Korean migrants returned to their home villages during the months of the summer harvest (July and August).[18]

FORCED LABOUR

The solutions employed by mine owners and the state to remedy the shortage of labour for the mines included various forms of compulsion or force. In this way the colliery owners were able to tie in a permanent supply of mining labour. In early modern Britain, systems of coercion were used to tie workers and their families to the mines, like the so-called "colliery serfdom" in eighteenth-century Scotland, and the "yearly bond" in the Durham mines.[19]

Systems of coercion of this kind were not confined to early modern Europe, however. In the coalfields of British India (Bengal), semi-feudal bonds were common in older collieries, in some cases even until the 1950s. Mine owners there had purchased large tracts of land near the pits and had developed a service tenancy arrangement, whereby peasants were granted a small piece of land in return for working a certain number of days in the company mine instead of paying rent, on pain of eviction.[20] In this way the

16. On this "lodge system", both at the iron mines and the coalmines, see Nimura Kazuo, *The Ashio Riot of 1907: A Social History of Mining in Japan* (Durham, NC, 1997), pp. 161–178.
17. Yukata Nishinarita, "Technological Change and Female Labour in Japan", UNU working paper (Tokyo, 1994), pp. 59–96; W. Donald Smith, "The 1932 Asō Coal Strike: Korean–Japanese Solidarity and Conflict", *Korean Studies*, 20 (1996), pp. 94–122, 96–98. On the early history and unevenness of Korean migration to the Kyūshū coalfield, see also the article by Tom Arents and Norihiko Tsuneishi in this Special Issue.
18. Michael A. Weiner, *The Origins of the Korean Community in Japan, 1910–23* (Atlantic Highlands, NJ, 1989), p. 66.
19. Alan B. Campbell, *The Lanarkshire Miners: A Social History of their Trade Unions 1775–1874* (Edinburgh, 1979), pp. 9–12; Sydney Webb, *The Story of the Durham Miners (1662–1921)* (London, 1921), pp. 7–15; Thomas S. Ashton and Joseph Sykes, *The Coal Industry of the Eighteenth Century* (Manchester, 1929), pp. 70–99.
20. Simmons, "Recruiting and Organizing an Industrial Labour Force", pp. 463–471; Simeon, *The Politics of Labour under Late Colonialism*, p. 26.

colliery owners were able to tie in a permanent supply of mining labour. The system had been applied by early starters in the Indian coalfields; for more recently established enterprises, like in the Jahria coalfield, other means of obtaining the desired number of workers had to be used, mainly in the form of subcontracting migratory peasant miners (see above).

In this Indian example, and also in the case of the Zonguldak coalfield in Turkey, described by Kahveci in this issue, economic and extra-economic coercion were used to mobilize local labour for the mines. We find several examples, also in Chinese coalmining, well into the twentieth century, be it in the form of convict labour, debt servitude, or servile labour.[21] In other cases, force was used to bring in migrant labour. In colonial Zimbabwe (Southern Rhodesia), the Wankie Colliery (opened in 1902) relied heavily in its early years on so-called *chibaro*, indentured labourers supplied by the Rhodesia Native Labour Board. In 1918 40 per cent of the black labour force at the Wankie Colliery still belonged to this category, as against 60 per cent "voluntary" labour, often migrants passing on their way from Northern Rhodesia to South Africa, who would work at Wankie for several months before resuming their journey. Thereafter, structural changes in the labour market freed the Wankie Colliery more or less from *chibaro* labour: by 1927 the percentage had dropped to 5.[22]

In the Dutch East Indies (Indonesia), the labour shortage the Ombilin coalmines (West Sumatra) faced when they first began operating was "solved" by the forced employment of convict labourers, both political and criminal prisoners, from other parts of the colony. Their number fluctuated up to 2,400 in 1898. Later, Chinese and Javanese "contract labourers", too, were employed. They were not "free", but bound to work for several years under the complete jurisdiction of the mine. Convict and contract labourers dominated the growing number of miners until the first half of the 1920s. After that, they gradually disappeared and were replaced by free labourers.[23]

Convict labour was, in fact, a fairly common recruitment device both in the start-up and the more advanced phases of coalmine development. In the nineteenth-century southern United States, convict labour drawn predominantly from among African Americans was regularly used in the coalmines of Georgia, Tennessee, and Alabama after the abolition of slavery

21. Tim Wright, *Coal Mining in China's Economy and Society 1895–1937* (Cambridge, 1984), p. 165.
22. Ian Phimister, *Wangi Kolia: Coal, Capital and Labour in Colonial Zimbabwe 1894–1954* (Harare [etc.], 1994), pp. 11 and 76; see also on the Rhodesian gold mines, Charles van Onselen, *Chibaro: African Mine Labour in Southern Rhodesia 1900–1933* (London, 1980), pp. 99 and 104–114.
23. Erwiza Erman, *Miners, Managers and the State: A Socio-Political History of the Ombilin Coal-Mines, West Sumatra, 1892–1996* (Amsterdam, 1999), pp. 36–41; idem, "Generalized Violence: A Case Study of the Ombilin Coal Mines, 1892–1996", in Freek Colombijn and Thomas J. Lindblad (eds), *Roots of Violence in Indonesia: Contemporary Violence in Historical Perspective* (Leiden, 2002), pp. 105–131.

(the employment of slaves had been common in the mines before).[24] Well into the twentieth century, convict labour played a fundamental role in setting the conditions under which free miners laboured, and provided a steady source of labour. With many black miners staying after their release, their experience as convict labourers in fact prepared large numbers of blacks for the slightly less harsh regime they would endure as free miners. So, in 1910 over 50 per cent of black coalminers in the Birmingham (Alabama) district had learned their trade as convicts. In this way the system offered both an instrument for disciplining the black labour force and for securing a steady flow of cheap labour for the mines.[25]

In Japan, labour scarcity at the start of the Hokkaido and Kyūshū coal-mines (from the 1880s) was also solved in this way. Later on, convict labour was replaced by a system of recruitment by labour contractors (see above), but this system confined the freedom of the miners to such an extent that it could also be considered a form of forced labour. During World War I coalmining grew strongly because of the economic boom and it became difficult to procure more labour from the agrarian villages in Japan itself. As Arents and Tsuneishi show in this Special Issue, labour shortages were now solved by transferring Korean migrants from rural areas in colonized Korea.[26] After 1939 the coercive mobilization of Koreans in the mines and other industries became increasingly important in the Japanese war economy. Between 1939 and 1945 more than 300,000 Koreans were sent to Japanese mines, most against their will. Koreans were almost exclusively used as underground face workers. In Hokkaido, for example, Koreans comprised over 40 per cent of the coalmining labour force, but they accounted for 60 to 70 per cent of underground workers.[27] Some 40,000 Chinese prisoners of war were employed in the Japanese mines as well.[28]

24. Ronald L. Lewis, *Black Coal Miners in America: Race, Class, and Community Conflict 1780–1980* (Lexington, KY, 1987), pp. 3–12; Alex Lichtenstein, *Twice the Work of Free Labor: The Political Economy of Convict Labor in the New South* (London, 1996); and the article by Joe Trotter in this Special Issue.
25. Lewis, *Black Coal Miners in America*, pp. 33–34; Brian Kelly, *Race, Class, and Power in the Alabama Coalfields, 1908–21* (Urbana, IL, 2001), pp. 90–94.
26. See also Yutaka Kusaga, *Transfer and Development of Coal-Mine Technology in Hokkaido* (Tokyo, 1982), pp. 24–26, 39–42, and 59–64; Weiner, *The Origins of the Korean Community*, ch. 3; Ken C. Kawashima, *The Proletarian Gamble: Korean Workers in Interwar Japan* (Durham, NC, 2009), pp. 25–45; Regine Mathias, *Industrialisierung und Lohnarbeit. Der Kohlebergbau in Nord-Kyūshū und sein Einfluss auf die Herausbildung einer Lohnarbeiterschaft* (Vienna, 1978), pp. 159–162; Michael Weiner, *Race and Migration in Imperial Japan* (London [etc.], 1994), pp. 112–113, 133–135, and 150.
27. Weiner, *Race and Migration in Imperial Japan*, p. 205; W. Donald Smith, "Beyond *The Bridge on the River Kwai*: Labor Mobilization in the Greater East Asia Co-Prosperity Sphere", *International Labor and Working-Class History*, 58 (2000), pp. 219–238, 223–226.
28. Laura E. Hein, *Fueling Growth: The Energy Revolution and Economic Policy in Postwar Japan* (Cambridge, MA, 1990), pp. 35–41.

Convict labour and other forms of forced labour were also introduced in the newly built Kuzbass basin in Siberia to meet the demands of forced industrialization in the Soviet Union in the 1930s, as Julia Landau details in her contribution to this Special Issue. In the German Ruhr, forced migrant labour, both civilian workers and prisoners of war, had already been used during World War I. These were mainly Belgians and Poles from the occupied Russian territories (at that time Poland did not exist as an independent state).[29] The experience with this kind of *Arbeitseinsatz* during World War I prepared the ground for the development of an extensive system of forced labour to support the war economy of Nazi Germany during World War II, both in Germany itself and in the European occupied territories.[30] In this system, ethnic discrimination and forced labour were closely interrelated as most of the deployed workers were so-called *Ostarbeiter* and prisoners of war from Poland, Ukraine, and Russia, and were considered by the Nazis to be of an inferior "race".

BRITISH AND OTHER MINERS IN WHITE SETTLER COLONIES IN THE EMPIRE

Much of the global expansion of coalmining in the nineteenth and twentieth centuries was possible only because of the migration of skilled groups of workers from Great Britain. They introduced mining skills and techniques, and often continued to hold privileged positions afterwards. The migration trajectories of British miners can be traced in almost every coalfield in the British Empire, but also in other parts of the world. One example is described by Clarice Speranza in this Special Issue in relation to the beginnings of coalmining in Brazil. In the Ukrainian Donbass (Donets basin) the first mines were opened in 1869 by the Welsh investor John J. Hughes (the place Juzovka was named after him), and he took some 100 Welsh and English workers with him.[31] Another example: in the early twentieth century the American-based Arctic Coal Company developed coalmining in the remote Spitsbergen Islands using experienced English miners from Sheffield. Common labourers were recruited in Norway (and also brought a habit of frequent strikes).[32]

29. Kai Rawe, *"… wir werden sie schon zur Arbeit bringen!". Ausländerbeschäftigung und Zwangsarbeit im Ruhrkohlenbergbau während des Ersten Weltkrieges* (Essen, 2005).
30. Klaus Tenfelde and Hans-Christoph Seidel (eds), *Zwangsarbeit im Bergwerk. Der Arbeitseinsatz im Kohlenbergbau des Deutschen Reiches und der besetzten Gebiete im Ersten und Zweiten Weltkrieg, Band I: Forschungen* (Essen, 2005). For the Belgian and French cases see also Nathalie Piquet, *Charbon – Travail forcé – Collaboration. Der nordfranzösische und belgische Bergbau unter deutscher Besatzung, 1940 bis 1944* (Essen, 2008).
31. Theodore H. Friedgut, *Iuzovka and Revolution*, II: *Politics and Revolution in Russia's Donbass, 1869–1924* (Princeton, NJ, 1994), p. 19.
32. Seth C. DePasqual, "Winning Coal at 78° North: Mining, Contingency and the Chaîne Opératoire in Old Longyear City" (MA thesis, Michigan Technological University, 2009), p. 28,

With the global expansion of coalmining from the nineteenth century onwards, British miners moved from coalfield to coalfield in British settler colonies such as South Africa, Canada, Australia, and New Zealand to develop the industry there. In the South African coalmines of Natal and Transvaal a high proportion of senior staff was Scottish; others came from Wales, Northumberland, Cornwall, and elsewhere in Britain.[33] In Australia, the coalfields of the Newcastle district in New South Wales were populated by English and Scottish miners, who also brought their tradition of trade unionism.[34] In the twentieth century Scottish migrants were still prominent in the Australian coalfields.[35] The West Coast mining district of New Zealand was an enclave of British mining practice as well. British colliers from Scottish and English coalfields had often first arrived in Australia.[36]

Also in the Canadian coalfields, both in the east (Nova Scotia) and the west (Vancouver Island), the British were the first to develop a mining industry and continued to arrive afterwards. Industrial mining in Nova Scotia started in the 1840s with experienced miners from Britain, who were later to form the higher strata of a hierarchy within the workforce.[37] The rapid expansion of the coal industry after 1900 brought a flood of new people into the area from other parts of Canada, the United States, the British Isles, France, eastern Europe, and elsewhere, but miners of Scottish descent continued to play an important role.[38]

Early recruitment of colliers for the coalmines on Vancouver Island started in 1854 from Staffordshire in England. As a result of chain migration their numbers swelled, with migrants being attracted from other British coalfields too. Soon, the whole of the British Isles were represented. Many "worked their way" through mining jobs in several colonies and

available at http://digitalcommons.mtu.edu/cgi/viewcontent.cgi?article=1307&context=etds, last accessed 3 August 2015.

33. Alexander, "Challenging Cheap-Labour Theory", p. 51; Peter Alexander, "Race, Class, Loyalty and the Structure of Capitalism: Coal Miners in Alabama and the Transvaal, 1918–1922", *Journal of Southern African Studies*, 30 (2004), pp. 115–132, 119 n. 20.

34. Ellen McEwen, "Coalminers in Newcastle, New South Wales: A Labour Aristocracy?", in Eric Fry (ed.), *Common Cause: Essays in Australian and New Zealand Labour History* (Sydney, NSW, 1986), pp. 77–92, 79–80; Robin Gollan, *The Coalminers of New South Wales: A History of the Union, 1860–1960* (Melbourne, VIC, 1963), pp. 17–19.

35. Andrew Reeves, "'Damned Scotsmen': British Migrants and the Australian Coal Industry, 1919–49", in Fry, *Common Cause*, pp. 93–106.

36. Len Richardson, "British Colliers and Colonial Capitalists: The Origins of Coalmining Unionism in New Zealand", in Fry, *Common Cause*, pp. 59–75; Len Richardson, *Coal, Class & Community: The United Mineworkers of New Zealand, 1880–1960* (Auckland, 1995), pp. 3–28.

37. Del Muise, "The Making of an Industrial Community: Cape Breton Coal Towns, 1867–1900", in Don Macgillivray and Brian Tennyson (eds), *Cape Breton Historical Essays* (Sydney, Cape Breton Island, 1981), pp. 76–94.

38. Paul MacEwan, *Miners and Steelworkers: Labour in Cape Breton* (Toronto, 1976).

countries of the Anglo-Saxon world. The British-born miners retained their prominence over the years. In 1881 the British colliers represented 79 per cent of the white workforce in the main Vancouver Island mining town of Nanaimo; in 1891 this was still 61 per cent. The other whites were from a variety of other countries (from Walloon Belgium, among others), or had been born in Canada itself.[39]

Unskilled, casual labour on Vancouver Island was at first recruited from the native population, providing an auxiliary source of labour, but from the 1870s the aboriginals were increasingly displaced by Chinese migrants. The Chinese performed mining tasks that were looked upon as humiliating by white miners. Efforts were repeatedly made to exclude Asian labour, but the Chinese remained a critical part of the collieries' workforce into the twentieth century, both above and below ground. The Chinese were employed especially in longwall mines, where craft labour had been replaced by semiskilled labour, under the supervision of a small number of whites.[40] White miners of British descent opposed the recruitment of Chinese labour, not only out of racial prejudice, but also in defence of craft positions.[41]

The South African sociologist John Hyslop has made a case for treating white workers of British origin in the settler colonies of the Empire as part of an "imperial working class" for which "whiteness" was a core component of identity.[42] This view is only partially convincing, as there were also British immigrants in South Africa, Canada, and Australia, who brought radical socialist and later communist ideas to the colonial coalfields and propagated interracial solidarity.[43] More importantly, without suggesting

39. John Belshaw, *Colonization and Community: The Vancouver Island Coalfield and the Making of the British Columbian Working Class* (Montreal, 2002), pp. 40 and 52–54, 59–60; *idem*, "The British Collier in British Columbia: Another Archetype Reconsidered", *Labour/Le Travail*, 34 (1994), pp. 11–36; Allen Seager and Adele Perry, "Mining the Connections: Class, Ethnicity, and Gender in Nanaimo, British Columbia, 1891", *Histoire Sociale/Social History*, 30 (1997), pp. 55–76, 67–69, and 73. Belgian miners were particularly active in the great miners' strike of 1891 in Nanaimo: *ibid.*, p. 59.
40. Belshaw, *Colonization and Community*, pp. 117–122.
41. *Idem*, "The British Collier in British Columbia", p. 35.
42. Jonathan Hyslop, "The Imperial Working Class Makes Itself 'White': White Labourism in Britain, Australia, and South Africa before the First World War", *Journal of Historical Sociology*, 12 (1999). pp. 398–421.
43. Neville Kirk, "The Rule of Class and the Power of Race: Socialist Attitudes to Class, Race and Empire", in *idem*, *Comrades and Cousins: Globalization, Workers and Labour Movements in Britain, the USA and Australia from the 1880s to 1914* (London, 2003), pp. 149–238; William Kenefick, "Confronting White Labourism: Socialism, Syndicalism, and the Role of the Scottish Radical Left in South Africa before 1914", *International Review of Social History*, 55 (2010), pp. 29–62; Jonathan Hyslop, "Scottish Labour, Race, and Southern African Empire c. 1880–1922: A Reply to Kenefick", *International Review of Social History*, 55 (2010), pp. 63–81; Lucien van der Walt, "The First Globalisation and Transnational Labour Activism in Southern Africa: White

that there was no racism involved, the opposition of white British miners to the entry of other ethnic and racial groups was inextricably linked to the defence of craft and skill in the mining industry.

AND IN THE UNITED STATES

The transfer of experience and technological skills, acquired at the coalface in the British mines, was essential for the development of the mining industry in the United States as well. The migration of British coalminers to the United States reached a provisional high in the 1860s and the early 1870s. In 1870 British immigrant miners (57,214) accounted for more than 60 per cent of all foreign-born miners (94,719) in the country. Once arrived, they moved from coalfield to coalfield in different US states. In Britain, emigration was sponsored by trade unions to reduce excess labour at British mines. Miners' leaders co-operated with agents, not only for American, but also for Nova Scotian (Canadian), New Zealand, and Australian coal companies in their recruitment efforts in England, Scotland, and Wales. Often British miners became union organizers in United States coalmining, and stayed in close contact with fellows and unions "at home".[44]

Many of these immigrant miners were young single men who travelled from mine to mine on a seasonal basis. Arriving with cheap tickets for the summer season, they would return to Britain for winter work, or travel a miners' circuit through different mining states. Depressions, like that of 1873, drove recently arrived migrant colliers back to their former homes in Britain. In this way transatlantic immigrant networks became conduits of British influence in American mining practices, not least in trade unionism.[45] Up to 1900, British-born immigrants were still dominant in coalmining in Illinois, Pennsylvania, West Virginia, and Kansas. Native-born miners were often also of British descent. Like everywhere else, ethnic networks were important in the migration patterns of British miners.[46] Welsh miners tended to cluster in communities around their own churches and to intermarry in their own group.[47] Welsh mine owners and managers often selected other

Labourism, the IWW, and the ICU, 1904–1934", *African Studies*, 66 (2007), pp. 223–251; Bill Freund, "Labour Studies and Labour History in South Africa: Perspectives from the Apartheid Era and After", *International Review of Social History*, 58 (2013), pp. 493–519, 500–501.

44. Amy Zahl Gottlieb, "Immigration of British Coal Miners in the Civil War Decade", *International Review of Social History*, 23 (1978), pp. 357–375.

45. John H.M. Laslett, "British Immigrant Colliers, and the Origins and Early Development of the UMWA, 1870–1912", in *idem* (ed.), *The United Mine Workers of America: A Model of Industrial Solidarity?* (University Park, PA, 1996), pp. 29–50, 30–31.

46. *Idem*, *Colliers Across the Sea: A Comparative Study of Class Formation in Scotland and the American Midwest, 1830–1924* (Urbana, IL [etc.], 2000).

47. Ronald L. Lewis, *Welsh Americans: A History of Assimilation in the Coalfields* (Chapel Hill, NC, 2008), p. 8.

Welshmen for their mining staff and workforce, thereby creating ethnic Welsh settlements.[48]

At the end of the nineteenth century, Italians, "Slav", and other migrants from southern and eastern Europe increasingly started to work in the coal-mines of the United States. By 1900 the combined total of Austro-Hungarians, Poles, and Russians in the anthracite mines of Pennsylvania had reached 31.3 per cent. Other mining districts, especially in the northern states, followed. The "Slav" and Italian migrant miners were mostly of peasant origin and unskilled. Their working in the mines went hand in hand with the introduction of coal-cutting machines and the deskilling of mine work. The proportion of British miners diminished, but they kept a position as foremen and skilled workers. A 1910 visitor to the Pennsylvania anthracite region summarized the resulting ethnic hierarchy: "Managers and superintendents: Welsh; foremen and bosses: Irish; contract miners: Poles and Lithuanians; outside laborers: Slovaks, Ruthenians, and Italians."[49] Welsh preponderance in supervisory roles was common throughout the coal industry prior to World War I. The Irish, "Slav", and Italian miners generally acted as labourers with a lower status. In these hierarchies social and ethnic differences went together.[50] However, despite the condescending attitude that Anglo-Saxon miners displayed towards the "new European" immigrants,[51] eastern European and Italian migrants soon took an active part in the miners' struggles and had to be accepted as members in the miners' union branches.[52]

Joe Trotter, in his contribution to this Special Issue, offers an overview of ethnic and race relations in the American coal industry and shows that relationships between "white" and African-American miners in trade unionism were much more ambivalent. While there were several coalmining districts, in Alabama for instance, where British miners participated in interracial unions,[53] the racial policies of organized labour were far from uniform. A debate on black workers, race, and organized labour in the United States, referred to as the "Gutman-Hill debate",[54] started several

---

48. *Idem*, "Networking among Welsh Coal Miners in Nineteenth-Century America", in Stefan Berger, Andy Croll, and Norman LaPorte (eds), *Towards a Comparative History of Coalfield Societies* (Aldershot, 2005), pp. 191–203.

49. Quoted in Laslett, "British Immigrant Colliers", pp. 46–47.

50. Lewis, *Welsh Americans*, pp. 189–249.

51. See also Michael A. Barendse, "American Perceptions concerning Slavic Immigrants in the Pennsylvania Anthracite Fields, 1880–1910: Some Comments on the Sociology of Knowledge", *Ethnicity*, 8 (1981), pp. 96–105.

52. Laslett, "British Immigrant Colliers", p. 49; see also Mildred A. Beik, "The UMWA and New Immigrant Miners in Pennsylvania Bituminous: The Case of Windber", in Laslett, *The United Mine Workers of America*, pp. 320–344.

53. Alexander, "Race, Class, Loyalty and the Structure of Capitalism", pp. 118 and 126.

54. Alex Lichtenstein, "Herbert Hill and the 'Negro Question'", *Labor: Studies in Working-Class History of the Americas*, 3:2 (2006), pp. 33–39. See also Joe William Trotter, *Coal, Class, and*

decades ago. It has continued in extended discussions about the importance of "whiteness" in American working-class history, especially after publication of David Roediger's *The Wages of Whiteness* in 1991.[55]

Price Fishback explained the difference in the experiences of African-American miners in the American coalfields in relation to racial discrimination and assimilation by the tightness or looseness of labour markets there. African Americans did better in the Alabama and West Virginia labour markets, because employers were constantly seeking new workers, and black migrants found ample employment. This contrasted with coalfields further north, where limits on employment growth constrained African-American immigration.[56] In West Virginia a large number of black miners worked side by side with other ethnic groups and were easily accepted into the miners' union, the United Mine Workers of America.

Fishback relates the arrival of different migrant groups in the United States mines to different phases of exploitation: most British immigrants came with coalmining experience and helped train American workers. They played a major role in the early development of the United States coal industry in the mid-1800s. Later, in the 1880s, and even more so between 1890 and 1910, in the Pennsylvania and Midwest mining regions inexperienced immigrants from eastern and southern Europe were employed on a massive scale to fill the need for unskilled labour. The coalfields in the low-wage Southern states (Kentucky, Virginia, West Virginia, Alabama) in turn attracted more African-American workers, migrating north from the Deep South.

THE POLISH DIASPORA IN EUROPE AND THE UNITED STATES

The Poles were the first and initially the most mobile among migratory mineworkers in Europe. From the last few decades of the nineteenth century they were mobilized on a massive scale to work in the coalmines of the Ruhr in Germany.[57] Polish migration to the Ruhr started in the 1870s

Color: Blacks in Southern West Virginia, 1915–32 (Urbana, IL, 1990); Daniel Letwin, *The Challenge of Interracial Unionism: Alabama Coal Miners, 1878–1921* (Chapel Hill, NC, 1998); Kelly, *Race, Class, and Power*, pp. 6–15 and 118–122.

55. David R. Roediger, *The Wages of Whiteness: Race and the Making of the American Working Class* (New York, 1991). For a review, see Eric Arnesen, "Up from Exclusion: Black and White Workers, Race, and the State of Labor History", *Reviews in American History*, 26 (1998), pp. 146–174; Bruce Nelson, "Class, Race and Democracy in the CIO: The 'New' Labor History Meets the 'Wages of Whiteness'", *International Review of Social History*, 41 (1996), pp. 351–374.

56. Price V. Fishback, *Soft Coal, Hard Choices: The Economic Welfare of Bituminous Coal Miners, 1890–1930* (New York [etc.], 1992), pp. 171–197.

57. Christoph Kleßmann, *Polnische Bergarbeiter im Ruhrgebiet 1870–1945. Soziale Integration und nationale Subkultur einer Minderheit in der deutschen Industriegesellschaft* (Göttingen, 1978); John J. Kulczycki, *The Foreign Worker and the German Labor Movement: Xenophobia*

with the recruitment of skilled miners from Upper Silesia (then still part of the German Empire), where coalmining had a much longer history. In the expansion phase following this initial immigration, however, most of the Polish migrants were unskilled workers, recruited from agricultural areas in West and East Prussia. At that time, almost all of them were Prussian citizens. By 1910, at least one-quarter of all Ruhr miners were Polish-speaking. Having arrived in the Ruhr, they formed ethnic communities, based on social organizations such as churches, trade unions, a Polish press, and sports clubs. As Diethelm Blecking reports in his article on Polish miners and sport in this Special Issue, the confrontation with a foreign and often hostile German milieu helped to foster a common national identity among these migrants, who had hitherto a locally oriented peasant background.

After World War I Poles from the Ruhr and from Poland itself moved to coalfields in northern France,[58] and to a lesser extent in Belgium and the Netherlands.[59] In the 1920s the number of Poles in the Ruhr was reduced to nearly one-third through re-migration and onward migration. For both economic and political reasons, many Polish workers from the Ruhr had moved to those mining areas in northern France that were suffering from a shortage of labour just after World War I.[60] As Philip Slaby makes clear in his article in this Special Issue, the German-Polish migrants, called "Westphaliens", brought a Polish press, social clubs, societies, and other organizations to France, and in this way were able to hold on to a Polish ethnic, religious, and national identity in a rather conservative fashion. This ethnicized segregation was consciously promoted by the mining companies, which sought both a fragmented workforce and ideological-cultural means to curb labour militancy.

and Solidarity in the Coal Fields of the Ruhr, 1871–1914 (Providence, RI, 1994); *idem, The Polish Coal Miners' Union and the German Labor Movement in the Ruhr, 1902–1934: National and Social Solidarity* (Oxford, 1997); Richard C. Murphy, *Gastarbeiter im Deutschen Reich: Polen in Bottrop 1891–1933* (Wuppertal, 1982), also in English: *Guestworkers in the German Reich: A Polish Community in Wilhelmian Germany* (New York, 1983); Wolfgang Köllmann, "Les mouvements migratoires pendant la grande période d'industrialisation de la Rhénanie-Westphalie", *Annales de Démographie Historique*, (1971), pp. 91–120.

58. Christoph Klessmann, "Comparative Immigrant History: Polish Workers in the Ruhr Area and the North of France", *Journal of Social History*, 20 (1986), pp. 335–353; Janine Ponty, *Polonais méconnus. Histoire des travailleurs immigrés en France dans l'entre-deux guerres* (Paris, 1988); Philip H. Slaby, *Industry, the State, and Immigrant Poles in Industrial France, 1919–1939* (Ann Arbor, MI, 2005).

59. Pien Versteegh, *De onvermijdelijke afkomst? De opname van Polen in het Duits, Belgisch en Nederlands mijnbedrijf in de periode 1920–1930* (Hilversum, 1994).

60. Donald Reid, "The Limits of Paternalism: Immigrant Coal Miners' Communities in France, 1919–45", *European History Quarterly*, 15 (1985), pp. 99–118, 100; Gary S. Cross, *Immigrant Workers in Industrial France: The Making of a New Laboring Class* (Philadelphia, PA, 1983), pp. 81–84.

As both employers and the French state were interested in recruiting Polish workers, a bilateral treaty was signed in 1919 to regulate the arrival of Polish citizens to the mines. This "Convention entre la France et la Pologne relative à l'émigration et l'immigration" can be considered the first in a system of state-regulated migration of mineworkers in Europe (see below). The employers cooperated in a Société Générale d'Immigration, which undertook a "systematic programme of prospecting" in Poland.[61] This resulted in a new wave of Polish outmigration of workers of peasant origin. Between 1920 and 1930 a total of 490,000 Polish migrants came to France, while about 60,000 left. A climax was reached in 1929 and 1930. The depression of the 1930s led to the expulsion of many of the Polish migrants who had arrived during the boom period in the 1920s. After 1937, when the French economy started to recover, the number of immigrant Poles rose again. Almost all migrants (92 per cent in Nord-Pas-de-Calais) worked in underground positions, while supervisory personnel were mostly French.[62] After World War II, however, the Poles left the French mines en masse, be it to their home country or to other jobs: while there had been 46,000 miners of Polish descent in 1946, there were only 283 in 1981.[63]

The new migrants arriving directly from Poland were more susceptible to social radicalization and rapprochement with the French labour movement than the Westphaliens. Some of the direct immigrants copied the Westphaliens' example and joined Polish clubs and societies; others adhered to French left-wing trade unions, and formed a Polish section of the Communist Party. In the 1930s a process of "depolonization" can be noticed. In the Popular Front period, communist influence among Polish immigrants reached its peak. In 1937, the circulation of the Polish-language newspaper issued by the Polish section of the PCF rose to 35,000.[64] Some authors consider the participation of Polish immigrant workers in French trade unions "to have contributed strongly to bringing together immigrant and French workers by treating them as equals".[65]

The first Polish mineworkers arrived in Belgium, at the Hainaut mines, before World War I. In the early 1920s Poles from the Ruhr and northern France also moved to the Belgian mines. In 1922 Belgian coal owners started to recruit in Poland itself. The number of immigrant Poles grew to several

61. Reid, "The Limits of Paternalism", p. 102; Cross, *Immigrant Workers in Industrial France*, pp. 55–63.
62. Ponty, *Polonais méconnus*, pp. 69–72; Klessmann, "Comparative Immigrant History", pp. 337–338.
63. Rolande Trempé, "La politique de la main-d'oeuvre de la Libération à nos jours en France", *Revue Belge d'Histoire Contemporaine*, 19 (1988), pp. 55–82, 70.
64. Klessmann, "Comparative Immigrant History", pp. 341–347; Reid, "The Limits of Paternalism", pp. 106–111.
65. Cited by Reid, "The Limits of Paternalism", p. 111.

hundred each year. Individual migration developed alongside organized recruitment. In September 1930 there were 11,993 Polish mineworkers in Belgium. In the depression years several thousand miners were dismissed again and had to return to Poland, but economic recovery in 1937 enabled a new recruitment campaign.[66] In the Netherlands, Poles had already begun to arrive before World War I as well, be it in relatively small numbers. Most of them came from the Ruhr. After World War I Dutch mining companies sent agents to the Ruhr and also to northern France to recruit Poles there. In the second half of the 1920s they started to recruit directly in Poland and in other countries in central, eastern, and southern Europe. As in Belgium, in the wake of official recruitment Polish migrants travelled from mine to mine in Germany, Belgium, and France. At its highest point there were some 1,200 Poles working in Dutch mines.[67]

Initially, the origin of Polish migration to the Ruhr and the Pennsylvanian anthracite region in the United States was quite similar. In the 1870s, both migrant groups tended to come from traditional mining areas in Upper Silesia. By the 1890s, however, the regions of origin were diverging sharply. In the Ruhr, almost all Polish migrants came from the German rural provinces of East Prussia, and because of the rapidly growing demand for labour in the Ruhr the number of Poles from the Prussian provinces migrating to the Pennsylvania coalfields decreased. The majority of Polish migrants to the United States now came from the Austrian (Galicia) and Russian empires.[68]

Both in the Ruhr and in Pennsylvania the Poles were the most numerous part of a highly diversified workforce in the mines. By 1914, at least twenty different languages were spoken in the Ruhr by migrants from the Netherlands, Belgium, and different parts of the Russian, Austrian, and German empires. Germans with local or regional roots had the highest status. In Pennsylvania "old" migrants from Great Britain and Ireland and their American-born children constituted the core of the "native" workforce, continuing to occupy the jobs with the highest status. In both regions, recently arrived Poles generally possessed the lowest social standing, at least until other immigrants began to arrive from the 1890s on; they suffered from significant discrimination because of their "foreign" language, religion, habits, and peasant background.[69] As a reaction, Poles

66. Frank Caestecker, *Alien Policy in Belgium, 1840–1940: The Creation of Guest Workers, Refugees and Illegal Aliens* (New York [etc.], 2000), pp. 47, 60, 67–68, 92–94, 117–123, 176–182, 216–225, and 243–345.

67. Serge Langeweg, *Mijnbouw en arbeidsmarkt in Nederlands-Limburg. Herkomst, werving, mobiliteit en binding van mijnwerkers tussen 1900 en 1965* (Hilversum, 2011), pp. 129–130, 140–148, and 153.

68. Brian McCook, *The Borders of Integration: Polish Migrants in Germany and the United States, 1870–1924* (Athens, OH, 2011), pp. 20–21.

69. *Ibid.*, p. 25.

developed an outspoken ethnic identity, supported by organized sociability. In pre-1914 Germany Poles established their own union, the Zjednoczenie Zawadowe Polski [Polish Trade Union], but in Pennsylvania they soon became involved in the undifferentiated United Mine Workers of America.[70]

STATE-REGULATED LABOUR MIGRATION TO NORTH-WESTERN EUROPE

Shortages of labour in several continental western European coalfields had already emerged in the expansion years before World War I, and they re-emerged after that war and in the 1920s. While in that period Great Britain and Germany were able to build a mining labour force from their own internal labour supply, France, Belgium, and the Netherlands witnessed severe labour shortages. To counteract these labour shortages in the interwar years, not only in the mining industry, western European countries developed systems of regulated migration based on bilateral treaties, especially with newly formed states in eastern Europe such as Poland, Yugoslavia, and Czechoslovakia, but also with Italy. These agreements set up official migration channels alongside spontaneous individual migration. State involvement was triggered by protectionist labour-market policies, increasing state involvement in welfare arrangements, and the concomitant costs of unregulated migration for both employers and the state.[71]

As mentioned above, the immigration agreement concluded between France and Poland on 7 September 1919 can be considered the first in a series of treaties of this kind. It was very soon followed, on 30 September, by a treaty with Italy, which in the early 1920s brought a first wave of Italian migrants to the coalfields in northern and central France, mainly from central and north-eastern Italy.[72] Belgium concluded an agreement with Italy to regulate migration in 1923.[73] In general, the Belgian state cooperated closely with employers' organizations in the mines, and this was also the case in the recruitment of smaller numbers from Czechoslovakia,

70. *Ibid.*, pp. 70–93.
71. Christoph Rass, "Temporary Labour Migration and State-Run Recruitment of Foreign Workers in Europe, 1919–1975: A New Migration Regime?", *International Review of Social History*, 57 (2012), pp. 191–224; *idem, Institutionalisierunsprozesse auf einem internationalen Arbeitsmarkt: Bilaterale Wanderungsverträge in Europa zwischen 1919 and 1974* (Paderborn [etc.], 2010).
72. Rudy Damiani, "Les Italiens: une immigration d'appoint", in Marie Cegarra *et al., Tous gueules noires. Histoire de l'immigration dans le bassin minier du Nord-Pas-de-Calais* (Lewarde, 2004), pp. 85–109; Rudy Damiani, "Les Italiens du bassin miner du Nord-Pas-de-Calais de 1939 à 1945", in Pierre Milza and Denis Peschanski (eds), *Exils et migration. Italiens et Espagnols en France, 1938–1946* (Paris, 1994), pp. 455–464.
73. Caestecker, *Alien Policy in Belgium*, pp. 62–65.

Yugoslavia, Hungary, and Poland.[74] In the Netherlands, in the second half of the 1920s the organized recruitment of foreign workers in their home countries replaced previous attempts to attract skilled migrants from the coalfields of the Ruhr and Nord-Pas-de-Calais. Recruitment campaigns by Dutch mining companies in Czechoslovakia, Yugoslavia, Poland, and Italy brought new groups of inexperienced migrant workers to the coalmines. The campaigns were organized jointly by employers' organizations, state officials, and institutions in the countries of origin, on the basis of bilateral agreements. However, during the depression of the 1930s most of the newly arrived migrants were dismissed and sent home.[75]

After World War II the system of bilateral migration agreements became a general device to recruit "guestworkers" for the north-west European mining industry from Mediterranean countries. It all started with Italy. Just after the war, urgent energy needs, both in France and Belgium, prompted governments to call for a *bataille de charbon* (a "battle for coal"), but labour supply in these countries fell short. Italy became the preferred country for the recruitment of migrant labour for the mines in France, Belgium, and somewhat later also in the Netherlands. In spite of attempts by Italy to include their citizens in the guidelines for the free movement of workers by the European Coal and Steel Community (1951 and 1957), national states held on to separate recruitment agreements.[76] France concluded an agreement with Italy on 26 February 1946 to arrange for the arrival of migrants in exchange for the delivery of a fixed amount of coal to Italy for each miner.[77] At first 20,000 were recruited. After November 1946 some 200,000 followed; most of them left again after the expiration of their contracts, however. Several new waves of Italians arrived in the 1950s. The employment of Italians in French coalmining rose to a highpoint of 11,023 in 1958; thereafter their number diminished to 1,687 in 1981.[78]

A few months later than France, on the 20 June 1946, Belgium concluded a comparable agreement with Italy on the recruitment of (initially) 50,000 miners, and a yearly (paid) export of 2 to 3 million tons of Belgian coal to Italy. Between 1946 and 1958 141,151 Italians were officially recruited to work in the mines, but this figure does not include the unorganized, spontaneous migration of individuals, arriving with the help of family members or acquaintances, whose number must have been considerable as well. As in France, because of the enormous turnover of

74. *Ibid.*, pp. 221–222.
75. Langeweg, *Mijnbouw en arbeidsmarkt*, pp. 144–150.
76. Simone A.W. Goedings, *Labor Migration in an Integrating Europe: National Migration Policies and the Free Movement of Workers, 1950–1968* (The Hague, 2005), pp. 60–61, 91–93, and 312–313.
77. Damiani, "Les Italiens", pp. 97–98.
78. Trempé, "La politique de la main-d'oeuvre", p. 70.

migrants a large difference arose between numbers recruited and those actually working at the end of each year.[79] The movement into and out of Belgian coalmines amounted to about one-third of the total number of underground miners in 1955–1956, twice the rate in France or Germany. Nevertheless, in Belgium the number of Italians working in the mines was much larger than in France: between 1948 and 1957 it fluctuated between 33,000 and 47,500 at the end of each year. After the Marcinelle disaster in 1956, which killed 269 miners, among them 136 Italians, the number of Italians employed in Belgian coalmines diminished from 44,000 in 1957 to 2,500 in 1975.[80] The Netherlands was a relative latecomer in the interstate quest for migrant workers from Italy: on 4 December 1948 an agreement was signed with the Italian government to recruit for the coalmines, although on a much smaller scale than in the French or Belgian cases:[81] in 1957 the number of Italians had risen to only 1,966.

The proliferation of these kinds of agreement for the state-sponsored recruitment of migrant workers has to be considered a response to shortages of unskilled or semiskilled labour in the mines.[82] Demand for unskilled labour had increased, relatively at least, because of the introduction of new mining methods and technologies. The Italian migrants were recruited mainly from the agrarian central and southern parts of the country, had no earlier experience with minework, and had to learn the skills on the job. This is one explanation for the high turnover, other explanations being the miserable conditions of their lodgings (often camp-like dwellings), poor working conditions, and their status as subordinate workers in general. As soon as new opportunities arose in their home country, the migration flow from Italy dried up. Western European countries started to negotiate with other countries in the Mediterranean periphery to find new supplies of mine labour. Instead of Italy, in the 1960s Spain, Yugoslavia, Greece, Tunisia, Turkey, and Morocco became preferred countries of recruitment for the coal and other industries in continental western Europe. This time, Germany, too, joined the group of recruiting countries. From each of these countries,

79. Anne Morelli, "L'appel à la main d'oeuvre italienne pour les charbonnages et sa prise en charge à son arrivée en Belgique dans l'immédiat après-guerre", *Revue Belge d'Histoire Contemporaine*, XIX (1988), pp. 83–130.
80. René Leboutte, "Coal Mining, Foreign Workers and Mine Safety: Steps towards European Integration, 1946–85", in Berger *et al.*, *Towards a Comparative History of Coalfield Societies*, pp. 219–237, 228–230.
81. Tesseltje de Lange, *Staat, markt en migrant. De regulering van arbeidsmigratie naar Nederland 1945–2006* (Amsterdam, 2007), pp. 69–70; Langeweg, *Mijnbouw en arbeidsmarkt*, pp. 186–192.
82. Leboutte, "Coal Mining, Foreign Workers and Mine Safety"; Christoph Rass and Florian Wöltering, "Migration und Sozialregion: Wanderungsbeziehungen zwischen europäischen und außereuropäischen Bergrevieren", in Angelika Westermann (ed.), *Montanregion als Sozialregion. Zur gesellschaftlichen Dimension von "Region" in der Montanwirtschaft* (Husum, 2012), pp. 59–89, 70.

"guestworkers", as they were called (from the German word *Gastarbeiter*), were again recruited on the basis of bilateral treaties to regulate migration according to the needs of the economy.[83]

In all coal-producing countries in western Europe (excluding Britain) "guestworkers" were employed in coalmining on a relatively large scale. To provide for workers in Germany, for instance, a German-Turkish "Regelung der Vermittlung türkischer Arbeitnehmer nach der Bundesrepublik Deutschland" [Settlement to Procure Turkish Employees for the Federal Republic of German] was signed in 1961 to regulate the selection and mediation of Turkish contract workers by German agencies in Istanbul and Ankara. By 1963 10,200 Turkish miners were already employed in German coalmining, the largest group among the 27,130 foreign workers in that industry.[84] After a relapse during the recession of 1966–1967, their number rose again, from about 5,200 in 1969 to 19,800 in 1973, accounting for 74 per cent of all foreign workers in coalmining.[85] The stark fluctuation of these numbers before, during, and after the recession of 1966–1967 reflects the general position of foreign workers as a flexible reserve army, both in coalmining and other sectors. Although by 1973 several German mines were staffed almost exclusively by miners of Turkish descent, in most cases Turks were to be found only at the lower end of the job ladder. As with the Moroccan workers in other European coal-producing countries, they were often employed to ensure exhausted or unprofitable mines could be closed down smoothly.[86]

Moroccan migrants were the last group of miners recruited for the coal industry on the basis of bilateral treaties. Their main destinations were France, Belgium, and the Netherlands. In the interwar years, small numbers had already arrived in the mining districts of northern France, and from there into Belgium.[87] In the late 1950s and early 1960s migration to northern France, Belgium, and the Netherlands started to grow, at first spontaneously, then in Morocco itself through recruitment by employers' organizations, but also through family networks. Once in the region, Moroccan migrants easily crossed the borders between France, Belgium, and the Netherlands, whose coalfields were situated relatively close to each other. Treaties with Morocco to regulate migration officially were signed in 1963 with France, in 1964 with Belgium, and in 1969 with the Netherlands.

---

83. Rass, *Institutionalisierunsprozesse auf einem internationalen Arbeitsmarkt, passim.*
84. Karin Hunn, *"Nächstes Jahr kehren wir zurück ...". Die Geschichte der türkischen 'Gastarbeiter' in der Bundesrepublik* (Göttingen, 2005), pp. 107–109.
85. *Ibid.*, p. 213.
86. *Ibid.*, pp. 219–221.
87. Marie Cegarra, *La mémoire confisquée: les mineurs marocains dans le Nord de la France* (Villeneuve-d'Ascq, 1999), pp. 45–46; *idem*, "Récession et immigration: les mineurs marocains dans les mines de charbon du Nord/Pas-de-Calais", in Jean-François Eck, Peter Friedemann, and Karl Lauschke (eds), *La reconversion des bassins charbonniers. Une comparison interrégionale entre la Ruhr et le Nord-Pas-de-Calais* (Villeneuve-d'Ascq, 2006), pp. 157–164.

The treaties enabled the entry of a growing number of Moroccan immigrants into the mines of these countries, in two waves: the first until the recession of 1966–1967, the second in the early 1970s. A total of 20,495 Moroccan immigrants arrived in France between 1960 and 1965; their number reached 78,000 in 1977.[88] Migration to Belgium and the Netherlands was less substantial in absolute terms (several thousands), but Moroccans became by far the largest group of foreigners in the Belgian and Dutch mines in the 1970s.[89] In the decaying coal industry in these countries, mining companies were unable to hold a local workforce. Miners and their sons took a bleak view of future opportunities in coalmining and started to look for employment outside the mines. Moroccan miners were brought in on short-term contracts to compensate for shortages of local workers and to help pit closures to proceed in an orderly manner.[90] In the 1970s they were recruited for the Lorraine coalmines in France with this same goal in mind.[91]

MIGRANTS IN THE MINING COMMUNITY

While debates on ethnic and racial discrimination and segregation, as against solidarity and integration, in miners' unions have a certain tradition in mining labour history, the focus of historical research since the 1990s has shifted from the relationship of class, race, and ethnic identity in workers' struggles to other aspects. New approaches have allowed scholars to shed light on issues such as racial discrimination, ethnic segregation, social integration, and the intricate processes of identity formation among migrants in the context of mining communities. At the same time, the concept of the "mining community" itself, as a closed, homogeneous, and often isolated settlement, dominant for a while in (especially British) sociology and mining history,[92] has come under scrutiny, precisely because of the diversity of its inhabitants.[93] As early as 1992 the late Klaus Tenfelde wrote:

> One such difference was that between residents and newcomers; another was the ethnic difference between, for example, the Irish [...] and the English and

88. Cegarra, *La mémoire confisquée*, p. 53.

89. Karim Azzouzi, "Les Marocains dans l'industrie charbonnière belge", *Brood en Rozen. Tijdschrift voor de geschiedenis van sociale bewegingen*, 9 (2004), pp. 35–53; Tanja Cranssen, "Marokkaanse mijnwerkers in Limburg, 1963–1975", *Studies over de sociaaleconomische geschiedenis van Limburg/ Jaarboek van het Sociaal Historisch Centrum voor Limburg*, 48 (2003), pp. 121–148.

90. *Ibid.*, pp. 145–146; Cegarra, "Récession et immigration", p. 127.

91. Piero-D. Galloro, Tamara Pascutto, and Alexia Serré, *Mineurs algériens et marocains. Une autre mémoire du charbon lorrain* (Paris, 2011), pp. 45–71.

92. The classic text is Martin Bulmer, "Sociological Models of the Mining Community", *Sociological Review*, 23 (1975), pp. 61–92. See also Norman Dennis, Fernando Henriques, and Clifford Slaughter, *Coal is our Life: An Analysis of a Yorkshire Mining Community* (London, 1956).

93. Mining communities in Britain are sometimes supposed to be less ethnically diverse than those in Europe and America. For an alternative view on the British case, see David Gilbert, "Imagined Communities and Mining Communities", *Labour History Review*, 60:2 (1995), pp. 47–55.

Americans, as well as between the Polish and the Germans. These ethnic differences weighed all the more heavily since [...] it was possible to link them to religious difference [...].[94]

The shift towards the study of migration and ethnicity in mining communities is clearly visible in the landmark volume on comparative coalfield history edited by Stefan Berger *et al.*, published thirteen years later (in 2005). Several chapters deal with "identities", "communities", and with the "interlocking spheres of workplace, neighbourhood, family, and working-class organizations", including the one by Leen Beyers on "ethnic, class and gender identities at street level" in the Belgian miners' colony (*cité*) of Zwartberg.[95] In this article she arrives at a fairly positive assessment of the inter-ethnic interaction between Flemish, Polish, Czech, and Italian neighbours. Elsewhere, she compares the construction and deconstruction of ethnic boundaries between second-generation migrants of Polish and Italian origin and Belgian nationals in this *cité*.[96] The time lag in the arrival of these different groups of immigrants also caused a time lag in the social integration of their children. However, both groups of migrants really succeeded in being accepted as "Belgians" only after the arrival of new groups of Islamic migrants, predominantly from Turkey. The (perceived) distinctiveness of these new outsiders led to the view by the local population (many of them former migrants or descendants of migrants) that migrants from former migration waves had successfully integrated.

Comparable issues have been raised in the German Ruhr in discussions on the similarities and differences between Polish migration in the more distant past and Turkish immigration in the recent past.[97] While historical

94. Klaus Tenfelde, "The Miners' Community and the Community of Mining Historians", in *idem* (ed.), *Towards a Social History of Mining in the 19th and 20th Centuries* (Munich, 1992), pp. 1201–1215, 1207. The volume itself, which brought together a selection of around seventy conference papers, contained only one on this issue of ethnicity: Mildred A. Beik, "The Competition for Ethnic Community Leadership in a Pennsylvania Bituminous Coal Town, 1890s–1930s", in *ibid.*, pp. 223–241.

95. Leen Beyers, "Everyone Black? Ethnic, Class and Gender Identities at Street Level in a Belgian Mining Town, 1930–50", in Berger *et al.*, *Towards a Comparative History of Coalfield Societies*, pp. 146–163.

96. Leen Beyers, "From Class to Culture: Immigration, Recession, and Daily Ethnic Boundaries in Belgium, 1940s–1990s", *International Review of Social History*, 53 (2008), pp. 37–61.

97. Aloys Berg, "Polen und Türken im Ruhrkohlenbergbau. Ein Vergleich zweier Wanderungsvorgänge mit einer Fallstudie über 'Türken im Ruhrgebiet'" (Ph.D. dissertation, University of Bochum, 1990); Diethelm Blecking, "Polish Community before the First World War and Present-Day Turkish Community Formation: Some Thoughts on a Diachronistic Comparison", in John Belchem and Klaus Tenfelde (eds), *Irish and Polish Migration in Comparative Perspective* (Essen, 2003), pp. 183–200; Leo Lucassen, "Poles and Turks in the German Ruhr Area: Similarities and Differences", in Leo Lucassen, David Feldman, and Jochen Oltmer (eds), *Paths of Integration: Migrants in Western Europe (1880–2004)* (Amsterdam, 2006), pp. 27–45; Klaus Tenfelde, "Schmelztiegel Ruhrgebiet? Polnische und türkische Arbeiter im Bergbau: Integration und

research, like that presented by Diethelm Blecking in this Special Issue, has established a clear relationship between the segregation of and discrimination against Polish miners before World War I and the emergence of a strong feeling of national identity among them, the supposedly easy integration of Polish migrants in the past has repeatedly been invoked in public discourse as a counter-story pointing to the lack of integration of their Turkish counterparts today. The supposedly opposite behaviour of Polish and Italian migrants on the one hand and Turkish migrants on the other serves in this discourse to disqualify the ability of Islamic migrants to adapt to "Western" culture. From a historians' perspective this is much more ambiguous, however.[98] In her article in this Special Issue on what the French call *la sociabilité sportive*, especially football, in the coalfield of Nord-Pas-de-Calais, Marion Fontaine argues that the possibilities open to migrants to participate in the sporting community depended on the social conditions in mining. Unlike the Polish footballers in the mining villages in the interwar years, migrants from the Maghreb (Morocco and Algeria) arriving after World War II could not be incorporated into professional football because the mining communities were already in dissolution owing to the decline of the mining industry since the 1960s.[99]

Marion Fontaine's case study points to the fact that opportunity structures and circumstances change considerably over time, which makes it difficult to compare (*ceteris paribus*, as it were) trajectories of migrants of different descent arriving in different periods of time. Other historians, however, have argued that the difference might not be that significant, because, depending on the time-frame under consideration, it often takes several generations for migrant minorities to overcome segregation and discrimination and to integrate socially and culturally.[100]

The comparability of "old" (nineteenth- and early twentieth-century) and "new" (late twentieth-century) migrants has been questioned, however, especially in the United States, where theories about a pattern of initial migrant segregation and subsequent integration over several generations have a long tradition, dating from the so-called Chicago School of migration research in the 1920s and 1930s.[101] In this debate, migration historians seem

Assimilation in der montanindustriellen Erwerbsgesellschaft", *Mitteilungsblatt des Instituts für soziale Bewegungen*, 36 (2006), pp. 7–28.

98. See, for instance, the uneasy integration of Italian migrants in the Walloon coalfields: Flavia Cumoli, "Perdus dans le paysage: la prolongation de la culture rurale italienne dans les bassins miniers de Wallonie", *Revue belge d'histoire contemporaine*, 37 (2007), pp. 419–443.

99. See also Marion Fontaine, "Les 'Polaks' et les 'Sang et Or': une lecture sportive de la relation aux étrangers dans une ville minière", in Judith Rainhorn and Didier Terrier (eds), *Étranges voisins. Altérité et relations de proximité dans la ville depuis le XVIIIe siècle* (Rennes, 2010), pp. 151–162.

100. Leo Lucassen, *The Immigrant Threat: The Integration of Old and New Migrants in Western Europe since 1850* (Urbana, IL, 2005).

101. *Ibid.*, pp. 5–8.

to be more confident about the applicability of this model, stressing parallels between the experiences of "old" and "new" migrants, than (several) social scientists, who argue that both present-day society and the (ethnic and religious) composition of the "new" immigrant groups in the United States (and also in Europe) differ dramatically from earlier ones. What seems important from a historical point of view, also in the context of ethnic relations among migrant miners, is that the social construction of ethnic and racial differences changed over time, for instance in the case of Irish, Italian, and "Slav" migrants in the United States, who were initially seen as racially inferior and who only gradually became "white".

This "process of whitening" has been explained partly by the mass migration of African Americans to the north, which enabled other (European) ethnic groups to be redefined as "whites" as opposed to "blacks". This is consistent with David Roediger's ideas about "whiteness" as a constructed racial identity in opposition to "blackness".[102] Roediger's arguments have been criticized, however, as rather one-dimensional, because they ascribe a uniform racial identity to an abstract "white" working class, which itself remained sharply divided along lines of ethnicity and other divisions.[103] Roediger himself cites the American writer Upton Sinclair, who in his novel *King Coal* gave a rather bleak picture of inter-ethnic relations in a Colorado coal town around 1917:[104]

> There were most rigid social lines in North Valley, it appeared. The Americans and English and Scotch looked down upon the Welsh and Irish; the Welsh and Irish looked down upon the Dagoes and Frenchies; the Dagoes and Frenchies looked down upon Polacks and Hunkies, these in turn upon Greeks, Bulgarians and "Montynegroes", and so on through a score of races of Eastern Europe: Lithuanians, Slovaks, and Croatians, Armenians, Roumanians, Rumelians, Ruthenians – ending up with Greasers, niggers, and last and lowest, Japs.[105]

CONCLUSION

What becomes clear from this overview is that there was a huge difference between the migration and settlement of skilled miners, like those from Britain but also from other countries, and the recruitment of groups of unskilled workers from rural areas. What stands out as common in the cases mentioned is that these recruitments were often targeted at ethnic groups of

102. Roediger, *Wages of Whiteness*.
103. Arnesen, "Up from Exclusion", p. 164.
104. David R. Roediger and Elizabeth D. Esch, *The Production of Difference: Race and the Management of Labor in US History* (Oxford, 2012), p. 89.
105. Upton Sinclair, *King Coal: A Novel* (New York, 1917), p. 53. "Dagoes" is contemptuous slang for Italians, Spaniards, or Portuguese; "Hunkies" is an ethnic slur used to refer to a labourer from central Europe; "Greasers" is a derogatory term for Mexicans.

a lower social status, not only because they were rural or unskilled, but also because they were considered inferior from a cultural or ethnic viewpoint.

Ethnic descent differentiated not only groups of migrants, however, but also an "established" workforce from "outsiders": ethnic minorities who were considered and treated as people of a lower status than the dominant ethnic group. In many cases the recruitment of new ethnic groups proceeded in parallel with technological innovations in the mining industry, which deskilled large parts of the work and required an enlargement of the workforce by unskilled or semiskilled workers. Examples include the massive recruitment of Koreans in Japan in the late 1920s, when work gangs in longwall mining replaced family teams at post-and-pillar mining; the employment of Chinese labourers in longwall mines on the Canadian west coast, replacing craft labour by semiskilled labour; the entry of "Slav" and Italian migrant miners in the Pennsylvania coalmines, which went hand in hand with the introduction of coal-cutting machines and the deskilling of mine work; and the recruitment of inexperienced Italian migrants in the French and Belgium mines after World War II, whose deployment had been made possible by the introduction of new mining methods and technologies.

The ethnic divisions in the workforce were therefore blurred with divisions of skill and hierarchy. This explains the negative, or sometimes even racist, attitudes of early arrivers, mainly skilled white miners, and their descendants, towards newcomers, not only blacks, as in South Africa and the United States, but also newly arrived migrants of other complexities and looks, such as eastern Europeans or Italians. Status and ethnic prejudice enforced each other also in the social relations between migrant families in the mining communities. The longer-term consequences of these divisions are, however, much less clear. Studies on the segregation and integration of different ethnic groups in European and United States coalmining give mixed results, both in relation to trade unions and daily life. Comparisons of "old" (late nineteenth- and early twentieth-century) and "new" (late twentieth-century) migration reveal great differences, which can perhaps be attributed to the shorter time-frame of the latter, but more likely to the persistent discrimination of the new migrant groups in Europe and the United States from the 1970s.

The picture, however, is far from complete, as it does not include knowledge about the dynamics in and around coalfields in other world regions. Coalmining (and mining in general) has had, and still has, a particular tendency to reshape both the natural and social surroundings of its locations, reshuffling, through the quest for a workforce amenable to the operator's needs, the ethnic and social composition of the mining communities many times over. The processes of segregation and integration, of exclusion and inclusion, and of solidarity and fragmentation, will thus be found in other parts of the world too. The degree to which other places follow the European and North American pattern remains to be ascertained.

IRSH 60 (2015), Special Issue, pp. 41–62 doi:10.1017/S0020859015000358
© 2015 Internationaal Instituut voor Sociale Geschiedenis

A Zambian Town in Colonial Zimbabwe:
The 1964 "Wangi Kolia" Strike

IAN PHIMISTER AND ALFRED TEMBO

Centre for Africa Studies, University of the Free State
205 Nelson Mandela Drive, Bloemfontein, South Africa

E-mail: phimister4@gmail.com; alfred.tembo4@gmail.com

ABSTRACT: In March 1964 the entire African labour force at Wankie Colliery, "Wangi Kolia", in Southern Rhodesia went on strike. Situated about eighty miles south-east of the Victoria Falls on the Zambezi River, central Africa's only large coalmine played a pivotal role in the region's political economy. Described by *Drum*, the famous South African magazine, as a "bitter underpaid place", the colliery's black labour force was largely drawn from outside colonial Zimbabwe. While some workers came from Angola, Tanganyika (Tanzania), and Nyasaland (Malawi), the great majority were from Northern Rhodesia (Zambia). Less than one-quarter came from Southern Rhodesia (Zimbabwe) itself. Although poor-quality food rations in lieu of wages played an important role in precipitating female-led industrial action, it also occurred against a backdrop of intense struggle against exploitation over an extended period of time. As significant was the fact that it happened within a context of regional instability and sweeping political changes, with the independence of Zambia already impending. This late colonial conjuncture sheds light on the region's entangled dynamics of gender, race, and class.

Until the proving and development over the past decade of gigantic coal reserves in Mozambique's Tete Province, the only coalmine of any significance in central Africa was Wankie, or "Wangi", since 1980 Hwange, Colliery in north-western Zimbabwe. Aside from scattered references in general histories, the colliery has been the subject of five historical studies, three of which were written by one of the authors of this article.[1] Only one study, a comparative examination of mining disasters, has looked at the period since 1954.[2] It is this

---

1. Ian Phimister, "Lashers and Leviathan: The 1954 Coalminers' Strike in Colonial Zimbabwe", *International Review of Social History*, 39 (1994), pp. 165–195; *idem*, *Wangi Kolia: Coal, Capital and Labour in Colonial Zimbabwe 1894–1954* (Johannesburg, 1994); and *idem*, "Global Labour History in the Twenty-First Century: Coal Mining and Its Recent Pasts", in Jan Lucassen (ed.), *Global Labor History: A State of the Art* (Bern, 2006), pp. 573–589. See also Charles van Onselen, "The 1912 Wankie Colliery Strike", *Journal of African History*, 15 (1974), pp. 275–289.
2. Ruth Edgecombe, "Dannhauser (1926) and Wankie (1972) – Two Mining Disasters: Some Safety Implications in Historical Perspective", *Journal of Natal and Zulu History*, 13 (1990–1991), pp. 71–90.

omission that the present article seeks in part to address. Wherever possible it does so by engaging with three overlapping historiographies. These comprise Zambian and Zimbabwean labour history, especially as regards questions of class and tribal representation in a context of migration and ethnicity;[3] the relationship between African labour movements and nationalist politics;[4] and the roles played by women in mining communities.[5] An overarching theme is how different ethnic groups lived together, and how they coped with racial discrimination and ethnic segregation. Unfolding in a specific place at a particular time, across an international border in a period of contested decolonization, it is precisely because these processes are both interrelated and contingent, as Frederick Cooper has observed elsewhere, that they deserve special scrutiny.[6]

Based on a wide range of sources, this study draws most heavily on the papers of the Associated Mineworkers of Rhodesia. Covering the strike and its aftermath in detail, these papers are presently privately held. Negotiations are underway for their deposit with the Contemporary Archives Centre of the University of the Free State, Bloemfontein, South Africa. This study also makes use of the papers of Garfield Todd, the Southern Rhodesian politician famous for his opposition to white minority

---

3. For Zambia see Ian Henderson, "Wage-Earners and Political Protest in Colonial Africa: The Case of the Copperbelt", *African Affairs*, 72 (1973), pp. 288–299; and Charles Perrings, *Black Mineworkers in Central Africa: Industrial Strategies and the Evolution of an African Proletariat in the Copperbelt 1911–1941* (New York, 1979). For Zimbabwe see, especially, Charles van Onselen's two articles, "The Role of Collaborators in the Rhodesian Mining Industry 1900–1935", *African Affairs*, 72 (1973), pp. 401–418, and "Black Workers in Central African Industry: Critical Essay on the Historiography and Sociology of Rhodesia", *Journal of Southern African Studies*, 1 (1975), pp. 228–246.

4. Among many studies engaging in part or whole with this question, see Robert Bates, *Unions, Parties, and Political Development: A Study of Mineworkers in Zambia* (New Haven, CT, 1971); Elena L. Berger, *Labour, Race and Colonial Rule: The Copperbelt from 1924 to Independence* (Oxford, 1974); Andrew Roberts, *A History of Zambia* (London, 1976); Peter Harries-Jones, *Freedom and Labour: Mobilization and Political Control on the Zambian Copperbelt* (Oxford, 1975); M.R. Mwendapole, *A History of the Trade Union Movement in Zambia up to 1968* (Lusaka, 1977); Jonathan Hyslop, "Trade Unionism in the Rise of African Nationalism, Bulawayo 1945–1963", *Africa Perspective*, 1 (1986), pp. 34–67; Brian Raftopoulos, "Gender, Nationalist Politics and the Fight for the City: Harare 1940–1950s", *SAFERE: Southern African Feminist Review*, 1 (1995), pp. 30–45; *idem*, "Problematising Nationalism in Zimbabwe: A Historiographical Review", *Zambezia*, 26 (1999), pp. 115–134; and Frederick Cooper, *Decolonization and African Society: The Labour Question in French and British Africa* (Cambridge, 1996).

5. Notably Valerie G. Hall, *Women at Work, 1860–1939: How Different Industries Shaped Women's Experiences* (Woodbridge, 2013); and Jane L. Parpart, *Labour and Capital on the African Copperbelt* (Philadelphia, PA, 1983). See also Teresa Barnes, *"We Women Worked So Hard": Gender, Urbanization, and Social Reproduction in Colonial Harare, Zimbabwe, 1930–1956* (Oxford, 1999).

6. Frederick Cooper, *Colonialism in Question: Theory, Knowledge, History* (Berkeley, CA, 2005), p. 206.

rule, also in private possession, as well as published primary material located variously in the National Archives of Zambia, Lusaka, and the National Archives of Zimbabwe, Harare. The latter includes: key commissions of enquiry; legislative assembly debates; reports of the government mining engineer; colliery and Anglo American corporation annual reports; and various published and unpublished brochures and memoranda about the colliery. Of these, the most useful was a thirty-three-page outline circulated in 1981 of the colliery's past and present position.[7] Particularly valuable were contemporary newspapers and periodicals, coming from throughout central and southern Africa, and from a variety of perspectives.[8] Interviews were conducted in the early 1990s with black and white miners who worked at the colliery between the 1950s and the 1970s. The transcripts are in the National Archives of Zimbabwe.

The first section outlines the colliery's origins and the region's political economy. It traces the history of the colliery from the end of the nineteenth century up to the early 1960s. Claiming that successive colliery companies exploited black miners with a ruthlessness not exceeded in any other sector of central and southern Africa's mining industry during the colonial era, it argues that the colliery's contested pasts are most usefully interpreted in the context of transnational political economy. By the first half of the 1960s, economic and political forces were pulling in different directions more strongly than ever before.

The second and third sections focus on the causes, course, and consequences of the strike itself. Particular attention is paid to competing interests within and beyond the sprawling confines of the colliery. A short conclusion attempts to explain the reasons for the strike, and its wider significance. This is done by locating it within the labour historiographies of Zimbabwe and Zambia, as well as alongside the wider themes noted above. Throughout, this case study turns on the contemporary insights of black miners, who, almost from the beginning, understood that the "Colliery stinks – Gu za unka e Malahl'eni".[9]

ORIGINS AND TRANSNATIONAL POLITICAL ECONOMY

Situated about eighty miles south-east of the Victoria Falls on the Zambezi River, Wankie Colliery, "Wangi Kolia", was central Africa's only large

7. National Archives of Zimbabwe, Harare, [hereafter, NAZ] Library, "Wankie – A Brief Review" (Wankie Colliery Company Limited, 16 December 1981), unpublished.
8. See, especially, *Northern News* (Northern Rhodesia/Zambia); *Bulawayo Chronicle, Rhodesia Herald* (Southern Rhodesia/Zimbabwe); and *Drum* (South Africa).
9. NAZ, NB 3/1/6, Native Commissioner, Sebungwe, to Chief Native Commissioner, Bulawayo, 23 March 1906, transl. by Native Commissioner, Sebungwe.

coalmine for most of the twentieth century.[10] As such, it played a pivotal role in the region's political economy. Before the opening of the Kariba hydroelectric dam scheme in 1960, the colliery's importance went unquestioned. In the estimation of one commission of inquiry, the dependence of colonial Zimbabwe and its neighbours on the Wankie coalfield was "absolute".[11] Afterwards, too, coal remained of great economic importance, certainly for Southern Rhodesia, if less so for the wider region. Many factories, quite apart from household cooking and heating, were coal-fired, as increasingly was the flu-cured tobacco industry, the colony's biggest earner of foreign exchange.[12]

Registered in London in 1899, the Wankie Colliery Company, in which Cecil Rhodes's British South Africa Company had been significantly interested from the start, was bought in 1950 by Powell Duffryn Ltd, one of several private companies looking to invest overseas following the nationalization of the British coalmining industry. In 1953 the colliery was bought up by Anglo American, a Johannesburg-based mining conglomerate anxious to safeguard coal supplies for its hugely profitable copper mines in Northern Rhodesia, colonial Zambia. By then, Wankie Colliery actually comprised three separate shafts or collieries: No. 1, which was the original mine; No. 2, which started production in 1927, was closed during the Depression, and restarted in 1937; and No. 3 colliery, which began production in 1953. With projected demand estimated in excess of 5 million tons per annum, Anglo American immediately embarked on a major programme of reorganization and expansion. All production calculations, however, were subsequently overturned by the development of the Kariba hydroelectric dam. No. 1 colliery was temporarily closed, only reopening once domestic Southern Rhodesian annual demand had recovered somewhat in the early 1960s to around 3.75 million tons.[13]

Throughout this period, Wankie Colliery Company was a highly profitable enterprise, regularly paying dividends. As the price of coal was regulated by a price agreement negotiated with the Southern Rhodesian government on the basis of the cost of production plus reasonable profit, the colliery's drive to increase its margins could bring it into conflict with the state, if the latter refused to play along. This was the case in 1957, when the government debated Wankie Colliery's wish to increase the price of coal. Although "there were no legal grounds for demanding it", ministers were informed that the colliery company had intimated that officials

10. R.L.A. Watson, "The Geology and Coal Resources of the Country around Wankie, Southern Rhodesia", *Southern Rhodesia, Geological Survey Bulletin*, 48 (1960), pp. 1–38.
11. *Report of the Wankie Coal Commission* (Salisbury, 1949), p. 9.
12. NAZ Library, *Wankie Colliery Company, Annual Report, 1961*, p. 5.
13. *Wankie. Southern Rhodesia's Great Colliery: Commonwealth Mining and Metallurgical Congress 1961* (Johannesburg, 1961), pp. 6–7.

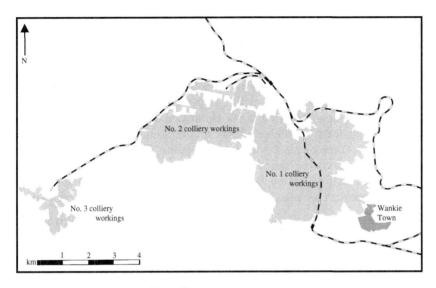

Figure 1. Wankie town and Wankie Colliery, 1964.

"should agree to an interpretation of Clause 20 [of the Price Agreement] which would concede the moral claims of the Company for an increase in the basic cost". Set against this, as the government realized, was the fact that in 1955 the colliery had paid a 5 per cent dividend, and in 1956 a 10 per cent dividend, on an increased capital of £4.4 million. "The Agreement was giving them [the colliery] a fair share of increased profit and had been designed as an incentive to further production", ministers agreed. "If the Company felt strongly about the matter it should proceed to arbitration which the Government were quite prepared to face."[14] This was exactly what the colliery company did, but for once its confidence was misplaced. Its request was denied.[15]

THE WANKIE LABOUR FORCE

Unable to raise the price of coal at will, the company kept expenditure on its black labourers within strict limits. In the first place, it reduced the numbers employed. From a peak of about 9,500 in 1953, the African workforce had fallen to 5,577 by 1962. In 1963 underground and surface workers totalled 4,906. This was achieved partly by shedding workers when non-core operations such as the brickworks were sold off, and partly through what

14. Todd Papers, Cabinet Minutes, 9 May 1957. These papers are in the possession of Judith Todd, Bulawayo, Zimbabwe.
15. *Ibid.*, 17 December 1957.

the company termed "the better utilisation of labour".[16] Such expenditure as there was on welfare was explicitly directed towards "administration, security, health and hygiene purposes".[17]

In the past, and indeed until the mid-1950s, the colliery had deservedly acquired a dreadful reputation for the appalling conditions in which its black miners worked and the casual brutality with which they were treated.[18] These conditions were now mitigated if not eliminated, and discipline and control modernized, at least by the standards of the Southern Rhodesian mining industry if not those of the Zambian Copperbelt. "We have worked towards setting things right on the basis that 25 percent to 30 percent of the Company's African employees would be provided with married accommodation", the colliery company's chairman reported at the end of the 1956 financial year.

> We also decided that in the interest of both health and control, single Africans should be fed by the Company rather than be given dry rations and allowed to cook for themselves. The commissioning of these new communal kitchens has undoubtedly resulted in a considerable improvement in efficiency at work and in general health. [...] These endeavours have undoubtedly resulted in a healthier, happier and more efficient labour force.

But try as the colliery company might, it could never be sure that "improvements will have placed the Company beyond any danger of labour unrest, because our labour force is inevitably open to influence from outside sources. We must, therefore, continue to ensure that the welfare of our African employees is under constant review."[19]

Similar claims were made in successive years. In 1957, the better health of unmarried workers was attributed to the "establishment of kitchens in the main compounds of the Colliery",[20] and in 1961 Wankie was described as "a happy and settled community, a situation [...] encouraged by the provision of social amenities". A 5 per cent wage increase in 1962 for all the colliery's black workers helped keep relations "satisfactory". As the company's chairman explained in his annual report, "Wankie is an isolated mine, and over the years we have given much attention to the provision of welfare, recreational and sporting facilities." This, he claimed had been

> [...] a considerable factor in helping to build a contented community, but the major factor has been the readiness of our employees to devote much of their spare time to the organisation of club and community activities. We have just completed a hostel to accommodate visiting teams and the African women's voluntary association have taken over the running of this.[21]

16. NAZ Library, *Wankie Colliery Company, Annual Report, 1963*, p. 9.
17. NAZ Library, *Wankie Colliery Company, Annual Report, 1956*, p. 12.
18. Van Onselen, "The 1912 Wankie Colliery Strike"; and Phimister, *Wangi Kolia, passim.*
19. NAZ Library, *Wankie Colliery Company, Annual Report, 1956*, p. 12.
20. NAZ Library, *Wankie Colliery Company, Annual Report, 1957*, p. 8.
21. NAZ Library, *Wankie Colliery Company, Annual Report, 1961*, p. 5.

By the end of the following year, thirty-one better quality houses for more senior African employees had been built, and a number of projects to provide additional amenities undertaken, "including the building of small village swimming baths". The colliery's relations with its black workforce were again described as satisfactory.[22]

Living conditions in the colliery compounds, only recently rebranded as villages, were obviously never as bucolic as suggested in corporate reports. In 1964, independent observers saw things rather differently. "The houses varied from reasonable enough whitewashed cottages, with brightly painted roofs, to gruesome brick hovels [...] bachelors are double-bunked eight to a room."[23] The improvements were anyway also about control, and here the colliery company's attempts to maintain discipline never faltered. It had long been the practice for experienced compound managers, backed up by company police, to use spies, but, as these were invariably exposed sooner or later, additional methods of surveillance and control were employed. Although the growing number of women and children in the various compounds made overall discipline much harder to enforce, black miners themselves were repeatedly denied the right to independent organization. Blaming the last major strike in 1954 on outside political agitators,[24] the colliery company always denied that low wages and poor working conditions had anything to do with that prolonged stoppage.

> The view is still emphatically held by the Company that the strike was part of a deliberate political manoeuvre [...] prompted from outside Wankie and had its origin in a combination of political factors and was in all probability staged in protest to Federation and as a "trial of strength".[25]

Apart from a wage increase that it was legally obliged to implement, the colliery company had otherwise rejected out of hand the findings and recommendations of the Native Labour Board appointed immediately after the 1954 strike.[26] It took particular exception to criticism of its system of "tribal representatives", whereby some miners were appointed "tribally" by

22. NAZ Library, *Wankie Colliery Company, Annual Report, 1963*, p. 9.

23. *Drum*, April 1964, p. 33. Though having published only one article on the 1964 Wankie strike, under the title "Behind the Big Strikes", *Drum*, a Johannesburg-based periodical as famous for its pointed criticism of white minority rule as for its sophisticated coverage of black urban life, is a particularly interesting source as it offers a contemporary voice free of racist condescension.

24. Phimister, "Lashers and Leviathan".

25. Associated Mineworkers of Rhodesia Papers [hereafter, AMR Papers], "Notes on Events Leading up to, and the Possible Causes of the Wankie Strike, February 1954", unpubl., Wankie, 7 January 1955, p. 1. The most pressing political factor in the region during this period was the creation of the Federation of Central Africa in 1953, consisting of Northern Rhodesia, Southern Rhodesia, and Nyasaland.

26. So-called Native Labour Boards were established in Southern Rhodesia after the 1946 railway workers' strike to determine African wages and conditions of service.

the company to act as intermediaries between workers and management. "The superimposition of Native Industrial Workers' Unions upon existing channels of communication", the Company insisted, "would serve only to weaken the existing medium of negotiation and communication between workers and Management."[27] So far as Wankie's management was concerned, "tribal rulers" reporting directly to the compound manager were the preferred channel of communication. Nor did the situation change significantly after legislation made possible the registration of so-called "multiracial" unions in 1961.[28] The Associated Mineworkers of Rhodesia, a small, white-led and avowedly non-political union, was permitted to establish a presence of sorts at the colliery. By 1964, however, only one in five miners were members.[29]

Convinced that its way was the only way, in the immediate aftermath of the 1954 strike the colliery company briefly toyed with the idea of employing indentured labour as a way of distancing itself from the government collective bargaining initiative noted above. Oblivious to its own unhappy past in this regard a generation previously,[30] the company thought of manning No. 3 Colliery entirely with "indentured Nyasaland [Malawi] natives, the reasons being that they thought indentured labour would be more reliable in times of trouble and could be called upon to keep essential services going". Although the proposal was shelved when wiser heads pointed out that "it might cause tribal trouble [...] especially if the native labour at the other two Collieries were organised on a different basis",[31] the colliery company continued to believe that its interests were best served by drawing on migrant labour from throughout the region. A long-term beneficiary of the southern African regional migrant labour system centred on the Witwatersrand goldmining industry, Wankie Colliery had always drawn by far the greater portion of its black labour force from north of the Zambezi River, from the territories that became Northern Rhodesia, modern-day Zambia, and particularly from its western province, Barotseland, home to the Lozi people.

Reluctant to meet the expense of a fully stabilized workforce, the company favoured the employment of single male migrant labourers. Married workers were in a minority. It was a policy with which successive Southern Rhodesian

27. AMR Papers, "Memorandum Submitted to the Select Committee Appointed by the Southern Rhodesian Parliament on the Native Industrial Workers Union Bill by the National Industrial Council of the Mining Industry", and Appendices, n.d. [February 1955]. This was a government initiative to legalize African trade unions.

28. NAZ Library, *Wankie Colliery Company, Annual Report, 1961*, p. 5. For a wider discussion see D.G. Clarke, "The Underdevelopment of African Trade Unions in Rhodesia: An Assessment of Working-Class Action in Historical Perspective", unpubl., 1974.

29. *Bulawayo Chronicle*, 5 March 1964.

30. Phimister, *Wangi Kolia*, pp. 30–43. See more generally Charles van Onselen, *Chibaro: African Mine Labour in Southern Rhodesia 1900–1933* (London, 1976).

31. Todd Papers, Cabinet Minutes, 3 August 1954.

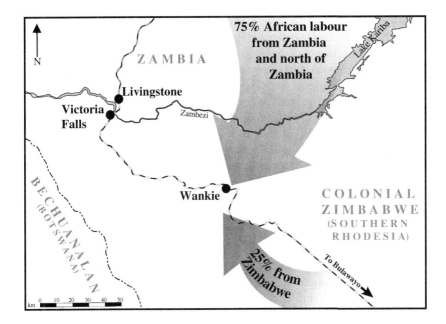

Figure 2. Wankie migration: sources of the colliery's African labour, 1964.

governments had sympathized. "Wankie had problems of its own", a cabinet meeting was told.

> Owing to the barrenness of the surrounding country and the absence of other occupations and industry the usual urban population could not be built up there unless at great expense to the Company. Families had to be supported and housed by the Colliery and there were no facilities for absorbing the adolescent labour thus available.[32]

But whatever cost advantages this had conferred in the past, it now left the colliery dangerously exposed to political upheaval. Fond of warning darkly about imagined political agitation, the company came face to face with its reality.

By the early 1960s, the African nationalist wind of political change acknowledged at the start of the decade by the British Prime Minister, Harold Macmillan, was blowing fiercely through central Africa.[33] Powerful enough to sweep away the short-lived Central African Federation of the two Rhodesias and Nyasaland (1953–1963), it was set to drive all before it north of the Zambezi. Nyasaland was about to become independent as

---

32. *Ibid.*
33. For Macmillan's acknowledgement in 1960 of African nationalism as a "political fact", see especially Larry J. Butler and Sarah Stockwell (eds), *The Wind of Change: Harold Macmillan and British Decolonization* (Basingstoke, 2013).

Malawi in July 1964 and Northern Rhodesia, under Kenneth Kaunda's United National Independence Party (UNIP), was set to follow suit as Zambia some three months later. Southern Rhodesia's white settlers, who for the previous forty years had enjoyed a significant measure of internal self-government, were determined to go their own way, however. Following the election in December 1962 of the extreme right-wing Rhodesian Front, and Britain's absent-minded award at the Victoria Falls conference in July 1963 of the bulk of the Federation's armed forces to Southern Rhodesia, tensions rose dramatically along the Zambezi River fault line between black nationalist and white-ruled Africa.[34] This was the increasingly fraught political background to the strike that convulsed Wankie Colliery in March 1964.

THE STRIKE OF 1964

The first overt signs of trouble erupted on the afternoon of Sunday, 1 March. A small open-air meeting of the Associated Mine Workers of Rhodesia (AMR), a multiracial, white-led union enjoying government recognition at a time when most African trade unions were either unregistered or banned,[35] was taken over by non-members, many of them women. Official speakers were unable to make themselves heard above shouts for money in lieu of the food rations distributed by the colliery company to married workers.

Consisting mainly of maize meal, meat, bread, and sugar, rations were issued from stores in each of the three colliery townships. But not only was the meat of such poor quality that some white settlers admitted they, too, would strike if they were forced to eat it,[36] quite often it did not reach those for whom it was intended. As one miner's wife, Ma-Nyambe Sitali-Wasamunu, remembered later, "Some officials sometimes abused distribution. There were times when workers came back from work and found that all the rations had been shared [...] hence the call for money in place of food rations."[37] The meeting broke up in uproar when a woman who had insisted that "she was satisfied with the rations because she was

---

34. See variously Philip Murphy (ed.), *British Documents on the End of Empire, Series B Volume 9: Central Africa Part 2: Crisis and Dissolution 1959–1965* (London, 2005); David Mulford, *Zambia: The Politics of Independence 1957–1964* (London, 1967); Larry W. Bowman, *Politics in Rhodesia: White Power in an African State* (Cambridge, MA, 1973); and John R. Wood, *The Welensky Papers: A History of the Federation of Rhodesia and Nyasaland* (Durban, 1983).

35. For details of the colony's restrictive industrial conciliation legislation, see Theodore Bull (ed.), *Rhodesian Perspective* (London, 1967), pp. 109–115. See also C.M. Brand, "Politics and African Trade Unionism in Rhodesia since Federation", *Rhodesian History*, 2 (1971), pp. 89–109.

36. *Drum*, April 1964, p. 33.

37. Interview, Ma-Nyambe Sitali-Wasamunu, 10 February 1991, transl. from Lozi by M. Mulabela.

sure of getting her food for her family" was set upon by other women and chased through the village. Taking refuge in the ration store, she was rescued by the compound manager and driven by car away from No. 2 Colliery. The remaining crowd of women then proceeded "to break up the store and obstruct the male single employees from obtaining food from their dining room".[38] Mine security police responded by firing tear gas to disperse the women.[39]

Overnight, No. 2 Colliery's black workforce, including the AMR's African members, decided to go on strike. A large crowd, comprising as many women and children as men, gathered in front of the colliery entrance. Attempts by Wankie's general manager and other officials to address the gathering were howled down. After some hesitation, a delegation of ten people, six of whom were women, were granted a meeting with management. The delegation was dismissively informed that grievances would not be discussed until the strike was called off.[40] When told that the delegation had failed to obtain anything more than a promise from management that complaints about the quality of meat rations would be looked into once the strikers had returned to work, the meeting ended "in disorder, with UNIP slogans being shouted and sung",[41] a first sign that support for Zambia's United National Independence Party played a role in the strike. A procession led by women then marched to No. 1 Colliery, "where they invaded the kitchen, threw sand and water in the food, ripped open mealie [maize] sacks and stoned the big, gloomy-looking ration building".[42] As Saela Mulemba recalled, "UNIP advised us. We demonstrated at the offices of the compound manager and demanded that African workers also be given money in place of food rations. We shouted at the compound manager and called him names for not heeding the demands of the people."[43]

On leaving, they were joined by black miners coming off shift. No. 1 Colliery was now also on strike. By the following day, Tuesday, 3 March, the strike had spread to No. 3 Colliery. A large crowd, once again including many women and children, refused to listen to committee members from the minority Associated Mineworkers of Rhodesia trade union urging them to return to work. Later that same day, AMR president, Howard Bloomfield, described by a *Drum* reporter as "a big man from an English coalmining area [who] lonewolfed about the compounds, but with little influence",[44] and local AMR leaders were again prevented from speaking.

38. AMR Papers, Report, "Wankie Colliery Strike from Monday 2nd to March 9th, 1964", p. 1.
39. *Northern News*, 5 March 1964.
40. *Rhodesia Herald*, 4 March 1964.
41. AMR Papers, Report, "Wankie Colliery Strike", p. 2.
42. *Drum*, April 1964, p. 33.
43. Interview, Saela Mulemba, 12 March 1991.
44. *Drum*, April 1964, p. 33.

"My Committee and I were lucky to escape injuries ourselves", wrote Bloomfield, "as the mob tried to overturn the car we were in and dented it with weapons".[45] Led by people wearing UNIP badges, the crowd then set about damaging mine buildings and machinery. There was little that the heavily outnumbered local police force could do, beyond watch from a distance, as large groups of men, women, and children roamed the streets well into the night.[46]

Over the next twenty-four hours, as unrest intensified, the number of strikers swelled. Although more than half the afternoon shift turned up for work at No. 1 Colliery, attitudes hardened on their return to surface. Earlier on Wednesday, 4 March, a large crowd of mainly women and children had staged a sit-down protest outside the No. 1 Colliery compound office, "singing UNIP songs and giving the party's fluttering hand sign".[47] Reinforced by units brought from Bulawayo, the nearest large city, and latterly from the capital, Salisbury (modern-day Harare), the police decided to move in. They began by arresting a man, subsequently identified as not employed by the mine, "for addressing a UNIP women's gathering". Baton charges were made to clear the area and tear gas was used.[48] In turn police were met with stones fired by small boys with catapults, "and when one policeman was cornered by the angry crowd, they opened fire, wounding two men".[49] Outraged miners returning to the townships called on other workers, including shop assistants and domestic servants, to join them.[50] So far as Wankie Colliery's black workers were concerned, the strike was now total.

Well before that point was reached, the colliery's white miners, helped by office staff and other settler volunteers, tried to keep coal production going.[51] Wankie's South African owner, the Anglo American Corporation, also mobilized white workers from other mines under its control in Southern Rhodesia. It did so with the full backing of the authorities in Salisbury. Insisting that the strike was illegal because arbitration procedures had not been followed, the government declared the colliery to be an essential service. It promptly placed Dakotas of the Royal Rhodesian Air Force at Anglo American's disposal. Just as dusk was falling on the evening of Tuesday, 3 March, the first of these venerable aircraft disgorged 25 white miners on to Wankie's dusty, unlit landing strip. Another 100 skilled workers from Salisbury, Gwelo (Gweru), and Fort Victoria

45. AMR Papers, Report "Wankie Colliery Strike", p. 3.
46. *Ibid.*
47. *Northern News*, 4 March 1964.
48. *Bulawayo Chronicle*, 4 March 1964.
49. *Drum*, April 1964, p. 33; and *Northern News*, 5 March 1964.
50. AMR Papers, Report "Wankie Colliery Strike", p. 5.
51. *Bulawayo Chronicle*, 3 March 1964.

(Masvingo) were due to arrive the following morning. "A spokesman for the management stressed that the miners were not coming as strike-breakers. 'They are here to keep essential services going. They are from copper mines owned by the company'."[52] "In the spirit of pioneer days", reported the *Sunday Mail*,

> [...] the [white] people of Wankie are pulling together – and enjoying it. Clerks have put down their pens to take up shovels, plumbers are wielding picks down the mine and women are doing jobs which before the strike they left to their houseboys. All are volunteers and not one receives a penny for their work.

Even the town's Anglican vicar did his bit at the company transport depot, "filling up trucks between his regular calls to the hospitals and other church duties". The Reverend G. Howard confessed: "I would have liked to go down the mine, but they wouldn't let me".[53]

At the end of each truncated shift, Wankie's white miners and volunteers alike returned to racially segregated amenities and housing. The low roofed bungalows set in spacious grounds enjoyed by white miners were very different from even the best housing reserved for the handful of senior African staff, and far removed from the overcrowded cottages and barracks occupied by most black miners. In former times, white miners' encounters with the colliery's authoritarian management were bruising enough, but by the 1950s and 1960s almost all settlers saw themselves as whites rather than workers, as a privileged aristocracy of labour. As one white miner remembered it, "life on the mine was superb [...]. We were just fat, happy cats in the sun."[54] Even if assaults by white miners on black workers were no longer as common as they had been in the recent past,[55] racial prejudice was rife. Voting solidly in the December 1962 election for the Rhodesian Front candidate,[56] many of the colliery's white miners staunchly supported white minority rule and the concomitant ideology. The AMR's self-conscious "multiracialism" rarely survived contact with the wider world beyond the immediate workplace. Striking black miners were on their own precisely because of the threat they posed to the white "Rhodesian way of life". The Minister of Mines understood this political fact only too well when publically thanking white miners for keeping essential production going.[57] For whites, the colliery was a very different place from the one experienced by black miners.

52. *Rhodesia Herald*, 3 March 1964.
53. *Sunday Mail*, 8 March 1964.
54. Interview, A.G. Koen, 16 February 1987.
55. Todd Papers, Cabinet Minutes, 25 May 1954.
56. F.M.G. Willson (ed.), *Source Book of Parliamentary Elections and Referenda in Southern Rhodesia 1898–1962* (Salisbury, 1963), p. 204.
57. *Rhodesia Herald*, 10 March 1964. For white and black miners undercutting each other's strikes, see for Southern Rhodesia/Zimbabwe, Ian Phimister, "White Miners in Historical Perspective: Southern Rhodesia, 1890–1953", *Journal of Southern African Studies*, 3 (1977),

Whereas white miners from Wankie and elsewhere could be mobilized easily, attempts to persuade the colliery's black miners to return to work failed. Repeated calls by the AMR's president, backed up by local AMR branch officials, for an end to the strike fell on deaf ears. A message from the general manager broadcast over the public address system covering the three colliery townships was ignored. His claim that miners' families were going hungry because of the strike was dismissed as manifestly untrue. Four days into the strike no one was starving. Miners were described as "buying heavily [...] from three local stores" to feed themselves and their families, some 9,000 people in total.[58] As late as Thursday, 5 March, reporters could see for themselves that there was still enough food. Admittedly, strikers "carefully counted their mealie [maize] cobs and the richer often helped the poorer with food [...] [and] some sold property to buy food", but for all that they had "no union, no official leaders, no meetings allowed, they were surprisingly solid".[59]

Nor did black mineworker solidarity waver in the face of threats by the settler government. Rushed to Wankie from Salisbury by a special RRAF flight on the morning of Tuesday, 3 March, the Southern Rhodesian Minister of Labour made three broadcasts over the public address system. Strikers were bluntly informed that they were acting illegally. "I must tell you that the Government is quite determined to uphold the law, and in terms of the law, the management is right to refuse to negotiate with you until you return to work." Before flying back to Salisbury the next day, the minister met the officers in charge of police operations, and mine management. He also found time to see the leaders of the two registered unions represented at Wankie, the Associated Mineworkers of Rhodesia, and the Salaried Staffs' Association.[60] No attempt was made to open negotiations with the striking miners.

But as the long, hot days wore on, police reinforcements continued to arrive. Speaker vans criss-crossed the townships ordering people to keep off the streets and stay indoors. These instructions were enforced by the night-time deployment of riot squads.[61] By the weekend of 7–8 March, journalists covering the strike were convinced that it had lost momentum.[62]

pp. 187–206; for Northern Rhodesia/Zambia, see Johan Frederik Holleman and S. Biesheuvel, *White Mine Workers in Northern Rhodesia 1959–60* (Leiden, 1973); and for South Africa, see Frederick A. Johnstone, *Class, Race and Gold: A Study of Class Relations and Racial Discrimination in South Africa* (London, 1976).

58. *Sunday Mail*, 8 March 1964. The three local stores were outside the colliery complex, and run by commercial retailers.

59. *Drum*, April 1964, p. 33.

60. *Rhodesia Herald*, 3 March 1964. See also Southern Rhodesia Information Services, Press Statement 216/64/DER, Minister Addresses Wankie Strikers. The Salaried Staffs' Association was a compliant grouping of technicians and middle managers.

61. *Bulawayo Chronicle*, 5 March 1964.

62. *Ibid.*, 7 March 1964.

From the start, the strike had been strongest in No. 2 Colliery, always identified as the "hard core of the strikers";[63] miners at the other two collieries had only walked out in the face of police brutality, and indeed power-station workers never joined in at all.[64] Although waverers were kept in line by threats and beatings,[65] commitment to the strike varied over time and place. Even at its greatest extent, immediately after police action on Wednesday, 4 March, when tear gas was used on women and children, and striking miners were baton charged and shot at, resolve was hard to sustain for any length of time across the three separate townships surrounding each colliery. The loss of a week's wages mattered a lot to underground workers whose starting pay was £3 17s 6d per month.[66]

Over the weekend, workforce divisions temporarily wiped away by police brutality began to re-emerge. Members of the AMR, usually the more skilled and better-paid workers, told their union representatives that they were prepared to call off the strike. On Friday, the AMR's president, Howard Bloomfield, claimed that there was "every sign that rowdyism is dead. Executives of the union and I received a good hearing by men in No. 3 colliery today." We told them, he added, that "we wanted to speak to men only and not to deal with Umfazis and picaninnis. The Africans understood that."[67] However, the tipping point for the "hard core" of strikers seems to have been the arrival of two officials from the Northern Rhodesian (soon to be Zambian) government on Saturday morning. Acting on the instructions of the Prime Minister, and President of UNIP, Kenneth Kaunda, they "urged Northern strikers to return to work".[68] Once miners from Zambia decided to return to work, other strikers quickly followed. On Sunday morning, domestic servants employed by the colliery's white miners, who had a history of taking strike action, began turning up for work.[69] During the rest of the day, the three colliery townships were described as quiet, and by nightfall it was generally agreed that the strike was over.[70] It had lasted for almost exactly one week.

---

63. *Rhodesia Herald*, 3 March 1964.
64. *Bulawayo Chronicle*, 5 March 1964.
65. *Rhodesia Herald*, 7 March 1964.
66. *Drum*, April 1964, p. 33. "£", "s", and "d" are the abbreviations for pounds, shillings, and pence, the pre-decimal currency system in use in the United Kingdom, many of its colonies, and Commonwealth countries up until the 1970s.
67. *Bulawayo Chronicle*, 7 March 1964. These were derogatory terms for African women and children, respectively.
68. *Northern News*, 9 March 1964.
69. See, especially, Ian Phimister and Brian Raftopoulos, "'Kana sora ratswa ngaritswe': African Nationalists and Black Workers: The 1948 General Strike in Colonial Zimbabwe", *Journal of Historical Sociology*, 13 (2000), pp. 289–324.
70. *Rhodesia Herald*, 9 March 1964.

AFTER THE STRIKE

On Monday, 9 March, there was a full turnout for the early morning shift. Ignorant from beginning to end of the intentions of its black workforce, top management at the colliery was taken by surprise. But conscious of the fact that nearly 20,000 tons of coal production had been lost owing to strike action, plus the cost of flying in white miners and accommodating them in Wankie's one hotel,[71] it speedily concluded negotiations with AMR officials. With immediate effect, food rations were replaced by cash. Married men would receive 4 shillings and 8 pence and single workers 2 shillings and 4 pence per shift.[72]

Although a company spokesman claimed, "a good atmosphere among all the men",[73] this surely was not widely shared at Wankie. The colliery company in particular exhibited a meanness of spirit when not exuding a sour vindictiveness. While thanking the AMR's president, Howard Bloomfield, in writing for his part in seeking a negotiated end to the strike, all Wankie's general manager could bring himself to enclose in the letter was a cheque for £75 for the union's benevolent fund.[74] A somewhat incoherent reply by Bloomfield in which he "let as many of our people know, both black and white, that we have management, who though at times on opposite sides, do have consideration for us, and what is more, appreciation of circumstances, and it is indeed a pleasure to discuss management of your calibre",[75] may have served merely to confirm Braithwaite in his estimation of the union. Certainly, it gave the company no pause for thought when pressing charges against the AMR's Wankie branch secretary.

Charged with holding an unauthorized and rowdy public meeting, the branch secretary's evidence in rebuttal revealed just how tightly the company attempted to bind its labour force: acknowledged as a "responsible" trade union and one recognized by the government, the AMR was nonetheless obliged to seek the compound manager's permission to hold meetings. If this was forthcoming, meetings had to be held in an open-sided tent, "because the company will not give us a building, for if we had one we could make it really private". But what the company gained by having union meetings more or less in the open where they could be monitored, it lost by having no controlled access to gatherings. People came and went as they pleased. "You can see what a battle it is to keep an eye on

---

71. *Sunday Mail*, 8 March 1964.

72. *Rhodesia Herald*, 10 March 1964; and *Chamber of Mines Journal*, 6:4 (April 1964).

73. *Bulawayo Chronicle*, 10 March 1964.

74. AMR Papers, T.A. Braithwaite, General Manager, Wankie Colliery Company Ltd, Wankie, to H.B. Bloomfield, President, Associated Mineworkers of Rhodesia, Gwelo [Gweru], 13 March 1964.

75. AMR Papers, H. Bloomfield, General Secretary's Office, Associated Mineworkers of Rhodesia, Gwelo [Gweru], to T.A. Braithwaite, General Manager, Wankie Colliery, Wankie, 23 March 1964.

all people, especially those who make it their business to sneak in", the branch secretary pleaded. When he further denied that "disturbances" had occurred, "only shouting, which is a common thing with the African even in his own home, and is a normal thing at a meeting anywhere trade unions hold their meetings, even with our Europeans at meetings as I well know", the local magistrate had heard enough. The case was dismissed.[76]

Management's post-strike message, though, was perfectly clear. Its line had to be toed at the colliery and its sister mines. At Mangula Mine, from which white miners had been sent to Wankie, AMR members, white and black, were harassed and sidelined. Towards the end of March, Mangula's AMR's branch secretary, Stephen Mugomeya, listed what he termed the "very severe incidents" at the mine.

> I have the following to give; (1) tribal chiefs, (2) the anti-unionism urged by the management, (3) union members threatened by the management not to bring their problems through union leaders but through tribal chiefs, (4) lack of understanding the work of union officials by the management, (5) mine management officials are trying to cause trouble so that they could lay the charge to union officials.

Yet however aggrieved Mugomeya was – "the use of tribal chiefs in our mining industry must be abolished; some stubborn managers must be dealt with" – his fundamental conservatism – "law and order in our mining industry must be maintained; illegal strikers must be dealt with" – completely passed management by.[77] No concessions were made. The system of "tribal elders" had long since been discredited and discarded on the Copperbelt. But deaf to miners' rejection of these unrepresentative "rulers", the Wankie Colliery Company persisted in dealing with them. "Unconstitutional", one striker had told the *Drum* magazine reporter, "They are saying we're acting unconstitutionally. But they do not tell us how we can be constitutional and be heard. Can you?"[78]

Both the Southern Rhodesian government and the Chamber of Mines, the industry's corporate voice, were equally determined to show who was still boss. In this, they found support from the Argus Group, controlling the colony's main daily newspapers. One editorial under the heading "Politics and the Wankie Strike", confident that "Rhodesians will echo the thanks sent by the Minister of Mines to those who kept essential production going", wondered "how much importance should be attached to reports of political agitation and the shouting of UNIP slogans?". Answering its own question, the editorial argued that

76. AMR Papers, Harry Thurbron, Evidence, 6 May 1964.
77. AMR Papers, S.T. Mugomeya, Branch Secretary, Mangula [Mangura], to General Secretary and Executive Council, Associated Mineworkers of Rhodesia, Gwelo [Gweru], 19 March 1964.
78. *Drum*, April 1964, p. 33.

[...] any dispute, whether over rations, money or the supply of soap, is capable of being turned into a political dispute by people to whom "politics" is a new and stimulating game. Judgement will have to be reserved on this question. It might be unduly alarmist to suggest that any large body of alien workers in Southern Rhodesia is a potential fifth column. On the other hand the case for employing indigenous labour wherever possible is strengthened.[79]

This was precisely what the government wanted to hear. The authorities in Salisbury had been shocked by the economy's vulnerability to the industrial action taken by Wankie's African coalminers, especially when they came from those regions that were already bound for independence. Despite official claims during the strike that there was "no threat to manufacturing industry, farming, hospitals and hotels",[80] it became apparent the following week just how low stockpiles of coal had fallen.[81] The *Bulawayo Chronicle* reported that the colliery was struggling to get the country's industry back on its feet. "Yesterday the Colliery's Bulawayo office switchboard was jammed with telephone calls pleading for immediate deliveries of coal [...] many factories have had to close down or cut back production through lack of fuel."[82] Warning the mining industry that "once there is any weakening or giving way to illegal strikes or political pressure, industry and the whole country would suffer enormously", the Minister of Mines urged big companies to make every effort to employ local labour, thus anticipating already the impending post-colonial constellation of Northern Rhodesia/Zambia.[83]

Nor was the Chamber of Mines backward in coming forward. Addressing a gathering of mining companies in April, the Chamber's president reaffirmed its commitment to "the policy of multi-racial trade unions and to the full use of the Industrial Conciliation Act and the machinery which it provides". "But as things stand in Southern Rhodesia at present", he explained,

[...] any unofficial strike is bound to have a substantial political content and even if in individual cases this is untrue, the professional agitator will always leap to exploit such a situation. I therefore wish to make it absolutely clear that the mining industry will make no concessions in the face of illegal strikes and I believe we have the full backing of the Government in taking up this position.[84]

The situation at that time, in which the mining industry as a whole employed 40,000 people, of whom some 68 per cent were foreigners, could

79. *Rhodesia Herald*, 10 March 1964.
80. *Ibid.*, 7 March 1964. See also, *Southern Rhodesia Legislative Assembly Debates* (Salisbury, 1965), 6 March 1964, Ministerial Statement on Wankie Strike.
81. *Citizen*, March 1964.
82. *Bulawayo Chronicle*, 11 March 1964.
83. *Rhodesia Herald*, 8 April 1964.
84. *Chamber of Mines Journal*, 6:4 (April 1964).

not continue. Rising unemployment in Southern Rhodesia and the sizeable wage bill being sent outside the country "would force the mining industry to review the position".[85] That moment came sooner rather than later. Even before Zambia became independent in October 1964, stricter immigration controls were imposed on the Zambian and Bechuanaland (Botswana) borders, resulting in a considerable reduction in the amount of migrant labour coming into Southern Rhodesia from those two countries and from Tanzania. As "lashers", that is, unskilled miners who shovelled coal, had traditionally come from north of the Zambezi River, the new government policy of restricting employment as far as possible to indigenous labour caused the colliery some difficulty. By the end of the year, it was reported as having been obliged by the new immigration restrictions "to enlist the aid of the Rhodesian African Labour Supply Commission to recruit labour for the colliery from the south eastern area of Rhodesia".[86]

CONCLUSIONS

According to *Drum* magazine, the strike was easy enough to explain:

> In air-conditioned offices and a hilltop hotel, a small army of embarrassed "experts" puzzled out how this strike was launched without any warning, sending the industrialist scurrying to his coal bunker to check on reserves. The answer was written on every lavatory wall. "Vote UNIP. Zambia is UNIP", it said in chalk and paint. Wankie, 60 miles inside Southern Rhodesia, is a UNIP town with most of its 4,000 labour force from across the border. Now Zambia is almost independent and Wankie is still the bitter underpaid place it was long before the last vicious 1954 strike.[87]

Drum's sharp-eyed account unquestionably captured the crucial transnational political dimension of the strike. Neither its wider context nor the settler state's harsh reaction is intelligible without it.

As noted above, there is some evidence that officials of the Northern Rhodesian Mineworkers' Union (NRMU) were seen around the colliery's No. 2 compound in the days immediately preceding demonstrations over rations, and the unambiguous oral testimony of several women that UNIP members urged them to march on the offices of the compound manager. This is supported by newspaper reports and at length by Bloomfield's first-hand account of the strike written for the AMR's executive council. Every observer remarked on the singing of UNIP slogans by many in the crowds and the prominent display on clothing of UNIP badges.[88] This close association

---

85. *Rhodesia Herald*, 8 April 1964.
86. NAZ Library, *The Chamber of Mines of Rhodesia, 1964 Annual Report*; and NAZ Library, *Report of the Chief Government Mining Engineer, Inspector of Mines and Explosives, 1964.*
87. *Drum*, April 1964, p. 32.
88. See, especially, AMR Papers, Report "Wankie Colliery Strike", p. 3.

between labour, organized and unorganized, and militant nationalist politics contradicts studies that have insisted that the relationship was fraught where it was not openly antagonistic.[89] Whatever divisions there may have been between the NRMU and UNIP on the Copperbelt were subsumed elsewhere at this time. More than this, it suggests that greater weight should be given to those instances when women activists in particular played leading roles in the politicization of African mining communities.[90]

The highly charged political atmosphere meant that from beginning to end the strike at Wankie was as much a confrontation about autonomy and respect as it was a dispute about terms of employment. The independently minded *Citizen* monthly news-sheet captured this perfectly. Summing up the strike, it explained that "the miners, it seems, are paid a certain wage in money and given food to the amount of £5, which money [...] is deducted from their wage". For the *Citizen* it was obvious that once the miners wanted their full wages in money, the colliery's management should have acceded to their request immediately.

> It is unheard of, even in Africa, that an employer should decree what his employee should eat. The employee earns his money by labour and he should be given the right to do just what he likes with it, he should especially have a choice of what goes down his throat.[91]

At the same time, grievances about conditions of service were inflamed not least because they were needlessly and heedlessly aggravated by the colliery company. "At the Wankie colliery the workers have got agreement to their demand for an end to the system whereby rations form part of their wages", commented Northern Rhodesia's national daily. "Since the [parent] company involved, Anglo American, agreed to this a year ago on the Copperbelt, it is hard to believe that they would not have conceded the point at Wankie too, without a strike to emphasize that the miners meant business."[92] Already, at the time of the 1954 strike, both food rations and so-called tribal elders had been sources of conflict.[93] Neither was addressed by the Company in the ensuing decade. Instead, the system of food rations was extended in the latter half of the 1950s as part of Wankie's pursuit of increased efficiency. Ultimately, this ensured that trouble in the compounds would involve everyone: men, women, and children.

89. For example, Bates, *Unions, Parties, and Political Development*, pp. 126–200; and Berger, *Labour, Race and Colonial Rule*, pp. 161–164 and 211–217.
90. See, especially, Harries-Jones, *Freedom and Labour*, ch. 1, "'Freedom and Labour': The Text of Foster Mubanga".
91. *Citizen*, March 1964.
92. *Northern News*, 11 March 1964.
93. Phimister, "Lashers and Leviathan", pp. 179, 184–185.

The prominent part played by women in the 1954 strike was more than replicated in 1964. At least as politicized as their menfolk, if not more so, six out of ten members of a strikers' delegation were women. Of particular note was the blurring of boundaries between private and public spheres. The fact that responsibility for household reproduction rested on women's shoulders placed special significance on the prompt and regular preparation of meals for men coming off shift. When this domestic routine was upset by the corrupt and irregular distribution of food, as well as threatened by the poor quality of such meat rations as did occasionally become available, it thrust women into direct confrontation with the colliery management. The action they took was immediate and violent, even if "reactive rather than proactive".[94]

Yet clashes also found expression through political mobilization and party slogans. The anti-colonial possibilities framed by UNIP were as attractive to women as they were to men. What Valerie Hall has found in her study about women in mining communities also holds true here: "mining women being, at one and the same time, the most domestic of working-class women and the most politically conscious".[95] Women's struggles over food and politics in mining communities remote in place and time from each other shared many similarities then. While no record has survived of colliery women working as UNIP activists, certainly nothing comparable to women's party roles on the Copperbelt from the late 1950s onwards, it does seem likely that black women rallied to party political calls.[96]

At the same time, the colliery company persisted in its belief that migrant labourers acted as tribesmen rather than as workers or miners. Ignoring all evidence to the contrary during and after the 1954 strike, a memorandum by the company the following year to the National Industrial Council of the Mining Industry asserted that:

> Native labour on any given mine is never homogenous, but [...] consists of members of a varying number of tribes, each of which is quite foreign to the other and speaks a different language. The present system takes account of this state of affairs, and of the primitive natives' natural inclination to act in concert with his

94. Hall, *Women at Work*, p. 78.
95. *Ibid.*, p. 21.
96. For the Copperbelt, see especially Harries-Jones, *Freedom and Labour*, *passim*. More generally see Jane L. Parpart, "The Household and the Mine Shaft: Gender and Class Struggles on the Zambian Copperbelt, 1926–64", *Journal of Southern African Studies*, 13 (1986), pp. 36–56. See also George Chauncey, Jr, "The Locus of Reproduction: Women's Labour in the Zambian Copperbelt, 1927–1953", *Journal of Southern African Studies*, 7 (1981), pp. 135–164. Among recent unpublished studies, see F. Sakala, "The Role of Women in Labour Stabilisation at Mufulira Mine, 1930 to 1964" (M.A. thesis, University of Zambia, 2001); and B. Dandule, "Women and Mineworkers' Struggles on the Zambian Copperbelt, 1926–1964" (M.A. thesis, University of Zambia, 2012).

fellow tribesmen, which it is claimed is the only true "collective" which the tribal native understands.[97]

But this was manifestly not the case, as any number of studies have demonstrated for west, central, and southern Africa.[98] No ethnic or linguistic differences divided the colliery's black miners during the strike. Black miners were united in their rejection of the "tribal rulers" foisted on them by the colliery company. Women who had come to Wankie from all over central Africa participated in the strike.[99] At the colliery, people from throughout Zambia came together in the same burial society, "Cigwilizano". One miner declared: "I forgot whether I was Lozi or no Lozi".[100] Nor did any other "tribal" issues shape the course of the strike.

Although one report speculated that trouble had been stirred up by "a pool of 500 unemployed men at the mine, who are called upon when there is any shortage of labour – they created the trouble with a view to stepping into full-time jobs",[101] the most telling division was not between employed and unemployed, but between black and white. Different black ethnic groups might all get along together in the colliery's various compounds or "villages", but white and black miners lived rigidly segregated lives. Relations at the workplace were tense, if less fraught than in the past. They certainly lent themselves to strike-breaking, as blacks saw it, or to the maintenance of essential services, as whites viewed it. For all that they were both bounded by patriarchy, the different spaces inhabited by the wives of white and black miners precluded anything remotely approaching sisterhood. If anything, racial attitudes were hardening at this time and place in central Africa. The narrow remit of liberal multiracialism precluded class solidarity as much as the unfolding ambition of African nationalism was to eschew it. In a polarized world of black and white nationalisms soon to be locked in mortal combat, miners' struggles were invariably racialized.

---

97. AMR Papers, "Memorandum Submitted to the Select Committee Appointed by the Southern Rhodesian Parliament on the Native Industrial Workers Union Bill by the National Industrial Council of the Mining Industry", 1955, p. 20.
98. See also in this same Special Issue, Carolyn A. Brown, "Locals and Migrants in the Coalmining Town of Enugu (Nigeria): Worker Protest and Urban Identity 1914–1929"; Van Onselen, "Black Workers in Central African Industry"; and Michael Burawoy, *The Colour of Class on the Copper Mines: From African Advancement to Zambianization* (Lusaka, 1972).
99. Interview, Saela Mulemba, 2 March 1991.
100. Interview, A. Kwibisa, 6 April 1990.
101. *Rhodesia Herald*, 7 March 1964.

IRSH 60 (2015), Special Issue, pp. 63–94 doi:10.1017/S0020859015000486
© 2015 Internationaal Instituut voor Sociale Geschiedenis

Locals and Migrants in the Coalmining Town of Enugu (Nigeria): Worker Protest and Urban Identity, 1915–1929

CAROLYN A. BROWN

Department of History, Rutgers, The State University of New Jersey
16 Seminary Place, New Brunswick, NJ 08901, USA

E-mail: cbrown@panix.com

ABSTRACT: This article focuses on the varied workforce in and around the Enugu Government Colliery, located in south-eastern Nigeria and owned by the British colonial state. Opened in 1915 at Udi and in 1917 at Iva Valley and Obwetti, the mines were in a region with a long history of slave raids, population shifts, colonization, and ensuing changes in local forms of political organization. The mines brought together an eclectic mixture of forced and voluntary unskilled labor, prisoners, unskilled contract workers, and voluntary clerical workers and artisans. Moreover, the men were from different ethno-linguistic groups. By taking into account this complex background, the article describes the gradual process by which this group of inexperienced coalminers used industrial-protest strategies that reflected their habituation to the colonial workplace. They organized strikes against the village men, who, as supervisors, exploited them in the coalmines. Their ability to reach beyond their "traditional" rural identities as "peasants" to attack the kinsmen who exploited them indicates the extent to which the complex urban and industrial environment challenged indigenous identities based on locality as well as rural status systems and gender ideologies. One of the major divisions to overcome was the one between supposedly backward "locals", men who came from villages close to the mine, and more experienced "foreigners" coming from more distant areas in Nigeria: the work experience as "coalmen" led "locals" to see themselves as "modern men" too, and to position themselves in opposition to authoritarian village leaders. The article thus traces the contours of the challenges confronting a new working class as it experimented with unfamiliar forms of affiliation, trust, and association with people with whom it shared new, industrial experiences. It investigates the many ways that "local" men maneuvered against the authoritarian control of chiefs, forced labor, and workplace exploitation by "native" and expatriate staff.

As I look back on these early days of our struggles to obtain a dignified and rightful place for our African workers, I think […] that the 1920s were critical for us. It was during this period that Nigerian workers began to understand what it meant to be an inferior, to be subject to the "busts" and the "booms" of Western capitalist manipulations. While the suffering of our workers was great, they learned to stand on their own feet. They expressed themselves by means of strikes and unrest which the British did not appreciate. More important than the strikes were the expressions of fraternal interest in workers elsewhere. *We did not have an effective trade union organization in the 1920s, but we had a lot of Nigerian workers who thought and acted like trade unionists.*

> Michael Imoudu, President of the Nigerian Railway Workers' Union[1]

In the summer of 1926 miners in eastern Nigeria, a remote outpost of the British Empire, demonstrated their "fraternal interest in workers elsewhere" by going on strike during the British General Strike in which the militant British coalminers had played a leading role. In mid-May the Colonial Office had asked the colliery to expand its operations to compensate for the loss of British coal used to bunker ships along the coast. The manager hired more workers, added a shift, and prepared to increase production. In July the "local" day laborers – tub, rail, and timber – walked off their jobs, demanding a 1-penny increase to raise their wages to 1 shilling and 3 pence per day. The strike was short – from 12–14 July – but successful, because it occurred during a period of high labor demand because of the British General Strike, and was especially significant because it was the first time the inexperienced "local" workers used a conventional form of industrial protest rather than deserting the mines and returning to their farms, as they had until this point. They understood that, although they were not skilled miners, without their tubs the hewers (miners) could not produce, and without their timber no new work faces could be opened, nor roadways reinforced. Moreover, they also recognized the administrative hierarchy of the state by refusing to meet with the local magistrate and insisted on meeting personally with the Resident of Onitsha Province.

The relationship between this consciousness and position in the workforce would be demonstrated in the next decade, when these same "unskilled" workers eloquently explained why their wage demands were reasonable. What was especially remarkable is that now the "locals" were showing the industrial sophistication of the more savvy "foreigners" – skilled men from more distant areas, who had been trained by missionaries and worked in capitalist workplaces where they cultivated a tradition of bothersome militancy.

This was the Enugu Government Colliery, an enterprise owned by the colonial state, which opened in south-eastern Nigeria in 1915. It was the only colliery in West Africa and was considered a vital resource during the world wars. Its coal had strategic value as the main fuel for the Nigerian Government Railway, the steamships that plied the coast, and, during World War II, the convoys and railways of Britain's West African colonies and their allies.

---

1. Personal communication, 24 June 1964, to Peter C.W. Gutkind, as cited in *The Emergent African Urban Proletariat*, Occasional Paper Series, No. 8, Centre for Developing-Area Studies, McGill University (Montreal, 1974), p. 7 (my italics).

When the colliery began production in 1915, the workforce was an eclectic mixture of forced and voluntary unskilled labor, prisoners, unskilled contract workers, and voluntary clerical workers and artisans. Moreover, the men were of different ethnic groups. The skilled artisans and clerks were either Yoruba, from western Nigeria, or Igbo, from more "civilized" and colonized areas of south-eastern Nigeria. This heterogeneous mixture of men with differing skills, under different systems of labor control, with differential commitments to wage labor, and familiarity with the capitalist workplace, created eclectic forms of protest and work cultures.

Although the workforce rarely exceeded 2,000 in the early decades and 7,000 later on, its power lay in its location in the West African political economy and attracted the concern of the highest levels of Britain's Colonial Office. The mines and the Nigerian Railway were "sister" state enterprises, and until 1937 both were administered by the Director of the Nigerian Railway. The railway was also the colliery's main consumer and transporter, creating a functional integration that linked the two industries' workers in protest. When the railway workers struck, coal could not be evacuated from the mines. When the mineworkers struck, the railway lacked the coal to run. The coal workers had little experience in wage labor and benefitted from the militancy of the railway workers from western Nigeria, who had worked on the western branch of the railway since its opening in the 1890s. In an export economy like Nigeria, workers in transport (i.e. railways, docks, etc.) and fuel production were in a key position. They were often the first labor sector to recognize their own power and to exert it.[2]

The discovery of coal some 135 miles from the Niger Delta led to the construction of a railway line to carry that coal to the coast. Railway construction took several years and did not reach the colliery until May 1916. Both industries used forced labor to introduce a "free labor market" that officials claimed signified the superiority of British "civilization" over the "primitive" slave-holding societies of eastern Nigeria. But despite the fact that "free labor" was promoted as a modernizing force, most of the workers were anything but "free". The labor market was actually a byproduct of the conquest.

This article describes the gradual process by which a group of inexperienced African coalminers in south-eastern Nigeria used industrial-protest strategies that reflected their habituation to the colonial workplace. Eventually, they organized strikes against the senior village men, who, as supervisors, exploited

---

2. After World War II a rash of general strikes ran through Africa. Timothy Oberst notes that many were led by transport workers; Timothy Oberst, "Transport Workers, Strikes and the 'Imperial Response': Africa and the Post World War II Conjuncture", *African Studies Review*, 31 (1988), pp. 117–133. On the importance of transport workers in late colonialism in different world regions, see also several of the contributions in Stefano Bellucci, Larissa Rosa Corrêa, Jan-Georg Deutsch, and Chitra Joshi (eds), "Labour in Transport: Histories from the Global South, c.1750–1950", Special Issue 22, *International Review of Social History*, 59 (2014).

them in the coalmines. Their ability to reach beyond their "traditional" rural identities as "peasants" to attack the kinsmen who exploited them indicated the extent to which the complex urban and industrial environment challenged indigenous identities based on locality, rural status systems, and gender ideologies. This forced some of the young men to be open to new forms of affiliation that were more appropriate to their new workplace and experiences as migrants in the city of Enugu. As they interacted with "foreign" men in the workplace and in the city, these young migrants used multiple, intersecting, and contradictory identities as bases of personal construction. Their senior rural leaders were confused and resentful of the challenges posed by these young men to the existing social and generational hierarchies, and tried to undermine industrial actions against the mines.

The article traces, too, the tortuous struggle of young migrant workers to reconcile rural social identities, rooted in regionalism and kinship, with their class position as labor in a despotic colonial industry. Because the colliery opened during the final phase of the conquest, it encountered problems in securing labor for the coalmines and the railway. Most of the workers and inhabitants of Enugu were Igbo, the largest ethnic group in south-eastern Nigeria, but the majority of the skilled workers and urban inhabitants were from more distant areas in south-eastern Nigeria. While government classified them as Igbo, to the local people they were "foreigners", because they spoke a different dialect, had a strange religion – Christianity – and were trained in sophisticated, modern skills that allowed them to hold the best jobs in the industry and in the town.

Additionally, the city also had a small group of skilled workers and clerks who were Yoruba, the largest group in western Nigeria. They had also been trained by missionaries and were employed as artisans on the railway and as clerks in the city. Finally, there was one other group, called the "Saro", a cosmopolitan African people descended from slaves who had been liberated from slave ships after Britain abolished the slave trade in 1807 and who were quite familiar with Western culture, British rule, and Christianity. To the "locals" they were all "foreigners", and they resented the imposition of a city of "strangers" on their land. These divisions between "locals" and "foreigners", as well as additional divisions among the "locals", became a barrier to solidarity, so needed in colonial industry. And these conflicts were exploited by government and "traditional" rulers, both of whom recognized in them a mechanism to control workers.

This study focuses on the first fourteen years of the Enugu Government Colliery, 1915–1929, when the industry introduced wage labor to rural communities in south-eastern Nigeria. The colonial state, motivated by early twentieth-century notions of "civilization" and racial hierarchy, organized local governance on the basis of erroneous assumptions about the structure of power in African villages. In a system called "indirect rule", it incorporated local "men of prominence" in the government project and imbued them with extraordinary powers that violated the most basic traditions of political power in local villages. Supposedly based on "native authorities", this system imposed colonial "chiefs", most of whom were former slave dealers, on all communities. Their brief was the daily and detailed operations of the unlawful and brutal state. Much of the power of the "chiefs" concerned the question of labor – supplying the thousands of workers needed by a state operating where no labor market existed. But their influence reached into colonial industries affecting the deployment of labor, systems of worker control, and industrial relations practices.

Connections between the coalmines' "native" staff and "chiefs"[3] were usually personal and close, thereby projecting industrial discipline into the rural villages, and in turn bringing rural systems of control into the workplace. The colliery manager encouraged this intervention by assuming a limited managerial style that mirrored the "indirect rule" practices being used to stabilize rural villages. The industry relied on the "boss boys" to handle workers' complaints, ignoring the fact that they themselves were the causes of most complaints.

Rural identities were powerful bases of personal affinity (and continue to be so even today). Even in the most cosmopolitan of African cities, men considered their natal villages to be their real "homes". It was in these villages that they expressed political power, attained prestige, exercised authority, and established gendered status. However, despite the power of rural affiliations for both local and foreign young men, those who worked in the coalmines and/or lived in the colonial city were more open to experimenting with new associations involving unfamiliar people who were considered "foreigners". The junior men who became coalminers and/or migrated to Enugu found in the city a particularly rich and dynamic environment, filled with new freedoms and opportunities for new forms of masculine invention. Additionally, subordinate men – the poor, slaves, and the young – discovered new opportunities to challenge the systems of oppression controlled by senior men in the villages. In this way wage labor and urbanization exacerbated the intergenerational conflicts between older men and their juniors and undermined rural systems of legitimacy and authority.[4]

There were some six strikes from January 1919 to early 1921, followed by a second wave in 1924–1925, and a final crisis in 1929. The protests by "foreign" clerks, artisans, and "pick boys" or miners in 1917, 1918, and 1919 had been

---

3. Despite the problematic character of the notion, "chief" is used without quotation marks hereafter.

4. One of the most serious points of contention concerned access to young fertile women as wives. In many cases senior men used both their power to restrict the younger men's ability to marry and their influence with the elder men of the young women's families to negotiate for their marriages. For a discussion of this tension see Lisa Lindsay and Stephen Miescher, "Introduction", in *idem* (eds), *Men and Masculinities in Modern Africa* (Portsmouth, NH, 2003), pp. 1–30, 1–9.

successful in securing pay increases to meet wartime inflation. But at that time the "locals" protested by deserting, returning to their farms and villages. However, the protests of the 1920s, the focus of this article, were more tenacious and widespread. Most importantly they were led by "locals", categories of labor heretofore uninvolved. These strikes established a "culture of protest" that characterized the industrial environment of the coal industry throughout its subsequent existence. The recurrent character of these industrial actions, the use of accepted forms of worker protest, the assumptions that workers made about the social responsibilities of the state, and their manipulation of the policy dissonance among state actors indicates a qualitative change in the consciousness of the workers. They operated from a position that as workers they deserved to live and work under certain conditions, and they wanted the state to secure these conditions on their behalf.

The emergence of "local" workers as the leadership of mine protest indicates the willingness of young men to trust new forms of alliances that they associated with "modernity" and "progress". As their income made its imprint on the development of local villages, they became "coalmen", associated with the transformation to a new world. As working men and urban migrants from the adjacent area formed alliances and relationships with other people from outside their natal villages, their senior rural leaders were confused by the influence that "foreigners" had over their men. To the workers this confusion became yet another indicator of the rural leaders' backwardness and inability to understand the new industrial realities.

Now these young men could utilize elements of the new political and economic system for personal improvement, especially to accelerate the attainment of male maturity. The early history of the "coal city" of Enugu thus exhibits not only the characteristic conflicts between "locals" and "foreigners", but also those arising from challenges posed by young men to the existing social and generational hierarchies.

THE PEOPLE OF SOUTH-EASTERN NIGERIA

The city of Enugu and the mines were located some 135 miles from the Bight of Biafra coast in the northernmost region of south-eastern Nigeria, called Igboland. This was an area occupied by the Igbo people, one of the three largest ethno-linguistic groups in contemporary Nigeria. Most labor for the coalmines and railroad was recruited from their villages. The Igbo lived in an area of some 15,800 square miles framed on the west by the Niger River (with some settlement on the western bank of the Niger River), the Benue to the north, the Cross Rivers to the east, and the Niger Delta to the south. The Delta was on the Bight of Biafra, and the hinterland sometimes carries that same name.[5]

---

5. This is the origin of "Biafra", the name of the breakaway region during the Nigerian Civil War (1967–1970). Enugu was the capital of this brief state. The literature on Biafra is extensive, but one

The Igbo are the largest group in south-eastern Nigeria. They and most of the other numerous ethno-linguistic groups in the area – Ibibio, Efik, Ogonni – had a similar socio-political organization of small autonomous village-groups, or clusters of villages, without chiefs.[6] Important political decisions were made by a series of overlapping associations and groups (male councils of elders, women's associations, age grades, associations of "native" doctors, etc.), each with specific responsibilities. The council of senior/elder men and some women, whose opinions were respected, included representatives of constituent villages. But no representative had the authority to make decisions without consulting the group. All the people in a compound, village, or village-group believed that they were descendants of a common ancestor whose several offspring established constituent villages of a "village-group" or "town". The whole system functioned gerontocratically: the oldest man in a compound, the oldest compound in a village, and the oldest village in a village-group had special authority and sacred power, though none could function autocratically. This all began to change during the trans-Atlantic slave trade and was transformed radically during colonial rule.

In Igbo villages power was especially diffuse since most villages had neither strong chiefs nor kings.[7] However, these were not villages of equality. By the nineteenth century a new class of wealthy slaving merchants, *Ogaranyan*, had forced a strengthening of authority based on wealth at the expense of seniority. Many *Ogaranyan* were involved in the internal slave trade, which expanded with the decline of the trans-Atlantic trade by the late nineteenth century. These savvy traders proved very skillful in hiding their activities and ingratiating themselves with the British invaders in 1900.[8] Aware of global economic trends, they were quick to supply services to the colonial soldiers. In return, officials assumed that they

of the best histories of this tragic event is Axel Harneit-Sievers, Jones O. Ahazuem, and Sidney Emezue, *A Social History of the Nigerian Civil War: Perspectives from Below* (Münster, 1997), and fictionalized by the remarkable young Igbo/American writer Chimamanda Ngozi Adichie in *Half of a Yellow Sun* (New York, 2007).

6. A village-group was a cluster of villages established by the descendants of a common ancestor. Thus kinship to the common ancestor became the central element of social cohesion of the group.

7. The exception is Onitsha, which was influenced by the Kingdom of Benin near the Niger River; Richard N. Henderson, *The King in Every Man: Evolutionary Trends in Onitsha Ibo Society and Culture* (New Haven, CT, 1972).

8. These men were surprisingly "modern". By World War I they were so familiar with British culture that early missionaries, upon visiting one in his remote home, found a Morris Minor parked in the yard, despite the fact that roads were quite primitive. They were especially astute at using "Western" commodities as prestige goods to secure clients and symbolize modernity. For a contemporary account of this encounter see Northwestern University Africana Library, Church Missionary Society Records, Microfilm Reel 204, Box G3.A3/0 1913–16 "Niger Mission", The Rev. Basden, "Report on a Visit to the Udi District", n.d. The records can be found in the Herskovits Library Collections, Northwestern University. The original documents are at SOAS, University of London.

were chiefs (despite there being no chiefs in pre-colonial Igbo villages). These were the men who would also supply drafted labor to the coalmines and infrastructural projects.[9]

The political fragmentation of Igboland as reflected in regional "ethnic" identities was related to the diverse ecology.[10] Igboland is located in the Guinea coastal climatic area, a region with a wide range of rainfall. Within this broad region are several micro-ecological zones with varying soil types, rainfall, and vegetation. As was the case throughout West Africa, communities based in the thick rainforests tended to be small and fragmented, while large, multi-ethnic states were clustered in the savannah region, where horses could become the crucial technology of empire building.[11] Although the Igbo shared some dialects and other cultural traits before the conquest, they never perceived themselves as one distinct "people", and they had historically organized their ever-shifting political alliances on a sharply defined regionalism. The key regional distinction was the "coast" versus the "interior".

"Coastal" society came to have a distinct meaning denoting groups who, by the twentieth century, had had some 400 years of contact with Europe, a contact that was reflected in their names, mercantile skill, and receptivity to European culture.[12] From the sixteenth century the coastal communities had come into closer contact with European traders, missionaries, and the precursors to colonial officials, and over time these regional identities had become more defined, reflecting differential levels of familiarity with European culture, labor systems, and the colonial economy. This familiarity

9. For a history of one such "big man" see Dillibe Onyeama, *Chief Onyeama: A Story of an African God* (Enugu, 1982).

10. I deliberately do not use the term "tribe" for a number of reasons, including its implication of primordialism and social stasis. Africanists have generally rejected this term because it has become clear that so-called tribal identity was constructed, is usually related to colonialism, and is not a useful category of analysis. For this debate see Archie Mafeje, "The Ideology of 'Tribalism'", *Journal of Modern African Studies*, 9 (1971), pp. 253–261; Leroy Vail (ed.), *The Creation of Tribalism in Southern Africa* (Berkeley, CA, 1989). For a discussion regarding the Igbo, see Douglas A. Anthony, *Poison and Medicine: Ethnicity, Power, and Violence in a Nigerian City, 1966 to 1986* (Portsmouth, NH, 2002).

11. This was the case with the Yoruba, who had been part of the Oyo Empire, a state created around 1100 and patrolled by a powerful cavalry. For a discussion of the relationship between ecology and political structure see Akin Mabogunje, "The Land and Peoples of West Africa", in Jacob F.A. Ajayi and Michael Crowder (eds), *History of West Africa*, I (New York, 1970), pp. 1–32.

12. The adoption of European names indicated the hybridity of these communities. Examples include the names of some traders, such as the Robin Johns, a prominent trading family, or Antera Duke. Coastal communities adopted elements of European culture as early as the sixteenth century. This included dress, housing styles (later even a kind of prefabricated Victorian house), and Christianity. On the Robin Johns see Randy Sparks, *The Two Princes of Calabar: An Eighteenth-Century Atlantic Odyssey* (Cambridge, MA, 2004); on Antera Duke see Stephen D. Behrendt, A.J.H. Latham, and David Northrup, *The Diary of Antera Duke: An Eighteenth-Century African Trader* (Oxford, 2012).

with Western culture was also to become a major influence on how workers engaged with the coal industry and the city.

THE IMPACT OF THE SLAVE TRADE

The most significant factor contributing to the divisive regional identities among the mine workforce was the region's role in the trans-Atlantic slave trade. Between the late eighteenth and mid-nineteenth centuries over 1.2 million (20 per cent) of the slaves crossing the Atlantic came from south-eastern Nigeria, and most were Igbo.[13] The internal trade continued into the nineteenth century, when slaving turned particularly violent as the Biafran hinterland became a palm oil producing area.[14] In a paradoxical way, the "legitimate" trade in palm products actually increased the demand for unfree labor in the palm belt.

The British conquest of Northern Igboland, the area of the subsequent Enugu colliery, incorporated the Udi district, a remote, impoverished area of relatively disadvantaged villages in comparison with groups from the coast. Moreover, Udi was still suffering from the after-effects of centuries of slave trading: Udi people had been a primary source for the Atlantic slave trade and were sold by middlemen to coastal traders. This association with slavery left an indelible mark upon the way they were viewed by other Igbo communities. Igbo from the more "civilized" areas of the south-eastern region – Onitsha, Owerri, Calabar – disparaged the people of Udi as being particularly "backward", "primitive", and "degraded", both because of their enslavement and because of their poverty. They called them "Wa Wa", a pejorative term meaning "primitive backward people". They had a reputation for kidnapping, lawlessness, and incessant warfare related to defense systems villages employed to prevent enslavement. They were the last group to be converted to Christianity and consequently lacked the skills to fill the most lucrative jobs that opened up in Enugu, and the skilled posts in the mines and railway.

In the late nineteenth century the destructive impact of the internal slave trade directed to the palm belt reached catastrophic proportions. Wealthy bandit traders, called *Awagwu*, created their own settlements of multiple wives, free dependents, and slaves, which they ruled with impunity. These marauding bandits operated totally outside the customary traditions of

13. The calculations of the trade from this area are undergoing constant revision owing to the major data projects that followed the Slave Voyages project directed by David Eltis (see www.slavevoyages.org), a multinational research effort that has allowed scholars to build, collaboratively, a more accurate quantitative estimate of slaves exported. See also Carolyn A. Brown and Paul E. Lovejoy (eds), *Repercussions of the Atlantic Slave Trade: The Interior of the Bight of Biafra and the African Diaspora* (Trenton, NJ, 2011).

14. One of the best discussions of this shift as well as of the internal political and social transformation is David Northrup, *Trade Without Rulers: Pre-Colonial Economic Development in South-Eastern Nigeria* (Oxford, 1978).

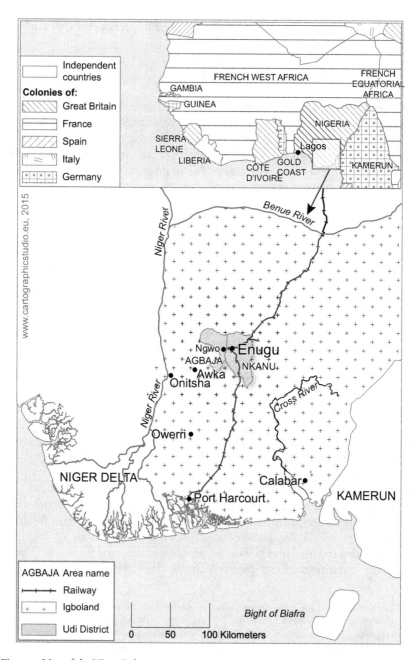

Figure 1. Map of the Niger Delta.

rural politics. They formed private militias, which they dispatched to raid villages and kidnap and sell adults and children, largely to the palm-producing areas near Owerri. This violence fundamentally changed both the governing system and the social stability of the region. The imprint was reflected in the architecture of the area, where watchtowers, maze-like compound entrances, and compact settlements became rural survival strategies. These bandits were particularly active in the area between Onitsha and Udi, where they destroyed villages, sending desperate refugees to areas like the Udi escarpment, a barren range of sandy hills to the west of the city of Enugu. Some of the prominent men who collaborated with the British invasion were from this group of *Awagwu*.[15]

As the global trade – initially the slave trade, later the palm trade – increasingly infiltrated village economies, wealthy merchants contested the political/ritual power of the elders and forced some accommodations to allow their wealth to translate into political power. The resulting *Ogaranyan* model of elite masculinity entailed heading a "big compound", an exaggerated polygamous household of many wives,[16] children, clients, and slaves, and being engaged in the conspicuous consumption of foreign commodities (i.e. bicycles, cars, Western clothes). Elite men tied to the mercantile economy differed significantly from those senior men who were "household heads" and whose status came from their ability to sustain and defend their household, to maintain personal autonomy, to avenge insult or violence, and to demonstrate commitment to the betterment of the corporate group.[17] In addition, the model of the *Ogaranyan* tied elite masculinity to the world market in ways that popularized gender relations based on substantial wealth. The *Ogaranyan* wore special clothes, danced exclusive dances, belonged to expensive associations, and were buried with considerable ceremony and expense.[18]

By the late nineteenth century elite masculinity impacted upon the aspirations of many men in a new way. The "big men" had transformed their wealth into political and spiritual power using prestigious "title"

---

15. The most prominent Udi trader, Onyeama Onwusi, became the most powerful of this group. See G. Ugo Nwokeji, *The Slave Trade and Culture in the Bight of Biafra: An African Society in the Atlantic World* (Cambridge [etc.], 2010).

16. See Jeff Guy, "Analysing Pre-Capitalist Societies in Southern Africa", *Journal of Southern African Studies*, 14 (1987), pp. 18–37. In the Udi area one chief was known for having eighty wives. The symbolism of this "conspicuous exhibitionism" was not lost on less wealthy men, and this form of elite masculinity became one of the models other men aspired to adopt.

17. For a discussion of this more "normal" male honor see Carolyn A. Brown, "A 'Man' in the Village is a 'Boy' in the Workplace: Colonial Racism, Worker Militance, and Igbo Notions of Masculinity in the Nigerian Coal Industry, 1930–1945", in Lindsay and Miescher, *Men and Masculinities*, pp. 156–174.

18. Ifi Amadiume, *Male Daughters, Female Husbands: Gender and Sex in an African Society* (London, 1987), p. 31.

societies, the most prominent being the *Ozo* title.[19] Before colonialism, few men could hope to attain the model of elite masculinity of the *Ogaranyan*, but regular wages opened this possibility to aspirants, especially as it offered an alternative way to marry, a prerequisite for mature adulthood. In fact, the state pulled into its new economy those young men who had not actually attained mature adulthood. Their conscription into wage labor by the *Ogaranyan* chiefs paradoxically empowered young men to challenge the power of their seniors in the village – in this way, the chiefs actually created their own nemesis. In fact, as we will see below, the workplace and the city of Enugu became incubators of an anti-chief/elder men sentiment, articulated largely by the Westernized elite and actively supported by young men.

The Udi district had been the northernmost wing of the supply system for the slave trade. The slave trade, however, was experienced differently by the two major Udi groups, the Agbaja and the Nkanu, called "clans" by anthropologists.[20] While the Agbaja became slaves, the Nkanu collaborated with slave traders. In the late eighteenth through the nineteenth century marauding militias pushed hundreds of refugees to the Udi escarpment, where they formed densely populated settlements. By 1900 the land was so infertile that it was virtually useless for farming.[21] In these villages, called the Agbaja, lived "locals" who would eventually supply the majority of the mines' labor force. But in the opening years of the mines, they would resist recruitment. However, this was unsustainable given the inability of young men to establish farms on the overcrowded escarpment. This was especially serious because farming was a precondition for young men to marry, establish their lineage, and form their own compounds and households, a prerequisite for social maturity.

---

19. Title societies were ranked associations in which entrance and ascent in rank depended on payment of an increasing level of fees. In the 1920s membership required a feast, followed one year later by £20 pounds in cash, 100 fowls, another feast, and payment to a person to perform facial scarification; P. Amaury Talbot, *The Peoples of Southern Nigeria* (London, 1969), III, p. 775.

20. The designation of "clan" was an example of the invention of categories to classify Igbo communities. It is characteristic of a particular form of "colonial knowledge" that was generated in the 1920s. See Dmitri van den Bersselaar, "Acknowledging Knowledge: Dissemination and Reception of Expertise in Colonial Africa", *History in Africa*, 33 (2006), pp. 389–393; also *idem*, "Missionary Knowledge and the State in Colonial Nigeria: On How G. T. Basden Became an Expert", *History in Africa*, 33 (2006), pp. 433–450; A.E. Afigbo, "Anthropology and Colonial Administration in South-Eastern Nigeria, 1891–1939", *Journal of the Historical Society of Nigeria*, 8 (1975), pp. 19–35.

21. In addition to land scarcity the escarpment suffered from severe erosion, which made migration a necessity to grow food. See David Grossman, "Migratory Tenant Farming in Northern Iboland in Relation to Resource Use" (Ph.D. dissertation, Columbia University, New York, 1968).

Marriage was an overwhelming preoccupation for young men, desperate to establish their independence and to take their place among the senior men in their village. While an older son in an extended family could look forward to inheriting the compound and land of the father,[22] the younger sons would have to forge their own way, colonizing new areas to establish their independence, found their own lineages, and establish farms. Fulfillment of the imperative to migrate from one's father/parents is reflected in the founding narrative of most Igbo village-groups.[23] In 1900 Agbaja's young men, thwarted in securing their own farming lands, were in a crisis. They were forced to migrate to the adjacent fertile plains of their neighbors, the Nkanu, who were the local middlemen selling slaves to the coast. Thus Agbaja men depended on access to land owned by the very people who had sold, and continued to sell, their people as slaves.[24] But Agbaja carried an even more humiliating burden: the more "civilized" Igbo of Owerri and Onitsha accused them of being so depraved as to violate sacred moral codes and sell some of their own children into slavery. It appears, however, that this was a tragic choice that they had to make to secure food to support the remaining family members.[25] The sale of kin was considered an ultimate indicator of social degradation.

Unlike the refugee communities of Agbaja, Nkanu settlements were on the adjacent fertile plains to which they dispatched slave families. As is the case in many slave-trading communities, by the nineteenth century Nkanu came to retain large numbers of slaves, locally called *Ohu*, who performed tasks judged "beneath" the status of the *Amadi*, the freeborn men. This gave Nkanu a particularly rigid and persistent form of slavery which defied British efforts, though indeed quite tepid, to end slavery and discrimination against descendants of slaves throughout the colonial period.[26] One consequence of the incorporation of slaves in freeborn villages was a series of very large segregated *Ohu* villages from which the *Amadi*

---

22. There was no land alienation. Extended families were given compound land and farmlands by the village council of men. But in the Agbaja area land shortage prevented all but the eldest sons from acquiring access to their fathers' land.

23. See the Intelligence Report for a number of "clans": Nigerian National Archives, Enugu [hereafter, NNAE], CSE 1/85/6114, H.J.S. Clark, Assistant District Officer, "Intelligence Report on the Ngwo Clan of Abaja Area, Udi Division, Onitsha Province".

24. Reuben Kendrick Udo, "The Migrant Tenant Farmer of Eastern Nigeria", *Africa*, 34 (1964), pp. 326–339.

25. W.R.G. Horton, "The *Ohu* System of Slavery in a Northern Ibo Village-Group", *Africa*, 24 (1954), pp. 311–336.

26. The ending of colonial slavery has been the subject of many studies in the last twenty years. We now know that in this area, as throughout the British colonies, the "Indian model" of colonial slave policy was employed. This involved criminalizing the sale of slaves and leaving it to the slaves to "free" themselves. Should owners try to resist, the colonial government would not use the courts to enforce their rights.

seized men to work on the railroad and later in the coalmines. While it is difficult to say exactly when slavery ceased to exist,[27] we do know that wage labor and the cash economy substantially eroded its moorings after World War I.[28]

The experience of Mazi Anyionovo Nwodo, an *Ohu* coalminer, illustrates the gradual transformation from slave to worker. His account refers to the 1920s:

> I and Edenwede Ogbu of Isigwe were pace setters sort of, to the *Ihus* or *Obias*.[29]
> We were the first set of people to enlist personally to the Europeans without the consent of the chief for their personal betterment. [...] I was among those sent by the chief to work in the construction of the railway line from Otakpa, now in Imo State. Otakpa was where the Nkanu people under Chief Chukwuani of Ozalla joined in the railway construction. [...] All payment for those that were sent out by the chief, whether on the coalmine or railway construction, was directed to the chief. We were left with nothing, but at a later date the chief started giving us small amounts of what each of us realized. This was after we had realized from the Europeans that we were paid for the job we had been doing for long. Because of the chief's action we deemed it unnecessary not to be obligatory to the chief.[30] In the circumstance, we started looking for our own greener pastures for personally paid jobs and the most possible area to look for jobs was in Enugu.[31]

Anyionovo Nwodo had escaped a system in which his "owner" attempted to profit from the agricultural labor he performed for him, as well to claim part of the wages he earned for paid colliery work.[32]

---

27. Slavery has proven to be an especially resilient form of coercive labor in the Nigerian context, which can easily be folded into family structures or marriage. For a discussion of the systems of disguise of actual slavery in the early colonial period (some of which continue today) see Robin Chapdelaine, "A History of Child Trafficking in Southeastern Nigeria, 1900s–1930s" (Ph.D. dissertation, Rutgers University, NJ, 2014).

28. For a discussion of the complicated meaning of "freedom" in the Enugu area, see Carolyn A. Brown, "Testing the Boundaries of Marginality: Twentieth-Century Slavery and Emancipation Struggles in Nkanu, Northern Igboland, 1920–29", *Journal of African History*, 37 (1996), pp. 51–80.

29. *Ihu* is another term used for slave in this area. *Obias* has a different history: the term means "stranger" and its use was a product of a period of violent struggle by the slave villages to force the state to outlaw the use of *Ihu* or *Ohu*, which clearly meant slave. I discuss this in Brown, "Testing the Boundaries".

30. This is Nigerian English.

31. Interview with Mazi Anyionovo Nwodo, Uhuona, Ugbawka, 18 August 1988. Interview conducted in Igbo. The translation into Nigerian English was made by the unidentified interviewer.

32. In some respects this resembled the "hiring out" system used during the nineteenth century in the US South, especially as slavery waned. Owners would allow their slaves to move to the city or off the plantation and perform labor for a wage. They were then required to pay their owner a percentage of their earnings, in something like "rent", for the freedom to earn a wage. See Richard C. Wade, *Slavery in the Cities: The South, 1820–1860* (New York, 1964).

This was a violation of the customary exploitation – "moral economy" – of slavery,[33] in which slaves could work a certain number of days on fields allocated to them and represented an intensification of exploitation for the *Ohu* men. As the *Amadi* tried to seize income the *Ohu* earned in wage labor, they sparked a revolt in many slave villages, especially in that of Anyionovo Nwodo. His village, Isigwe, was physically distant from that of their owners, which gave them an opportunity to experience daily autonomy over their internal affairs, a process that encouraged solidarity and a collective consciousness. In 1922 the people of Isigwe were in the forefront of the insurrection when the *Ohu* from Nkanu finally rose up against their owners' claim on their wages.

Tensions continued to build up as earnings from coalmining emboldened the *Ohu* to demand social equality with the *Amadi*. Incomprehensible to the British, they fought most hard to protect their families from kidnapping and sale, to retain their wages, to have full access to land (without the conditionality of slave labor), and the right to join the same types of prestigious male associations that distinguished the most prominent *Amadi*. The *Amadi* were enraged, and seized and sold several *Ohu* children. The *Ohu*, in turn, expelled the *Amadi* from their segregated village.[34] The conflict continued for most of the decade until the state brokered an agreement for land to establish separate *Ohu* villages, but they were never accepted as equals of the *Amadi*.[35]

The history of enslavement was humiliating to the Agbaja men and appeared to be but one additional attribute of their "backward" and "immoral" culture. Additionally, they were unfamiliar with the cultures, technologies, and religions of the more "civilized" areas. This disparity became even more intolerable from the late nineteenth century when they interacted with the more modern "foreigners", ironically in a city – Enugu – built on the land of the marginal Agbaja villages. The British had unwittingly built a modern industry and city on the foundation of the nineteenth-century economy – slavery – that had instilled terror, dislocation, and internal discrimination in the self-same area. As colonial rule took root, it intensified the pre-existing regional disparities between the prosperous slave-dealing (and later palm-trading) coastal trading states and the poor hinterland areas, like Udi, ravaged

---

33. Slaves (and their families) worked on their owners' fields a certain number of days per week and the rest of the time they could work on fields designated for their own use. By charging them part of their wages, *Amadi* violated their right to the product of their labor during their own time.
34. There is a detailed discussion of the revolt, which erupted in 1920 and continued with increased intensity until 1922, when the area was in civil war. For a discussion of *Ohu* men demanding full equality and social acceptance (a demand which the freeborn community never conceded), see Brown, "Testing the Boundaries".
35. When I conducted interviews in this area, freeborn descendants quickly noted that any prestigious associations established by the descendants of *Ohu* were invalid and fraudulent.

by slaving. This was the difference between the "local" population (and workers) and the "foreigners", i.e. those who had come from regions further away, like Onitsha and Owerri, to fulfill jobs.[36] To the people of Udi, Enugu was "their town".

THE INVENTION OF CHIEFS AND THE CREATION OF NEO-TRADITIONAL LABOR SYSTEMS

The northern area of south-eastern Nigeria was the last region to be incorporated into the Nigerian colony. While Britain's conquest of south-eastern Nigeria began in 1900, the invasion did not reach Udi, the future area of the coalmines, until 1904, and even then the conquest proved ephemeral as annual military expeditions occurred for four years. Resistance did not end in 1908, however, when initial hostilities concluded. Even then, despite the overwhelming military superiority of the troops it took a decade before the area could be considered "pacified" (in 1914). In the midst of the conquest, officials set the political reconstruction in place; "indirect rule", as it was called, established chiefs' courts to adjudicate disputes, levy fines, and to conscript labor.

In 1914 Frederick Lugard became Governor General of Nigeria and centralized more power in the hands of the chiefs.[37] This increased the burden on the people of a partnership of despotism between an outlaw state and the local collaborators that it recognized. For those so anointed, the tasks of governing were lucrative but formidable and risky, for despite the military superiority of the state, Europeans were too few on the ground when villagers decided to end, once and for all, a chief's despotic rule. While bludgeoned into submission in the "pacification" of the region, the local people were forced, in defeat, to become "free laborers" for a myriad of colonial projects. This occurred in the first year of the war.

The Enugu Government Colliery opened in 1915 under military guard and defeated villages were forced to supply labor in retribution for their resistance. But the Udi villages rose up again – in an event called "the Udi business" – triggered by the government deployment of colonial troops to the eastern border with German Kamerun. The desperate shortage of coal reserves forced the Colonial Office to open the colliery despite this unsettled context and the financial constraints of the war. Supplies of Welsh coal, the favored source, were far from secure, given hostilities. Since local labor was up in arms, officials

---

36. For the history of these two areas see Adiele E. Afigbo, "Southeastern Nigeria in the 19th Century", in Jacob F.A. Ajayi and Michael Crowder (eds), *History of West Africa*, II (London, 1987, 2nd edn), pp. 429–484.
37. For a discussion of the Lugardian reforms see Carolyn A. Brown, *"We Were All Slaves": African Miners, Culture, and Resistance at the Enugu Government Colliery* (Portsmouth, NH, 2003), pp. 80–84.

recruited workers from Onitsha, a large market town on the Niger River, and later from Owerri, an important commercial center in the palm belt to the south nearer the coast. Colonial chiefs became labor recruiters and young men and slaves were the usual target.

Colonial rule was more established in Onitsha and Owerri, and their men, while from the same ethnic group – Igbo – as Enugu's "locals", were far more habituated to wage labor, even in its conscripted form. In addition to these groups of Igbo men there were men from other areas of Nigeria. Railway workers, skilled artisans, and clerks came to the city from the distant cosmopolitan Yoruba city of Lagos in the west (370 miles away). Christianized Yoruba and "Saro", descendants of slaves captured from ships that violated Britain's 1807 abolition of the slave trade, became the city's "foreign" elite. To the local communities, the men from Onitsha, Owerri, and Lagos were "foreigners" who occupied their land and farms, and monopolized the highest paying jobs in "their" city of Enugu. Thus, from the very beginning, the colliery workforce had a "local–foreigner" division that challenged the development of a solidarity the workplace otherwise encouraged.

Workers were paradoxically empowered by the inferior quality of Enugu coal, which was sub-bituminous "soft" coal that broke easily, disintegrating with each handling into ever smaller – and less usable – chunks. It was also prone to spontaneous combustion, a dangerous attribute given the wooden railway wagons that transported coal to the coast. Despite these limitations, Udi was a large, secure regional source of coal when war jeopardized the sea lanes that brought the superior Welsh coal. Because of its fragility and combustibility, purchasers intentionally held small reserves, a practice that made the market especially vulnerable to work stoppages. Miners grew to recognize this strategic advantage, and although they were relatively inexperienced and isolated on the "fringes of empire", Enugu coal workers quickly reflected the activist image of British miners that so menaced Britain's energy source. Enugu miners similarly leveraged the power that their inferior product gave them in the regional transport system. They used this knowledge skillfully to create an industrial tradition of troublesome militancy that gave them a national reputation as a strategically powerful sector of Nigeria's working class. They organized frequent work stoppages, manipulated state officials, and selected as leaders men capable of defending their interests as workers. These patterns would be visible in the first locally led strikes in the 1920s.[38]

The complexity and fluidity of Igbo political systems (colonially perceived as "anarchic" and "chaotic") frustrated both early government officials and anthropologists who were creating "colonial knowledge" to

---

38. When the state authorized trade unions in 1938 and 1939, they tended to locate sophisticated and militant leaders among the corps of men being trained in the "Nigerianization" initiative.

develop working instruments of local government. They invented
categories – such as "tribe" – to refer to virtually every corporate settlement
of several lineages. They could not reach a consensus on whether the Igbo
were "one tribe" or dozens of "sub-tribes", each with its own ethnographic
profile.[39] Despite their fraudulence, these categories became the foundation
for the "indirect rule" model of local government. This system was
embedded in the philosophical foundations of the evolving schools of early
twentieth-century imperial ethno-historical research.

From 1899 to 1906 the main proponent of indirect rule, Frederick Lugard,
had been the High Commissioner of the Protectorate of Northern Nigeria. As a
military man he was partial to the ordered (and authoritarian) governing system
created in Nigeria's Muslim north. In 1914 he became Governor General of a
unified Nigeria and was perplexed by the plethora of governing forms that had
developed under colonial rule in the south-east. He began a centralization process in 1912 (acting as Governor of the two protectorates of Northern and
Southern Nigeria) that removed European officers from the courts, gave more
authority to the chiefs, and laid a foundation for corruption, extortion, and
terror, all emanating from the "native courts" controlled by these chiefs.[40] As
noted above, "indirect rule" was the guiding principle for industrial relations in
the coal industry. The colonial "warrant chiefs" (government-appointed chiefs
who were given a warrant to symbolize the authority of their position) became
labor recruiters and were given the power to recruit and discipline labor through
their "boss boys", who brought crews of drafted young men to work. There
they supervised them at work and in the labor camps, controlled by the chiefs.

In many cases the chiefs were from within the *Ogaranyan* class, and they
relished this legitimacy conferred by the colonial state. They responded to
the state's first labor demands, which were rationalized as punishment for
resistance, by seizing young men and slaves. The labor needs were many:
unskilled labor to develop the infrastructure, for head porterage, to clear

39. One study that follows this format is Percy Amaury Talbot, *The Peoples of Southern Nigeria*,
4 vols (London, 1969).

40. Native courts were part of the indirect rule that was practiced throughout Nigeria. The
government appointed men as chiefs and gave them the right to try certain types of cases in the
districts over which they reigned. The courts included a chief, a clerk, usually a Saro or literate
local, and messengers who canvassed the area delivering court warrants and arresting defendants.
The system bred corruption and permitted the chiefs, clerks, and messengers to extort fines from
the population, to demand women as wives, and to draft young men to work in their fields. In
1912 they became even more corrupt because Lugard prevented the District Officers from
attending the courts. The educated elite in Lagos was especially incensed by these reforms, because
Lugard refused to allow any lawyers to attend the sessions and ignored their calls to eschew
"traditional" institutions that they felt represented authoritarian "traditions" and corrupt
practices. Chiefs used the courts to get money, to lend money to indigent defendants, and to create
near fiefdoms. The major study is Adiele Eberechukwu Afigbo, *The Warrant Chiefs: Indirect
Rule in Southeastern Nigeria 1891–1929* (London, 1972).

streams and bush paths, and to build roads. Government buildings and official quarters needed to be built, and the infrastructure for the coalmines and the railway constructed. One example of such a labor-recruiting chief was Chief Njemanze of Owerri. He had been a powerful slave trader, who worked with the Aro slavers, an enterprising Igbo clan who controlled slave procurement – in the area's periodic market system.[41] After the British Aro Expedition in 1901–1902 he switched sides: he helped guide the troops to Aro Chukwu, the Aro capital, and convinced villages not to contest the armies.[42] Later on, Njemanze sent several hundred workers to Enugu, including a number of tradesmen whose mission-trained skills made them especially valuable to the railway operations. Another case is that of Eze Okoli, a famous *dibia* ("native" doctor) from Nnoli near Onitsha. He was especially helpful to the British. He embraced Christianity, took private lessons in English, and supplied troops for the Cameroon campaign in World War I.[43] Okoli sent hundreds of young men to Enugu to work in the mines.

In the Udi area two prominent men, Chief Chukwuani Nwangwu of Nkanu and Chief Onyeama Onwusi of Agbaja, both *Ogaranyan*, shifted from being slave dealers to labor recruiters, calling up hundreds of men for forced labor and/or local slavery. Both had been prosperous slave and palm traders, and had supplied railway workers from the Agbaja and Nkanu areas of Udi. Now as chiefs, both claimed "customary" rights to conscript workers, although in reality no *Ogaranyan* could claim labor beyond his own household. In ignorance, colonial field officers assumed that in supplying workers they were merely exercising the same "customary" rights as a "house" head on the coast.[44] The chiefs claimed the authority vested in several labor laws that allowed the state to conscript labor. These included the Masters and Servants Act, Roads and Creeks Ordinance, and the so-called House Rules Ordinance, which enabled the chiefs to conscript workers, establish courts in the labor camps, and manage the labor camps using their own paramilitary groups to keep order.[45]

41. For a discussion of this sophisticated slave procurement system of the Aro see Northrup, *Trade Without Rulers*, ch. 5.
42. Afigbo, *The Warrant Chiefs*, p. 64.
43. Amadiume, *Male Daughters, Female Husbands*, p. 138.
44. Coastal "houses" were commercial institutions that emerged with the slave trade and expanded with the palm oil trade. They evolved from a segmentary kin-based compound (which continued to exist in the interior) into a hierarchal "house" of slaves. The most detailed explanation is in Kenneth O. Dike, *Trade and Politics in the Niger Delta, 1830–1885: An Introduction to the Economic and Political History of Nigeria* (Oxford, 1956).
45. This triumvirate of laws were the legal framework for Britain's forced-labor policies. For a discussion of how these three laws worked against African labor, see Brown, *"We Were All Slaves"*, ch. 2; also Tekena N. Tamuno, *The Evolution of the Nigerian State* (New York, 1972).

Chief Onyeama used his *Ogwumili* force,[46] a private militia of "enforcers" and labor headmen, to insure that workers, once in the labor camps, complied with his regulations. Onyeama also invented an elaborate labor-recruitment system emanating from his native court. He contacted subordinate chiefs, instructing them to call up men within specific age grades,[47] who then had to report to a series of transit camps where agents checked off their names on the list for their villages.[48] He also used his court to enforce workplace discipline, all with the tacit approval of the political officers. Onyeama and other chiefs were allowed to make deductions from the workers' wages to cover costs of food and other, less legal, expenses.[49]

While the chiefs conscripted their men for the mines and other projects, they also wreaked havoc in the rural villages. Legal prohibitions notwith-standing, *Amadi* still enforced slavery in their villages, relying upon the fears of colonial officials that public emancipation would create social disorder.[50] Attempts by the *Amadi* to change the terms of slavery to give them more control over their erstwhile workers led to a major revolt in 1920–1922, which required a military patrol for several months and resulted in the deaths of many *Amadi* and *Ohu*. In addition, traditional practices in the native courts controlled by the warrant chiefs were increasingly violated. Most warrant chiefs operated with impunity, even after the uprisings during World War I, when many of them were either killed or run out of their villages.[51] They leveled false charges against men, collected fines, or demanded a daughter as a wife. Others became moneylenders, requiring pawns to work off the interest on usurious loans.[52]

---

46. Only anecdotal information is available about Onyeama's *Ogwumili* force. See Onyeama, *Chief Onyeama*, p. 40; Robert L. Tignor, "Colonial Chiefs in Chiefless Societies", *Journal of Modern African Studies*, 9 (1971), pp. 339–359, 350; Felix C. Mgboh, "The Biography of Chief Onyeama: A Research Paper Presented to the Department of History-Civics Alvan Ikoku College of Education, Owerri", June 1980 (unpublished), p. 12.
47. Age grades were groups of men and women who were initiated into adulthood during the same year. They were formed every several years and were often named after some event. Those born around the time of the Spanish flu of 1919 were named "Fluenza".
48. Interview with C.O. Ude, Amokwe, Udi, 23 February 1972; interview with Chief J. Nwankwo, Eke, Udi, 7 March 1972; interviews conducted by Innocent Uzoechi, both cited in Innocent F.A. Uzoechi, "The Social and Political Impact of the Eastern Nigerian Railway on Udi Division, 1913–1945" (Ph.D. dissertation, Kent State University, 1985), p. 125.
49. NNAE, ONDIST 12/1/1562, Colliery Manager to District Officer, 17 February 1920, enclosure in Acting District Officer to Resident Onitsha, 16 February 1920.
50. The British also hesitated to institute a public emancipation for fear of having to pay the compensation to slave owners that they had encountered in the West Indies. See Suzanne Miers and Richard Roberts, *The End of Slavery in Africa* (Madison, WI, 1988).
51. Akinjide Osuntokun, "Disaffection and Revolts in Nigeria during the First World War, 1914–1918", *Canadian Journal of African Studies*, 5 (1971), pp. 171–192.
52. Pawnship was a practice in which a debtor gives a relative to the creditor until the loan is repaid. The labor of the pawn did not pay off the loan principal but the loan interest.

Despite all of these problems and signs of unrest, officials allowed the native court system to continue and consolidate. At one point they even paid Udi's two chiefs to supply targeted numbers of workers for the mines. In the slave villages in Nkanu, *Amadi* chiefs used the courts to extort money from their slaves, which became another contributing factor to the violent 1920 revolt. Significantly, this helped *Ohu* to embrace their identity and mobilize throughout Nkanu, forming a social movement that expanded beyond the slaves to include other poor sectors of the communities.[53]

Despite all the problems with corruption, child stealing, extortion, and violence by the chiefs, what would finally end the warrant chieftaincy system was the 1929 uprising by thousands of Igbo, Ibibio, and Efik women who, fearing that chiefs would tax them, rose up and brought down the entire local government structure in one fell swoop.[54]

"COME TO THE CITY AND BE FREE!": CLERKS, RUNAWAY SLAVES, AND RURAL DISSIDENTS – ENUGU AS A CENTRE OF ANTI-CHIEF PROTEST

The city of Enugu began as a cluster of labor camps located on land secured from a group of local men claiming to be chiefs.[55] The camps were located near the railway station and the entrance of the Udi mine, which opened in 1915. Additional camps were set up in 1917, when two new mining sites – Iva Valley and Obwetti – were opened. The pioneer settlers of the new city of Enugu were a polyglot population of European military officers, "foreigners" from Lagos, Onitsha, and Owerri, and a few "locals", including village dissidents (mostly younger men from the local surroundings) who wanted to escape the abuses of senior men and chiefs in the village.

During World War I Enugu grew rapidly into a cosmopolitan city. In relation to its surroundings, it was indeed a "foreign" town. Until the 1940s, the majority of the Igbo inhabitants were either from Owerri or from Onitsha, both areas about 100 miles away from Enugu.[56] After the war the rural officials noted the presence of new men who were emerging as troublesome challengers to the chiefs' control in the villages. The city had become a den of sedition, with clerks and other "foreigners" campaigning against the "traditionalism"

---

53. See Brown, "Testing the Boundaries".
54. The literature on this "Women's War" is quite extensive. See, for instance, Judith Van Allen, "'Sitting on a Man': Colonialism and the Lost Political Institutions of Igbo Women", *Canadian Journal of African Studies*, 6 (1972), pp. 165–181; Misty Bastian, "Vultures of the Marketplace: Southeastern Nigerian Women and Discourses of the *Ogu Umunwaanyi* (Women's War) of 1929", in Jean Allman, Susan Geiger, and Nakanyike Musisi (eds), *Women in African Colonial History* (Bloomington, IN, 2002), pp. 260–281.
55. For most of the colonial period the people of Udi initiated multiple court proceedings to get this transaction invalidated.
56. Calculations included in NNAE, Paul E.H. Hair, "Enugu" (n.d. mimeograph).

of the chiefs. The young coalminers repeated these critiques, which fit quite comfortably with their own disagreements with the elderly chiefs and senior men in their villages. In the villages the "coal men" were a proud, contentious group that articulated the political perspective of young and politically marginal men. This was the inevitable consequence of the industry's existence amid the contradictions of a bankrupt rural policy and the corrupt hierarchies it created. The miners assumed an identity that opposed exploitative chiefs, thereby undermining local government. One pensioner proudly noted: "The miners were most modern and powerful. Because they were always after democracy. And they don't allow the chief by opposing him to harass his people. And they always succeeded in opposing him."[57]

By the end of World War I Enugu had all the trappings of a fully segregated colonial town: a "native" and European area, separated by the customary "neutral zone";[58] several trading firms; mission schools; labor camps for the railway and mines; a police force; prisons; and other government agencies.[59] Like most colonial cities, residential segregation – the European reservation – was an important representation of imperial power and a showcase for the "superiority" of European civilization. This representation of "white" authority was but a façade to the reality of fragile political control in a territory that far exceeded the scope of British military resources. Such representations of the dichotomy between European/African, colonizer/subject, and black/white were especially important in spaces where Africans and Europeans were in daily contact – the city and the colonial workplace.[60]

By 1927 the city had grown to 10,000 inhabitants, 7,000 of whom worked in various government departments.[61] In 1929 the city changed qualitatively, when Enugu became the administrative capital of south-eastern Nigeria. The variety of jobs in government gave Enugu's African population a class complexity uncommon in most Nigerian cities. Most workers were accustomed to negotiating with political officials during disputes and had begun to develop a set of expectations for their treatment by the state. The industrial component of the city gave this government town its "edge", with most workers looking to the coalminers as leaders in labor conflicts. Added to

57. Interview conducted in English with Augustine Ude, Umuagua, Udi, 5 August 1975. Ude began work as a messenger in the colliery in 1919 when only ten years old.
58. Philip D. Curtin, "Medical Knowledge and Urban Planning in Tropical Africa", *The American Historical Review*, 90 (1985), pp. 594–613.
59. NNAE, Hair, "Enugu", pp. 162–163.
60. On the spatialized representation of colonial relations, see the instructions Governor General Lugard sent to his officials: Frederick Lugard, *The Political Memoranda: Revision of Instructions to Political Officers on Subjects Chiefly Political and Administrative, 1913–1918* (London, 1970, 3rd edn); also see Maynard W. Swanson, "The Sanitation Syndrome: Bubonic Plague and Urban Native Policy in the Cape Colony, 1900–1909", *Journal of African History*, 18 (1977), pp. 387–410; and Curtin, "Medical Knowledge and Urban Planning in Tropical Africa".
61. NNAE, Hair, "Enugu".

the thousands of coalminers were several hundred clerks employed through the government agencies from throughout the coastal regions of the colony. They and the artisans saw themselves as part of an enlightened group with skills that were valuable, if not indispensable, for the smooth operation of the industry and the colonial state. As "foreigners" they had an awareness of colonial society that came from their earlier exposure to mission education and colonial administration.

The clerks were loyal members of the colonial civil service, but they were critical of the racial hierarchies of colonial society, which they considered to be quite "un-British". When the white civil service struck for more wages after the war, they launched their own protest, adding a demand for the end of job discrimination. They were enemies of "traditionalism", and most especially of the rural chiefs, and contributed to a general environment of resistance and protest characteristic of urban life. They were just the type of African that officials viewed with foreboding – "detribalized" Africans free of the moderating influence and control of their chiefs. But they played a contradictory role in the city. They formed urban associations that became an important pillar of urban order for a beleaguered colonial administration, reliant on "native" allies, both rural and urban. In return for this assistance they expected to receive more political authority. This, the state was reluctant to grant.

The jobs in government agencies also meant that male workers could now imitate the "big compound" of the *Ogaranyan*, with many wives, children, and dependents. In fact, officials found that government workers' households were two to three times larger than those of other workers. This status model destroyed all British attempts to regulate housing occupancy as a way of controlling the city. One worker's experience expressed these new possibilities. He was from Udi and chose to marry six wives. He proudly expressed his successful attainment of rural elite masculinity emulating the *Ogaranyan*:

> The development of [the] coal industry did a lot to my village. But for coal industry civilization would have not reached us as early as it had reached us. The coal industry initiated me into Ozo title. I am Ozo Samuel N. Onoh. I was able to train up my children, build good houses. We contributed money and build schools and churches.[62]

The authorities had built the colonial state on a foundation of rural authoritarianism, creating chiefs where none had existed before, and giving them powers far beyond those of any group in Igbo village government. This rural transformation made the city into a refuge for rural dissidents,

---

62. Interview conducted in English with Samuel N. Onoh, Ngwo-Etiti, Nigeria, 9 August 1975. Onoh began work in 1915 as a tubman and worked up through the ranks until he became an underground foreman after World War II.

some from the local areas, and others from more distant "foreign" communities. A few were women who were unhappy with their marriages or marriage prospects, many more were young men fleeing the exactions of autocratic chiefs and slaves deserting their masters. In the city, these rural dissidents joined with the clerks, and participated in a cultural and political struggle over the nature of work and urban life. For the men from local areas minework rotated with farming, and their commitment to the job fluctuated with the farming seasons. For "foreigners", the distance from home was so great that they were forced to become more acclimatized to life and work in the city. However, they, like most migrants to African cities, nonetheless considered their natal village to be their home.[63]

Many of the young men refused to work regularly, rebuffed missionary attempts at conversion, and clustered in slum settlements that defied administrative control. In so doing, Africans resisted colonialist attempts to instill industrial time into their culture, to restrict access to space through the marketplace, and to restructure their households into nuclear families as against polygynous rural norms.

Both the colliery and the city emerged under the watchful eye of the Governor General Frederick Lugard. Lugard's personal interest in the city and the industry arose from his belief that while wage labor was of educative value for African labor, Africans should remain socially rooted in their rural communities away from the "dangerous" temptations of urban life. Lugard found that it was very difficult to prevent a permanent urban-based working class from developing.[64] Despite his efforts to keep the numbers of urban Africans to a bare minimum, his rural policies pushed them into the city.

To Lugard's dismay, the clerks and artisans were from the Lagos elite that had mobilized so vigorously against the conquest and the discrimination in government employment. Furthermore they had declared war on Lugard, whom they attacked in their press as the archetypal arrogant imperialist.[65] Lugard hated the Westernized elite for being "Africans out of place", far too arrogant for "natives". To him, they were "natives", and no amount of English competence, Western clothes, and sophisticated literacy would make them equal to the "real" British. Similarly he hated the artisans

---

63. The natal village looms large in the identities of most African urban dwellers, historically as well as today. They return to the village for important meetings, and migrants build a house there even if they spend their entire life in the city. During the colonial period women returned to give birth, and everyone is buried there. Even today, when someone dies abroad their family or migrant community will collect money to repatriate the body.

64. Frederick Cooper, "Urban Space, Industrial Time, and Wage Labor in Africa", in *idem* (ed.), *The Struggle for the City: Migrant Labor, Capital, and the State in Urban Africa* (Beverly Hills, CA, 1983), pp. 7–50.

65. Fred I.A. Omu, *Press and Politics in Nigeria 1880–1937* (Atlantic Highlands, NJ, 1978).

(i.e. skilled African workers) who, like the clerks, became a thorn in his side by organizing protests against racial discrimination and poor salaries.[66] As Enugu grew at an extraordinary pace, it created a receptive context for these new traditions of resistance. Thus, while Lugard was busily trying to stabilize rural Igboland around colonial chiefs, the clerks and coalminers were making the city a center of dissent that gave voice to the complaints of the young men who were the chiefs' victims.

The first contingent of railway clerks and artisans in Enugu originated from mid-nineteenth century Lagos and had gradually dispersed throughout the coast, settling in several cities in eastern Nigeria – Calabar, Onitsha, Owerri, and Enugu. These were a transnational group of men from communities in Britain's black Atlantic empire: a sprinkling of West Indians, Creoles/Saro from Sierra Leone, returnees from Brazil (called *Amaro*), Yoruba men from Lagos, and Igbos from the more "civilized" areas on the coast and the cosmopolitan market town of Onitsha on the Niger River. They had a profound belief in personal and group improvement, independence, "progress", self-reliance, "civilization", and the supremacy of British culture as the pinnacle of civilization. When they arrived at the coalmines early in World War I, the city of Enugu did not formally exist. They relished the opportunity to "tame" the countryside, to carve this modern industry out of the forest; in this way they fulfilled an aspect of Victorian manhood – the mastery over the self and the environment. In the 1930s officials noted that these men saw themselves as "pioneers", who had carved the mines and city out of the "bush", at a time when the locals were still "cannibals".[67]

During the war the clerks organized new home-town ("tribal") associations to provide mutual aid, assist in urban socialization, and finance development projects in the home villages, which heightened their prestige in rural politics while they were away. The first urban *Nzuko* or "meetings" were formed in 1915 by Westernized men from Owerri. The form soon spread to other groups of "foreign" residents of Enugu.[68] *Nzuko* also allowed the "respectable" members of migrant communities to assist in controlling and socializing the young.[69]

---

66. Arnold Hughes and Robin Cohen, "An Emerging Nigerian Working Class: The Lagos Experience, 1897–1939", in Peter Gutkind, Robin Cohen, and Jean Copans (eds), *African Labor History* (Beverley Hills, CA,1978).
67. University of Liverpool, Paul E. Hair Collection, Charles H. Croasdale, "Report on the Enugu Colliery, 1938", n.d., pp. 40–41.
68. The "locals" from the surrounding areas, however, continued to participate in rural associations where, as coalminers, they could leverage their wages and prestige as "modern" men to secure authority in the village. The literate clerks were the associations' leaders, but membership was multi-class, being based on the natal village.
69. For a discussion of this, see Brown, *"We Were All Slaves"*, pp. 105–106. For a discussion of the contradictions between "sons abroad" and the village leaders, see Dmitri van den Bersselaar,

Nzuko represented a new type of men, migrant workers, those whose absence from the village prohibited their daily involvement in rural politics but whose missionary education, industrial training, or wage labor made them intermediaries between the village and the new economy and political apparatus.[70] As an institution, the *Nzuko* allowed urban and wage-earning men to exhibit collectively some of the characteristics of "big men". They redirected financial resources with largesse to "bring the village up". This element of helping the collective was an important demonstration of a wealthy man's moral power. The Owerri men were the first to form *Nzuko*, which enabled them to support "modern" projects, such as schools, maternity clinics, and road construction. At the same time, their claims of "modernity" introduced new criteria for male maturity. This enabled young men to challenge the power of senior men in the village councils.

Nzuko meetings opened an important social environment in which both elite and working-class masculinity could be performed,[71] especially by the clerks, who avidly demonstrated their command of Western meeting protocols. While the clerks were especially keen to laud their sophistication over the illiterate workers, the postwar economic conditions were encouraging a coalition of these different groups. Although class distance had initially been of crucial importance to the self-identity of the proud clerks, discriminatory wages and residential segregation blurred these divisions. Wartime inflation further depressed their discriminatory wages, putting the "respectable" lifestyle that so defined their identity beyond their reach. This forced them to live in the same squalor as the unskilled urban workers, their inferiors.

While they felt superior to the manual workers, the literate *Nzuko* leaders nonetheless opened an avenue for the politicization of these illiterate men. This enabled the elites' values, political expectations, and gender ideologies to filter into the discourse of illiterate workers. Importantly, their meetings became a context in which clerks and artisans demonstrated new ideas about the expectations, role, and responsibilities of "modern" African men. Their relationship with colonial officials was ambivalent: while they saw themselves as assisting in preserving urban order, a function appreciated by the state, they became an organizational platform through which "Westernized" Africans could leverage their power in the transformation of

---

"Imagining Home: Migration and the Igbo Village in Colonial Nigeria", *Journal of African History*, 46 (2005), pp. 51–73.

70. See Audrey C. Smock and David R. Smock, "Ethnicity and Attitudes Toward Development in Eastern Nigeria", *The Journal of Developing Areas*, 3 (1969), pp. 499–512; Immanuel Wallerstein, "Voluntary Associations", in James S. Coleman and Carl Rosberg (eds), *Political Parties and National Integration in Tropical Africa* (Berkeley, CA, 1964), pp. 318–339.

71. The performative aspect of masculinity is discussed in Lindsay and Miescher, "Introduction", in *idem*, *Men and Masculinities*, pp. 1–9.

the colony. In fact, during World War II they coalesced into Nigeria's first nationalist party. In the meantime, Enugu's unskilled miners would "borrow" the *Nzuko* form to create their first workers' organizations.

THE EROSION OF VILLAGE-BASED IDENTITY: UDI'S "NEW" MINERS ATTACK "NATIVE" SUPERVISORS

The first industrial strikes (1917–1919) were led by artisans and clerical workers seconded from the railway. Although both looked down on the unskilled workers, they nonetheless influenced the forms of protest that would later be adopted by the more "local" underground laborers. In 1919 the locals did not participate in a series of strikes related to the inflationary spiral of the war and the consequent postwar unrest among both African and European civil servants.[72] The center of the strikes was in Lagos, where in 1918 Africans in the Nigerian Civil Service Union petitioned for salary increases and protested against discriminatory treatment – though to no avail.[73] In any case, these early industrial strikes were led by the "foreign" artisans and organized by the industrial derivatives of the home-town unions, the *Nzuko Ifunyana*. The strikes were caused by a number of factors: food shortages, payment in unpopular paper money, and the harsh measures used by "native" foremen to control the workers. The new industrial *Nzuko* synthesized Western voluntary associational forms with Igbo principles of corporate affiliation.

This formation of an autonomous workers' association, free from the interference of the chiefs or their "boss boys", was one indicator of the influence of seasoned workers and clerks on the less experienced miners. The postwar agitation expressed personal and collective definitions of "just" and "unjust" compensation and treatment for employees within an evolving set of expectations of the colonial state. The forms of protest reflected differential employment patterns, residential options, and variations in the regional significance of and familiarity with wage labor. These ideas about appropriate treatment and compensation were first expressed by urbanized "foreign" clerical, artisan, and skilled underground workers, but by the mid-1920s this protest culture had been rapidly embraced by local men, despite their continued affiliation with

---

72. The Nigerian staff's key demand was for the end of job discrimination; Wogu Ananaba, *The Trade Union Movement in Nigeria* (New York, 1969), p. 11.

73. There were a whole series of discriminatory practices that elicited African protest. Africans had not received a wage increase since 1906, and there was a ceiling of £300 per year on African employees, regardless of qualification and job. Africans did not qualify for a pension until they had completed thirty-seven years of service. Most died before they could receive it. They also complained that the use of the word "native" when referring to African medical officers was derogatory. See Akinjide Osuntokun, *Nigeria in the First World War* (London, 1979), pp. 296–297; Matthew A. Tokunboh, *Labour Movement in Nigeria: Past and Present* (Lagos, 1985), p. 22.

collaborative leaders in their village. This model of protest was an important dimension of the response of African workers to colonial capitalism.

Of the three strikes after World War I, only the first, in 1920, was led by "foreign" workers. At this time most "local" workers followed their normal pattern of protest and chose desertion. However, although the first strike was unsuccessful in securing the restoration of a rate cut made at the beginning of the recession that started in 1920, it demonstrated the forms of protest appropriate to the colonial workplace.[74] There is little archival documentation about the strike. We know only that skilled underground workers or hewers, "foreigners" from Awka, Owerri, and Onitsha town, participated in the strike. The management rejected the demands, dismissed the protesting miners and station magistrate, and four policemen chased them into the woods.[75] One of the leaders singled out by management, European staff, and African headmen was Edward Okafor of Umouji (Onitsha division). He was dismissed for insubordination and blacklisted in all other government departments. When the other hewers threatened another strike that April, the management decided to hire only Agbaja men, who they assumed would be less activist.[76]

In following this policy the colliery manager acceded to a request by representatives of the Agbaja clan group, who argued that, since the mines were on their lands, they should be given preference in all hiring. Within five years the Agbaja constituted the majority of the underground work-force, both skilled and unskilled, and the "foreigners" held only the clerical and administrative positions.[77]

This expectation of Agbaja docility proved short-lived. In the aftermath of the British General Strike of 1926, the Agbaja day laborers walked off their jobs in July, demanding a 1-penny increase. This would have raised their paltry wages to 1 shilling and 3 pence per day. Agbaja men had held a series of underground support jobs, often called "dead work", that supported the "pit boys" (hewers).[78] They were all on daily wages rather than the hewers' tonnage rates and could therefore not increase their incomes by working harder. At the same time, the payment of day wages to

---

74. Little remains in the archives about these events, and only tangentially relevant documents exist in colonial records. See, for instance, NNAE, ONDIST 12/1/1562, Resident to Colliery Manager, 11 March 1925; Colliery Manager to Resident, 12 March 1925.

75. NNAE, NRUCAR 1924/25; Agwu Akpala, "The Background of the Enugu Colliery Shooting Incident in 1949", *Journal of the Historical Society of Nigeria*, 3 (1965), pp. 335–363, 347.

76. For a detailed account of this first rash of strikes after World War I, see Brown, "*We Were All Slaves*", ch. 4.

77. NNAE, File no. PA 260, Resident to Executive Enugu, "Labour Force Colliery Department, Towns of Origin", 28 March 1925 (destroyed), as cited in Akpala, "The Background to the Enugu Colliery Shooting Incident", p. 339.

78. For a discussion of the use of childlike terms to describe adult men see Brown, "A 'Man' in the Village".

such a broad spectrum of the underground workforce encouraged solidarity and collective action. As increased effort had no impact on income, securing higher wage rates was the only way that these workers could increase their wages. Clearly, the "backward" Agbajas had learned from the "foreigners" and from their own experience in the mines. They no longer deserted, as they had in the past, but recognized the power of stopping production to underscore their demands.

A second series of strikes was related to rampant corruption and the chiefs' agents in the mines. The management structure and system of industrial relations at Enugu was an industrial application of "indirect rule": work in the mines exposed the men to a complex system of extortion and corruption, a fact that was understood by management but, as long as it secured industrial discipline, was of little concern. In fact abusive practices in the system of labor recruitment and control at the colliery were just an industrial expression of the problems inherent in the indirect-rule system at large. African intermediaries were given many managerial functions, with little European supervision. The chiefs' "boss boys" and various other "native" supervisors handled daily colliery operations. With the general manager insulated from the daily supervision of the men, a culture of predation emerged in which both Africans and Europeans used corruption, extortion, and physical violence to push the workers to produce.

Of all the supervisory staff, the men complained most bitterly about the exploitation of the "boss boys". From the position of the worker, the "boss boy" was the most powerful "native" supervisor in the mine. He decided who worked and where they would work. He was responsible for discipline, which he could enforce outside the workplace in the villages with the help of the chief and native courts. His power over individual men, exercised through physical violence, was ominous and arbitrary. Ultimately it was the "boss boy" who had the power in production and control over the hewers' wage-earning capacity.

In September 1929 the "local" hewers walked out of the mines to protest the illegal deductions from their pay by the "local" "boss boys". This was the most significant strike, from the perspective of regional and "local" identity, as it suggested that clan/village affiliation was not as secure a basis for industrial peace as in the past. The Agbaja workers launched a full frontal attack against the men who recruited and victimized them. Under the industrial application of "indirect rule", men like the "boss boys" could extort money from the workers without any managerial oversight. If a miner refused to pay a bribe, the "boss boy" retaliated by placing him on a difficult workface where he would be unable to hew large amounts of coal.

The "boss boys" and headmen selected their work crews daily from the men in the labor camps, and they alone knew who was in their crew.[79]

---

79. Croasdale, "Report on the Enugu Colliery", p. 25.

In some cases they received the wages for their entire work crew.[80] The consequences were predictable, as one miner noted:

> The Colliery was paying its workers by the month. The boss-boys and headmen exploited this and often arranged to dismiss laborers a few days before pay day and take on other men. The headmen then drew the pay for the whole month and kept for themselves that of the dismissed men. The paying officer could not check this because he did not know the laborers individually.[81]

Alternatively, the "boss boys" could arrange with the European overmen to have the miners fired. Neglect by management was not coincidental, but expressed a generalized assumption that the "boss boys", as men from the village, should be given carte blanche in the mines.

Similar accusations were raised against the interpreters, again local men who were intermediaries between their crews and European overmen. One Agbaja tubman complained:

> Interpreters caused the sudden dismissal of many workers. They really were very wicked to workers. When they find one resting in the working place and if such a one refuses to bribe him he would accuse such a one [of] sleeping on duty or accuse him of one serious offense which will lead to his dismissal. They always report them to the Europeans who dismissed such a one.[82]

Both "boss boys" and interpreters were of inestimable value to management, especially when they functioned as informers on the miners. They attended workers' meetings and informed on the ringleaders, who were subsequently dismissed. To counter this, the workers attempted to use "traditional" methods of securing solidarity and began using oath-taking at their secret meetings.[83] But as the colliery workers became more conscious and organized, curtailment of these corrupt practices was considered a priority, with claims of clan affinity (and corresponding obedience) losing their power.

CONCLUSION

This article has traced the contours of the challenges confronting a new working class as it experimented with unfamiliar forms of affiliation, trust, and association with people with whom it shared new, industrial experiences. This has included investigation into the many ways that local men maneuvered against the authoritarian control of chiefs, forced labor, and workplace exploitation by "native" and expatriate staff. The management and the collaborating rural leaders wanted to continue to use village loyalty as an

80. NNAE, OP 45/1921, Railway Construction: Recruitment of Labour and Arrangements for Control Thereof, cited in Akpala, "Enugu Colliery Shooting Incident", p. 341.
81. Interview conducted in English with Chief Thomas Ozobu, Imezi Owa, Udi, 21 June 1975.
82. Interview conducted in English with Anieke Chiegwu, Umuagba Owa Imezi, 7 July 1975.
83. Interview conducted in English with Bennett U. Anyasado, Mbieri, Owerri, 23 July 1975.

enduring basis for industrial organization and worker control. But as early as 1919 the "pull" and legitimacy of the village governing system was already under strain. A political official complained about the problems "colliery boys" caused for the chiefs in the village-groups most heavily involved in the industry:

> This system of boys [in Enugu-Ngwo, Abor and surrounding towns] living in their town and working at the mines is not one I prefer. The trouble is that the colliery boys living in the towns will not obey the chiefs who complain to the Political Officer that these boys are loafing in the towns and will not obey them.[84]

Too disruptive to live in the village, too threatening to the tenuous urban order to live in the city, the mineworkers challenged all imperial fantasies and stereotypes about the nature of African workers. Their very existence as workers contradicted the ideological assumptions officials had about African society and the patterns of authoritarian rule that officials tried to insinuate into village politics. The miners' insistence on "democracy" challenged what colonial authorities assumed was an endemic authoritarianism rooted in African society.

Initially most local workers were quite unfamiliar with the capitalist workplace. But the "foreign" artisans – the skilled African workers from other cities and often with a remarkably cosmopolitan background – exhibited a working-class identity that had been encouraged by their education in mission-run technical schools. They were rational, independent, self-improving men, whose pride in performing a skilled task resonated with some aspects of local Igbo masculinity, facilitating a synthesis of gender ideologies. These "foreigners" demonstrated the effective forms of worker protest and organized the industry's first strikes during World War I.

While "white" bosses used race, class, and gender ideologies to construct repressive systems of labor control in the new colonial workplace, African miners countered by creating eclectic models of masculine prestige, which they demonstrated in the villages. They became providers of "development" and village uplift, thereby using industrial jobs to achieve the valued accomplishments of men in Igbo culture. In this respect they invented forms of self-representation that merged local and foreign gender ideologies arising from work, rural culture, and the influence of the more established industrial workers who came at the beginning of coalmining in Enugu.

As the colliery and the city entered the tumultuous decade of the 1930s, the hold of clan identity on the workers was clearly losing currency. Many young men saw themselves as a different breed. As noted above, even as early as the first years of World War I, District Officers complained that

---

84. The National Archives, Kew, Public Records Office, CO 657/4, Nigerian Railways and Udi Coal Mines Administrative Report, 1919, E.M. Bland, General Manager, p. 96, as cited in Uzoechi, "Eastern Nigerian Railway", p. 208. By "towns" the author does not refer to Enugu but to rural settlements.

young men had already begun to challenge rural leaders, who they felt were so ignorant and so archaic that they could not really understand the industry. For those in the industry, the conflicts they encountered with their clan mates in the workplace pushed them to question the ability and legitimacy of senior village leaders and those wealthy men, *Ogaranyan*, who tried to advise them on the problems they encountered in the workplace. Rather, they trusted the workplace commonalities they had with men from "foreign" areas of Igboland, and drew upon their expertise in crafting movements of solidarity and handling problems with management. The experience of working in this industry and living in Enugu led them to abandon rural patterns of affiliation and political leadership based on kinship, age, and wealth, and encouraged them to join in solidarity with co-workers and leaders from areas that had been considered foreign or even hostile before.

This history of labor's struggles during the first few decades suggests that by assuming the identity of "industrial workers" Udi men were able to reconstruct themselves as "coalmen", men who both ran a crucial industry and were impressive promoters of modernization – both social and political. The mines gave them an opportunity to celebrate a skill, hidden in the darkness of the mines, and to confront this dangerous and mystical workplace with the courage and self-confidence that few other workers could claim. In this respect Igbo notions of male "bravery" and "commitment" merged with workplace identities in the mines.

IRSH 60 (2015), Special Issue, pp. 95–119 doi:10.1017/S0020859015000346
© 2015 Internationaal Instituut voor Sociale Geschiedenis

Labor Control and Mobility in Japanese-Controlled Fushun Coalmine (China), 1907–1932*

LIMIN TEH

Institute for Area Studies, Leiden University
Arsenaalstraat 1, 2311 CT Leiden, The Netherlands

E-mail: l.m.teh@hum.leidenuniv.nl

ABSTRACT: The prevalence and persistence of labor contractors in China's mining industry during the first half of the twentieth century is frequently attributed to foreign management's avoidance of directly managing Chinese laborers. However, in Japanese-controlled Fushun Coalmine, Japanese management's reliance on labor contractors over four decades (1907–1945) represented an expansion in management's reach in labor management. In this article, I examine the period of Japanese control (1907–1932), during which Japanese mine managers resorted to bureaucratic means to control labor contractors. Using labor process theorists, particularly Richard Edwards, to read company archival documents, I argue that salient features of the Chinese labor market, namely Chinese migrant labor's mobility and international competition for Chinese labor, compelled Japanese managers to extend control over labor contractors.

The greedy, cruel, and parasitic labor contractor looms large in Fushun mineworkers' cultural memory. A compilation of Fushun area folk songs, collected between 1984 and 1986, contains several songs about labor contractors. One such song is *Daguihen* ["Mean Big Boss"]:

Mean big boss, mean big boss	*Daguihen, daguihen*
Cheats us with his abacus! What a cheat!	*Suanpanzi neng chi ren! Neng chi ren!*
Coal is produced as fast as flowing water,	*Bie kan meitan ru liushui,*
Yet we miners have no money to bury our parents.	*Kuanggong wuqian zang bieqin.*[1]

Dagui, or big boss, was what miners called labor contractors. According to the editor's annotations, this song originated among Chinese mineworkers in the

---

* I would like to thank Ad Knotter and David Mayer for their hard work in molding my rough draft into a presentable article. I would also like to thank all participants in the "Migration and Ethnicity in Coalfield History" workshop, held at NIAS, The Netherlands, 5–6 November 2014, which Ad Knotter organized.
1. Sun Hongjun (ed.), *Fushun minge* [Fushun Folk Songs] (Fushun, 1986), p. 59.

Longfeng underground pit of Fushun Coalmine in north-east China (Manchuria) when it was under Japanese control, eventually gaining popularity among all Chinese mineworkers in Fushun because its lamentation of the contractors' "brutal exploitation" [*canku boxue*] resonated with the miners.[2] The miners' recognized their tragic lives in the song: they labored to produce vast quantities of coal, yet the contractor paid them so little that they could not even afford to bury their parents.

Other songs used the predator motif to emphasize the contractors' greediness, cruelty, and parasitism. One song, titled *Kuanggong buru zuo ma niu* ["Miners are like horses or cows"], compared miners to horses and cows, and contractors to tigers and wolves.[3] Another song, *Gongren nan taitou* ["Workers cannot hold their heads up high"], decried *guizi* ["Japanese devils"] for eating workers' flesh and Chinese labor contractors for gnawing workers' bones, making it impossible for workers to stand up for themselves.[4] Implied in this song is the dependence of Chinese contractors on their Japanese masters. Too weak to be masters in their own right, these contractors derived their authority from becoming lackeys for the Japanese colonizers.

Predictably, Japanese mine management presented a drastically different picture of labor contractors. To Japanese mine management, labor contractors were integral – though low-level – functionaries in a modern bureaucracy. A Chinese-language textbook for Japanese personnel in Fushun Coalmine offers an apt instance of such representation. In a section with the heading, "What a contractor should know", a Chinese contractor details his duties:

> The most important duty is the matter of recruitment. You must find on your own the workers you need. As a *batou* [contractor], you must properly supervise your workers in the underground pit by following directives from the Japanese and directing your workers accordingly. As a *batou*, you should readily train the mineworkers under your supervision. As a *batou*, on a regular basis, you must work closely with the Labor Affairs Department to diligently supervise your workers' morals and to guide their thoughts.[5]

In the latter half of this dialogue, the Chinese contractor excuses himself from the conversation, announcing that he has to attend a *batou* meeting.[6] Like a bureaucrat, the labor contractor performs his duties, follows directives, coordinates with other bureaucrats, and attends meetings. At the

2. *Ibid.*
3. *Ibid.*, p. 67.
4. *Ibid.*, p. 64.
5. Minami manshū tetsudō kabushiki būjun tankō shōmu ka [South Manchuria Railway General Affairs Department], *Nichi-Man taiyaku kōzan yōgoshū* [Japanese–Chinese Parallel Text, Mining Vocabulary] (Būjun, 1935), p. 158.
6. *Ibid.*, p. 161.

same time, the control function refers not only to the behavior of the workers but also to their thoughts and minds.

The discrepancy between these two representations of labor contractors reflects the power dynamics of the economic relations binding management and workers. Mine management, driven by the profit imperative, saw labor contractors as an extension of a bureaucracy committed to extracting maximum labor power from mineworkers, who surrendered all control over themselves in exchange for wages. As such, the editor of the volume on Fushun folk songs is right in noting that mineworkers resented labor contractors as much as they resented Japanese mine management. But this interpretation misses fundamental shifts in the forms of labor control and the nature of mining work that occurred in Fushun Coalmine. That labor contractors became bureaucrats is a notable development. The regimentation and scrutiny of mining work is another significant change. To mineworkers, these changes meant little except for making their work even more unpleasant.

In this article, I investigate how the labor contractor became a bureaucrat in Fushun Coalmine. The bureaucratization of the labor contractor position was part and parcel of the bureaucratization of labor control in the mine. Drawing from labor process theory, I argue that bureaucratization stemmed from conflicts and contestations among actors inside and outside the workplace. As developments in Fushun Coalmine illustrate, mine management's desire to exert control over a highly mobile workforce, who expressed their resistance by, for example, singing subversive folk songs and by leaving at will, provided the impetus for bureaucratization, which was further propelled by international politics.

The article begins with sections on the historiography of labor contractors in modern China and on theories of labor control and bureaucratization. This is followed by a discussion on the challenges that geology and migration presented to Japanese management. Subsequent sections explain how management used bureaucratization to control migration flows to Fushun and how international politics further catalyzed the bureaucratization process. Finally, I examine mineworkers' mobility as a counterpart to bureaucratization and labor control.

CONTRACTORS AND THE CHINESE INDUSTRIAL WORKER

During the early phases of economic modernization in late nineteenth- and early twentieth-century China, the industrial workforce came from traditional craft industries, the urban population, and the countryside. To recruit these workers, factory management relied on three methods of labor recruitment: direct hiring, apprenticeship, and labor contractors. Of the three methods, the labor contractor system was the most prevalent. Labor contractors, known as *baogong* or *batou*, had precedents in Chinese economic history. Because the contract system had been an institution in the Chinese traditional economy, Chinese modernizers in the 1920s and 1930s viewed it as a vestige of China's past that impeded economic development.[7] Boris Torgasheff, a mining consultant based in China, claimed that contractors prevented the introduction of technological change in mines. He argued that a modern mining labor force could be created only when mine management directly recruited and supervised mine labor.[8] Not surprisingly, when organizing Anyuan mineworkers in the 1920s the Chinese Communist Party leaders, especially Liu Shaoqi, railed against the contractors for their collusion with mine owners and secret societies.[9]

For labor historians, the prevalence of labor contractors in the modernizing Chinese economy reflected conditions specific to the Chinese context and were not indicative of a structural deficiency in Chinese modernization. As Chesneaux explains in his landmark work on the Chinese labor movement, the labor contract system was particularly common in foreign-owned factories, since foreign management had little knowledge of and contacts in local society, and so had to rely on third-party intermediaries to procure its labor supply.[10]

In his study of the contract labor system in the pre-1937 Chinese mining industry, Tim Wright, however, contends that foreign ownership only partially accounted for the widespread use of this labor recruitment method. Wright discovered that Chinese-owned mines were just as likely to use labor contractors as foreign-owned mines. Rather, the prominence of a contract system was generally due to problems in "the early stages of a country's industrialization", and not to a country's history, culture, or society. Based on his comparison of the labor contract system in the Chinese mining industry with other instances worldwide, Wright concludes that the emergence of a regional or national labor market would provide industries with a steady supply of skilled labor, thereby rendering the contract system irrelevant. In other words, the contract system functioned as a stop-gap measure at a time when demand for labor far exceeded supply, and fragmentations in the labor market prevented direct hiring.[11]

7. Gu Zhanran, "Zhongguo baogongzhi [China's Contract Labor System]", *Duli pinglun*, 1 (1932), pp. 10–16.
8. Boris Torgasheff, "Mining Labor in China, Pt 2", *Chinese Economic Journal*, 6 (1930), pp. 510–541.
9. The Anyuan coalmine is located in the present-day city of Pingxiang, Jiangxi province. See Elizabeth Perry, *Anyuan: Mining China's Revolutionary Tradition* (Berkeley, CA, 2012).
10. Jean Chesneaux, *The Chinese Labor Movement, 1919–1927* (Stanford, CA, 1968), p. 60.
11. Tim Wright, "A Method of Evading Management: Contract Labor in Chinese Coal Mines before 1937", *Comparative Studies in Society and History*, 23 (1981), pp. 656–678.

By putting the Chinese instance in a global context, Wright's account highlights important similarities between the pre-1937 Chinese economy and other industrializing economies. But his conclusion leans too heavily on classic economic theory which treats labor markets as commodity markets, and supposes that the market mechanism would eventually resolve problems of inefficiency such as the labor contract system. This conception of the labor market limits our understanding of it.[12] The buying and selling of labor power entails more than a simple transaction of money for commodity; it takes place at the intersection of complex social processes. Because of the social nature of labor, changes in labor markets and labor relations come about as a result of conflict and contestation between workers, employers, households, organizations, and states.[13] Conflict and contestations between these actors contributed as much as local conditions to shaping the peculiarities of labor markets, labor recruitment methods, and labor control.

LABOR CONTROL AND BUREAUCRATIZATION

During the years 1907–1932, Japanese mine management, in a long drawn-out process, transformed labor contractors from independent third-party contractors (who would oversee labor recruitment, supervision, and welfare) to salaried pit foremen with clearly defined responsibilities in labor recruitment and supervision. This transformation belongs to a broader change in the mine's labor control that bears much resemblance to what sociologist Richard Edwards called "bureaucratic control". Changes in the labor contract system accompanied other measures to standardize wages, to regulate labor recruitment and the allocation of jobs, and to install a clear hierarchy of authority that subordinated Chinese contractors to Japanese management.

Bureaucratization is often presented as antithetical to efficiency, which is the guiding principle of scientific management and a fundamental requirement for making profits. Yet, as corporations grow in scale, they become more bureaucratized. Management resorts to bureaucratic means, like rules and procedures to ensure uniformity in decision-making. To account for this change in labor control during the twentieth century, Richard Edwards identified three types of labor control: simple, technical, and bureaucratic.

Under simple control, the owner or manager exercises direct control over labor, oftentimes in person. Because bosses personally intervene "to exhort

---

12. Cf. David Harvey, *The Urban Experience* (Baltimore, MD, 1989), p. 19; Jamie Peck, *Work-place: The Social Regulation of Labor Markets* (New York, 1996).
13. Mark Granovetter and Charles Tilly, "Inequality and Labor Processes", in Neil J. Smelser (ed.), *Handbook of Sociology* (Newbury Park, CA, 1988), pp. 175–221, 179–180.

workers, bully and threaten them, reward good performance, hire and fire on the spot, [and] favor loyal workers", they "generally act as despots, benevolent or otherwise", with "little structure to the way power was exercised and workers were often treated arbitrarily".[14] In contrast, technical and bureaucratic controls utilize impersonal forms of technology and bureaucracy to structure the exercise of power. Technical control involves the embedding of controls in the "physical structure of the labor process", and therefore "the assembly line [becomes] the classic image [of technical control]".[15] Bureaucratic control is defined by the "institutionalization of hierarchal power", which means that "'rule of law' – the firm's law – replaces 'rule by supervisor command' in the direction of work, the procedures for evaluating workers' performance, and the exercise of the firm's sanctions and rewards; supervisors and workers alike become subject to the dictates of 'company policy'".[16] These three forms of labor control correspond to the evolution in capitalist production from small, unmechanized factories to large, mechanized factories owned by modern corporations.

Edwards's typology of labor controls under capitalist production is not the only account of how corporate management in the twentieth century became large bureaucracies,[17] and the concept of bureaucratic control has been criticized,[18] but I hesitate to reject wholesale Edwards's concept of bureaucratic control. The point about rules and procedures as a means of labor control is still valid, especially when these rules and procedures become the basis of management's claim to control. Management introduces rules and procedures to the labor process – hiring, allocation of jobs, organization of work, and oversight of work – in order to legitimize its own role and to delegitimize the roles of the individual foreman or contractor. The outcome, of course, is that management, if it takes its own premises seriously, has to submit to these rules and procedures, alongside everyone else. In other words, bureaucratization is not an abstract force acting on the labor process, but an integral component of conflict and contestation among contending actors.

In Fushun Coalmine the introduction of rules and procedures reflected the endeavor of Japanese managers to insert themselves into the labor process and to diminish the influence of individual contractors. Bureaucratization spanned two decades and entailed two processes.

14. Richard Edwards, *Contested Terrain: The Transformation of the Workplace in the Twentieth Century* (New York, 1979), p. 19.
15. *Ibid.*, p. 20.
16. *Ibid.*, p. 21.
17. See, for instance, Michael Burawoy, *Manufacturing Consent: Changes in the Labor Process under Monopoly Capitalism* (Chicago, IL, 1979).
18. See, for instance, Granovetter and Tilly, "Inequality and Labor Processes", pp. 179–180.

Figure 1. The location of Fushun in north China/Manchuria.

One was management's piecemeal takeover of most contractors' duties in relation to labor recruitment, supervision, and welfare, and the other was the incorporation of contractors into management.

FUSHUN COALMINE

The city of Fushun (Figure 1) is located in the Hun River Valley, between Shenyang (the provincial capital) and the Changbai Mountains, a mountain range that separates China and Korea. The city sits on top of a coalfield formed about 50 to 60 million years ago and discovered at the end of the nineteenth century. A handful of Chinese businesses first mined outcroppings in the coalfield in 1900 and quickly encountered financial difficulties. Loans from Russian investors sustained these companies for a few years until Japanese victory in the Russo-Japanese War (1904–1905) transferred ownership into Japanese hands. The South Manchuria Railway Company (SMR), a joint-stock company that the Japanese state formed and controlled, took over these companies. For the next forty years, the SMR managed

Fushun Coalmine through the tumult of the Japanese invasion in 1931 and the establishment of the nominally independent Manchukuo nation-state in 1932 until the Japanese empire fell in 1945.

During the first two decades of control, Japanese engineers and mine managers faced the unique challenge of twin abundance: energy resources and labor. The coalfield in Fushun possessed an exceptionally thick coal seam relatively close to the earth's surface. The main coal seam spanned about 16 kilometers in length and 3 kilometers in width, and measured in depth 24 meters at its thinnest and 146 meters at its thickest. Japanese geologists initially estimated the deposit at 1.2 million tons.[19] This estimate was revised in the 1920s to 750 million tons and subsequently in the 1980s to 950 million.[20] Coal analysis indicated that Fushun coal contained minimal sulfur and moisture, possessed a high heating point, and thereby belonged to the class of bituminous coal. These inherent qualities of Fushun coal made it suitable for making coking coal, heating furnaces, powering steam engines, and generating electricity. When Japanese management took over mining operations in 1907, the mine was producing about 234,000 tons of coal. Thirty years later, in 1937, the mine reached its peak output of 10.34 million tons, accounting for one-quarter of the entire coal output in Manchuria and China.[21]

The technical solutions to mining Fushun's thick coal seam inevitably shaped the organization of mining work. The corresponding mining techniques – long-wall mining, inclined shaft, sand filling-in, and open-cut – demanded a highly structured organization of work and a highly regimented approach. A sharp division of labor emerged especially in the underground pits, separating hewers from haulers, timberers, sweepers, and odd-job generalists.[22] At the same time, precise times for eight-hour work shifts, safety equipment and

19. The South Manchuria Railway, *Manchuria: Land of Opportunities* (New York, 1922), pp. 34–35.

20. The 1930s estimate was provided by Japanese geologists and engineers to William M. Quackenbush and Quentin E. Singewald, members of the US Army's Mining and Geological Division. See William M. Quackenbush, "Fushun Coalfield, Manchuria, Report no. 68, 17 February 1947", Tokyo General Headquarters, Supreme Commander for the Allied Powers, Natural Resources Sect. [1947]. South Manchuria Railway documents on Fushun Coalmine used in this article have been consulted at the United States Library of Congress, Jilin Province Academy of Social Sciences, and the Liaoning Provincial Archives. The estimate in the 1980s is reported in Edward A. Johnson, "Geology of the Fushun Coalfield, Liaoning Province, People's Republic of China", *International Journal of Coal Geology*, 14 (1990), pp. 217–236.

21. Minami manshū tetsudō kabushiki bujun tankō [South Manchuria Railway Fushun Coalmine], *Bujun tankō tōkei nenpō* [Fushun Coalmine Annual Statistics] (Fushun, 1942); Tim Wright, *Coal Mining in China's Economy and Society, 1895–1937* (Cambridge, 1984), Appendix B.

22. This high degree of specialization intensified in the 1930s with the introduction of electric- and steam-powered hand tools in underground pits. I discuss this in greater depth in my dissertation: Limin Teh, "Mining for Differences: Race, Chinese Labor, and Japanese Colonialism in Fushun Coalmine, 1907–1945" (Ph.D., University of Chicago, 2014).

checks, and strict work rules were introduced. As such, mineworkers in Fushun Coalmine were subjected to a discipline that was more commonly found on a factory assembly line than in traditional mines. To the newly recruited mineworkers who had never encountered such discipline, it might not be an exaggeration to say that they found themselves no more than cogs in a wheel. More than a few recruited mineworkers rejected this discipline and left. I discuss this common practice of leaving in greater detail below.

LABOR SUPPLY AND MIGRATION

The second abundance that challenged mine managers was the great quantity of Chinese labor due to longstanding migration from north China to Manchuria.[23] Manchuria was a peripheral frontier whose population base was too low for emerging industries like Fushun Coalmine, while the region to its south, north China, was far more densely populated. From 1890 to 1941 about 25 million people travelled between Manchuria and north China, with 8 million settling permanently in Manchuria and 17 million returning to north China. According to historians Diana Lary and Thomas Gottschang, the migration to Manchuria was one of the largest population movements in twentieth-century world history.[24]

To SMR management, this migration proved as much a boon as a bane. Takeo Itō, the head of the SMR research bureau, articulated the positive perspective of this migration. In his autobiography, Itō commented that "Chinese laborers, not only longshoremen, but also as wagon drivers, factory workers, and coalminers, came pouring into Manchuria. And peasants and laborers on the Chinese mainland were an inexhaustible supply."[25] At the same time, this "inexhaustible supply" of labor came with problems. Another SMR researcher, Isamu Abe, complained that "whereas Manchuria does not lack unskilled hands such as coolies there are very few who are more or less experienced in factory work".[26] Abe's complaint about the perceived flaws of Chinese migrant labor is elaborated in another company report comparing Japanese and Chinese workers. In this report, the SMR observed that Japanese workers "show a tendency to remain stationary", and their "efficiency may be 30 to 40 per cent higher than the

23. The macro-region of north China consists of Hebei, Shandong, Henan, and Shanxi provinces. Hebei and Shandong were the main provinces that sent migrants to Manchuria in the first half of the twentieth century.

24. Thomas R. Gottschang and Diana Lary, *Swallows and Settlers: The Great Migration from North China to Manchuria* (Ann Arbor, MI, 2000), p. 2.

25. Ito Takeo, *Life along the South Manchurian Railway: The Memoirs of Ito Takeo* (Armonk, NY, 1988), p. 48.

26. Isamu Abe, *The Economic Development of Manchuria: Japan's Contributions* (Dairen, 1931), p. 26.

Chinese".[27] Conversely, Chinese workers were regarded as highly mobile and inefficient.

Japanese management frequently relied on the racial ideology of Japanese imperialism to validate their claims about the inferiority of Chinese labor. As historians of Japanese imperialism and Sino-Japanese relations have argued elsewhere, the racial ideology that underpinned Japanese imperial expansion into China crystallized with the Japanese victory in the First Sino-Japanese War (1895–1896).[28] This victory confirmed, in the eyes of Japanese elites, Japan's ascendancy and imperial China's rapid descent. Subsequently, science and history were mobilized to construct a racial ideology that justified Japanese superiority and Chinese inferiority. Whereas the racial ideology of Western imperialism ascribed negative meanings to somatic attributes of its colonized subjects, the racial ideology of Japanese imperialism ascribed negative meanings to the cultural attributes of its Chinese subjects. Hence, the source of Chinese inferiority was Chinese culture. Accordingly, Japanese management in Fushun explained that "because their outlook on life is unstable, the Chinese workers tended to be dull-witted, ill-tempered and unsystematic".[29] Culture is substituted here with the code phrase "outlook on life".

These traits of Chinese migrant labor, however, lay not with "culture" or "race", but in migration itself. Migration from north China to Manchuria had a history that predated Japanese arrival in 1905 and was based on institutions that were independent of Japanese control. This migration became such a widespread social phenomenon that it acquired a proper name. To migrate to Manchuria is to *chuang guandong*, or to travel east past the gates, though the verb *chuang* connotes intrusion or forceful entry. When the Japanese arrived in 1905, they stimulated this migration by improving the existing transportation infrastructure and by enlarging the demand for labor. Although Chinese migrants rode in Japanese-owned steamships and railroads to work in Japanese-controlled factories and mines, the forces that drove these migrants from their homes in north China and the dynamics that regulated the migrants' movement were far beyond Japanese control.

27. The South Manchuria Railway, *Third Report on Progress in Manchuria, 1907–1932* (Dairen, 1932), p. 117. The SMR distributed these English-language annual reports to libraries worldwide. This was likely part of the Japanese government's broader campaign to demonstrate to Western nations Japan's role in modernizing China.
28. Mark Peattie, "Introduction", and "Japanese Attitudes Towards Colonialism, 1895–1945", in Ramon H. Myers and Mark Peattie (eds), *The Japanese Colonial Empire, 1895–1945* (Princeton, NJ, 1984), pp. 3–60 and 80–127; Stefan Tanaka, *Japan's Orient: Rendering Pasts into History* (Berkeley, CA, 1995).
29. Minami Manshū Tetsudō Kabushiki Kaisha [South Manchuria Railway] [Mantetsu], *Minami Manshū Tetsudō Kabushiki Kaisha Dainiji Jūnenshi* [Second Ten-Year History of the South Manchuria Railway] (Dairen, 1928; repr. Tokyo, 1974), p. 570.

The migrants from north China to Manchuria were of two types: sojourning workers and settlers. The former made up the majority, especially in the 1900s and 1910s. Almost all of them came from farming households. They resorted to supplementing their household incomes with seasonal work in Manchuria when crop yields, falling cotton prices, and heavy taxes deteriorated living conditions. For those whose farming plots were simply too small to yield enough income, they sought seasonal work in hopes of purchasing more land. Regardless of the reason for their leaving, these sojourning workers eventually returned to tend their land.[30]

The number of permanent settlers and temporary migrants increased dramatically in the twentieth century when the political and economic conditions in north China plunged to previously unknown depths. The Qing state's collapse in 1911 precipitated almost two decades of continuous warfare among rival regional warlords. In the period 1912–1930, there were only two years, 1914 and 1915, during which military conflict did not occur in north China.[31] These warlords also intruded into the lives of ordinary Chinese in other ways, from heavy taxation to forced conscription to plundering villagers' provisions for their armies. Compounding the problems of warlordism was a series of natural disasters visited upon the region. These natural disasters – flooding, drought, hail, and locust infestation – depressed crop yields and displaced millions.[32]

While worsening political and economic conditions in north China forced millions to leave their farmlands, the growing Manchurian economy lured those displaced to Manchuria in search of employment and political stability. Between the Russo-Japanese War in 1905 and the Japanese invasion in 1931, Manchuria's economy flourished. Japanese enterprises like the SMR embarked on large-scale urbanization and industrial projects that created plenty of jobs for migrant workers from north China. Jobs in these Japanese-owned industrial enterprises paid higher wages than those in Chinese-owned enterprises, and required fewer daily working hours. In 1929, a Chinese worker in a Japanese-owned enterprise earned an average daily wage of ¥0.61 and worked an average of 9.58 hours daily, whereas a Chinese worker in a Chinese-owned enterprise earned an average daily wage of ¥0.36 and worked an average of 11.28 hours.[33] Chinese migrant workers – both temporary sojourners and permanent settlers – flocked to these higher-paying jobs in Manchuria's growing industries.

30. Gottschang and Lary, *Swallows and Settlers*, p. 41.
31. Fan Lijun, *Jindai guannei yimin yu zhongguo dongbei shehui bianqian* [Modern Migration from within the Great Wall and the Development of North-East Chinese Society] (Beijing, 2007), p. 144.
32. Gottschang and Lary, *Swallows and Settlers*, pp. 56–59.
33. South Manchuria Railway, *Third Report on Progress in Manchuria*, pp. 157–159.

Facilitating this population movement was an infrastructure of transportation and communication, consisting of buffalo carts, railways, steamships, and inns. In addition to its relatively comprehensive coverage of the
routes traveled, this transportation infrastructure was also surprisingly
affordable. Three large transportation companies – Shandong Railroad,
Dalian Steam Shipping Company, and SMR – dominated the market. In
1918, these three companies offered Shandong migrant workers heading to
Fushun an attractive package of discounted railway and steamship tickets at
the price of ¥1.50. This was the equivalent of three days' work for a hewer in
Fushun Coalmine and seven days' work for a hewer in Zichuan Coalmine
in Shandong, about 780 kilometers from Fushun.[34] So low were transport
costs that travel times were probably more prohibitive. It took up to ten
days to travel the shortest distance from Zhifu in Shandong province to
Fushun, and more than ten days for those migrants living in remote villages
far from transport routes.

LABOR CONTRACTORS

Recruitment for this migration relied on existing networks in rural society.
Similar to other instances in the global history of migration, social networks
based on native place and kinship were activated to sustain the migration
from north China to Manchuria. Existing native place and kinship ties
enabled returning migrants to recruit others from their villages and families
by sharing stories of success and information about the destination.[35]
In rural north China, where native place and kinship often overlapped,
villagers were more likely to trust returnees than random strangers, even if
the returnee did not hold any position of authority in village society. This
made returnees ideal recruiting agents. The enterprising ones parlayed
their position, knowledge of local society, and contacts in Manchuria's
flourishing industries into careers as labor contractors.

For Japanese industrial enterprises in Manchuria this recruitment
dynamic proved beneficial in securing a steady labor supply. Because
contractors need not be authority figures in their village, any enterprising
worker could become one, and consequently there was no shortage of
contractors. Moreover, Japanese management was able to handpick
those contractors who seemed most trustworthy in view of the inevitable
(and potentially detrimental) allegiances these had to family and village
societies. The career paths of two contractors in Fushun Coalmine, Zheng
Fuchen and Xu Diankui, illustrate the convenient overlapping of migration
and labor recruitment. Zheng was originally from Kaiping, where the first

---

34. Fujihirada Bunkichi, *Manshū ni okeru kōyama rōdō sha* [Mineworkers in Manchuria]
(Dairen, 1918), pp. 31–33.
35. *Ibid.*, p. 49.

modern coalmine in China was started in 1877, while Xu moved from his birthplace in Shandong to Xinqiu (today a district in Fuxin, Liaoning province), where his father worked as manager of a coalmine.[36] Having come from mining communities in Kaiping and Xinqiu, to Japanese management they proved attractive candidates as labor contractors. They knew enough about mining techniques to train and supervise others at work. More importantly, their knowledge of these communities made labor recruitment easy. By the late 1910s, both men had become powerful contractors in Fushun Coalmine, each overseeing 500 to 700 mineworkers. Most of their workers came from their own native places.[37]

Contractors shared native place and even kinship ties with the migrants, but these ties were not binding to the point of coercion. They possessed limited control over the recruited migrants, especially after the migrants arrived in Manchuria. As noted in Gottschang and Lary's work, migrants moved easily and freely upon their arrival in Manchuria, leaving jobs they found unsuitable for more lucrative ones, including banditry.[38] In the first decades of the twentieth century, Japanese officials reported at least 300,000 migrants entering and at least 200,000 leaving Manchuria annually.[39] As these figures suggest, the migrating population was highly mobile. The contractor's weak hold over the recruits was largely because of the low hurdles and risks involved in making this journey. As mentioned earlier, the transportation and communication infrastructure was established and affordable. Furthermore, there was hardly any state oversight on population movement to and inside of Manchuria. Until 1932, the absence of a centralized state in Manchuria meant that there were no controls over population movement within, and in and out of Manchuria. The paucity of statistical figures on migration, especially by the Chinese state, exemplifies the state of affairs. It was only after 1932 that the Manchukuo regime imposed control over the mobility of labor, but with limited success.

BUCREAUCRATIZATION OF LABOR CONTROL IN FUSHUN COALMINE

Despite the shortcoming of the labor contractors in terms of actual labor control, dependence on them was widespread in Manchuria's industries, especially in Japanese-owned enterprises. Almost all Japanese enterprises relied on the labor contract system for labor recruitment. The exception was

---

36. *Ibid.*, pp. 49–50.
37. Yu Heyin, *Kuang ye baogao: Fushun meitan* [Report on Mining: Fushun Coalmine] (Beijing, 1927), p. 146.
38. Gottschang and Lary, *Swallows and Settlers*, p. 58.
39. See Appendix A in Gottschang and Lary, *Swallows and Settlers*, for detailed figures of entries and departures from Manchuria 1891–1942.

Fushun Coalmine. Unlike its peers, Japanese management in Fushun Coalmine sought to rectify the shortcomings of labor contracting by extending bureaucratic control over the contractors. Because labor contractors interfaced between the worlds of Japanese-controlled Fushun Coalmine and Chinese migration to Manchuria, mine management assumed that control over contractors would grant it control over the migration.

From the time the SMR took over Fushun Coalmine, Japanese mine management was far from content with the autonomy that labor contractors enjoyed, conveying its dissatisfaction in action and in words. In 1908, mine management introduced a parallel system of direct hiring, with the company directly employing 25 per cent of all mineworkers.[40] A Japanese-language company report published in 1909 included a lengthy discussion on labor contractors taking advantage of mineworkers, such as shortchanging workers' wages by manipulating the complex currency situation in Manchuria, and labor contractors' inconsequential contribution to production output.[41] Mine management observed no difference in the output of direct hires and contract workers. This experiment probably emboldened Japanese mine managers to take further action to regulate labor contractors' role in providing jobs, wages, and welfare.

In 1911 Japanese mine management introduced major changes that drastically curtailed contractors' influence over mineworkers. Through a series of measures, the responsibilities of labor contractors (such as wage payment, labor recruitment, labor welfare, and labor treatment) were gradually taken over. First, mine management converted all mineworkers to the status of "direct hires", which meant that all mineworkers, including those hired under the labor contract system, received their wages directly from mine management.[42] This seemingly trivial administrative move actually deprived contractors of a source of power. Contractors had frequently used this ability to determine and distribute wages to their advantage. By withholding or docking wages, they usually forced workers submit to them.

Second, mine management began assuming responsibilities traditionally associated with labor contractors, namely opening a labor recruitment center in Zhifu to recruit miners directly in Shandong.[43] Third, the company embarked on constructing housing and other facilities for its miners. Two- and

---

40. Minami manshū tetsudō kabushiki būjun tankō [South Manchuria Railway Fushun Coalmine], *Bujun tankō* [Fushun Coalmine] (Dairen, 1909), p. 227.
41. *Ibid.*, pp. 249–250.
42. Minami Manshū Tetsudō Kabushiki Kaisha [South Manchuria Railway] [Mantetsu], *Minami Manshū Tetsudō Kabushiki Kaisha Jūnenshi* [Ten-Year History of the South Manchuria Railway] (Dairen, 1919, repr. Tokyo, 1974), p. 497; Fujihirada, *Manshū ni okeru kōyama rōdō sha*, pp. 241–247; Yu, *Fushun meitan*, p. 145.
43. Mantetsu, *Jūnenshi*, p. 495.

three-story tall dormitories with modern amenities such as steam heating and running water were built. A hospital was opened to provide free medical treatment to sick or injured miners. And an entertainment complex that housed a stage for Chinese operas and supplied free musical instruments to those interested in learning to play them was erected.[44] In doing so, Japanese management signaled a desire to reduce its dependence on Chinese contractors by obtaining its labor supply and providing for its laborers themselves. Fourth, management issued regulations on the treatment of newly recruited miners. In these regulations, management inveighed against the abuse of newly recruited miners and spelled out punishment for the guilty. The regulations also entitled new recruits to two months' fixed income, regardless of output. These regulations demonstrated management's efforts to cultivate loyalty among new hires and isolate abusive contractors.[45]

Most significant in the expansion of Japanese managerial reach were the standardization of contractors' wages and the subordination of labor contractors to Japanese management's authority. On 10 September 1911 mine management issued "Regulations on Mining Workers' Contractors" [*saitan kukō hatō kisoku*], which separated contractors into two groups, large contractors and small contractors, with the latter assisting and subordinate to the former. [46] The new regulations stated that a small contractor could supervise no more than fifty men, though there were no restrictions on the number of men that a large contractor could supervise. Monthly salaries for both groups of contractors were capped at 3.5 per cent of mineworkers' gross salaries. Under the new regulations, the chain of command began with the Japanese colliery manager at the top, followed by the large contractor and then the small contractor. Japanese colliery managers had the right to dismiss contractors for poor performance. It is impossible to ascertain how effective these regulations were in limiting the contractors' influence in the workplace, but it is possible to state that these regulations marked the end of contractors' autonomy and the start of their careers as company bureaucrats.

Between 1917 and 1927, mine management expanded and intensified the bureaucratization of labor recruitment. In 1917, it issued new regulations on this issue.[47] Under these regulations, management reimbursed new hires and contractors for all costs incurred in their journeys to and from Fushun. With mine management paying for travel costs and reimbursement standardized, the contractors lost control over the right to charge recruits

44. *Ibid.*, p. 497.
45. Fujihirada, *Manshū ni okeru kōyama rōdō sha*, p. 243.
46. Repr. in Yu, *Fushun meitan*, pp. 166–167, and Fujihirada, *Manshū ni okeru kōyama rōdō sha*, pp. 245–246.
47. Fujihirada, *Manshū ni okeru kōyama rōdō sha*, pp. 61–64.

for bringing them to Fushun. In addition, these new regulations further deprived contractors of the right to decide whom to hire, and required contractors to send prospective workers to a recruitment center or branch office, where Japanese SMR staff evaluated them before approving them for employment in a coalmine. Evaluation of a miner's eligibility for employment entailed subjecting the prospective mineworker to a battery of tests to ascertain that his physical fitness and health were up to the company's standards. Those found to have lung disease, syphilis, or opium addiction were immediately rejected.[48] No longer did contractors have the final say in a miner's hiring. But to ensure that contractors were motivated to retain these recruits at the workplace, mine management implemented an incentive scheme that rewarded contractors and recruits for working thirty days in the mine.

The next step in bureaucratizing labor recruitment was to eliminate contractors as intermediaries altogether. Recruitment centers and mine-approved shops replaced contractors as proxies in recruiting and evaluating prospective miners. To this end, mine management issued regulations and procedures in 1925 to encourage workers to come to the mine of their own accord, without recruiters. As with all new hires, those who arrived on their own had their travel costs reimbursed. But before they arrived in Fushun, they had to go to recruitment centers in large cities like Qingdao or to retail shops acting as proxies for the mine. In order to become a mine-approved agent, the retail shop's owner had to be recommended by a labor contractor and personally submit a written request, and the shop had to be located at a busy intersection of a town. As mine-approved agents, these shops fingerprinted prospective workers and issued them departure certificates containing their names, ages, and fingerprints. These shops then had to inform, probably by telegraph, the mine's so-called Chinese Labor Department [C. *huagong bu*; J. *kakō bu*] of the workers' arrival.[49] Upon arrival, the workers had to submit their departure certificates to the Chinese Labor Department, which then verified their identities before issuing them with identity cards. For each worker who completed thirty days' work, the worker and the shop received a bonus.[50]

This system was predicated on migrant workers already knowing about the mine and its hiring practices. To ensure that knowledge about mine

---

48. Mantetsu, *Jūnenshi*, p. 567.
49. The Chinese Labour Department dealt only with Chinese migrant workers. The General Affairs Department [C. *shuwu bu*; J. *shōmu bu*] dealt with Chinese permanent employees and Japanese employees of all ranks.
50. *Regulation No. 1145, "Terms of Provisional Regulations on Rewarding Chinese Miners who Paid for their own Fare to the Coalmine"*, repr. in *Mantie midang: mantie yu laogong* [Secret Archives of the South Manchuria Railway: South Manchuria Railway and Labor] (Guilin shi, 2003), I, pp. 1–8.

recruitment practices was not restricted just to select individuals, Japanese management regularly advertised its recruitment policies. These advertising broadsheets announced the names of mine-approved proxy recruiters, that the mine reimbursed travel costs, that prospective hires needed guarantors, and that new hires had to complete thirty days of work before receiving their travel reimbursement.[51] By making the recruitment procedures public information, mine management pre-empted greedy contractors from taking advantage of prospective hires' ignorance while simultaneously rendering contractors all but irrelevant in the recruitment process.

FINGERPRINTING AND IDENTITY CARDS

Mine management's most ambitious intervention in regulating labor recruitment and mobility was the introduction of mandatory fingerprinting and identity cards in 1924. Under this new fingerprinting policy, the hiring department had to take two sets of fingerprints when it decided to hire a Chinese worker. Only the worker's left index finger was printed at this initial stage of implementation. One record (later whole sets of fingerprints) would be filed at the hiring department and another at the Chinese Labor Department, which would use the fingerprints to check the worker's background. If criminal activity was discovered in the worker's records, the worker was immediately fired.[52] In the following year, mine management increased the amount of information recorded about every Chinese worker. After the worker had the prints of all his fingers taken, he had to provide the following information: department of employment; job title; job number; pay range; full name; age; place of origin; current residence; and full name of father, mother, wife, and son. This newly expanded identity card formed the basis of a rudimentary personnel file, in which management would record employment dates, reasons for dismissal, resignation, and transfers, as well as workplace fatality and injury. With information about a worker's past employment record on file, mine management could easily determine if the worker had been previously fired, transferred from another pit without permission, or stolen a dead worker's identity card.[53] Mine management claimed to have disqualified from employment 1,640 Chinese workers, out of all 34,955 workers hired in 1925, on the basis of these workers' records.[54]

51. An example of such an advertisement is repr. in Yu, *Fushun meitan*, pp. 167–168.

52. Mantetsu, *Dainiji Jūnenshi*, p. 572.

53. "Fushun meikuang zhiwen guanli guicheng zhaiyi [Translated excerpt of the Fushun Coalmine Regulation on Supervision of Fingerprinting], Fu da No. 640, 1925.24", repr. in Xie Xueshi (ed.), *Mantie shi zhiliao* [Materials on the History of the South Manchuria Railway] (Beijing, 1987) pp. 315–316.

54. Minami Manshū Tetsudō Kabushiki Kaisha Būjun tankō [South Manchuria Railway Fushun Coalmine], *Sakugyō nenpō: Taishō jū yon nendo* [Annual Report on Operations, 1925], p. 6,

Kuribayashi Kurata, the chief of Fushun Coalmine's Chinese Labor Department, outlined the company's reasons for introducing fingerprinting and identity cards. Fingerprinting facilitated the identification and "elimination of bad elements" [*furyō bunshi haijo*].[55] Those considered "bad elements" included those who did not pay back money borrowed from friends and *batou*, who were involved in strikes or labor activism, and who were fugitives fleeing the Chinese criminal justice system. Obtaining the fingerprints of each Chinese worker would facilitate the identification and elimination of these "bad elements" because, as Kuribayashi points out, they were "unchanging for life" [*shyūsei fuhen*] and "unique for tens of thousands of people" [*manjin fudō*].[56]

In addition to the policing of Chinese labor, Kuribayashi also argued that fingerprinting would improve Japanese management of Chinese labor. Fingerprinting allowed management to treat its very large labor force with precision. In 1927, Fushun Coalmine employed about 42,701 Chinese workers. Given the large number of Chinese workers, fingerprinting assisted Japanese management in properly meting out punishments and rewards. Also, the new fingerprinting system allowed mine management to investigate why Chinese workers left employment. The new system required the recording in each worker's personnel file of the reason for terminating employment. This would allow a better understanding of the high turnover rate. Lastly, the introduction of fingerprinting would prevent Chinese workers from taking advantage of the mess hall. Each Chinese miner paid 11 *sen* a day for his meals in the mess hall. Without proper means of identifying workers who had paid and eaten, mine management could not prevent Chinese workers from either taking a second helping or sneaking someone else into the mess hall.

It is noteworthy that Kuribayashi's arguments were presented to the *Minami manshū kōgyōsha konwakai* [South Manchurian Industrialists' Club, hereafter *konwakai*]. Formed in May 1926, the *konwakai* was a regular gathering of representatives from Japanese industrial enterprises in southern Manchuria, including the Manchuria Spinning Company and the Manchuria Candy Manufacturing Company, Anshan Steelworks, Benxihu Coal and Steel Company, and SMR branch operations like Fushun Coalmine. The purpose of these gatherings was to share and collaborate on issues related to labor management.[57] The agenda of the first two meetings concerned the high turnover rate among Chinese employees at these

Library of Congress MOJ1633; Būjun tankō [Fushun Coalmine], *Sakugyō nenpō: Taishō jū san nendo* [Annual Report on Operations, 1924], p. 6, Library of Congress MOJ1632.

55. Kuribayashi Kurata, "Konwakai ni shimon jisshi nitsuite [Concerning the Implementation of Fingerprinting, Discussed at the Casual Forum]", [1927], repr. in *Mantie midang*, p. 50.

56. *Ibid.*, p. 52.

57. Repr. in *Mantie midang*, Item 2.1, p. 11.

enterprises. Kuribayashi's presentation was to persuade other enterprises to adopt fingerprinting and identity cards as measures to contain labor mobility.

The problem of labor mobility was so severe that all members of the *konwakai* readily agreed to have their Chinese workers fingerprinted. In fact, the SMR also joined in this effort by issuing a company-wide directive on 4 August 1927 that required all its Chinese employees to be fingerprinted according to the procedure established at Fushun Coalmine.[58] Clearly, labor mobility affected all industrial enterprises, but the labor turnover rate was particularly high in Fushun Coalmine, which accounts for mine management's vigorous efforts to control the movement of Chinese migrant labor.

INTERNATIONAL POLITICS, NEW RECRUITMENTS, AND BUREAUCRATIZATION

The accelerated pace of bureaucratization in labor recruitment coincided with the expansion of recruitment areas. In the years 1916–1918, British and French recruitment of Chinese labor in the mine's traditional recruitment areas in Shandong, which had, as described above, a long history of out-migration to Manchuria, forced Japanese management to consider new areas. Various factors led management to settle on the parts of Hebei province that had no tradition of outmigration to Manchuria. The decision attracted the attention of the Chinese state, which then demanded that Japanese management share information about the recruiters.[59] Hence, the confluence of international politics resulted in mine management's trend toward bureaucratization being accelerated.

The last two years of World War I brought equal measures of fortune and misery to the mine's Japanese managers.[60] Although the main theater of the war was thousands of miles away in Europe, it still affected China and the rest of Asia. The Great War caused economic recession in China and Manchuria, as fighting drastically lowered European demand for goods and commodities from Asia. When the war drew to a close, pent-up demand worldwide and reconstruction efforts in Europe stimulated economic recovery in Asia. As factories in China and Manchuria strove to meet increasing domestic and international orders, their need for coal increased accordingly. For Fushun Coalmine to meet the growing demand, it had to raise mining capacity. Since the open-cast pit in Guchengzi was far from

---

58. "Jitatsu dai 61 go [Directive No. 61]". Repr. in *Mantie midang*, Item 9.2, p. 61.
59. Information about recruiters and recruited workers is listed in the Fushun Mine Director's correspondence to the Republic of China Ministry of Foreign Affairs, dated 2 March 1921, 03-03-015-04-021, Institute of Modern History Archive, Academia Sinica, Taipei.
60. Mantetsu, *Jūnenshi*, p. 541.

completion, the only viable solutions for Fushun mine management were to open up more underground workings and to hire more workers for them. Two new pits were opened in 1917 and 1918, Longfeng and Xintun respectively. Hiring grew in scale and scope in the late 1910s. The mine employed 37,057 Chinese workers in 1919, which was almost twice the total number of Chinese workers employed in 1916.[61]

While the end of warfare unleashed rapidly growing demand for Fushun coal, it also created conditions that threatened the supply of Chinese labor in Shandong. With the creation of the laborers-as-soldiers program in 1915, a portion of the labor supply in Shandong was diverted to Europe. Under this program, the Chinese state allowed Britain and France to obtain much needed manpower by recruiting Chinese laborers and students in Shandong in exchange for both countries' support for China's campaign to regain Shandong from Japan. This program sent about 140,000 Chinese, with the majority from Shandong, to Britain and France between 1916 and 1921.[62] Although the gross figures for laborers recruited under this program paled in comparison to the figures for north China–Manchuria migration, the proximity of French and British labor recruitment campaigns in Tianjin and Weihaiwei respectively adversely affected Japanese labor recruitment in Yantai.

This unexpected turn of events compelled Japanese management at Fushun Coalmine to broaden its recruitment areas. Despite the mine's pressing need for more laborers and the competitive pressures of French and British recruitment, Japanese management imposed restrictions on its search for new labor sources. It was not interested in expanding its recruitment campaign to Japan. Japanese labor was an expensive alternative. Not only were Japanese workers' transportation costs higher, their wages and living costs were higher too. Since its formation in 1905, the SMR, including Fushun Coalmine, instituted different wage scales for Japanese and Chinese employees, with Japanese wages at least three times higher than Chinese wages. In 1926, the average daily wage for a Japanese worker was ¥2.48 while that for a Chinese worker was ¥0.68.[63] Indeed, in its 1908 cost-reduction efforts SMR management replaced its Japanese employees in less skilled positions with Chinese workers.[64]

Japanese management in Fushun Coalmine was not keen on extending its recruitment area to Korea either. As compared with Japan, Korea was closer

61. *Bujuntankō tōkei nenpō Shōwa 15 nen* [Fushun Coalmine Annual Statistics: 1942], Library of Congress MOJ1548.

62. Xu Guoqi, *Strangers on the Western Front: Chinese Workers in the Great War* (Cambridge, MA, 2011), p. 42.

63. Mantetsu, *Jūnenshi*, p. 140.

64. Yoshihisa Tak Matsusaka, *The Making of Japanese Manchuria, 1904–1932* (Cambridge, 2000), p. 143.

to Manchuria and Korean labor cost less than Japanese. When Japan annexed Korea as its formal colony in 1919, Japanese companies also faced fewer barriers to Korean markets, including labor. In the late 1910s, all mines in Manchuria experienced labor shortages, but none of the Japanese-controlled mines in nearby Anshan and Benxihu expanded their recruitment areas in Korea. According to Fujihirada Bunkichi, an SMR staff member who in 1918 prepared a report on mining labor in Manchuria, Japanese managers in Anshan and Benxihu mines thought poorly of the Koreans they had hired. They found them to be "nasty drunks", who frequently fought and quarreled among themselves, "lazy", and lacking Chinese workers' "capacity for work".[65] The same attitude was prevalent in Fushun.

Apart from this reluctance to use Korean laborers, Japanese management in Fushun did not wish to compete with Japanese-controlled mines in Manchuria for labor and thus it specifically prohibited its recruiters from poaching workers in Anshan and Benxi mines. This meant that Fushun mine management had to expand its recruitment territory further into rural counties in Shandong and Hebei provinces that had, up to this point, not participated in the seasonal migration to Manchuria. Within a span of eight years (1914–1921), the number of counties in Shandong represented among mineworkers grew from eleven in 1914 to twenty-six in 1921, the number of counties in Hebei grew from four in 1914 to thirteen in 1921, and the number of counties in Manchuria grew from one in 1914 to six in 1921.[66] Figure 2 illustrates the growing spatial spread of counties from which mineworkers originated. In 1914, Shandong mineworkers were from Jimo or counties in central Shandong along the Jinan–Qingdao railway line, while Hebei and Manchuria workers were from Chaoyang, Lingyuan, Linyu (in present-day Qinhuangdao), Fuxin, or Jinxian (present-day Jinzhou). In 1921, increasing numbers of Chinese mineworkers came from western and south-western Shandong, southern and north-eastern Hebei (especially the areas near Tangshan, where Kaiping Mines were located), and counties in Manchuria near the mine.

The expansion into territories formerly untouched by Fushun recruiters and the migration to Manchuria roused the suspicion of local Chinese government officials. The mine's recruitment in Hebei prompted the governor Zhu Jiabao to contact the Republic of China Ministry of Foreign Affairs (MFA) on 16 December 1916, requesting a formal investigation.[67] The ministry confirmed the legality of Japanese recruitment, but added a demand for Fushun mine management to provide Chinese officials with information

65. Fujihirada, *Manshū ni okeru kōyama rōdō sha*, p. 18.

66. Yu, *Fushun meitan*, p. 149.

67. Xu Youchun, *Minguo renwu da cidian* (Shijiazhuang, 1991), p. 198.

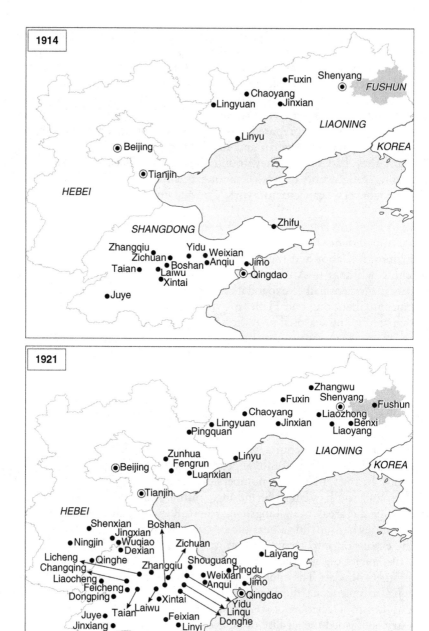

Figure 2. Distribution of mineworkers' places of origin, 1914 and 1921.

on labor recruiters' names, age, place of origin (specifying province, county, and village), name of underground pit where recruiter worked, the labor contractor (*batou*) in charge of the pit, the month that the recruiter arrived, and the number of workers recruited.[68] Surprisingly, Japanese mine management complied and supplied Chinese officials with the requested information. According to the mine director's report, 360 recruiters under the supervision of 16 contractors were sent to over 200 villages located in 38 different counties in north China, netting a total of 11,400 men. Judging from archival records, the ministry and local Chinese officials did not do anything with the information supplied, except to file it in the Ministry of Foreign Affairs archives.

Regardless of how precise recordkeeping was or how the collected information was used, this episode reveals another instance of bureaucratization as an attempt at asserting control. It must be remembered that asserting control and gaining control are two different matters. The Chinese state did not, through this small act, stop future recruitment attempts or reverse the trend of increasing Japanese incursion into Chinese sovereignty in Manchuria. Similarly, in its more grandiose plan of bureaucratization Japanese management failed to control labor mobility, let alone slow the rate of labor turnover.

PERSISTENT LABOR MOBILITY

In 1926, Yu Heyin, a Chinese government official, was sent to survey Fushun Coalmine. Yu noted that Chinese mineworkers in Fushun were "frequently on the move". As he reported, "of the 12,000 miners presently employed in the mine, more than 40,000 men had already come and left", which meant that "over 120 men entered or left employment on a daily basis".[69] Employment tenure was brief; no miner stayed for longer than six months. The company's statistics of miners hired and dismissed confirm Yu's observations. The earliest figures for labor mobility are from the year 1912, when the mine needed 7,282 workers. To meet the mine's labor demand, 30,751, workers were employed and 29,679 left voluntarily and involuntarily.[70] These figures meant that the company hired 4.2 workers for a single position. Put differently, it had to hire at least four times to fill a single position in a calendar year. This frequency of hiring translated into an employment stint of only 86.9 days.

This pattern of labor mobility held for the next two decades, even during peak recruitment years. In one of these peak years, 1920, underground mining required 11,349 workers. To meet this demand, 58,809 workers

68. Fushun Mine Director to MFA, 2 March 1921, 03-03-015-04-021, Institute of Modern History Archive, Academia Sinica, Taipei.
69. Yu, *Fushun meitan*, p. 176.
70. Fujihirada, *Manshū ni okeru kōyama rōdō sha*, p. 84. For a clarification of these calculations see ch. 3 of Teh, "Mining for Differences".

were hired – 15,190 recruits came by way of the company's recruitment network and 43,619 arrived on their own. However, 57,828 left, at various points of their employment, voluntarily and involuntarily. These figures indicate that the company had to hire 5.18 workers for each mining position. In other words, the company had to hire at least five times to fill a single mining position in a calendar year. This meant that the average miner's tenure was seventy days. When recruitment slowed due to decline in coal demand, hiring was less frequent and miners stayed a little longer at the job. Two years after coal demand and labor recruitment peaked in 1920, the coal market slumped and recruitment shrunk. Only 8,260 miners were needed in 1922. Yet, 26,556 men were hired to fill these positions and 26,343 departed at some point during their employment. SMR had to hire only 3.21 workers for a single mining position in that calendar year, half the figure for the peak year of 1920. Contributing to the slow-down in hiring was the lengthening of the miners' employment tenure. The hired miner stayed for 113 days on the job in 1922, which is 43 days longer than 1920.[71]

A factor contributing to the high turnover rate, the government official Yu pointed out in 1926, was that many miners were from farming backgrounds. Since farming was their primary occupation, they often came in the autumn after the crops' harvest and left in spring in time for the start of the planting season. The migrant workers that the mine recruited in its expansion westward in 1917 – 1927 were even more likely to return to their farmlands. As Yu's remarks intimated, the migrant workers who came from poorer regions were content to have earned a month's wages. As for the few who were not farmers, Yu explained that they were mostly from Shandong province and were familiar enough with the geography and economic situation in Manchuria to seek out better opportunities elsewhere. As for those with previous mining experience, Yu found that these allegedly experienced hires had worked in traditional mines that were shallower and the mining work organized differently. Their experience did not prepare them for deep underground mining work that was intense and demanding. Lastly, Yu also noted that those from poorer regions west of Fushun were often content with only 20–30 *yuan* in their pockets and would not stay longer.[72] In short, the migrants' farming background, mobility, and their resistance to industrial discipline explained their reluctance to root themselves in Fushun coalmine.

CONCLUSION

When the Japanese-state-controlled South Manchuria Railway Company took over Fushun Coalmine in 1907, labor supply for the mine was based on a well-established migration pattern between north China and

71. Mantetsu, *Dainiji Jūnenshi*, p. 586.
72. Yu, *Fushun meitan*, pp. 146, 176.

Manchuria. Mobilized and mediated by labor contractors originating themselves from the villages in the recruitment areas, peasants and laborers from the Chinese mainland formed a seemingly inexhaustible supply. The high turnover and mobility of these migrants, however, also caused severe problems for Japanese management in building a steady and efficiently organized labor force. Controlling these mobile migratory miners became its main preoccupation. Its main targets were the labor contractors, who had traditionally occupied a quasi-independent intermediary position between management and migrant workers. Fushun managers assumed that control over contractors would grant them control of migration.

Their method was a conscious policy of centralization of labor control after 1911. All mineworkers became "direct hires", and wages were no longer paid by the contractors but by the mine itself. Fushun opened its own recruitment agencies in Shandong and other recruitment areas as centers for recruiting and evaluating prospective miners, thereby replacing contractors. Contractors were incorporated in the mine's hierarchical structure, and became subordinate to the Japanese authorities in the mine. Last but not least, to administer and control the whole recruitment process, Japanese management introduced fingerprinting as part of an elaborate system of workers' registration. This transformation can be considered a manifestation of a more general trend in the development of labor control in capitalist business from "simple" to "bureaucratic", as described by the sociologist Richard Edwards.

These measures hardly affected the movement of Chinese migrants however. Labor mobility remained a challenge to Japanese management. Because it constantly struggled with the mobility of Chinese labor, Japanese management never succeeded in raising labor productivity. Given that labor mobility persisted throughout the four decades of Japanese management, it is safe to conclude that mine management's bureaucratic measures – from incorporating labor contractors into management to fingerprinting – failed. Chinese workers chose their own way and stuck to their mobility patterns, in spite of all Japanese investments in recruitment procedures and administrative control.

IRSH 60 (2015), Special Issue, pp. 121–143 doi:10.1017/S0020859015000437
© 2015 Internationaal Instituut voor Sociale Geschiedenis

The Uneven Recruitment of Korean Miners in Japan in the 1910s and 1920s: Employment Strategies of the Miike and Chikuhō Coalmining Companies

TOM ARENTS

Graduate School of Regional Management,
Sapporo Gakuin University
Bunkyōdai 11, Ebetsu-shi, 069-8555, Japan

E-mail: tom_arents@hotmail.com

NORIHIKO TSUNEISHI

Graduate School of Architecture, Planning and Preservation,
Columbia University
1172 Amsterdam Avenue, NY 10027, New York, USA

E-mail: nt2296@columbia.edu

ABSTRACT: After Japan's colonization of Korea in 1910, many Korean peasants lost their land owing to the changes imposed in agriculture, and several Japanese coalmining companies started to recruit them as a colonial surplus population. Despite the low wages they offered, not all of the companies relied on Korean miners – the distribution of this workforce was strikingly uneven. Focusing on the mines of Chikuhō and Miike in the Fukuoka prefecture during the 1910s and 1920s, this article argues that the distribution of Koreans was a consequence of uneven capital accumulation among different mining companies. This unevenness reflected the differing wages and recruitment policies of these companies. Correlating earlier groups of cheap labourers, such as convict workers, to this history, we suggest some explanations as to why some mining companies brought Korean workers into the coal-production process as an immediately available, cheap, and disposable workforce, while others did not.

In the first half of the twentieth century, Korean migrants became a vital workforce for coal production in Japan. In the period of Japanese colonization of the Korean peninsula between 1910 and the end of World War II, many Korean peasants lost their lands to a handful of rich landowners. According to Ken Kawashima, a historian of Korean immigration in Japan, they turned into a "colonial surplus population", i.e. an extensive pool of cheaply available workers created, directly and indirectly, by the

Japanese colonization.[1] These impoverished Korean peasants were recruited as wage labourers to work in different coalmining sites across Japan's empire, from the Kyūshū and Hokkaidō islands to South Sakhalin, which occupied part of present-day Sakhalin (see Figure 1).

While some of the existing scholarship on the history of Japan's coal production underplays, if not almost completely ignores, the role of Korean workers,[2] other scholarship emphasizes the ways in which the colonial workforce was mobilized, racially discriminated against, and exploited as a cheap labour force by Japanese mining companies.[3] While sympathizing with those scholars, the present article will further complicate this narrative by revealing how, since the annexation of the peninsula in 1910, Korean workers were unevenly distributed across different mining companies. The use of Korean workers was thus not a generalized phenomenon.

The varying distribution of Korean workers during the first few decades of colonization is often ignored in existing scholarship.[4] In the late 1930s, when Japan intensified its war efforts, virtually all major Japanese mining companies began to rely on the colonial workforce as forced labourers to cover wartime labour shortages. Before the late 1930s, however, Korean miners were unevenly distributed across different companies. This article will focus on this earlier period, raising the question of why, if Korean miners were indeed a cheap workforce, not all companies used them to maximize their profits. If, from the perspective of Marxian political economy, capital's driving force is to "absorb the greatest possible amount of surplus labour", why did not all companies follow this logic?[5]

In order to explain the problem of uneven distribution, we will focus on two coalmining regions in south-western Japan, the Miike and Chikuhō regions in the Fukuoka prefecture, located on Kyūshū island. Both had been major coal-mining regions since the mid-nineteenth century, and stayed so until the last pit at the Miike Mine closed in 1997. The Miike Mine was the largest coalmine in Japan. It was operated by Mitsui Kōzan, which was part of Mitsui Zaibatsu.[6]

---

1. Ken Kawashima, *The Proletarian Gamble: Korean Workers in Interwar Japan* (Durham, NC, 2009), pp. 25–28.

2. For example, Mikio Sumiya, *Nihon Sekitan Sangyō Bunseki* [An Analysis of the Japanese Coal Industry] (Tokyo, 1968).

3. For example, Yasuto Takeuchi, *Chōsa: Chōsenjin Kyōsei Rōdō 1: Tankō-hen* [Investigation: Forced Labour of Koreans 1: Coalmine] (Tokyo, 2013).

4. William Donald Smith points out the uneven distribution in passing, but does not investigate this topic in detail. See his "Ethnicity, Class and Gender in the Mines: Korean Workers in Japan's Chikuhō Coal Field, 1917–1945" (Ph.D. dissertation, University of Washington, 1999), p. 76.

5. Karl Marx, *Capital*, I (London, 1990), p. 342.

6. The notion of *zaibatsu* indicates a business conglomerate that emerged in the late nineteenth century in Japan. Mitsui Zaibatsu was one of the largest of these conglomerates. Led by Douglas MacArthur (Supreme Commander for the Allied Powers) following the Second World War, all *zaibatsu* were dissolved in 1947.

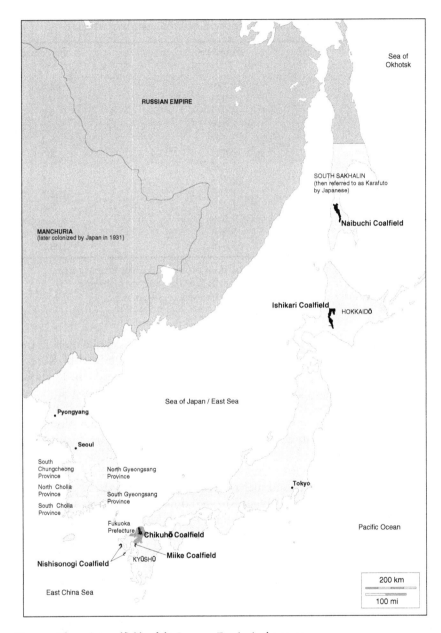

Figure 1. The major coalfields of the Japanese Empire in the 1910s.

In the Chikuhō region, meanwhile, there were several mines of varying size, administered by different companies. Among them were Mitsui Kōzan as well, next to Mitsubishi Kōgyō, a company owned by Mitsubishi Zaibatsu, and Asō

Table 1. *Places of origin of miners in the Chikuhō coalfield in 1928.*

Birthplace	Number	Percentage
Japan		
Fukuoka	28,280	44.4
Kumamoto	5,973	9.4
Oita	5,933	9.3
Hiroshima	4,278	6.7
Ehime	3,337	5.2
Saga	2,853	4.5
Kagoshima	2,202	3.5
Nagasaki	1,494	2.3
Miyazaki	1,305	2.1
Shimane	1,317	2.1
Yamaguchi	1,048	1.6
Korea	5,626	8.8
TOTAL	63,646	100.0

Source: Fukuoka Chihō Shokugyō Shōkai Jimukyoku [Fukuoka Employment Bureau], *Chikuhō Tankō Rōdōsha Shusshinchi Shirabe* [Survey of Home Prefectures/Country of Chikuhō Miners] (Fukuoka, 1928), p. 6.

Shōten, a smaller company that had emerged from within Chikuhō itself. In the 1910s and 1920s the mines in this region employed a large pool of Korean miners, alongside Japanese miners, both from within and outside the Fukuoka prefecture. A survey in 1928 indicated that almost 9 per cent of the miners originated from Korea (Table 1). According to this survey, the majority of these Koreans were from the provinces of North and South Cholla and North and South Gyeongsang, where according to Kawashima "peasant immiseration was greatest [during the interwar period]".[7]

While many companies in Chikuhō, such as Mitsubishi Kōgyō and Asō Shōten, employed a large number of Korean workers as early as the late 1910s, during World War I, Mitsui Kōzan did not rely on them at Miike in the 1910s and 1920s, nor at their mines in Chikuhō. This article argues that the uneven recruitment of Korean workers was a consequence of uneven capital accumulation among those companies, and was related to the availability of workforces and the wage level at their mines.

This research first examines what preconditions prevailed at Miike and Chikuhō when the aforementioned companies began developing their respective mines in the late nineteenth century. Varying geographies, production processes, and workforces caused different historical trajectories. In the following section we will show that the labour force employed by Mitsui Kōzan at the Miike Mine consisted of immediately available, cheap,

7. Kawashima, *The Proletarian Gamble*, p. 50.

and disposable Japanese miners: convict workers, and later also female pit workers, who were deployed when the use of prisoners had become restricted. We will then demonstrate how profits made at the Miike Mine at the expense of these cheap workers financially fuelled Mitsui's other mines in the Chikuhō region, offering the company the possibility of paying the employees at those mines relatively high wages. As wages were a decisive factor in recruiting as well as in retaining miners, Mitsui Kōzan was able to keep enough Japanese miners in Chikuhō under the company's rather discriminatory guiding precept of *Seihyō-Shugi* (which might be translated as "elite troop-ism").

Conditions at the Mitsubishi Kōgyō and Asō Shōten mines in Chikuhō around the time of Japan's annexation of Korea in 1910 differed from those at the Mitsui Kōzan mines. Compared to Mitsui Kōzan, wages at their mines were lower, which also implies that these two companies must have been less successful in securing a stable workforce of Japanese miners. We suppose that, because of the lack of a stable Japanese workforce, the two companies turned to the vast pool of the Korean colonial surplus population, produced by Japan's colonialism, as an immediately available labour supply. In a peculiar way, the Korean workers conjured up the role that the convict and other, non-convict miners had played for Mitsui Kōzan at Miike a few decades earlier. Productivity and the use of labour differed in these companies and mining sites, depending on their own preconditions and corresponding capital accumulation. This is the history of economic unevenness at work within Japan's capitalism during the interwar period, seen through the lens of immediately available, cheap, and disposable workforces.

PRECONDITIONS AT MIIKE AND CHIKUHŌ

Located relatively close to each other in the Fukuoka prefecture, Miike and Chikuhō were two of Japan's major coalmining regions (see Figure 2). The history of coal production at both locales predated the Meiji Restoration, which replaced the Tokugawa shōgunate with the imperial state in 1868. Administered by local clans during the Tokugawa era (1603–1868), coal production at that time was still insignificant in both regions, relying on manual labour with insufficient machinery. For Miike and Chikuhō to become prominent for what they are known for in Japan – the production of coal – both regions needed to wait for large capital, machineries, and infrastructures to be introduced.

At Miike in 1873 the new Meiji state intervened in the mine to extract coal for export. The quality of the bituminous coal from the Miike Mine was high. Also, as the mine was located by the Ariake Sea at the border of the present Fukuoka and Kumamoto prefectures, it was relatively easy to transport coal to the nearby Ōmuta port. Thanks to this location and the

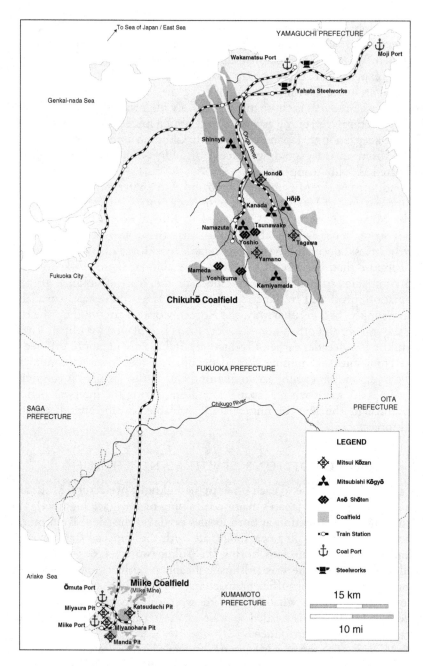

Figure 2. Mines and pits in the Miike and Chikuhō coalfields administrated by Mitsui Kōzan, Mitsubishi Kōgyō, and Asō Shōten.

high quality of coal, the amount of coal exported from Miike increased from 409 tons in 1877 to 217,302 tons in 1888.[8] Coal from the mine was sent to foreign trading ports, such as Hong Kong and Shanghai, by the Mitsui Bussan trading company, another key company owned by Mitsui Zaibatsu and which had been in charge of exports since the mid-1870s. As exports grew, the total output of coal further increased. Concomitantly, large amounts of capital were invested to mechanize the mining process, introducing, for instance, the steam-generated water pump. Financed and administrated by the state, the Miike Mine had the most advanced mechanical production process and by the late 1880s it yielded the largest tonnage of coal of all Japan's mines.

In 1888, with the profits gained through the trading business of Mitsui Bussan, Mitsui Zaibatsu won the bid over Mitsubishi Zaibatsu and purchased the Miike Mine from the state, taking over the operation fully the following year. After the takeover, Mitsui formally established the Mitsui Kōzan mining company in 1892. Since Mitsui Kōzan inherited all the existing infrastructure and workforce from the state, the company was able to jumpstart its operation. Included in the workforce were convict workers, as shown in the following section. The company further invested in new machinery (including the mechanical winch), the opening of new pits, and the construction of the Miike port in 1908. As a result of these investments, the Miike Mine continued to be Japan's main coal-producing mine in terms of output.

In the Chikuhō region, although located at a relatively short distance from Miike, the state was much less involved in the operation of mines after the Meiji Restoration in 1868. Mines previously owned by local clans during the Edo period became available for local merchants, allowing for the advent of endogenous mining companies. Without sufficient private capital of their own, these companies continued to rely on the primitive means of production carried over from the previous era. Their operations were far less industrialized than those of the state-owned Miike Mine. Devoid of large investments by the state, it took a longer time to develop the Chikuhō mines and to accumulate large capital.

The major obstacles in the region were the small size designated by the state to each mining concession and the large distance to the nearest port. The small concessions did not allow for a greater production of coal, and the transportation of coal to the port through the Onga river and its tributaries took a long time and thus was costly. These spatial and geographical circumstances were not attractive enough for the large companies to consider investing. These impediments began to dissolve only when the Sentei Kōku Sei [Coalmine District Reformation] was enacted by the state in 1888 to enlarge the minimum mining concession, and railway lines were

---

8. Sumiya, *Nihon Sekitan*, p. 121.

constructed to connect the mines to the Moji port and Wakamatsu port, which were built around 1890.

A few months after the enactment of the Sentei Kōku Sei, Mitsubishi Zaibatsu bought the Shinnyū Mine and Namazuta Mine, followed by the Kamiyamada Mine and Hōjō Mine in 1895. A few years later, Mitsui Kōzan also advanced into the region, purchasing the Yamano Mine in 1896 and the Tagawa Mine in 1900.[9] Also, a handful of local companies, wealthy enough to increase their coal production, further expanded their operations. Asō Shōten was one of those endogenous companies, whose advent further industrialized the region. By 1895, Chikuhō, together with Miike, was producing almost one-half of all coal extracted in Japan, fuelling the furnaces, for example, of the Yahata Steelworks (inaugurated near Chikuhō in present-day Kitakyūshū city in 1901).

Still, Chikuhō's growth was uneven. The larger companies, such as Mitsui Kōzan, were able to increase coal production quickly, while other companies with less capital had a different pace as well as size of production. Diverse conditions at the start of the industrialization of the mines allowed for the coexistence of multiple companies, big and small, jostling each other in the region. This economic unevenness among different companies in the region continued throughout the interwar period.

Along with geography and production, another major difference between the Miike and Chikuhō mines was the availability of labour. The mining process in both areas continued to rely heavily on human labour, regardless of the extent of mechanization at each mine. Procuring a guaranteed workforce in Chikuhō continued to trouble all companies, even during the interwar period when labourers seemed most readily available. The proximity of the mines in the region made it easy for the miners to leave one mine for another, and thus the retention of miners was a serious issue for the companies. In contrast, Mitsui Kōzan was able to overcome the difficulty of maintaining a stable workforce, at least at Miike, by employing convict workers, provided by the state. This enabled the company to accumulate more capital earlier and quicker than the other companies in Chikuhō. In addition, Mitsui Kōzan was virtually the only employer in Miike. Surrounded by farmlands with a surplus agrarian population, the mine was able to monopolize the supply of labour.

CHEAP AND DISPOSABLE LABOUR AT MIIKE

When the state began administrating the Miike Mine in 1873, the majority of the workforce consisted of peasants who had been mining coal during the

9. Chikuhō Sekitan Kōgyō-shi Nenpyō Hensan Iinkai [Committee for the Compilation of a Historical Chronology of the Chikuhō Coal Industry] (ed.), *Chikuhō Sekitan Kōgyō-shi Nenpyō* [Historical Chronology of the Chikuhō Coal Industry] (Fukuoka, 1973), pp. 168–180.

off-season of their farm work. In order to increase coal production further, the state needed a more stable workforce and to that end it turned to prisoners.

As soon as the state began operations in 1873, fifty prisoners were taken to the mine to transport coal to the nearby port. As far as the mining process was concerned, although the state introduced machinery into some of the major pits, the hauling and hewing of coal continued to rely on manual labour. Also, the underground water needed to be pumped out manually from the pits, as the steam-generated water pump was not widely available at that time. These jobs were not attractive, especially with the high temperature and humidity underground, making it even more difficult for the state-owned mine to find enough new miners. Hence, utilizing its juridical and prison apparatus, the state disciplined more prisoners to work in the mines to keep production going under these harsh conditions. Accordingly, the number of convict workers increased further in the following years.

Both the availability and the low cost of convict workers at the Miike Mine were crucial preconditions for Mitsui to continue mining after the takeover from the state. When the company purchased the mine in 1888, it made sure it applied for permission to use convict workers. Although there are no exact figures, the wages for convict workers were roughly half those of non-convict miners.[10] Based upon the low cost of the convict workers, Mitsui Kōzan was able to increase its profits. At its peak during the 1890s, convict workers constituted almost 70 per cent of the pit workforce. In this period, the company opened more pits and production at the mine drastically increased.

Every time a new pit was opened, and a new workforce was urgently needed, convict workers were relocated from the previous pit to work there for several years, until the company introduced new machinery, opened another pit, or hired non-convict workers. By using immediately available and cheap convict labour, Mitsui Kōzan was able to increase production further as well as to expand its capital. Simultaneously, convict workers were mobilized as a highly disposable workforce.

Two factors rendered convict workers no longer the "best option" at the Miike Mine. One was prison reform, the other was mechanization. In 1899 the state enacted the Prison Law (Kangoku Hō). As this law restricted the use of convict workers to a maximum of 400, Mitsui Kōzan needed to discharge many of them. This change of policy also reflected the impact of growing public criticism of the use of prisoners as

10. Tetsuya Hashimoto, "Mitsui Kōzan to Shūjinrōdō" [Prison Labour at Miike Mine], *Shakai Keizaigaku-shi* [Social Economic History], 32 (1966), pp. 398–418, 403.

Table 2. *Number of workers at the Miike Mine, 1894–1930.*

Year	Pit workers		All workers	
	Convict	Non-convict	Male	Female
1894	1,290	622	4,287	81
1896	1,457	475	4,734	83
1897	896	420	5,080	81
1898	838	545	4,936	79
1899	[n.a.]	[n.a.]	5,077	75
1900	[n.a.]	[n.a.]	4,520	572
1901	[n.a.]	[n.a.]	5,205	681
1902	276	1,209	6,018	871
1903	266	1,229	6,235	1,139
1908	148	2,000	8,352	1,971
1913	180	4,052	11,740	3,041
1918	121	4,143	12,310	3,335
1923	100	2,658	12,147	2,694
1928	115	2,224	9,807	1,329
1930	99	1,711	9,392	530

Source: Mitsui Kōzan, *Gojūnen-shi Kō, 1ohen, Rōmu* [Draft of 50-Year History of Mitsui Kōzan, X, Labour Management] (Tokyo, 1943).[11]

forced labour.[12] Nevertheless, as the company continued to use convict workers until 1930, albeit in smaller numbers (see Table 2), the juridical or ethical motives were not the only explanation for discharging convict workers. The introduction of machinery was equally crucial. The installation of a huge steam-generated water pump in the early 1890s was a decisive moment for the industrialization of the Miike Mine. Clearing the underground water no longer required human labour, making the convict workers partially dispensable.[13] At the same time, the convict workers were still needed for hewing and hauling, which continued to rely on manual labour. However, they were not considered ideal by the company. This was the occasion when Mitsui turned fully to non-convict workers, first female then male miners.

As shown in Table 2, the number of convict workers drastically decreased from 1898 to 1902, largely due to the Prison Law. In stark contrast, while there were only 75 female workers in 1899 when the law was enforced, the number skyrocketed to 572 in the following year. Those women workers, who likely came from peasant households nearby, were paid less than their

11. This and the other printed and unprinted documents authored by Mitsui Kōzan used in this article can be consulted at the Mitsui Bunko [Mitsui Archives], Tokyo.
12. Naoki Tanaka, *Kindai Nihon Tankō Rōdōshi Kenkyū* [Labour History of Japanese Coalmining] (Tokyo, 1984), p. 269.
13. Hashimoto, "Mitsui Kōzan to Shūjinrōdō", p. 416.

male counterparts, and in this respect they shared features with the convict workers. When in 1901 the remaining convict workers at the Katsudachi pit were relocated to the Miyanohara pit, the company soon lifted a ban on using female workers in the Katsudachi pit.[14] These female workers were obviously brought into the production process to compensate for the dwindling number of convict workers upon the passage of the reform law.

Female workers represented more than the mere replacement of the convict workers, however. Along with the water pump, the mechanical winch was introduced during the mid-1890s. It automated the transportation of coal from the main shaft inside the pit to the surface. As this task had presumably been handled by the convict workers before, the machine replaced some of their labours. On the other hand, the installation further intensified the use of manual labour in the underground pit to keep pace with the machine. In this way, the mechanization of transport created more jobs for the coal haulers, who transported coal from the coalface to the main shaft manually. As this work required less skill and probably less strength compared with the work of the coal hewer, Mitsui Kōzan turned to female workers for the hauling jobs. By assigning these jobs to women, the company was able to optimize the production process.[15]

Furthermore, the company had another motive for incorporating female miners. To increase production and the return on the investment in new machinery, the company needed to hire more male hewers. To secure a stable workforce of male miners, the company strategically hired their wives as haulers. Especially in "room and pillar" mining – still the predominant method around 1900 – pairs of married couples were assigned to respective "rooms", where a husband worked as a hewer and his wife as a hauler. Together they formed a "family-style employment structure based upon a dual-income household".[16] The increase in the number of female workers in 1900 marked Mitsui Kōzan's initial move toward this structural change – that is, the expansion of its workforce by discharging convict workers.

Table 2 shows that, while there were around 1,457 convict pit workers (hewers and haulers) at the peak of their employment in 1896, their number decreased quickly in the following years. In contrast, although the number of male workers, surface and underground combined, at Miike decreased

14. Mitsui Kōzan, *Shūto Saitan no Yurai* [The Origin of Convict Miners] (Tokyo, n.d. [1943]), p. 4. The Katsudachi pit is also colloquially called the Kaddachi or Katsudate pit. The Miyanohara pit was referred to as the Miyahara pit in the past.

15. Yutaka Nishinarita, "Sekitan Kōgyō no Gijutsu Kakushin to Joshi Rōdō" [Technological Development and Female Labour in the Coal Industry], in Nakamura Masanori (ed.), *Gijutsu Kakushin to Joshi Rōdō* [Technological Development and Female Labour] (Tokyo, 1985), pp. 71–105, 75.

16. *Ibid.* All translations from Japanese are ours.

from 5,077 in 1899 to 4,520 in 1900, perhaps because of the Prison Law, thereafter it increased again to 5,205 in 1901. Notably, the number of non-convict pit workers reached 2,000 by 1908 and continued to increase in the following years. Within a few years of the Prison Law, the non-convict miners, male and female together, exceeded the number of convict miners at the peak of 1896. This trend suggests that, even without the Prison Law, the supply of convict workers alone would not have been enough to increase production at the mine.

For example, had Mitsui Kōzan continued to use convict workers in its newly opened Manda pit in 1903, one of the largest pits at the Miike Mine, the company would have needed to bring more prisoners from elsewhere, which would have cost more since it would have entailed, for example, constructing new corresponding facilities. Therefore, with or without the Prison Law, it is highly probable that the reliance on prisoners became an obstacle to the prospective growth of the mine. Although the wages of the prisoners were lower than those of the non-convict miners, the need for enhanced capital accumulation rendered convict workers "unattractive" in the long run: there were extra costs attached to them and they were considered less productive than non-convict labourers. Sooner or later, the company would have required non-convict workers.

The simultaneous use of convict and non-convict miners must have caused problems too. Their presence in a pit perhaps made it more difficult for the company to secure a stable labour force, for it is not hard to imagine that toiling side by side with prisoners in the same pit was not appealing to others. This explains why, after 1901, all convict workers were relocated to the Miyanohara pit, which was destined to be closed.[17] As the company had calculated that the Miyaura pit and the Manda pit were more productive, non-convict workers were assigned to these pits. In a way, the Prison Law conveniently shrank the pool of convict workers and made it easier for the company to insulate them from the others. Doing so enabled Mitsui Kōzan to recruit more non-convict hewers, while using the labour of the prisoners at the waning pit until the end (the Miyanohara pit closed in 1931).

At the same time, there is no doubt that Mitsui Kōzan had gained tremendous profits from the forced labour of the convict workers. By the early 1910s, the Miike Mine became the cashbox for the company. It yielded approximately 2,000,000 tons of coal by 1912, the largest volume of any of Japan's mines. This abundant production and capital accumulation at the Miike Mine greatly helped the subsequent operation of their mines in Chikuhō.[18] Thanks to the convict workers in Miike, the company became

---

17. *Ibid.*, p. 22.
18. See Hideki Hatakeyama, *Kindai Nihon no Kyodai Keiei: Mitsubishi Zaibatsu no Jirei Kenkyū* [Giant Enterprise in Modern Japan: A Case Study of Mitsubishi] (Tokyo, 2000), p. 7.

wealthy enough to hire non-convict workers and managed to increase production at its mines. Furthermore, the convict wages functioned as a benchmark for the company, leading it to lower the cap on wages for the subsequent non-convict Japanese miners.[19] In a way, the convict workers defined the labour conditions of those who followed.

WAGES

Having discharged the majority of the convict workers, since the dawn of the twentieth century Mitsui Kōzan began hiring former peasants from the vicinity of the Miike Mine. "With regard to the employment of miners", wrote an office manager of the company, "one of the difficult parts is their wage."[20] The manager reasoned that the company should not hire "experienced" persons since they "try to leave the mine". Instead, it had to look for "unsophisticated" peasants, for they tended to stay longer and "the company does not have to raise the wage [to attract them]".[21] From these passages, we can surmise how important it was for the company to secure a stable workforce and how the wage was the crucial factor for both the miners and the company.

Interestingly, the officer wrote in the same report that, "as persons often come from Chikuhō to steal miners [from the Miike Mine], the company should always tighten security".[22] This remark suggests that the mines in Chikuhō (at least those not pertaining to Mitsui Kōzan) had more difficulty in retaining enough miners. As wages were the crucial factor for both the employment and retention of miners, in this section we will briefly look at the wages of miners at the different mines in the Chikuhō region in the early 1910s. As will be shown later, the varying wage scales across the companies reflected their respective employment strategies toward Korean miners later on.

Table 3 presents the average daily wages for male miners at Chikuhō mines in 1912, two years after the annexation of the Korean peninsula. The table makes clear that wages fluctuated from one company to another. The highest wages were paid in the three mines of Mitsui Kōzan, averaging 0.78 yen. Mitsubishi Kōgyō and Asō Shōten (or their predecessors) paid the lowest wages, averaging 0.68 yen and 0.61 yen respectively.[23]

19. Toyoo Shindō, *Akai Botayama no Hi: Chikuhō Miike no Hitobito* [Red Fires of Coal-slag Heap: People in Chikuhō and Miike] (Tokyo, 1985), p. 154.
20. Mitsui Kōzan, *Miike Kōgyōsho Enkaku-shi: Rōmu*, III [History of the Mitsui Mine: Labour Management, III] (Tokyo, 1943), p. 637.
21. *Ibid.*, p. 638.
22. *Ibid.*
23. In 1912 the Mitsubishi mines were administered by the Mitsubishi Co., and the Asō mines were administered by Taichi Asō, a founder of Asō Shōten. Both Mitsubishi Kōgyō and Asō Shōten were formally established in 1918.

Table 3. *Wages for male pit workers paid at different Chikuhō mines in 1912.*

Company*	Mine	Miners	Wages (yen)	Company	Mine	Miners	Wages (yen)
Mitsui	Tagawa	1,402	0.845	Meiji	Meiji‡	1,194	0.830
	Yamano	844	0.695		Hōkoku	857	0.778
	Hondō	861	0.810		Akaike	279	0.700
Mitsubishi	Shinnyū	918	0.679	State-owned	Shinbaru Kaigun#	569	0.779
	Namazuta	1,370	0.640		Futase	1,425	0.742
	Hōjō	520	0.711	Iwasaki	Iwasaki	326	0.685
	Kamiyamada	441	0.660	Arate	Arate	296	0.695
	Kanada	530	0.687	Itō	Nakazuru	355	0.735
Asō	Mameda	346	0.597	Miyoshi	Miyoshi	277	0.714
	Yoshio	652	0.620		Takamatsu	174	0.613
Kaijima	Ōnoura	1,647	0.780	Hori	Gotoku	248	0.748
	Ōtsuji	497	0.700	Koyanose	Koyanose	407	0.793
Furukawa	Furukawa†	536	0.760	Kurauchi	Mineji	1,205	0.750
	Shimoyamada	557	0.730		Ōtō	401	0.880
Sumitomo	Tadakuma	815	0.740	Nakano	Aida	157	0.550

* Regarding the ownership of each mine, we relied on the information for 1913. Hence, some mines might have been owned by different companies in 1912.
† The figures are for three Furukawa-owned mines: Shiogashira, Shakanō, and Katsuno.
‡ The figures include the numbers of and wages for pit timberers and haulers.
# The mine was located in the present-day Kasuya district, west of the Chikuhō region.
Source: Chikuhō Sekitan Kōgyō-shi Nenpyō Hensan Iinkai [Committee for the Compilation of a Historical Chronology of the Chikuhō Coal Industry] (ed.), *Chikuhō Sekitan Kōgyō-shi Nenpyō* [Historical Chronology of the Chikuhō Coal Industry] (Fukuoka, 1973), p. 255.

As it is not likely that the higher wages paid by Mitsui Kōzan were a consequence of longer working hours, they do suggest that there were differences in productivity between Mitsui Kōzan and other companies. Whatever the reasons for the varying productivity, our contention is that the corresponding higher wages at the Mitsui Kōzan mines in Chikuhō would have been impossible without the profits at the Miike Mine. Without the state-funded start of production and the labour of convict workers at Miike, Mitsui Kōzan would have been unable even to purchase those mines in Chikuhō in the first place. Thanks to the preconditions at and the continual prosperity of the Miike Mine, the mines operated by Mitsui Kōzan in Chikuhō had access to enough capital possibly to invest in better machinery and to spend on the wages of their workers.[24] Accordingly, as we will

24. The wages at the Miike Mine were in fact lower than some of those at Mitsubishi's mines in Chikuhō. This might be due to the geographical location. As the only mine in the region, the

demonstrate below, the company was able constantly to increase the number of Japanese miners and production throughout the rest of the 1910s.

Judging from the wages paid in 1912 at the Mitsubishi Kōgyō and Asō Shōten mines in Chikuhō, these were not as economically prosperous as the Mitsui Kōzan mines. This might have been due to the geological conditions of the mines, the scarcity of capital, or all of those factors combined. Without the preconditions of Miike and subsequent capital accumulation, both companies inevitably had to build their respective production lines from what they had available, for which Korean miners became an indispensable workforce.

UNEVEN DISTRIBUTION OF KOREAN MINERS

Table 4 shows the distribution of Korean miners across the larger mines in Miike and Chikuhō in the late 1920s. As becomes clear from the table, Mitsubishi Kōgyō and Asō Shōten relied on heavily colonial labour, while the Miike Mine employed only 7 Koreans, a negligible number considering that there were over 11,000 workers at this mine (surface and underground combined). Although the table does not include the figures for the Mitsui Kōzan mines in Chikuhō (Tagawa and Yamano), it is likely that the percentages of Koreans there were equally negligible.

The virtual absence of Korean miners at the Mitsui Kōzan mines was the consequence of the company's guiding precept, *Seihyō-Shugi*. In an overview of its fifty-year history, Mitsui Kōzan itself defined the ideal labourer – *Seihyō* (elite troop) – as somebody with a "trustworthy personality, sound thought, and strong body".[25] Korean miners apparently did not fit this criterion. According to the company's own historical overview, Mitsui Kōzan first recruited 102 Korean miners in 1917 at its Kawakami Mine in South Sakhalin, then part of Japan's colonial empire along with the Korean peninsula (see Figure 1). This resulted in a series of conflicts, including a massive brawl with Japanese miners. Adding to the worries of the company were the language barrier and the apparently high illiteracy rate among Koreans, which in its view hampered the Koreans' "working efficiency". Following these experiences and the principle of *Seihyō-Shugi*, Mitsui Kōzan thus decided not to employ colonial workers

---

Miike Mine monopolized the demand for labour and might not have had to compete with other mines by raising wages.

25. Mitsui Kōzan, *Gojūnen-shi Kō, 10hen, Rōmu* [Draft of 50-Year History of Mitsui Kōzan, X, Labour Management] (Tokyo, 1943), p. 147. Since this document was prepared in 1943, it is not certain whether the term *Seihyō-Shugi* had already been used in the late 1910s. Although it might have been retrospectively defined, we use the term to characterize Mitsui's discriminative management policy also in the 1910s and 1920s.

Table 4. *Korean miners in some major mines in Miike and Chikuhō, March 1928.*

Company	Mine	All miners Total	Korean miners Underground	Surface
Miike				
Mitsui	Miike	11,136*	5	2
Chikuhō				
Mitsui	Tagawa	7,156*	[n.a.]	[n.a.]
	Yamano	3,650*	[n.a.]	[n.a.]
Mitsubishi	Kamiyamada	2,657	218	121
	Namazuta	4,543	1,494	244
	Shinnyū	2,846	873	71
	Hōjō	2,746	392	21
Asō	Yoshio	2,995	48	90
	Yoshikuma	1,614	96	[n.a.]
	Tsunawake	983	110	16
Kaijima	Ōnoura	9,512	58	154
Nakajima	Iizuka	5,801	1,687	81

*These figures refer to the number of workers at the respective mines for the whole of 1928, while all other figures indicate the numbers during March of the same year.
Sources: Fukuoka Chihō Shokugyō Shōkai Jimukyoku [Fukuoka Employment Bureau], *Kanai Zaijū Chōsenjin Rōdō Jijō* [Working Conditions of Korean Workers in Fukuoka] (Fukuoka, 1930), pp. 83–89, available at the Digital Library from the Meiji Era, http://kindai.ndl.go.jp/, last accessed 15 June 2015; Yutaka Nishinarita, "Sekitan Kōgyō no Gijutsu Kakushin to Joshi Rōdō" [Technological Development and Female Labour in the Coal Industry], in Nakamura Masanori (ed.), *Gijutsu Kakushin to Joshi Rōdō* [Technological Development and Female Labour] (Tokyo, 1985), pp. 71–105; Mitsui Kōzan, *Gojūnen-shi Kō.*

any more (a policy that, in any case, was altered in the late 1930s when the Japanese war effort intensified).[26]

Obviously, *Seihyō-Shugi* was a racially ethnically discriminative precept, deeming all Korean miners "unproductive". Leaving its discriminatory aspect aside, however, what made *Seihyō-Shugi* possible in the first place? What deserves attention here are both the preconditions and the effects of this policy. Mitsui Kōzan fully understood that the Korean workers could have become an immediately available and cheap workforce, as their recruitment fee was also lower. Moreover, in the company's view, they adapted more easily to bad working conditions compared with Japanese miners.[27] Still, the company considered relying on Japanese miners, "unsophisticated peasants", or skilled coal hewers a better employment

26. *Ibid.*, p. 47.
27. *Ibid.*

strategy, although this was more expensive. It is clear that this policy of ethnic homogenization of the workforce and its benefits were made possible by the company's preconditions at Miike and resulting capital accumulation, enough to recruit "elite troops".

In order to measure the capital accumulation and corresponding productivity, the Mitsui Yamano Mine and some Mitsubishi mines in Chikuhō will provide a useful contrast here. As already indicated in Table 3, the Yamano Mine was the least productive among the Mitsui Kōzan mines in Chikuhō in 1912. Still, Table 5 shows that the Yamano Mine managed to increase its coal output from 373,629 tons in 1916 to 453,029 tons in 1920 in response to the swelling demand for coal due to World War I. During the same period, as evident from the same table, the output from the Namazuta Mine, one of the most mechanized Mitsubishi Kōgyō mines in the late 1910s, increased only from 449,331 tons to 470,504 tons. Therefore, despite the low productivity earlier in the decade, the Yamano Mine was able to catch up quickly with one of Mitsubishi's most industrialized mines by 1920.

As the Yamano Mine then still heavily relied on manual labour, this growth in production must have involved securing more underground pit workers.[28] Wage thereby becomes the indicator of how successful their recruitment was. As Table 5 shows, while the price of rice – a metonym for the miners' standard of living – was rising, the Yamano Mine increased wages for their miners during the period: from 0.79 yen in 1916 to 2.53 yen in 1920, consistently higher than the average wage in Chikuhō. Accordingly, the total number of workers also increased, from 3,410 in 1917, to 4,423 in 1919 and 4,750 in 1920.[29] This makes a good contrast with the Mitsubishi Kōgyō Shinnyū Mine. Although by the mid-1910s the Shinnyū Mine offered the highest wages among the Mitsubishi mines in Chikuhō, the average wage remained lower than that paid by the Yamano Mine. Moreover, while the difference in wages between the two mines was not large in 1916, it became more pronounced in the period leading up to 1920. These comparisons seem to indicate that the expansion of production as well as the recruitment and retention of an ethnically homogeneous labour force at the Mitsui Kōzan mines was perhaps realized more smoothly through higher wages.

Although we do not have much data on the wages of workers at Mitsubishi Kōgyō, this comparison with Mitsui Kōzan at least allows a glimpse of their productivity and employment conditions. Judging from their wages (Table 5), we can surmise that the company must have been less

---

28. The Tagawa Mine (Mitsui Kōzan) and the Namazuta Mine (Mitsubishi Kōgyō) had already introduced the coal cutter in 1917. See Yoshihiro Ogino, *Chikuhō Tankō Rōshi Kankeishi* [History of Labour Relations in Chikuhō Coalmines] (Tokyo, 1993), p. 144.
29. Mitsui Kōzan, *Gojūnen-shi Kō.*

Table 5. *Productions, value, and wages at mines of Mitsui, Mitsubishi, and Asō.**

Company	Mines		1916	1917	1918	1919	1920	1925	1926	1928	1930
Mitsui	Miike	Total output (tons)	1,898,192	2,007,934	1,885,881	1,970,266	1,932,798	2,152,771	2,810,529	2,355,513	2,269,485
		Total value (yen)	8,963,467	13,045,367	22,700,893	32,845,139	35,306,376	20,986,849	20,474,377	22,721,475	18,673,132
		Average wages (yen)	0.76	0.89	1.27	2.15	2.80	2.53	2.59	2.84	3.04
	Tagawa	Total output (tons)	973,571	988,464	886,526	927,819	986,583	1,047,179	1,019,156	1,116,937	1,039,353
		Total value (yen)†	4,201,206	6,440,731	10,219,879	14,335,762	16,954,619	9,657,247	8,929,372	9,880,330	7,665,115
		Average wages (yen)	0.85	1.19	1.85	2.35	2.51	2.02	2.03	2.33	2.33
	Yamano	Total output (tons)	373,629	406,289	409,438	396,699	453,029	586,407	596,800	586,511	533,972
		Total value (yen)	1,037,241	1,924,189	3,600,665	5,307,001	6,070,581	4,368,875	4,424,376	4,488,768	3,148,149
		Average wages (yen)	0.79	1.15	1.69	2.19	2.53	2.29	2.3	2.34	2.24
Mitsubishi	Shinnyū	Total output (tons)	385,434	364,779	351,314	397,046	373,747	555,491	574,929	432,270	409,476
		Total value (yen)	1,330,768	1,850,750	3,659,854	5,974,378	5,632,923	4,523,644	4,577,145	3,403,570	2,604,127
		Average wages (yen)‡	0.74	1.04	1.34	–	2.35	1.56	1.18	–	2.24
	Kamiyamada	Total output (tons)	184,626	165,185	169,689	199,388	211,650	276,841	276,572	363,604	322,083
		Total value (yen)	641,747	854,520	1,749,806	3,025,357	3,278,008	2,119,848	2,141,129	2,904,399	2,052,646
		Average wages (yen)	–	0.92	–	–	–	1.78	–	–	–
	Namazuta	Total output (tons)	449,331	442,117	475,067	461,939	470,504	615,409	606,150	739,173	604,399
		Total value (yen)	1,587,860	2,376,388	5,202,670	7,318,585	7,638,911	4,765,994	4,579,086	5,860,095	4,025,848
		Average wages (yen)	–	0.95	–	–	–	1.75	–	2.07	–
Asō	Tsunawake	Total output (tons)	79,619	119,350	143,952	137,821	128,599	251,488	284,031	297,349	281,878
		Total value (yen)	251,982	589,551	1,479,278	1,964,032	1,800,649	1,821,557	1,986,437	2,049,550	1,531,901
		Average wages (yen)	–	1.18	–	–	–	1.78	1.80	–	–
	Yoshio	Total output (tons)	269,936	300,741	295,829	260,970	236,254	259,661	260,098	302,920	322,608
		Total value (yen)	741,853	1,284,758	2,830,505	3,572,883	3,161,819	3,476,692	1,831,618	2,134,592	1,788,931
		Average wages (yen)	–	1.04	–	–	–	1.64	–	1.52	–
Average daily wages for a miner in Chikuhō (yen)#			0.74	1.07	1.55	2.31	2.47	1.91	1.84	2.28	2.01
Average price of rice (yen/shō)§§			0.13	0.19	0.3	0.43	0.44	0.42	0.42	0.32	0.27

* All wages, values, and prices are nominal. Unless otherwise noted, the average wages indicate the daily average wages among both coal hewers/haulers and male/female miners.

† The figure for 1920 is the total sales price for the amount of coal (1,002,366 tons) sold at market.

‡ The average for 1925 was for the whole mine, while the remaining averages were the wages at the mine's Pit No.1. The figure for 1926 was calculated in the following way: the average monthly wage for male miners (23.62 yen)/the estimated average number of working days in a month (20 days) = 1.18 yen.

The figure for 1926 was taken from *Chikuhō Tankō Rōdō Jijō*. For the remaining years, we follow the hypothesis put forward by Ogino (1993): Ogino considers the average wages at the Ōnoura Mine's Sugamuta Pit, which was owned by Kaijima & Co, to be the average wages for a miner in Chikuhō. For the figures for 1925, 1928, and 1930 we took the average wage for the whole Ōnoura Mine. For 1928 we added the highest wage and the lowest wage for male and female miners, and divided the figure by four.

§ Again following Ogino, these figures are the average price of rice at Moji in Fukuoka, taken from *Fukuoka-ken Tōkeisho* [Statistical Report for Fukuoka]. We calculated the average price of rice (yen/shō) as follows: the average price of rice (yen/koku) / 100 (shō/koku). Miners are believed to have consumed up to 1 shō (c.1.6 kg) of rice a day.

Sources: Shōkōshō Kōzankyoku [The Mining Division of the Ministry of Commerce and Industry], *Honpō Kōgyō no Sūsei* [Current State of the Mining Industry in Japan], available at http://www.meti.go.jp/statistics/tyo/honpouko/tokei.html, last accessed 15 June 2015; Nōshōmushō Kōzankyoku/Shōkōshō Kōzankyoku [The Mining Division of the Ministry of Agriculture and Commerce/Commerce and Industry], *Honpō Jūyō Kōzan Gairan* [List of Important Mines in Japan], available at the Digital Library from the Meiji Era, http://kindai.ndl.go.jp/, last accessed 24 July 2015; Yoshihiro Ogino, *Chikuhō Tankō Rōshi Kankei-shi* [The History of Industrial Relations in the Chikuhō Coalmine] (Fukuoka, 1993), ch. 2; Mitsui Kōzan, *Gojūnen-shi Kō*, and *idem*, *Mitsui Tagawa Kōgyōsho Enkaku-shi* [History of the Tagawa Mine] (Tokyo, 1943); Osaka Chihō Shokugyō Shōkaijo Jimukyoku [Osaka Employment Bureau], *Chikuhō Tankō Rōdō Jijō* [Working Conditions in the Chikuhō Coalmine] (Osaka, 1926), available at the Digital Library from the Meiji Era, http://kindai.ndl.go.jp/, last accessed 15 June 2015; *Fukuoka-ken Tōkei-sho* [Statistical Report for Fukuoka], available at the Fukuoka Data Web, http://www.pref.fukuoka.lg.jp/dataweb/nenkan-pdf.html#M14, last accessed 24 July 2015; Nobuo Ayukawa, "Senkanki no Chikuhō Shotankō niokeru Kōfu Tōkatsu – Nayaseido kara Chokkatsuseido e" [The Management of Coalminers in Chikuhō during the Interwar Period – From the Naya System to Direct Employment System]", in *Chōsa to Kenkyū: Keizaironsō Bessatsu* [Survey and Research: Economic Theory Collection Special Issue] (1997), XII, pp. 10–26.

successful in securing labour throughout the 1910s, especially compared with Mitsui Kōzan. The labour shortage must have been a serious issue, especially when demand for coal began to soar in 1916. It is thus not surprising that the company began recruiting Korean workers on a large scale precisely during this period.

At the end of June 1917 the Mitsubishi Kōgyō Kamiyamada Mine recruited just over 200 Korean miners to supplement the existing workforce. According to a government survey at the time, there were 1,825 miners, underground and surface included, working at the mine in 1917.[30] In previous years, the mine had apparently been running at an economic loss, which explains why the average wage for a pit worker was one of the lowest among the Mitsubishi mines.[31] In fact, while the value of total output from the Kamiyamada Mine was increasing, due to rising coal prices, the actual output of coal declined, from 184,626 tons in 1916 to 165,185 tons in 1917 (see Table 5). This indicates that the mine had insufficient capital to offer higher wages, and accordingly that there were not enough miners to sustain production. The Korean workers seem to have come in the midst of this crisis and, notably, the mine's output began to recover in the following years, rising from 169,689 tons in 1918 to 211,650 tons in 1920. Although the deployment of Koreans was probably not the only reason, their labour, however transitory, must have served in the recovery, as a "colonial gift".

In fact, in September 1917, the Kamiyamada Mine was indicted by a court for imposing a sanction on twenty-five "abductors", who had kidnapped [mostly] Korean miners from them.[32] The incident indirectly reveals how desperately the mine needed these migrant workers and how jealously the company tried to retain them. Subsequently, at the beginning of the following year, Mitsubishi Kōgyō applied for permission to recruit more Korean workers for the Namazuta Mine and Shinnyū Mine from the South Gyeongsang province as well as from the South Chungcheong province in Korea (see Figure 1). The Korean workers were recruited to keep the mine's production in pace with the increasing demand for coal – quite similar to how convict workers had been mobilized to assist the mechanization process at the Miike Mine a few decades earlier. Table 5 further shows that, even after 1920, wages at the Mitsubishi Kōgyō mines, especially those like the Shinnyū Mine which depended heavily on Korean workers, remained low. In other words, Mitsubishi Kōgyō must have been less successful than Mitsui Kōzan in securing its workforce during this period.

---

30. See Chikuhō Sekitan Kōgyō-shi Nenpyō Hensan Iinkai, *Chikuhō sekitan kōgyō-shi nenpyō*, p. 281, and Nōshōmu Shō Kōzan Kyoku [Mining Division of the Ministry of Agriculture and Commerce], *Honpō Jūyō Kōzan Yōran* [List of Important Mines in Japan] (Tokyo, 1918), p. 907.
31. Hatakeyama, *Kindai Nihon no Kyodai Keiei*, p. 23.
32. Chikuhō Sekitan Kōgyō-shi Nenpyō Hensan Iinkai, *Chikuhō Sekitan Kōgyō-shi Nenpyō*, p. 283.

As far as Asō Shōten is concerned, we do not have enough documentation to demonstrate when and under what circumstances Asō Shōten began recruiting Korean labourers to their respective mines.[33] Although the company was historically notorious for uncompromisingly low wages – it was often referred to as the "despotic mine" (*assei no yama*) – Table 5 surprisingly shows that the wages in its Yoshio Mine and Tsunawake Mine were not drastically lower than those at the mines owned by Mitsui Kōzan in the late 1910s.[34] However, neither coal output nor the corresponding value of the coal produced at the two mines increased as much as they did at Mitsui or Mitsubishi. Moreover, as indicated in Table 5, average wages at the Asō mines dropped below the average at Chikuhō, almost the lowest among the three companies by the late 1920s, at which point Asō Shōten was already relying on Korean miners. It is highly probable that the company, much more than Mitsubishi Kōgyō, suffered from labour shortages in those years, and that the availability of Korean labour was a matter of life and death for the survival of their mines.

In sum, the colonial surplus population remained a vital source of labour throughout the 1920s at the lower-wage mines of Asō Shōten and the Mitsubishi Kōgyō. The existing scholarship problematizes the way in which these companies took advantage of the "ethnic difference" and exploited Korean miners as a cheap workforce. Yet, as Donald Smith writes, it is hard to track down exact figures for the wages of Korean miners during the interwar period, largely because of the scarcity of archival sources.[35] What can be said, based on the information available, is that the labour of the colonial miners enabled Asō Shōten and Mitsubishi Kōgyō to manage their mines without drastically increasing wages and helped these companies to keep wages down even for the Japanese miners. In that sense, the Korean immigrant miners played a role similar to that of the convict workers at Mitsui Kōzan in the late 1890s.

CONCLUSION

As the annexation of Korea in 1910 further reconfigured the economic structure of the then agrarian countryside of the Korean peninsula, many impoverished peasants lost their lands. Those peasants became a colonial surplus population in need of jobs to sustain their lives. Just as, a few decades earlier, the legal system had provided Mitsui Kōzan with an allotment of convict workers, colonialism in effect produced a vast pool of

---

33. According to Yasuto Takeuchi, several sources indicate that the company first used Korean miners in the late 1910s; Takeuchi, *Chōsa: Chōsenjin Kyōsei Rōdō*, I, p. 181.
34. Eidai Hayashi, *Chikuhō Gunkanjima: Chōsenjin Kyōsei Renkō, Sonogo* [Chikuhō and Gunkanjima: The Forced Recruitment of Koreans, and After] (Fukuoka, 2011), p. 53.
35. Smith, "Ethnicity, Class and Gender in the Mines", p. 69.

immediately available labour with a low recruitment fee.[36] For companies such as Mitsubishi Kōgyō and Asō Shōten, the Korean surplus population was a colonial gift they could not resist.

In our view, the uneven distribution of the Korean workforce in Chikuhō during the colonial period was related to the "monopolization" of convict workers at Miike a few decades earlier. The unevenness reveals the ways in which companies capitalized on respective preconditions and their effect on employment strategies. Such an analysis could potentially be expanded to include other companies or coalfields in Japan itself, such as Ishikari (Hokkaidō) and Nishisonogi (Nagasaki), but also in Japan's former colonies (for example, South Sakhalin or Manchuria).

From the late 1920s the companies initiated, under the banner of a "rationalization policy" (*gōrika seisaku*), a reduction of the workforce and a mechanization of the mining process by introducing, for example, the coal cutter and the conveyor belt. The chronic economic recession of this period urged the companies to carry out this rationalization process. While replacing the labour of underground workers with machinery, in 1930 Mitsui Kōzan decided to impose a "ban" on the use of female pit miners, along with the remaining convict workers. Senior workers, long-time employees, and high-wage earners were also fired. Instead, the company kept only the core workforce (*chūken rōdōsha*) – "robust healthy [male] workers in their 20s and 30s" – and thus further solidified the principle of *Seihyō-Shugi* by homogenizing the workers in relation to age and gender.[37]

At the Mitsubishi Kōgyō mines, too, many Korean workers were discharged, beginning in the late 1920s, due to the recession.[38] Although we cannot investigate here in depth what was at work in these layoffs, through this policy Mitsubishi Kōgyō established its own version of *Seihyō-Shugi*; it proved how disposable immigrant labour was in the face of socio-economic troubles. Although their wages were most likely the lowest, the company, by discharging them, could save the jobs for Japanese miners – the "elite troops" who were becoming militant during the recession.

Thus, each company had – though in different ways according to the moment, the circumstances, and its own possibilities – ways to secure a reserve of a particular type of workforce; defining them by criminality, gender, ethnicity, nationality, or age and, depending on the amount of their capital accumulation, these companies sought to construct alterity through those distinctions to establish considerable wage differentials. Although the economic benefits of this constellation were important, over time the

36. For further information on the recruitment of Korean workers, see Kawashima, *The Proletarian Gamble*, pp. 28–43.
37. Mitsui Bunko, *Mitsui Jigyō-shi* [History of the Mitsui Enterprise], III, pt. 2 (Tokyo, 1994), p. 95.
38. Smith, "Ethnicity, Class and Gender in the Mines", p. 119.

companies tended to dispose of these "non-elite" groups of workers and to replace them with a more homogenized workforce (male, young, Japanese) – sometimes accompanied by a rhetoric of miners as vanguard workers. Thus, both the evolving logic of capital accumulation and the circumstances (infrastructure, economic situation, state policy, workers' resistance) saw companies making, at given moments, different valuations and subsequent adjustments in relation to the workforce composition.

IRSH 60 (2015), Special Issue, pp. 145–164 doi:10.1017/S002085901500036X
© 2015 Internationaal Instituut voor Sociale Geschiedenis

The Dynamics of Race and Ethnicity in the US Coal Industry

JOE WILLIAM TROTTER, JR

*Center for Africanamerican Urban Studies and the Economy (CAUSE),
Department of History, Carnegie Mellon University
5000 Forbes Avenue, Baker Hall 240, Pittsburgh, PA 15213, USA*

E-mail: trotter@andrew.cmu.edu

ABSTRACT: By the turn of the twenty-first century, scholars had transformed our understanding of class, race, and ethnicity in the rise and demise of the US coal industry. Under the twin impact of the modern Black Freedom Movement and the rise of the New Labor History, studies of American labor and race relations fragmented during the late twentieth century. Following the lead of pioneering labor historian Herbert Gutman, one influential body of scholarship resuscitated the early history of the United Mine Workers of America and accented the emergence of remarkable forms of labor solidarity across the color line during the industrial era. Before this scholarship could gain a firm footing in the historiography of labor and working-class history, however, social activist and labor scholar Herbert Hill forcefully argued that emerging emphases on interracial working-class cooperation downplayed the persistence of racial divisions even during the most promising episodes of labor unity. In significant ways, the Hill–Gutman debate fueled the florescence of whiteness studies and the myriad ways that both capital and labor benefitted from a racially stratified workforce. Based upon this rapidly expanding historiography of coalminers in America, this essay explores how the overlapping experiences of black and white miners established the foundation for modes of cooperation as well as conflict, but the persistence of white supremacist ideology and social practices repeatedly undermined sometimes heroic movements to bridge the chasm between black and white workers.

During the late twentieth century, a variety of studies transformed our knowledge of class, race, and ethnicity in the development of the US coal industry from its dramatic expansion after the Civil War through its rapid demise in the years after World War II. As early as 1968, social and labor historian Herbert Gutman urged scholars of the US working class to focus attention on the largely hidden history of interracial solidarity in the coal industry, particularly the role of the United Mine Workers of America (UMWA). In a variety of coalmining strikes in the northern and southern coalfields, including West Virginia and Alabama, Gutman underscored the emergence of unity among black and white miners. He also insisted that such actions represented viable alternatives to the system of ethnic and racial stratification in the workforce and community life of coalmining towns.[1]

A plethora of studies soon followed Gutman's lead.[2] These studies accented the occasions when class solidarity, spurred by the organizing activities of the UMWA, submerged the color line and challenged the authority of coalmine operators. Before such understandings of interracial solidarity in coalminers' lives and struggles could take hold, labor analyst Herbert Hill offered a stinging critique of the shortcomings of research inspired by Gutman's agenda for a new history of coalminers. Hill underscored the persistence of racial hostility within the coalmining workforce as well as the union despite moments of substantial evidence of unity across the color line.[3]

At about the same time, historian David Roediger and others produced studies emphasizing the salience of "white privilege". The notion of white privilege incorporated workers as well as elites across all sectors of the American economy, society, and politics, including the coercive powers of the state.[4] Partly under the impact of Hill's critique and the emergence of "whiteness" scholarship, a fresh wave of studies offered increasingly complicated portraits of labor relations in the coalfields of industrial America. By the turn of the twenty-first century such studies largely rejected scholarly inquiries into "relations between black and white workers as either harmonious or antagonistic".[5] Contemporary scholarship

1. Herbert Gutman, "The Negro and the United Mine Workers of America: The Career and Letters of Richard L. Davis and Something of their Meaning, 1890–1900", in Julius Jacobson (ed.), *The Negro and the American Labor Movement* (Garden City, NY, 1968), pp. 49–127. Reprinted in Herbert Gutman, *Work, Culture, and Society in Industrializing America: Essays in American Working-Class and Social History* (New York, 1976), pp. 121–208.

2. Early studies following Gutman's lead include: David A. Corbin, *Life, Work, and Rebellion in the Coal Fields: The Southern West Virginia Miners, 1880–1922* (Urbana, IL, 1981); Paul Worthman, "Black Workers and Labor Unions in Birmingham, Alabama, 1897–1904", *Labor History*, 10 (1969), pp. 375–407; Stephen Brier, "Interracial Organizing in the West Virginia Coal Industry: The Participation of Black Mine Workers in the Knights of Labor and the United Mine Workers, 1880–1894", and Daniel P. Jordan, "The Mingo War: Labor Violence in the Southern West Virginia Coal Fields, 1919–1922", both in Gary M. Fink and Merl E. Reed (eds), *Essays in Southern Labor History* (Westport, CT, 1977), pp. 18–43, and 102–143.

3. Herbert Hill, "Myth-Making as Labor History: Herbert Gutman and the United Mine Workers of America", *International Journal of Politics, Culture, and Society*, 2 (1988), pp. 132–200; Nell Irvin Painter, "The New Labor History and the Historical Moment", *International Journal of Politics, Culture, and Society*, 2 (1989), pp. 367–370.

4. David Roediger, "History Making and Politics", *International Journal of Politics, Culture, and Society*, 2 (1989), pp. 371–372; idem, *The Wages of Whiteness: Race and the Making of the American Working Class* (London, 1991); Peter Kolchin, "Whiteness Studies: The New History of Race in America", *Journal of American History*, 89 (2002), pp. 154–173; Eric Arnesen, "Whiteness and the Historians' Imagination", *International Labor and Working Class History*, 60 (2001), pp. 3–32; and responses to Arnesen's essay by James Barrett and others, *ibid.*, pp. 33–80.

5. Daniel Letwin, *The Challenge of Interracial Unionism: Alabama Coal Miners, 1878–1921* (Chapel Hill, NC, 1998), p. 6. For more examples of studies in this vein see Karin A. Shapiro,

underscores the distinctive experiences of each group; it acknowledges deep cleavages along the color line; and it notes how the rigors of life and labor in the coal industry (including the ongoing alliance of capital with the military might of the state) nonetheless helped to create a work culture and politics that cut across racial and ethnic divisions.

Drawing upon this expanding body of recent scholarship on the coal industry as well as upon my own earlier research on coalminers in southern West Virginia, this essay addresses a series of debates in the historiography of coalminers in America. First and most important, it confronts the class–race debate ignited by Herbert Hill when he challenged Gutman's interpretation of labor and race relations in the US coal industry. This article reinforces Hill's emphasis on the deep racial divide in both the coalmining workforce and the union, but it also accents the powerful role that the UMWA played in galvanizing interracial unity compared with other industrial unions such as the steelworkers and meatpackers at the time.

While this article identifies the color line as the most enduring and pronounced division among coalminers in industrial America, it rejects the conclusion that the entrenched racial hostility of white workers, employers, and the state largely obliterated the influence of black miners over their own lives. On the contrary, African-American miners forged a variety of strategies for shaping their own experience in the coalfields. Their efforts included the construction of their own coalmining communities as well as membership in the UMWA when and where possible. In other words, despite powerful recent critiques decrying the limits of an entire generation of scholarship accenting the self-activities of poor and working-class people,[6] this essay underscores the need for ongoing if more nuanced treatments of this indelible thread in black workers' culture and politics.

Black miners' history was by no means as uniform or monolithic as sometimes suggested in labor and working-class studies. In addition to highlighting the "agency" of black workers, this study addresses questions of variation across regions as well as time in the lives of black no less than white miners. African Americans first entered the coalfields as enslaved people before the Civil War. In the wake of emancipation, they encountered intense labor exploitation and inequality in the Alabama fields, a measure of

---

A New South Rebellion: The Battle against Convict Labor in the Tennessee Coalfields, 1871–1896 (Chapel Hill, NC, 1998); Brian Kelly, *Race, Class, and Power in the Alabama Coalfields, 1908–21* (Urbana, IL, 2001); Ronald L. Lewis, *Black Coal Miners in America: Race, Class and Community Conflict, 1780–1980* (Lexington, KY, 1987); Crandall A. Shifflett, *Coal Towns: Life, Work, and Culture in Company Towns of Southern Appalachia, 1880–1960* (Knoxville, TN, 1991); Joe William Trotter, Jr, *Coal, Class, and Color: Blacks in Southern West Virginia, 1915–1932* (Urbana, IL, 1990).

6. For a provocative critique of this notion see Walter Johnson, "On Agency", *Journal of Social History*, 37 (2003), pp. 113–124.

equality in southern West Virginia, and a pattern of stiff resistance and exclusion in Pennsylvania, Ohio, and Illinois.

Finally, this essay calls attention to the ethnic fragmentation of the immigrant and American-born white coalmining workforce. Before the gradual emergence of the UMWA, substantial conflict characterized the life and labor even of English-speaking miners. Until the 1960s, however, a voluminous immigration historiography tended to homogenize the experiences of diverse immigrant groups from the British Isles – English, Scottish, and Welsh, although not of the Irish. According to this body of scholarship, British migrants were "absorbed into the general mass of native [American] citizens", and largely lost their identity "almost immediately". It was the arrival of "new immigrants" from southern, central, and eastern Europe that touched off virulent relations among white workers.[7]

During the late twentieth century, immigration historians shifted their attention away from a preoccupation with the "assimilation" of migrants and immigrants into the established culture, politics, and society of the United States. New research focused on conflict and the persistence of old-world forms of politics and institutions in the rapidly industrializing nation.[8] In sum, informed by these larger currents in US labor, ethnic, and social history, this essay explores the numerous ways that perceived ethnic and racial differences shaped miners' experiences, while emphasizing the distinctive history of African-American coalminers and their communities based upon the pervasive ideology and practices of white supremacy.

WHITE MINERS' ETHNICITY, CONFLICT, AND SOLIDARITY

During the antebellum years, the US coal industry gradually developed on the basis of British immigrant miners in the anthracite district of Pennsylvania. By the 1840s, some 6,800 coalminers produced nearly 2 million tons of coal in the United States. In the antebellum South, namely Virginia and Alabama, enslaved African-American workers supplemented the early white

---

7. John J. Bukowczyk, "Introduction, Forum: Thomas and Znaniecki's *The Polish Peasant in Europe and America*", *Journal of American Ethnic History*, 16 (1996), pp. 3–15; Ronald L. Lewis, *Welsh Americans: A History of Assimilation in the Coalfields* (Chapel Hill, NC, 2008), p. 4. For helpful theoretical and empirical assessments of assimilationist theory, see also, respectively, Alice O'Connor, *Poverty Knowledge: Social Science, Social Policy, and the Poor in Twentieth-Century US History* (Princeton, NJ, 2001), and Mildred A. Beik, *The Miners of Windber: The Struggles of New Immigrants for Unionization, 1890s–1930s* (University Park, PA, 1996).

8. Jon Gjerde, "New Growth on Old Vines – The State of the Field: The Social History of Immigration to and Ethnicity in the United States", *Journal of American Ethnic History*, 18 (1999), pp. 40–65. For an initial synthesis of this scholarship, see John Bodnar, *The Transplanted: A History of Immigrants in Urban America* (Bloomington, IN, 1985).

coalmining workforce.[9] Following the American Civil War, the US coal industry dramatically expanded. In the eastern Pennsylvania anthracite region alone, coal production rose from 13 million tons in 1870 to 54 million tons in 1910. At the same time, the anthracite coalmining workforce increased from 36,000 to over 140,000 miners. In addition to American-born migrants from nearby farms and rural settlements, immigrants from England, Scotland, Wales, and Ireland dominated the early postbellum coalmining workforce.[10]

Nationality, race, and ethnic differences produced significant levels of economic competition, as well as social and political conflict in the US coal industry. While diverse English-speaking immigrants from the British Isles and their American-born counterparts would soon develop forms of solidarity that mitigated their differences, this outcome was by no means a foregone conclusion. In the Mahoning Valley region of Ohio, the Welsh not only spoke their own language, they also "conducted their union meetings entirely in Welsh". In 1874, according to an Illinois miner, each ethnic group forged its own separate institutional and community life: "The English have the St Georges, the Scotch the St Andrews, the Welsh the S. David's, and the Irish the St Patrick's."[11]

Despite evidence of nationality and ethnic conflicts in the early postbellum coalfields of the United States, British- and American-born miners soon developed bonds of solidarity in their escalating encounters with the owners of the coalmines. During the final decades of the nineteenth century, they forged a collective identity around their work in the mines, partly honed in the fires of British collieries before migration to America. In 1871 John Hall, an English-born miner, underscored the link between his work as a miner in the United States and his home in England. "I am a miner [...]. I was a miner in the old country, from which I migrated in 1848. I have mined coal in Pennsylvania and also western Virginia. I began mining work when eight years old."[12]

British miners viewed themselves as fiercely "proud", "literate", and "skilled" craftsmen. They also described themselves as "experienced" and independent "contractors, not mere wage earners". In his groundbreaking study of Welsh miners in the US, historian Ronald Lewis provides a close and detailed transnational portrait of how the British miners "transferred their scientific knowledge of underground mining to America as well as

9. Priscilla Long, *Where the Sun Never Shines: A History of America's Bloody Coal Industry* (New York, 1989), pp. 3–5, and 19–23. See also Ronald L. Lewis, *Coal, Iron, and Slaves: Industrial Slavery in Maryland and Virginia, 1715–1865* (Westport, CT, 1979); Robert S. Starobin, *Industrial Slavery in the Old South* (New York, 1970).

10. Long, *Where the Sun Never Shines*, pp. 3–5, and 56–57.

11. Lewis, *Welsh Americans*, pp. ix–x, and 1–9.

12. *Ibid.*, pp. 51–90; John Hall is quoted from Long, *Where the Sun Never Shines*, p. 7.

their practical skills as craftsmen".[13] Skilled "pick miners", as they were sometimes called, not only exercised considerable control over their own daily production of coal and drove up the cost of their labor, they also largely set their own work schedules. As such, they made decisions, too, about the time devoted to their own leisure, home, business, community, and organized labor activities away from the pits. Indeed, some miners earned enough money to purchase and furnish their own homes.

Until the closing decades of the nineteenth century, English-speaking immigrant and American-born colliers made up the majority of the total coalmining workforce. In addition to pioneering such widely dispersed coalfields as those in the eastern Pennsylvania anthracite district, they initiated coal production in the emerging bituminous coalfields of western Pennsylvania, Ohio, Illinois, and Indiana; the Appalachian South; and the western states of Colorado, Washington, and parts of Wyoming.[14] In the Colorado coalfields, the number of coalminers increased from no more than about 1,500 in 1870 to a peak of nearly 16,000 in 1910. In Colorado and elsewhere, British, Irish, and Welsh miners formed the artisan core of the initial coalmining workforce.[15]

By the turn of the twentieth century, a variety of forces gradually transformed the character of the US coal industry and undercut the pivotal role of English-speaking and American-born white miners within the workforce. In both the anthracite and bituminous coalfields, the British and American-born "aristocrats" of the coalmining workforce confronted increasing challenges to their precarious hegemony. As early as 1890, introduction of the coal-undercutting machine dramatically reduced demand for experienced pick miners and opened the door for the recruitment of a large, ethnically and racially diverse, and less skilled hand-loading workforce. The percentage of the coal mechanically undercut for loading increased to nearly 25 per cent in 1900 and to over 80 per cent by 1930. The new machinery increased the daily output of the individual miner from 2.57 tons in 1891 to 3.71 tons by the beginning of World War I.[16]

---

13. John H.M. Laslett (ed.), *The United Mine Workers of America: A Model of Industrial Solidarity?* (University Park, PA, 1996), p. 14; Lewis, *Welsh Americans*, pp. 59–60, 120–121.

14. John H.M. Laslett, "Introduction: 'A Model of Industrial Solidarity': Interpreting the UMWA's First Hundred Years, 1890–1990", in *idem, The United Mine Workers of America*, pp. 1–25; *idem, Nature's Noblemen: The Fortunes of the Independent Collier in Scotland and the American Midwest, 1855–1889* (Los Angeles, CA, 1983), pp. 1–9; Maier B. Fox, *United We Stand: The United Mine Workers of America 1890–1990* (Washington DC, 1990), pp. 21–23, 56–74, and 82–101; Perry K. Blatz, *Democratic Miners: Work and Labor Relations in the Anthracite Coal Industry, 1875–1925* (Albany, NY, 1994), pp. 1–35.

15. Thomas G. Andrews, *Killing for Coal: America's Deadliest Labor War* (Cambridge, MA, 2008), pp. 95–96, and 102–103.

16. Keith Dix, *What's A Coal Miner to Do? The Mechanization of Coal Mining* (Pittsburgh, PA, 1988), pp. 6–7, 28–32, and 217.

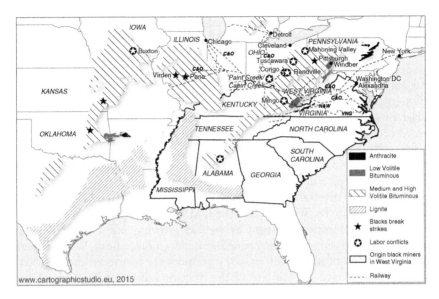

Figure 1. The US coal industry.

Closely intertwined with the expansion of the undercutting machine was massive migration from rural America as well as immigration from eastern, central, and southern Europe to meet the coal industry's growing demand for low-wage hand loaders and general laborers. In rapid succession, operators recruited trainloads of Italian, Slav, Polish, Hungarian, and other new European immigrants for work in the coalmines. Founded in 1897, for example, the coal town of Windber, Pennsylvania, had deep roots in the new immigration. In 1910, according to historian Mildred Beik, four southern, central, and eastern European groups made up nearly 85 per cent of the town's total foreign-born population and about 45 per cent of its total population.[17]

Established British- and American-born English-speaking white miners resisted the impact of both technological changes and massive southern, central, and eastern European immigration on their work, livelihood, and communities in coalmining towns. British colliers not only openly disdained the new workers as "ignorant", untrained miners who threatened their safety underground, they also regarded new immigrant culture,

17. Beik, *The Miners of Windber*, pp. xx–xxx, and 1–51; *idem*, "The UMWA and New Immigrant Miners in Pennsylvania Bituminous: The Case of Windber", and John H.M. Laslett, "'A Parting of the Ways': Immigrant Miners and the Rise of Politically Conscious Trade Unionism in Scotland and the American Midwest, 1865–1924", in Laslett, *The United Mine Workers of America*, pp. 320–325, and 417–437.

work habits, and adherence to Catholicism as a threat to Anglo-Saxon Protestantism. As historian John H.M. Laslett notes, established British colliers responded to the increasing influx of new people with "a mixture of condescension and contempt". In some cases, these workers upped sticks and moved west, describing the new immigrants in nativistic terms as the "Slav invasion". Violence against Slavs by earlier British and particularly Welsh miners resulted in the Latimar Massacre on 10 September 1897, when armed coal company guards murdered nineteen Slav strikers in cold blood in the anthracite coalfields of Pennsylvania.[18]

After a period of intense economic, social, and political resistance to the new immigrants, British colliers gradually accepted Italians, Poles, Slavs, and other immigrants into the United Mine Workers of America (UMWA) union, organized in 1890. By World War I, the UMWA had organized old and new immigrants of European descent as well as growing numbers of African Americans. Following the massacre of Slav miners, noted above, Welsh miners joined their Slav brothers and walked out under the banner of the UMWA. Although challenged by the rise of the militant Industrial Workers of the World (IWW), founded in 1905, the UMWA became the most ethnically and racially diverse union in the US labor movement. While the UMWA faced an ongoing uphill battle against the coal operators' immense capital and police power, as well as struggling for control over company-owned towns, organized miners achieved significant success in the bituminous coalfields of western Pennsylvania, Ohio, Illinois, and Indiana, though they were far less successful in the anthracite fields of eastern Pennsylvania.[19]

Despite the increasing movement of new immigrants into the coalfields as well as into the UMWA, they nonetheless faced stiff barriers breaking into the higher-skilled, managerial, and supervisory jobs both before and after joining the union. They also confronted obstacles, including ethnic segregation in the housing, institutional, cultural, and political life of coalmining towns. At the Windber mines, new immigrants constituted 99 per cent of all miners in 1910, but they made up only about 10 per cent of mine foremen and assistant foremen. Company housing policy also separated English-speaking and earlier immigrant miners from their new immigrant counterparts. At the same time, the Berwind-White Coal Company reinforced the growth of nativist organizations like the Patriotic Order of the Sons of America during the opening decades of the twentieth century and the Ku Klux Klan during the 1920s. Furthermore, English-speaking residents also dominated the town's government, fire, and police departments.[20]

18. Lewis, *Welsh Americans*, pp. 236–237; Blatz, *Democratic Miners*, pp. 55–60.
19. Lewis, *Welsh Americans*, pp. 238–239; Isaac Cohen, "Monopoly, Competition, and Collective Bargaining: Pennsylvania and South Wales Compared", in Laslett, *United Mine Workers of America*, pp. 415–416; Long, *Where the Sun Never Shines*, pp. 248–249, and 321–323.
20. Beik, "The UMWA and New Immigrant Miners in Pennsylvania Bituminous", p. 329.

AFRICAN AMERICANS AND THE LIMITS OF
WORKING-CLASS UNITY

The incorporation of new immigrant miners into the labor movement of coalmining towns produced some (though insufficient) benefits, but it was the color line that emerged as the most salient social division that fragmented the coalmining working class. Nonetheless, similar to the larger US coal industry, the experiences of African-American miners varied considerably from region to region and across time. Distinct patterns of "race, class, and community conflict" emerged in the coalfields of "Deep South" Alabama and the Chesapeake region as well as in the north-east and mid-west.[21] As alluded to above, the first generation of black miners entered the coal industry as enslaved workers in eastern Virginia, the Kanawha Valley, western Virginia, and north-central Alabama. Enslaved antebellum miners gave way in the postbellum years to a predominantly black prison "convict" coalmining labor force on the one hand and a sharply racially stratified free coalmining working class on the other.

Free black miners faced a strictly enforced lower wage rate than white workers. They also encountered discriminatory coal-weighing scales based on race, and a racially exploitative "contract" labor system. In the contract arrangement, regular white coal loaders hired black workers as lowly paid helpers and largely passed on the most arduous work of coalmining labor to their black counterparts. Partly because of this anti-black racial imperative, particularly in the coal strikes of 1894 and 1908, coal operators effectively used the "social-equality" issue as a wedge to divide workers and undermine public support for the union cause. Thus, in the Deep South coalfields, the convict lease system only disappeared during the 1890s and the early twentieth century; and it was not until the 1930s that white workers gradually challenged the "social-equality" notion and forged stronger ties with black miners across the color line.[22]

Whereas black workers confronted extreme forms of exploitation in the Alabama coal industry, they were largely excluded from the anthracite

---

21. Lewis, *Black Coal Miners in America*, pp. iv–xv.
22. *Ibid.*, pp. viii–xv; Lewis, *Coal, Iron, and Slaves*, pp. 3–10; Letwin, *The Challenge of Interracial Unionism*, pp. 1–30; Kelly, *Race, Class, and Power in the Alabama Coalfields*, pp. 3–15. In her groundbreaking study of resistance against convict labor in Tennessee, historian Karin Shapiro shows how black and white miners forged greater interracial solidarity in the east Tennessee coal towns of Coal Creek, Briceville, and Oliver Springs than they did in the southeastern town of Tracy City. See Shapiro, *A New South Rebellion*, pp. 12–13. Coal companies provided wider screens for weighing coal mined by blacks than they did for whites, thus creating a racial differential in pay. Such practices reinforced the idea that white men were both materially and socially "superior" to black workers. Thus, any evidence of black–white solidarity through labor unions flirted with the idea of social equality of all workers and threatened white-worker privileges such as discriminatory weighing practices. See Lewis, *Black Coal Miners in America*, p. 47.

region of Pennsylvania and only slowly moved into the bituminous fields of western Pennsylvania, Ohio, Illinois, Iowa, and Indiana in small numbers. However, as diverse groups of white miners slowly bridged their differences, created more potent forms of labor solidarity, and walked out on strike for better pay, living, and working conditions in coal towns, northern coal operators turned increasingly to black workers as strikebreakers. Beginning during the 1880s, coal companies regularly imported black workers to break strikes in the Pittsburgh district, the Tuscarawas Valley of Ohio, Virden and Pana in Illinois, and parts of Oklahoma and Kansas. In the small coalmining town of Buxton, Iowa, the coal company imported southern black workers to break the strike among white miners during the 1890s. Blacks soon became the single largest ethnic group in the town's workforce before the town's demise during the 1920s.[23]

In the Pittsburgh district, strikebreaking persisted into the 1920s (including most notably the coal strikes of 1922, 1925, and 1927). Strikebreaking entailed a substantial incidence of violence between striking white workers and African Americans as well as between white workers, company guards, and police. As economists Abram L. Harris and Sterling Spero noted in their historical study, *The Black Worker* (1931), in western Pennsylvania between September 1927 and February 1928 the results of African-American strikebreaking activities "were written largely with violence, bloodshed, loss of life, and the destruction of property". Similar to the earlier reactions of British miners to their southern, central, and eastern European counterparts, old and new white miners of various nationalities and ethnicities treated African-American migrants as a "foreign invasion" of their "homes". During labor disputes, white workers often declared in the face of black workers, "I do not mind the white scab, but I be damned if I will stand for a Negro scab." For their part, black strikebreakers sometimes boldly retorted, "You would not work with me before the strike. Now I have your job and I am going to keep it."[24]

Despite the recurring use of black strikebreakers in the coalfields, the United Mine Workers nonetheless reached out to African Americans and opened its doors to black workers earlier than steel, meatpacking, and other mass production industries. From its founding in 1890, the UMWA pledged "to unite in one organization, regardless of creed, color or nationality, all workmen [...] employed in and around coal mines". Moreover, the union

---

23. Sterling D. Spero and Abram L. Harris, *The Black Worker* (1931; repr. New York, 1968), pp. 210–213; Bruce Nelson, *Divided We Stand: American Workers and the Struggle for Black Equality* (Princeton, NJ, 2002), p. 167; Dorothy Schwieder, Joseph Hraba, and Elmer Schwieder, *Buxton: Work and Racial Equality in a Coal Mining Community* (Ames, IA, 1987), pp. 3–12, 209. See also Dorothy Schwieder, *Black Diamonds: Life and Work in Iowa's Coal Mining Communities, 1895–1925* (Ames, IA, 1983).
24. Spero and Harris, *The Black Worker*, p. 233; Nelson, *Divided We Stand*, p. 167.

sought to insure equality of work opportunities among miners in practice. The UMWA constitution included a clause stating that, "No member in good standing who holds a dues or transfer card shall be debarred or hindered from obtaining work on account of race, creed or nationality." African-American membership in mine unions increased from about 1,000 at the union's founding to about 5,000, before declining during the mid-1920s. Black miners not only joined the union, they participated in large-scale strikes in the northern and southern coalfields, including the bloody confrontations in Alabama in 1908 and West Virginia (particularly the Paint Creek Cabin Creek Strikes of 1912–1913 and the Mingo Coal War of 1921).[25]

Coalminers developed some of the most remarkable episodes of interracial as well as interethnic solidarity in the US labor movement. The UMWA soon employed blacks as union officers, including locals with predominantly immigrant members. African-American facility in English made them preferred representatives in some locals with majority immigrant miners. In 1891, the Rendville, Ohio, miner Richard L. Davis was elected to the executive board of the UMWA District Six (Ohio). He held the Ohio post for six years, and in 1896 and again in 1897 he was elected to the national executive board, the highest position ever held by an African American in the UMWA. Davis's influence was felt at the local, regional, and national levels. He advised miners during bitter industrial disputes in West Virginia, western Pennsylvania, and Alabama as well as Ohio. In 1892, for example, when owners sought to segregate one mine in Rendville by using black laborers exclusively, paying those workers lower wages and forcing them to work under poorer conditions than had been the case in integrated mines, Davis rallied black and white workers against the company's effort to divide workers along racial lines.

In another instance Davis opposed the development of segregationist policies in Congo, Ohio. After calling attention to segregated housing, he observed a similar pattern in the mines and urged an end to such racial stratification. Davis resolutely and consistently opposed exclusionary hiring practices, advocated the election of blacks to leadership positions in the union, and protested white miners' discriminatory attitudes and behavior toward black workers. On one occasion, he rebuked his white counterparts for referring to black men in derogatory language, "I assure anyone that I have more respect for a scab than I have for a person who refers to the negro in such way, and God knows the scab I utterly despise."[26]

25. Spero and Harris, *The Black Worker*, pp. 356–357. See also Letwin, *The Challenge of Interracial Unionism*, pp. 89–123; Corbin, *Life, Work, and Rebellion in the Coal Fields*, pp. 45–46, 65–77, 87–101; Shapiro, *A New South Rebellion*, pp. 31–32, 229–230.
26. Richard L. Davis's coalmining career is well-documented in the columns of the *United Mine Workers' Journal (UMWJ)* and the *National Labor Tribune (NLT)*. See also Gutman, "The Negro and the United Mine Workers of America".

Although the UMWA forged some of the nation's most significant movements for labor solidarity across the color line, it nonetheless failed to stem the development of racially and ethnically divided coalmining towns. Segregated and unequal work, living, family, and community environments greeted black miners across regions and from place to place within the coalfields of the North and South. According to Spero and Harris:

> [...] the most frequent complaint one got from the Negro unionist in the coalfields was his inability to use his union card at some mines where the employment of a Negro had caused the white union miners to strike, or where it was believed by the operators that the employment would cause a strike.

Black miners regularly complained of the union's "inability or unwilling-ness to draw any distinction between the absence of racial discrimination in constitutional principle and the appearance of it in every day fact".[27]

MINING ALONG THE COLOR LINE: THE CASE OF SOUTHERN WEST VIRGINIA[28]

A closer look at the southern West Virginia coalfields reveals both the promise and limits of coalmining work, unionization, and efforts to secure the full emancipation of the black worker during the industrial era of US history. African Americans gained a firmer (but still precarious) footing in the mines of southern West Virginia than they did further south and north. Beginning slowly during the Civil War and early postbellum years, black migration to the Mountain State accelerated during the late nineteenth and early twentieth centuries. Under the impact of the expanding bituminous coal industry, the black population dramatically increased, rising from 25,800 in 1880, to over 64,000 in 1910, and to nearly 115,000 in 1930. At a time when most industrial firms in the nation excluded black workers from employment, both the rail-road and coal industries hired large numbers of African Americans to open up the bituminous coalfields of southern Appalachia. African Americans helped to lay track for the Chesapeake & Ohio, the Norfolk & Western, and the Virginian railway lines. Work on the Chesapeake & Ohio line also produced the black folk hero John Henry. Most important, however, growing numbers of black railroad men remained behind as part of the expanding coalmining labor force. Blacks made up over 20 per cent of West Virginia's total coal-mining labor force from the 1890s through the early twentieth century.[29]

---

27. Spero and Harris, *The Black Worker*, pp. 336–337.
28. For this analysis of coalmining in southern West Virginia, I am indebted to the University of Illinois Press for permission to reprint portions of my book, *Coal, Class, and Color: Blacks in Southern West Virginia, 1915–1932*.
29. James T. Laing, "The Negro Miner in West Virginia" (Ph.D. dissertation, Ohio State University, 1933), pp. 64–69; J.M. Callahan, *Semi-Centennial History of West Virginia*

The nearby states of Virginia, Kentucky, and Tennessee sent the lion's share of black migrants to West Virginia before World War I. During the war and its aftermath, however, rising numbers of black migrants from the Deep South states of Alabama, Georgia, and Mississippi supplanted the Upper South sources of black migrants. Based substantially on the labor of rising numbers of black workers, coal production increased from less than 5 million tons in 1885 to nearly 40 million in the southern counties of the state alone by 1910. Although the industry would experience recurring upswings and downswings in the demand for coal, southern West Virginia mines produced over 120 million tons in 1925.

Important social, cultural, and political factors reinforced the attractiveness of West Virginia as a target of black migrants. Racial lynchings were fewer, educational opportunities were greater, and voting was not restricted by race, unlike elsewhere in the South. Although it frequently overstated the case, during the 1920s the Bureau of Negro Welfare and Statistics (BNWS), a state agency, repeatedly emphasized the political and social attractions of West Virginia.[30]

In addition to the economic conditions from which they came, the recruitment and advertising campaigns of coal companies provided important stimuli to black migration. At the height of World War I, such advertising intensified. Professional labor recruiters for the coal companies encouraged southern blacks to move to the coalfields. Coal companies also enlisted the support of middle-class black leaders. Especially important was the regional black weekly, the *McDowell Times*, which circulated in West Virginia and nearby Virginia. During World War I, the *McDowell Times* editorially proclaimed: "Let millions of Negroes leave the South, it will make conditions better for those who remain."[31] In lengthy articles, the *McDowell Times* celebrated the movement of blacks into the various coal camps, such as Glen White, Raleigh County:

> The old saying that "All roads lead to Rome" surely has its modern analogy [...] "All railroads seem to lead to Glen White" for every train drops its quota of colored folks who are anxious to make their homes in the most beautiful spot in the mining district of West Virginia.[32]

The *McDowell Times* columnist, Ralph W. White, stated simply: "To one and all of them we say WELCOME."[33]

(Charleston, WV, 1913); A.A. Taylor, *The Negro in the Reconstruction of Virginia* (Washington DC, 1926); Corbin, *Life, Work, and Rebellion in the Coal Fields*, ch. 7.

30. West Virginia Bureau of Negro Welfare and Statistics (hereafter, WVBNWS), *Biennial Report* (Charleston, WV, 1921–1922), p. 5, and *Biennial Report* (Charleston, WV, 1925–1926), p. 8.

31. "The Exodus", *McDowell Times*, 18 August 1916. Unless indicated otherwise, none of the newspaper articles quoted here have a specified author.

32. "Southern Exodus in Plain Figures", *McDowell Times*, 1 December 1916.

33. Ralph W. White, "Another Lesson [...]", *McDowell Times*, 20 July 1917. See also "Colored Folks Enjoying Universal Industrial and Social Advancement", *McDowell Times*, 28 July 1917.

Despite the optimistic portrayals of the *McDowell Times*, a substantial degree of private and public coercion underlay the recruitment of black labor. Operators often advanced the migrants transportation fees, housing, and credit at the company store. Using privately employed detectives from Baldwin-Felts, a private agency infamous for its brutal anti-labor activities, some coal operators were notorious for their violent control of black workers.[34] In 1917, the West Virginia legislature enacted a law to "prevent idleness and vagrancy [...] during the war and for six months thereafter. All able bodied men between 18 and 60 years of age, regardless of color, class or income must toil thirty-five hours each week to support themselves and their dependents."[35] Moreover, West Virginia had passed a prohibition law in 1914, and some of the prohibition arrests, convictions, and sentences to hard labor on county road projects were scarcely veiled efforts to discipline and exploit the black labor force. Even the local black weekly soon decried the arrest of what it condescendingly called "a lot of ignorant men and depriving their families of support for months and in some cases years". According to the state commissioner of prohibition, southern West Virginia had the highest incidence of arrests, convictions, and sentences to hard labor on county road projects.[36]

Although some black miners felt the impact of public and private coercion, most migrants chose southern West Virginia voluntarily, using their network of kin and friends to get there. After arriving, they often urged their southern kin and friends to join them. Acute contemporary observers understood the process. In his investigation of the great migration, the US attorney for the Southern District of Alabama reported that at least 10 per cent of those who had left had returned, but half of the returnees had come back for relatives and friends. "It is returned negroes who carry others off."[37]

34. United States Senate Committee on Interstate Commerce, *Conditions in the Coal Fields of Pennsylvania, West Virginia, and Ohio* (Washington DC, 1928). For excerpts from the committee hearings, see *United Mine Workers Journal*, 1 March 1928. See also "Testimony of J.H. Reed", in United States Senate Committee on Education and Labor, *West Virginia Coal Fields* (Washington DC, 1921), pp. 479–482.

35. "Idlers between Ages of Eighteen and Sixty Will Be Forced to Work", *McDowell Recorder*, 25 May 1917. See also T. Edward Hill, "Loafers and Jonahs", *McDowell Times*, 25 May 1917; "Dig Coal or Dig Trenches is the Word to the Miner", *Raleigh Register*, 12 July 1917.

36. Quote from: "Educate All the People", 16 April 1915. See also "To Whom it May Concern", 29 January 1915; "Good People of McDowell County Outraged", 17 May 1918, all in *McDowell Times*; State Commissioner of Prohibition, *Biennial Report* (Charleston, WV, 1921–1922).

37. Robert N. Bell, US Attorney, Northern District of Alabama, to US Attorney General, 25 October 1916; and Alexander D. Pitts, US Attorney, Southern District of Alabama, to Samuel J. Graham, US Assistant Attorney General, 27 October 1916, both in National Archives, Washington DC, Department of Justice, Record Group No. 60, Straight Numerical File No. 182363. See also Otis Trotter, *Keeping Heart: A Memoir of Family Struggle, Race, and Medicine* (Athens, OH, 2015), Introduction; Salem Wooten, interview by author, 25 July 1983;

COAL LOADING

Coal loading was the most common, difficult, and hazardous job in the mine. Yet, black men often preferred it because it paid more than other manual labor jobs and "provided the least supervision with the greatest amount of personal freedom in work hours".[38] As one black miner recalled, coal loaders could make more money because they were paid by the ton, and could increase their wages by increasing their output.[39] On the other hand, while average wage rates for coal loading were indeed higher than those for most outside jobs, inside work was subject to greater seasonal fluctuation and greater health hazards than outside positions.[40] Although coal loading was classified as unskilled work, it did require care and skill. It took over an hour of preparation before the miner could lift his first shovel of coal. The miner deployed an impressive repertoire of skills: the techniques of dynamiting coal, including knowledge of various gases and the principles of ventilation; the establishment of roof supports to prevent dangerous cave-ins; and the persistent canvassing of mines for potential hazards. Referring to the training he received from his brother, Salem Wooten recalled: "The first thing he taught me was [...] my safety, how to set props and posts. Wood posts were set up to keep the slate and rocks from caving in on you [...] safety first."[41]

Wooten's brother also taught him techniques for blasting coal: how to drill holes with an auger and place several sticks of dynamite in them properly; how to judge atmospheric conditions and be accurately sensitive, not only to his own safety, but also to the safety of fellow workers. Salem Wooten also learned the miner's distinctive vocabulary of terms, such as "bug dust", particles of coal remaining after machines undercut the coal; "kettlebottom", a huge fossilized rock, responsible for numerous injuries and even deaths when it dislodged from the roof of mines; and the frequently shouted "Fire! Fire in the Hole!", warning fellow workers of an impending dynamite blast.[42] In small numbers, African Americans also

---

Thelma O. Trotter, conversation with author, 1 August 1983; Solomon Woodson, conversation with author, 9 November 1985.

38. James T. Laing, "The Negro Miner in West Virginia", *Social Forces*, 14 (1936), pp. 416–422, 418.

39. North Dickerson, interview by author, 28 July 1983.

40. Laing, "The Negro Miner" (1936); Dickerson, interview by author, 28 July 1983.

41. Wooten, interview. Similar statements were made in other interviews: Charles T. Harris, interview by author, 18 July 1983; Leonard Davis, interview by author, 28 July 1983; Watt Teal, interview by author, 23 July 1983. For general insight into the miners' work, see Carter Goodrich, *The Miner's Freedom* (1925; repr. New York, 1971), and Keith Dix, *Work Relations in the Coal Industry: The Handloading Era, 1880–1930* (Morgantown, WV, 1977), chs 1 and 2.

42. Wooten, interview. While some scholarly accounts refer to the particles left by the under-cutting machine as "duck dust", black miners used the term "bug dust". See Laing, "The Negro

worked in skilled positions as machine operators, brakemen, and motor-men. Labor advertisements sometimes specified the broad range of jobs available to African Americans: "Coal Miners, Coke Oven Men, Day Laborers, Contract Men and Helpers, Motormen, Track Layers, Machine Runners, Mule Drivers, Power Plant Men, and other good jobs to offer around the mines".[43]

However skillful black loaders may have become, coal loading took its toll on the health of black men. Some men literally broke themselves down loading coal. Pink Henderson painfully recalled:

> My daddy got so he couldn't load coal. He tried to get company work [light labor, often on the outside] but the doctor turned him down, because he couldn't do nothing. He done broke his self down [...] My brothers done the same thing. They used to be the heavy loaders.[44]

Moreover, all coal loaders, black and white, careful and careless, were subject to the inherent dangers of coalmining: black lung, then commonly called "miners' asthma", the slow killer of miners caused by the constant inhalation of coal dust; explosions, the most publicized and dramatic cause of miners' deaths; and slate falls, the largest and most consistent killer of miners. All miners and their families had to learn to live with the fear of death, although few fully succeeded. As one black miner and his wife recalled: "That fear is always there. That fear was there all the time, because [...] you may see [each other] in the morning and never [see each other] any more in the flesh."[45]

Miner" (1933), p. 171; Dix, *What's a Coal Miner to Do?*, ch. 1; and Goodrich, *The Miner's Freedom*, p. xx.

43. For examples of advertisements see: "Safety First"; "Go North"; "Wanted"; "Employment Office"; "Wanted Sullivan Machine Men", *Logan Banner*, 8 June 1923. For African Americans in skilled positions see: interview with William M. Beasley, 26 July 1983; interview with Roy Todd, 18 July 1983; Dix, *Work Relations in the Coal Industry*, ch. 1; Laing, "The Negro Miner" (1933), pp. 264–265; Price V. Fishback, "Employment Conditions of Blacks in the Coal Industry, 1900–1930" (Ph.D. dissertation, University of Washington, 1983), ch. 6.

44. Interview with Pink Henderson, 15 July 1983; interview with Walter and Margaret Moorman, 14 July 1983.

45. Quoted from: Henderson, interview; Walter and Margaret Moorman, interview. See also Fishback, "Employment Conditions", pp. 182–229; Ronald D. Eller, *Miners, Millhands, and Mountaineers: Industrialization of the Appalachian South, 1880–1930* (Knoxville, TN, 1982), pp. 178–182. For recurring reports of black casualties, see "Six Miners Killed in Explosion at Carswell", *Bluefield Daily Telegraph*, 19 July 1919; "Gary (Among the Colored People)", 11 December 1923; "Compensation for Six Injured Miners", 10 December 1923; "Russel Dodson Killed Monday by Slate Fall", 14 July 1925; "Walter McNeil Hurt in Mine", 22 July 1925, all in the *Welch Daily News*; "Negro Miner is Killed at Thorpe", 12 June 1929; "Colored Miner Killed Friday in Slate Fall", 5 March 1930; "McDowell County Continues Out in Front in Mine Fatalities", 24 July 1929; "Negro Miner Electrocuted in Tidewater Mines", 9 October 1929; "Hemphill Colored Miner Killed in Mining Accident", 8 January 1930, all in *McDowell Recorder*.

COMMUNITY, CULTURE, AND POLITICS

Under the impact of the expanding bituminous labor force, increasing numbers of black migrants perceived southern West Virginia as a permanent place to live and work. Coalmining was an overwhelmingly male occupation, with few opportunities for black women outside the home. Yet, black women played a crucial role in the settlement of African Americans in the coalfields. Before migration to southern West Virginia during the war years, Catherine Phillips married John Henry, who worked in a nearby sawmill in rural western Virginia. Catherine raised crops for home consumption, performed regular household chores, and gave birth to at least three of the couple's eight children. In 1917, she took care of the family by herself for several months while John Henry traveled to southern West Virginia, worked in the coalmines, and finally returned for her and the children.[46] Upon arriving in the southern West Virginia coal towns, along with their regular domestic tasks women nearly universally contributed to the diets of their families and the earnings of their men through cultivating, harvesting, and canning the produce of vegetable gardens, including sometimes abundant crops of corn, beans, cabbage, collard, and turnip greens, supplemented by a few hogs, chickens, and sometimes a cow.[47]

As the number of black coalminers and their families expanded, they established their own institutions and launched political movements to secure full citizenship rights and equal treatment in coalmining towns. African Americans developed a variety of class and multi-class institutional and political responses to racial inequality in the Mountain State. While black business and professional men often dominated leadership positions in black institutions, black coalminers, their wives, and other female relatives constituted the core of African-American culture and politics in the region. Predominantly Baptist and African Methodist Episcopal, membership of black religious organizations climbed from less than 15,000 in the pre-World-War-I years to nearly 33,000 in 1926. Membership of black fraternal orders and mutual benefit societies reached similar proportions, about 32,000, before declining during the late 1920s.

The emergence of West Virginia branches and affiliates of the National Association for the Advancement of Colored People (NAACP) and the Universal Negro Improvement Association (i.e. the Garvey Movement), the McDowell County Colored Republican Organization, and the black weekly *McDowell Times* rounded out the institutional life of blacks in West Virginia before the onslaught of the Great Depression. Under the editorship of Matthew Thomas Whittico, a graduate of Lincoln University in

---

46. Lester and Ellen Phillips, interview by author, 20 July 1983.
47. In their book of poetry, the Peters sisters illuminated the role of coalfield women's gardening and household activities. See Peters Sisters, *War Poems* (Beckley, WV, 1919), particularly p. 7.

Pennsylvania, the *McDowell Times* voiced the civil rights struggles of blacks in West Virginia.

Unlike their counterparts in most southern states during the era of Jim Crow, lynchings, and disfranchisement, African Americans in West Virginia not only gained jobs in the region's major industrial sector, they also retained the franchise. Based on the activities of black men and women, elites and workers, African-American political campaigns produced significant results in the Mountain State. Black coalmining communities not only built an alliance with the Republican Party, they also elected their own representatives to state and local offices. In 1918, for example, blacks sent three black men to the legislature: the Charleston attorney T.G. Nutter, the Keystone attorney Harry J. Capehart, and, most significantly, the coalminer John V. Coleman of Fayette County. Black legislators spearheaded passage of a state anti-lynching law, a statute barring the showing of inflammatory films such as *The Birth of a Nation*, and entitlements for the expansion of old and the creation of new social welfare and educational institutions. By 1930, African Americans also claimed access to two state colleges (West Virginia State and Bluefield State); a tuberculosis sanitarium; homes for the deaf, blind, aged, and infirm; schools for delinquent youth; a Bureau of Negro Welfare and Statistics; and an expanding number of public elementary, junior high, and high schools.[48]

THE GREAT DEPRESSION AND AFTER

During the Great Depression of the 1930s, blacks shouldered a disproportionate share of the unemployment and hard times. Their percentage in West Virginia's coalmining labor force dropped from over 22 per cent in 1930 to about 17 per cent in 1940. The depression and World War II also unleashed new technological and social forces that transformed the coal industry, and stimulated massive out-migration in the postwar years. Loading machines rapidly displaced miners during the 1940s and 1950s. Black miners recall that the mine management always put the loading machines first where blacks were working.[49]

Mechanization further decimated the black coalmining labor force. The percentage of black miners in West Virginia dropped steadily to about 12 per cent in 1950, 6.6 per cent in 1960, and to 5.2 per cent in 1970. By 1980, African Americans made up less than 3 per cent of the state's coalminers. To be sure, the white labor force had also declined, dropping by nearly 36 per cent, but the numbers of black miners had declined by

---

48. Joe Trotter, "Introduction: African Americans in West Virginia", in A.B. Caldwell, *History of the Negro: West Virginia Edition* (Morgantown, WV, 2012), pp. xvi–xvii.
49. Lewis, *Black Coal Miners in America*, p. 170.

over 90 per cent. Under the leadership of John L. Lewis, the United Mine Workers of America adopted a policy on technological change that reinforced the unequal impact of mechanization on black workers. As Lewis put it, "Shut down 4,000 coalmines, force 200,000 miners into other industries, and the coal problem will settle itself."[50]

As West Virginia's black coalmining labor force declined, racial discrimination persisted in all facets of life in the Mountain State. In 1961, according to the West Virginia Human Rights Commission, most of the state's public accommodations – restaurants, motels, hotels, swimming pools, and medical facilities – discriminated against blacks. Most importantly, as blacks lost coalmining jobs, they found few alternative employment opportunities. The state's Human Rights Commission reported that, "Numerous factories, department stores, and smaller private firms had obvious, if unwritten, policies whereby blacks were not hired or promoted to jobs of importance or positions in which they would have day-to-day contact with white clientele."[51]

Many coalminers and their families moved to the large metropolitan areas of the north-east and mid-west. Small networks of West Virginia blacks emerged in cities such as Cleveland, Chicago, Detroit, and New York. Others moved to the nearby Upper South and border cities of Washington DC, and Alexandria in Virginia. Still others moved as far west as California. Indicative of the rapid outmigration of West Virginia blacks, the state's total African-American population dropped from a peak of 117,700 in 1940 to 65,000 in 1980, a decline from 6 per cent to 3 per cent of the total. The dwindling number of African Americans who stayed behind struggled to maintain black churches, newspapers, and other community-based institutions.

In 1988, the First Baptist Church of Charleston hosted the First Annual Conference on West Virginia's Black History. Spearheaded by the Alliance for the Collection, Preservation, and Dissemination of West Virginia's Black History, subsequent annual conferences have featured a variety of papers, speeches, and comments on the state's black heritage. They have also reflected an enduring commitment to African-American institutions, values, and beliefs in southern West Virginia in particular and West Virginia in general. Mountain State blacks not only struggled to retain their own institutions, they also joined the Miners for Democracy, an interracial rank-and-file movement against the growing anti-democratic impulses within the leadership of the United Mine Workers of America. But the industrial era had slipped away without a viable economic alternative to fill the void left by the departure of "king coal".

---

50. Dix, *What's a Coal Miner to Do?*, p. 160.
51. See Joe William Trotter, Jr, "Historical Afterword", in Ancella R. Bickley and Lynda Ann Ewen (eds), *Memphis Tennessee Garrison: The Remarkable Story of a Black Appalachian Woman* (Athens, OH, 2001), pp. 223–224.

CONCLUSION

Characterized by enduring patterns of class, ethnic, and racial conflict and inequality, the history of the US coal industry represented not one but many stories. The first generation of British and diverse English-speaking miners emerged at the pinnacle of the early coalmining workforce as skilled craftsmen, supervisors, and managers, while the later arrival of new immigrants from southern, central, and eastern Europe entailed an uphill battle breaking into the coal industry, first as coal loaders, and later as supervisory and managerial employees. But it was the color line that defined the staunchest barriers blocking the upward mobility of workers in the US coal industry. Even so, black coalminers' experiences varied from region to region and within the same locale.

Few blacks found jobs in the northern anthracite region and only small numbers entered the bituminous fields of the north and mid-west. By contrast, large numbers of black workers entered the southern Appalachian coalfields of Alabama and West Virginia. In Alabama, many black miners labored as convict workers alongside a free labor force that was itself racially divided between blacks and whites; the latter gained access to a formally instituted wage scale that paid them uniformly higher wages than their black counterparts. In southern West Virginia, black and white workers received the same wage for performing the same work, but Mountain State black miners nonetheless faced ongoing difficulties in using their union card to move around and obtain work during downturns in the coal economy.

Despite important regional and subregional differences in the coal industry, African-American coalminers not only joined the UMWA, they also forged their own communities in the face of different levels of economic inequality, institutional segregation, and discrimination. These highly organized black workers' struggles for freedom and equal rights gained their greatest expression in the southern Appalachian coalfields, but they also characterized life in the northern and midwestern fields. In the years after World War II, as increasing mechanization and de-industrialization undercut the coal-loading workforce, black coalmining communities declined at a faster rate than their white counterparts. Those who stayed in the coalfields built upon the institutional, political, and cultural foundation established by miners during the industrial era. At the same time, they forged new social struggles within the emerging context of the post-industrial era. How well they ultimately succeed in rebuilding their communities and modes of solidarity is yet to be seen. In that, the color line continues to persist. As in the past, this line is both tenaciously sharp and, at the same time, varyingly dotted.

IRSH 60 (2015), Special Issue, pp. 165–183 doi:10.1017/S0020859015000371
© 2015 Internationaal Instituut voor Sociale Geschiedenis

European Workers in Brazilian Coalmining, Rio Grande do Sul, 1850–1950

C L A R I C E   G O N T A R S K I   S P E R A N Z A

Pelotas Federal University
Rua Cel. Alberto Rosa 154, Pelotas, Rio Grande do Sul, Brazil

E-mail: clarice.speranza@gmail.com

ABSTRACT: Coalmining in Brazil began in the mid-nineteenth century in the municipality of São Jerônimo, Rio Grande do Sul, the country's southernmost state. European workers were brought in and joined Brazilian workers, mostly local peasants with no experience in mining. This article discusses the role played by the immigrants in the making of a working class in the coalfields of southern Brazil. The research on which this article is based draws on numerous sources, including lawsuits and the application forms used to request professional licences. It focuses on ethnic and racial ambiguity, and on political strategies. The identity of the miners in the region is commonly represented as an amalgam of all ethnic groups, but this article shows that this self-propagated solidarity and cohesion among workers had its limits.

In the Brazilian city of Arroio dos Ratos, on a small hill surrounded by wooden houses and cobblestone streets, a bronze, slightly larger-than-life statue of a coalminer, wearing ankle-length trousers, an undershirt, a cap, and bearing a haversack, symbolizes the greatest pride of this small town of 13,000 inhabitants. The monument was inaugurated by the local city council in 1974, during the Brazilian military dictatorship (1964–1984), to glorify local workers, who, according to the bronze plaque at the foot of the statue, had done such "fruitful work during a century of coal extraction, for the sake of the wealth and progress of this region and of the country".[1]

The statue evokes a distant past of wealth and struggle in Arroio dos Ratos. Coalmining in Brazil started in this area in the nineteenth century, with the country's first coalmine; it subsequently also saw the construction of the country's first coal-fired power plant. This coalmining was concentrated in just a few towns, including Arroio dos Ratos and Butiá, all in the former municipality of São Jerônimo. By 1943, when coal production in the region peaked, there were over 7,000 workers in the mines. Today,

---

1. All translations from the Portuguese are mine.

some coalmining in a few opencast pits continues in neighboring towns, but the Arroio dos Ratos mines are exhausted, and former underground mines in the region are now used for purposes considered less noble: to store the domestic garbage produced by the 1.4 million inhabitants of the nearby city of Porto Alegre, capital of Rio Grande do Sul, the southernmost state of Brazil.

The statue represents the miner as a proud, but at the same time humble, worker. He seems calm and obedient, but also courageous; he is a hero. What is more, the coalminer's identity prevails over all other ethnic, racial, and cultural identities; he is an amalgam of them all. As with all stereotypes, this representation obscures differences and tensions among the diverse groups of workers who had arrived at the mines in Rio Grande do Sul in waves.

Contrary to the established image of harmony and assimilation, the construction of the working class in these mining localities started from the initial exclusion of the locally available workforce – referred to in Brazil as *trabalhadores nacionais*,[2] or "national workers" – who were generally viewed as incapable and indolent. From the start, European workers were recruited, many of them, but not all, experienced miners. These workers had to face appalling working conditions and authoritarian working relations inherited from centuries of slavery in the country. Because of the specific characteristics of underground coalmining, immigrants started to interact with laborers from diverse origins, generating conflicts but also solidarity among them.

European newcomers to Brazil were generally valued, not only because of their expertise, but especially as promoters of the "whitening" of Brazilian society.[3] In a country where "work" was associated with slavery and the Afro-Brazilian population, those workers had to differentiate

2. This expression has different meanings according to the historical context. In the late nineteenth century it referred to the "national element" (born in Brazil, generally of mixed race or former slaves), always viewed unfavorably compared with immigrants. By the 1930s and 1940s, "national worker" had more positive connotations, and was increasingly used in the context of a state policy that aimed at controlling and incorporating immigrants into the "national element" through repression and acculturation. Currently, the expression "national worker" is most commonly used in economic and demographic research as meaning available labor in Brazil (irrespective of where people are born). On discussions of the "national element", see Manoel Luís Salgado Guimarães, "Nação e Civilização nos Trópicos: o Instituto Histórico e Geográfico Brasileiro e o projeto de uma história nacional", *Estudos Históricos*, 1 (1988), pp. 5–27. On the policy of "nationalizing" immigrants, see Giralda Seyferth, "Os imigrantes e a campanha de nacionalização do Estado Novo", in Dulce Pandolfi (ed.), *Repensando o Estado Novo* (Rio de Janeiro, 1999), pp. 199–228.

3. On whitening policies in Brazil, see Thomas Skidmore, *Black into White: Race and Nationality in Brazilian Thought* (Durham, NC, 1993), as well as Lilia Moritz Schwarcz, *The Spectacle of the Races: Scientists, Institutions, and the Race Question in Brazil, 1870–1930* (New York, 1999), and Andreas Hofbauer, *Uma história de branqueamento ou o negro em questão* (São Paulo, 2006).

themselves from people of African or mixed descent, with whom they often worked side by side.

This article seeks to understand the part played by European workers in the making of a working class in the coalfields of southern Brazil between 1850 and 1950 by looking at their role in social practices and coalminers' struggles. How did they relate to other groups and identities in southern Brazil's mining population in this period? As in other mining societies, as Stefan Berger has pointed out, the Brazilian coalfields were characterized by an intense "ideas interchange" among different nationalities of workers, which "led to the selective appropriation of 'foreign' models by indigenous societies".[4] For copper mining in Chile, Thomas Klubock observes that "the structures of feeling and political culture of the community were composed by often competing and contrasting ideological formations and by interpenetration of both class and non-class discourses and practices".[5]

Characteristics pertinent to mining work in general were, of course, also present in Brazil, such as intensive work, dangerous and unhealthy working conditions, large mining companies, company villages, strict control of work and family life, political activism, and solidarity. The peculiarity and wealth of experience of the Brazilian miners, however, resided in the fact that their working community was created in a cultural context marked by ethnic and racial ambiguity. In Brazil the "mixing of races" is considered a primordial value in defining national identity, but racism is as much denied as it is present.

COALMINING IN RIO GRANDE DO SUL

The coal outcrops in southernmost Brazil were discovered in the late eighteenth century but remained unexplored until the mid-nineteenth century. Located at the border with Uruguay and Argentina, the province of Rio Grande do Sul was one of the last territories of Brazil to be populated. In the south of the region, bordering Uruguay, large farmers raised livestock on extensive landholdings. In the north, colonies of immigrants, who had started to arrive from Germany and Italy around 1835, owned smaller properties. These immigrants were involved in agriculture and commercial activities, but often lived a culturally isolated life.

Rio Grande do Sul is a border region and in preceding centuries had been the location of several wars with the *platinos* countries of Uruguay,

---

4. Stefan Berger, "Introduction", in Stefan Berger, Andy Croll, and Norman LaPorte (eds), *Towards a Comparative History of Coalfield Societies* (London, 2005), pp. 1–11, 4.
5. Thomas Miller Klubock, *Contested Communities: Class, Gender, and Politics in Chile's El Teniente Copper Mine, 1904–1951* (Durham, NC, 1998), p. 6.

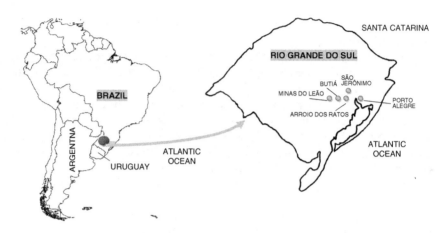

Figure 1. Coal extraction in Rio Grande do Sul (to 1950).

Argentina, and Paraguay. Its indigenous population had been practically decimated, or mixed with immigrants from the São Paulo region, other Latin American countries, Portugal, and Spain. A beef jerky (dried meat) industry had prospered in the first half of the nineteenth century. It was based on slave labor and had generated a concentration of Afro-Brazilians, especially around the city of Pelotas.[6]

The coalmining region is located in the centre of the state, near its capital Porto Alegre (Figure 1). Before the mines were opened the area was sparsely populated by subsistence farmers of mixed descent. Around 1889 new immigrant colonies were created in the region of Barão do Triunfo, within the municipality of São Jerônimo, with German, Italian, and Spanish immigrants. This diversity was not accidental: "there was a prevalence of favoring mixture, to avoid the potential formation of racial and national minority communities".[7]

It was a British miner, James Johnson, who first introduced excavation techniques and established a coalmining enterprise in the region in the mid-nineteenth century. Born in Cornwall and brought to Brazil by a Brazilian aristocrat, Johnson encouraged British investment in coalmining in Brazil.[8] After discovering coal seams in Rio Grande do Sul and in the neighboring region of Santa Catarina, he started exploration himself.

---

6. For a general overview of the region's history see Sandra Pesavento, *História do Rio Grande do Sul* (Porto Alegre, 1997); Fábio Kuhn, *Breve história do Rio Grande do Sul* (Porto Alegre, 2011).
7. Carlos Alfredo Simch, *Monografia de São Jerônimo* (Porto Alegre, 1961), p. 97.
8. Mário Belolli, Joice Quadros, and Ayser Guidi, *História do carvão de Santa Catarina* (Florianópolis, 2002), p. 35.

In 1853, Johnson brought ten to twelve families of miners from Wales to work in the first coalmine.

The president of the province of Rio Grande do Sul, Cansação de Sinimbu, subsequently put Johnson in charge of all local coal extraction.[9] Mine operations were still extremely primitive. Coal was transported in horse-drawn wagons or shipped on waterways to the centre of the town of São Jerônimo, and later to Porto Alegre. In 1866 the regional government granted Johnson and a Brazilian associate the right to explore the area of Arroio dos Ratos. In the following years, Johnson returned to London, where he succeeded in raising the capital he needed to start a mining company. The Brazilian Imperial Collieries Company Limited was created in 1872 and built a railroad connecting the coalfield to São Jerônimo town. This first initiative soon backfired, however: Johnson's company went bankrupt the following year.

A subsequent company, Holtzweissig & Co., brought workers and tools from Europe,[10] using German capital, but it, too, failed. In 1883 it was succeeded by the Companhia das Minas de Carvão de Pedra de Arroio dos Ratos, the first with Brazilian capital. After the collapse of the Brazilian monarchy and the advent of the republic in 1889, the company changed its name to Companhia Estrada de Ferro e Minas de São Jerônimo (CEFMSJ).

In the 1930s coalmines in the region started to expand vigorously, supported strongly by tax incentives granted by the federal government. In 1932, an important Brazilian group took ownership of all Arroio dos Ratos and Butiá coalfields (exploited since 1906 in a rudimentary way) and began to explore them more intensively through the Carbonífera Riograndense. The founding of the Consórcio Administrador das Empresas de Mineração (Cadem) in 1936 paved the way to further growth. After Cadem had merged with CEFMSJ and the Carbonífera Riograndense, it virtually monopolized Brazilian production until 1945. In the 1930s and 1940s the mining villages of Arroio dos Ratos and Butiá grew in size and became more urbanized, under the watchful eye of these mining companies. From cemetery to police department, from grocery store to cinema, everything depended on or was controlled by Cadem. From 1932 to 1939 the region produced 82 per cent of all coal mined in Brazil.[11] In 1936, as part of the nationalist policies of the first presidency of Getúlio Vargas (1930–1945), a federal decree increased the minimum consumption of Brazilian coal in the country from 10 to 20 per cent. Production at Rio Grande do Sul's

9. E.S. Eugenio Dahne, *A mineração de carvão e as concessões da Companhia no estado do Rio Grande do Sul – Brazil* (Porto Alegre, 1893), p. 8.
10. *Ibid.*, p. 9.
11. Ministério das Relações Exteriores (Brazil), *Brazil 1940/41: An Economic, Social and Geographic Survey* (Rio de Janeiro, 1941), pp. 271–272.

coalmines peaked in 1943, when 1.34 million tons of coal were mined there (around 65 per cent of all Brazilian coal production).[12]

After World War II, oil began to replace coal, and demand for coal decreased. In 1947 the state created a publically owned coal company. After a few years, Santa Catarina, a state neighboring Rio Grande do Sul, took over as the country's leading coal-producing state, producing coal more suitable for use in steel mills. The underground mines in Rio Grande do Sul were decommissioned in the first few years of the twenty-first century. Today, there is only surface mining in a few cities in the state (Butiá, Charqueadas, Cachoeira do Sul, Candiota, and Minas do Leão). They are exploited by Copelmi (formerly Cadem) and Companhia Riograndense de Mineração (a publically owned company).

EUROPEAN IMMIGRATION, MINING SKILLS, AND THE "WHITENING" OF THE LABOR FORCE

Coalmining demanded a large workforce. Faced with this challenge, in 1889 CEFMSJ agreed with the government to establish five settlements in the region, each with 1,000 workers, to provide dwellings for the workers to be recruited for the coalmines. These would come from Europe, from the remaining Portuguese or Spanish colonial possessions,[13] or from other Brazilian regions, in a proportion of 80 per cent "foreigners" to 20 per cent "nationals". As a consequence, a large number of immigrants were engaged, both in agriculture and coal extraction. In exchange, the government awarded the company a range of benefits, such as public lands and tax reductions.[14]

The immigrant miners initially enjoyed some advantages owing to their skills. In 1892, CEFMSJ management justified a wage increase by the difficulty of "finding in the land practical miners for the service".[15] Foreign miners were seen as potential instructors to the locals, and were always considered superior to the local population – who were not even considered "workers". To the government, employers guaranteed that they would bring to Brazil only miners "selected on the basis of their qualifications and morality, whose teaching and example has already formed local people who once lived in inactivity".[16]

---

12. Clarice Gontarski Speranza, *Cavando direitos: as leis Trabalhistas e os conflitos entre os mineiros de carvão e seus patrões no Rio Grande do Sul (1940–1954)* (Porto Alegre, 2014), pp. 50–51.

13. The intention of the company, expressed in the text of the agreement, seems contradictory to the general Brazilian policy which encouraged European immigration and tried to prevent the arrival of immigrants from other world regions, especially from Asia and Africa, where there were numerous Portuguese colonies. Whatever the intentions of the company, there is no evidence of mineworkers from any region other than Europe.

14. Dahne, *A mineração*, p. 53.

15. *Ibid.*, p. 89.

16. *Ibid.*, p. 98.

The beginnings of coalmining in Brazil coincided with the onset of industrialization in the country. This was a particularly significant moment in Brazil's labor relations, marked by a reconfiguration of the working classes after the abolition of African slavery in 1888, and the rise of pro-immigration policies. It is impossible to talk about labor in Brazil without referring to the enduring role of slavery in the country. Brazil was the most important destination for African slaves in the Americas, with an estimated 5.5 million people brought from Africa between 1550 and 1866,[17] and it was the last country in the Americas to abolish slavery. At the same time, the Brazilian slave system showed high numbers of manumissions, especially in the nineteenth century. Free and slave labor coexisted throughout the nineteenth century, and there was significant mobility between slavery and freedom. While manumissions were frequent, freedom was precarious and re-enslavement common. In 1872, of Brazil's 9.93 million inhabitants 58 per cent were Afro-descendants (*preto*, or *pardo*), totalling 5.76 million people. Of this total, 1.51 million were slaves and 4.25 million were free (either because they had obtained freedom for themselves or because they were descendants of former slaves).[18]

In the years before the abolition of slavery, the Brazilian elite began to defend the idea that black people had been "corrupted" by slavery, a logic sustained by a eugenic discourse. Political measures were taken to promote racial "whitening". European immigrants, considered synonymous with "white people", became the workers of preference for the fledgling industry. European immigration was encouraged, while immigration from Africa, the Middle East, or Asia was severely repressed.[19] Although slaves had never been deployed in the coalmines, social relations in the region cannot be understood without taking the prevalent cultural perspective of that period into account, which regarded the "white" (equated to European) population as superior to the native mixed population.

Among the various nationalities arriving at the Brazilian coalfields, the Spaniards were the most numerous. The largest influx of Spaniards to Brazil was from 1891 to 1920, when over 431,609 immigrants arrived from Spain. Brazil had established a recruiting office in Malaga in 1896.[20] In the 1920

---

17. Based on http://www.slavevoyages.org/tast/assessment/estimates.faces, accessed 31 December 2014.

18. *Censo Demográfico 1872*. http://www.nphed.cedeplar.ufmg.br/pop72/index.html, accessed 31 December 2014. On manumissions see, for example, Sidney Chalhoub, "The Precariousness of Freedom in a Slave Society (Brazil in the Nineteenth Century)", *International Review of Social History*, 56 (2011), pp. 405–439; Robert Slenes, "A 'Great Arch' Descending: Manumission Rates, Subaltern Social Mobility, and the Identities of Enslaved, Freeborn, and Freed Blacks in Southeastern Brazil, 1719–1888", in John Gledhill and Patience Schell (eds), *New Approaches to Resistance in Brazil and Mexico* (Durham, NC, 2012), pp. 100–118.

19. Skidmore, *Black into White*; Jeffrey Lesser, *Immigration, Ethnicity, and National Identity in Brazil, 1808 to the Present* (New York, 2013), pp. 60–88.

20. *Ibid.*, pp. 108–110.

Brazilian census, the town of São Jerônimo was listed as the third most important destination for Spanish immigrants in Rio Grande do Sul, after the state's capital Porto Alegre and the industrial centres of Rio Grande and Pelotas. São Jerônimo had a population of 22,719, with 1,318 foreigners. With 504 Spaniards, almost 10 per cent of all Spanish immigrants were concentrated in Rio Grande do Sul.[21]

A sample based on files of requests for professional licences in Rio Grande do Sul between 1933 and 1943 shows the predominance of Spaniards among immigrant coalminers (see Table 1).[22] The thirty-nine files relating to immigrant miners in São Jerônimo contain data from the following countries: Spain (15); Poland (6); Portugal (4); Uruguay (4); Lithuania/Russia (4); Germany (2); Austria (1); Romania (1); Czechoslovakia (1); Hungary (1). Although these data should be viewed with caution,[23] they indicate that several Spanish workers came from traditional coalmining towns in northern Spain (Ourense, Leon, Lugo), or from near Leon and Asturias,[24] which suggests that they were skilled workers. Most of them had arrived between 1910 and 1920, aged between twenty and thirty. The presence of children points to family migration. After 1920 the arrival of Polish, Russian, and Lithuanian immigrants became more common. The proximity of the Uruguayan border explains the presence of Uruguayans from the border towns of Rivera and Treinta y Tres.

---

21. I am grateful to Regina Weber (Universidade Federal do Rio Grande do Sul) for allowing me to use these data, which she has compiled in the context of her research project "Spaniards in Southern Brazil: Immigration and Ethnicity".

22. In 1932 the Brazilian government created the professional licence (*carteira profissional*), a booklet recording data on the identity of the individual worker and on his professional life. Such licences were not new, but they had previously been issued by unions and associations. The new licences enabled Getúlio Vargas's government to gain more effective control of information on workers. The licence was issued by the regional labor departments on request for workers aged over sixteen who worked in commerce and industry. The licence application forms contained questions on, for example, name, place and date of birth, skin color, nationality of spouse, number of children, name of employer, position held, and wages (after 1944). The regional labor departments (Delegacia Regional do Trabalho, DRT) were government agencies responsible for issuing the professional licences in each state; until 1940 the agencies were called regional labor inspectorates (Inspetoria Regional do Trabalho). The DRT archive contains around 627,200 application forms for professional licences in Rio Grande do Sul, dating from 1932 onward. They are held by the Historical Documentation Centre (Núcleo de Documentação Histórica) at Pelotas Federal University (UFPel) (hereafter, DRT-NDH/UFPel). Data taken from documents dated between 1932 and 1943 have already been processed to a digital database.

23. The files for the period 1933 to 1943 have been only partially preserved (about 25 per cent of all licences issued during the period in Rio Grande do Sul). Furthermore, professional licences were not mandatory at that time, and workers had to pay for them. Nevertheless, many workers and unions chose to promote the licences, because the documents were seen as a way of ensuring the effective implementation of labor legislation (such as the Vacation Law). The professional licence, or Carteira de Trabalho e da Previdência Social is still in use today in Brazil.

24. For an account of the politically highly contentious history of coalmining in Asturias, see Adrian Shubert, *The Road to Revolution in Spain: The Coal Miners of Asturias, 1860–1934* (Urbana, IL, 1987).

Table 1. *Sample of foreign coalminers in Rio Grande do Sul, 1933–1943*

Country/city of birth	Year of arrival	Age on arrival	Number of children	Age at registration	Year of registration
Spain					
Tudela de Navarra	1899	23	0	61	1937
Lugo	1908	8	3	34	1934
Ourense	1910	20	2	43	1933
Rodelas	1912	20	2	42	1934
Ourense	1913	20	0	44	1937
No information	1913	24	6	53	1942
Brollon	1914	29	2	49	1934
Leon	1917	21	4	38	1934
Ourense	1925	15	0	25	1935
Almeria	1927	19	1	27	1935
Cotova (Córdoba?)	1928	25	0	31	1934
Melon	1928	18	0	25	1935
Barcelona	1929	34	0	42	1937
Cristina	1929	26	0	31	1934
Ourense	1936	33	0	34	1937
Poland					
Opole	1912	17	4	40	1935
Plonia	1927	23	0	30	1934
Ulów	1929	23	2	28	1934
No information	1929	26	2	32	1935
Zakopane	1938	53	3	56	1941
Unknown	Unknown	–	0	20	1942
Portugal					
Villa da Feira	1905	11	5	40	1934
Coimbra	1913	3	1	24	1934
Pinheiro Novo	1913	23	5	44	1934
Unknown	1939	27	0	27	1939
Russia					
Marijampolė (now Lithuania)	1922	21	2	33	1934
Unknown	1923	35	1	48	1936
Kaukas (Kaunas?) (Lithuania)	1929	27	0	32	1934
Germany					
Unknown	1891	2	6	45	1934
Lehne (Lehnstedt?)	1927	28	0	36	1935
Austria					
Hulweis (?)	1913	19	0	41	1935
Hungary					
Badonos (?)	1924	27	3	37	1934
Lithuania					
Tanlichen (Šalčininkai?)	1928	18	0	25	1935
Czechoslovakia					
Unknown	1927	20	0	28	1935
Romania					
Kiseenev (Kishinev?) (now Moldova)	1924	26	1	36	1934
Uruguay					
Rivera	1909	4	1	28	1933
Treinta y Tres	1910	9	1	33	1934
Rivera	1921	26	3	39	1934
Unknown	Unknown	–	0	28	1933

Source: Author's survey created from a database based on files at the Regional Labor Department (Delegacia Regional do Trabalho), DRT-NDH/UFPel. The forms were apparently completed by Brazilian officials on the basis of information given orally by workers. Foreign languages were usually "translated" according to Portuguese orthography, and in some cases it is difficult to identify the city of origin.

As the years went by, expertise and skill became less important as a reason for recruiting immigrants. Attracted by advantages such as low-priced housing, electric lighting, medical assistance, education, and salaries higher than those in agriculture, many inhabitants of nearby immigrant colonies or local rural workers began to seek employment in the mines. The arrival of workers from Europe after 1935 had the goal of replacing striking workers, often summarily dismissed. Immigration was also considered a strategy to cope with high turnover and mortality rates.

After World War II, Brazilian mining companies started to recruit workers from European countries affected by the war. In 1945, for example, Cadem asked the Brazilian federal government to permit 500 Poles to enter Brazil who apparently wished to leave Poland following the Soviet occupation of their country. A director of one coalmining company contacted a Polish troop commander in London, trying to attract former Polish soldiers to the Brazilian mines. In the following years, many Poles, Ukrainians, and Yugoslavs would arrive in order to work in the Brazilian coalfields.[25]

STRIKES AND RIOTS

European immigrants faced a harsh life and poor working conditions in Brazil. Rioting in response to working conditions was serious and frequent throughout the country. The exhausting work, carried out in such a cramped underground environment, with high rates of disease and workplace accidents, combined with low wages, were the main reasons for this disaffection. Because of these low wages, double or even triple shifts were common among the miners – the fact that this practice was called *doble* (the Portuguese word *duplo* was never used) is an indication of Spanish influence in work practices.

The first miners' strike in Brazil occurred in 1895. A group of twenty European workers from the nearby immigrant colonies of Jaguari and Lucena[26] were the leaders of the movement. "They were workers, *but* socialists",[27] said a CEFMSJ report, adding:

> [...] desiring to earn too much quickly, and always disaffected, they completely disorganized the service. Whenever national staff were recruited, they took the opportunity to compel the manager to increase the prices paid per ton of coal

25. Marta Cioccari, "Do gosto da mina, do jogo e da revolta: um estudo antropológico sobre a construção da honra numa comunidade de mineiros de carvão" (Ph.D. dissertation, Rio de Janeiro, Museu Nacional, 2010), p. 109.
26. The Lucena settlement was located in the north of Santa Catarina, a state (at that time, province) neighboring Rio Grande do Sul. It was founded between 1890 and 1891 with British, Polish, and Russian immigrants. The Jaguari settlement, consisting mostly of Italians, Poles, and Germans, was established in 1889 and was located in the mid-west of Rio Grande do Sul (in what today is the municipality of Jaguari).
27. My italics.

mined, and the wages of all staff. By the end of 1893, when our staff had been recruited for the third time, we had to pay them 1$200 *réis* per ton and 8$000 *réis* per square metre of underground gallery in the *Fé* coal pit.[28]

The report mentions earlier episodes of repeated mobilization among miners under European immigrant leadership. Apparently, disaffection peaked in June 1895, when the strike began, with massive support from Brazilian workers, including children and older miners:

[...] on 1 May, they presented new demands, organizing marches with red-coloured flags and anarchist demonstrations, and in early June they recruited all our national miners, train drivers and locomotive stokers, blacksmiths, carpenters, national and foreigner employees, including old people and 13-year-old boys. They took horses, mules, and carts from the company. When they were alone in the field, they declared they would not work anymore and would not allow any employee to work without a raise of 25 per cent! So they remained on strike for over 15 days.

This strike occurred during the final days of the Federalist Revolution.[29] That "national" workers, engaged in this revolution, apparently also supported the strike seems to have alarmed employers. Consequently, "at this dangerous moment, the manager decided to pay the most quarrelsome workers [their remaining salaries] and lay them off", the company report said. The report also expressed concern among employers about European miners and their integration in Brazil: "From this fact, we learned that immigrant miners are socialists expelled from the coalfields in Europe, because miners in Europe are well-paid workers, surrounded by comforts and only expatriate themselves spontaneously if attracted by greater advantages than those in their home country". At least four other strikes before 1934 pointed to the growing organization among miners and their dissatisfaction with working conditions and wages.[30]

Little by little, from the beginning of the twentieth century the positive view of immigrants began to change. Both in the mines and in the country as a whole, Europeans began to be seen not only as useful trainers of local labor

---

28. São Jerônimo Railroad Company and Coalfield Report, regular session 1895 (Rio de Janeiro, Jornal do Brasil, 1895), pp. 12–13, Rio Grande do Sul State Museum of Coal Archive. The following quotations are from the same document. The *réis* was Brazil's currency from 1833 to 1942. Due to devaluation, the *mil-réis* (Rs 1$000) became the common basic currency unit in the second half of the nineteenth century. In 1942 the *réis* was replaced by the *cruzeiro* (Cr$).

29. The Federalist Revolution was a bloody civil war (which left an estimated 10,000 dead) fought in Rio Grande do Sul in 1893. See Joseph Love, *Rio Grande do Sul and Brazilian Regionalism, 1882–1930* (Chicago, IL, 1971); Luiz Alberto Grijó, *Capítulos da História do Rio Grande do Sul* (Porto Alegre, 2004).

30. On the strikes in the 1930s see Felipe Figueiró Klovan, "Sob o fardo do ouro negro: as experiências de exploração e resistência dos mineiros de carvão do Rio Grande do Sul na década de 1930" (M.A. thesis in history, UFRGS/PPG, 2014).

but also as dangerous elements that could menace discipline at work. Between 1907 and 1921 several laws were passed allowing for the deportation of foreign workers involved in riots. The legislation also allowed for the dissolution of any union-type group performing actions considered harmful to public order. In 1931 a law was issued that prescribed a mandatory proportion of two-thirds native Brazilians to one-third immigrants for employment in industry. In the late 1930s, during the Estado Novo dictatorship (1937–1945), ethnic community building was forbidden so as to promote assimilation and ethnic mixing as an expression of Brazilian nationality.[31]

Because of repression by the mining companies and the intense control of workers and their families, it was only in 1934, long after the first clashes mentioned above, that a miners' union could officially be founded.[32] Before, workers were forced to meet secretly in the woods at night, hiding from the company's management. In later interviews retired miners commented on the decisive importance of Spanish workers in this organization.[33] In fact, the union's first president was Deotino Rodrigues, who had been born in Ourense (Spain) and migrated to Brazil in 1910 at the age of twenty.

The miners' union did not restrict membership by ethnicity or nationality. Nonetheless, many of its leaders were from Europe. In 1937, for example, among the eighteen union leaders laid off because of a mobilization three years earlier, five had surnames denoting a European origin or ancestry (Wodacik, Caldellas, Martinez, Covales, and Splanick).[34] It is noteworthy that the most popular miners' leader, Manoel Jover Telles, was the son of Spanish migrants. He led strikes during the Estado Novo dictatorship (1937–1945), was elected to parliament in 1947, and was an important leader of the Brazilian Communist Party from the 1950s to the 1970s. His father, Jeronimo, had come from Linares, an Andalusian town in Spain, settling first in São Paulo before moving to Rio Grande do Sul in the early 1920s. Like Asturias, Andalusia had a strong mining tradition, with a powerful anarchist and socialist movement. In spite of his Brazilian nationality, one of the nicknames given to Jover Telles was "Spanish prince".[35]

31. Endrica Geraldo, "O 'perigo alienígena': política imigratória e pensamento racial no governo Vargas (1930–1945)" (Ph.D. dissertation, Unicamp, 2007); Giralda Seyferth, "The Diverse Understandings of Foreign Migration to the South of Brazil (1818–1950)", *Vibrant: Virtual Brazilian Anthropology*, 10:2 (2013), pp. 118–162.

32. The union's official name was Sindicato dos Trabalhadores na Indústria em Extração do Carvão de São Jerônimo; see Alexandro Witkowski and Tassiane Melo Freitas, *Sobre os homens desta terra – A trajetória de fundação do sindicato dos mineiros de Butiá no Rio Grande do Sul* (Porto Alegre, 2006).

33. Testimonies were given to the Oral History Centre (CHO) of Rio Grande do Sul, in 2002, and are available at the Archive of Museu Estadual do Carvão (State Coal Museum).

34. Klovan, "Sob o fardo do ouro negro", p. 197.

35. Éder da Silva Silveira, "Além da traição: Manoel Jover Telles e o comunismo no Brasil do século XX" (Ph.D. dissertation, Unisinos, São Leopoldo, 2013), pp. 83–85 and 213.

Strikes and demonstrations for higher wages and better working conditions became more frequent after the end of World War II, when democracy was restored at the end of the Estado Novo dictatorship and the Communist Party was briefly legalized (from 1945 to 1947). In June 1947, Cadem complained to the local police that sixteen of the fifty-nine European immigrants who had recently arrived from Austria, Poland, and Ukraine[36] had refused to work owing to "incitement by bad elements". The group had arrived in Brazil through the mediation of the Intergovernmental Committee on Refugees (founded in 1938 and becoming, in the immediate postwar period, a predecessor to the UNHCR).[37]

To gain support in its confrontations with employers, the miners' union sponsored and encouraged lawsuits in the labor courts (established in 1941), and contacts with political leaders. The union called for the intervention of the Ministry of Labor and the Regional Labor Office, both created during the first government of Getúlio Vargas (1930–1945), to improve working conditions in the mines.[38] This legal strategy adopted by the miners' union did not in any way mean a break with past struggles. The first Vargas government (which ruled dictatorially from 1937–1945 as the Estado Novo) intervened in industrial relations, inspired by a corporatist perspective aimed at promoting "harmony between capital and labor".[39] Despite its fascist inspiration, this model offered scope for action and claims by workers, and some protection against employers. More importantly, it sought social appreciation of the worker and of work, something unheard of in a country where these concepts had always been associated with slavery.

During World War II coalminers were considered "heroes" and "soldiers of production" by sacrificing themselves in work. Although they were controlled and repressed, they were valued as citizens, on condition of their obedience to employers and loyalty to the government. However, as this discourse was appropriated by the workers themselves, this did not lead to harmony but, combined with poor working conditions and the ineffectiveness of most of the newly created protection laws, instead sharpened conflicts between employers and employees. The use of the law and legal instruments in the labor courts became important in the formation of class-consciousness among miners, as well as among other Brazilian workers.[40] It counteracts the idea of passivity, which, through the lens

---

36. According to a local historian, the population offered food and clothing to help the foreigners upon their arrival; Gertrudes Novak Hoff, *Butiá em busca de sua história* (Butiá, 1992), p. 62.

37. Cioccari, "Do gosto da mina", pp. 122–123.

38. Speranza, *Cavando direitos*, pp. 132–138.

39. Robert Levine, *Father of the Poor? Vargas and his Era* (New York, 1998), p. 81.

40. On the importance of the law and the system of labor courts in regulating (formal) labor relations in Brazil over many decades, see John French, *Drowning in Laws: Labor Law and*

of "populism", had previously been attributed to workers in Brazil during that period.[41] In the case of coalminers, the use of labor courts was never dissociated from direct action such as strikes, demonstrations, and occupations, almost all of which attracted broad support among workers.[42]

VULNERABILITY, DIVERSITY, AND SEGREGATION

The situation of immigrants in the mines clearly reflected the Brazilian dynamics of assimilation and the differentiation of immigrant workers. As Jeffrey Lesser claims, the identity of origin often accompanied later generations born in Brazil. Foreign-born Brazilians are not usually referred to as, for example, "German-Brazilian" or "Italian-Brazilian", but mostly as "Germans" or "Italians". A foreign origin is seen as a status symbol, however poor migrants had been at the time of migration itself.[43] An immigrant background may, however, also be used pejoratively. Alexandre Fortes has shown how in southern Brazil immigrants from eastern Europe were called indistinctly *polacos*, generating confusion and ethnic ambiguity.[44] One example is an incident during the 1946 strike, when the miner Alexandre Kalinski, who had abandoned the strike, was repeatedly called *polacos* by labor activists, despite his being born in Brazil.[45]

Assimilation and acquiring a "Brazilian" identity did not exempt immigrants from vulnerability in industrial relations, especially during World War II. The war gave companies a pretext to dismiss non-nationals perceived as subversive. In August 1943, for example, Cadem asked the police to arrest the Hungarian worker Axis Vassal, who was actually known by his Brazilian name, José Varga. He had come to Brazil long before the war and had worked in the mines since 1925. The main problem

---

Brazilian Political Culture (Chapel Hill, NC, 2004); Angela de Castro Gomes and Fernando Teixeira da Silva (eds), *A Justiça do Trabalho e sua história* (Campinas, 2013).

41. On "populism" and the ensuing debates in relation to labor in Brazil, see Francisco Weffort, *O populismo na política brasileira* (São Paulo, 2003); John French, *The Brazilian Workers' ABC: Class Conflict and Alliances in Modern São Paulo* (Chapel Hill, NC, 1992); and Jorge Ferreira, "O Nome e a coisa: O populismo na política brasileira", in *idem* (ed.), *O Populismo e sua história: debate e crítica* (Rio de Janeiro, 2001). For another view, denoting the political culture of Brazilian workers as *trabalhismo* (laborism), see Jorge Ferreira, *Trabalhadores do Brasil – o imaginário popular* (Rio de Janeiro, 1997).

42. Speranza, *Cavando direitos*, pp. 275–283.

43. Lesser, *Immigration, Ethnicity, and National Identity*, p. 3.

44. Alexandre Fortes, *Nós do Quarto Distrito – A classe trabalhadora porto-alegrense e a Era Vargas* (Rio de Janeiro, 2004), pp. 119–176.

45. Lawsuit 84/46, São Jerônimo Court Labor Lawsuits (1938/1947), Memorial da Justiça do Trabalho no Rio Grande do Sul (Labor Courts Archive in Rio Grande do Sul, hereafter, MJT-RS). These lawsuits have been made available on CD-ROM.

seemed to be that he had "anarchist tendencies" and caused "agitation among the workers".[46]

In contrast, other immigrants played an important role in the coalfield hierarchy, disciplining workers or punishing strikers. Examples can be found in labor lawsuits since the 1940s. In a labor lawsuit filed by a Brazilian worker against the Companhia Carbonífera Riograndense in 1941, a Spaniard acting as a mine foreman testified in favor of the company. He had already been living in Brazil for twenty-eight years. In 1947, another Spaniard, in charge of a drilling crew, appeared as a key witness for the mining companies in several labor lawsuits.[47] He had arrived in Brazil from Asturias in 1917, at the age of twenty-one. The trajectories of these two Spaniards exemplify how some immigrants became company men, while others openly challenged their employer's authority.

In the early twentieth century, the Catholic Church had few supporters among miners in the region. The workers were exposed to only "the smallest degree of religious instruction", and most families had "almost complete religious indifference and were devoted to spiritualism and Protestant practices", wrote Edmundo Rambo, the first chaplain of Arroio dos Ratos in 1932.[48] The Catholic Church could count on employers for support however. They financed the construction of the churches of St Theresa in 1930 (in Butiá) and St Joseph in 1944 (in Arroio dos Ratos). They also promoted the feast day of St Barbara (4 December). Furthermore, Carbonífera Riograndense and the archdiocese signed an agreement to establish religious services in Butiá, with the company paying the costs.[49] In 1955 a chapel dedicated to St Barbara was built in Butiá at the initiative of a chief engineer, who also organized annual celebrations for the saint.[50]

As in other mining communities, São Jerônimo workers founded leisure associations (mostly with the support of employers). The oldest, Última Hora [Last Hour], was founded in 1933 in Arroio dos Ratos by Spanish workers as a typical Brazilian carnival club. This society congregated workers of several nationalities, including native Brazilians. As in other Brazilian cities, there was also a club for black workers only: Tesouras [Scissors].

Because mining company documents have been lost, and in the absence of specific government data, it is hard to find information on black workers in

---

46. José Varga Dossier, Archive of Museu Estadual do Carvão (State Coal Museum), Arroio dos Ratos (Rio Grande do Sul).
47. Lawsuit 02/41; 6/46; 142/46; Declaration 23.005, 5 Series, Book 461, São Jerônimo Labor Court Lawsuits (1938/1947), MJT-RS.
48. Quoted from Ervino L Sulzbach, *Arroio dos Ratos – Berço da Indústria carbonífera nacional* (Arroio dos Ratos, 1989), p. 132.
49. Hoff, *Butiá em busca*, p. 58.
50. *Ibid.*, p. 65.

Figure 2. Miners working underground.
Archive of Museu Estadual do Carvão (State Coal Museum), Arroio dos Ratos (Rio Grande do Sul). Used with permission.

the mines. Photographs taken in the mines clearly show white and black miners working together. However inadequate, our sample of 472 miners (which is based on applications for professional licences between 1933 and 1944) includes 114 people of Afro-Brazilian descent. The vast majority originated from nearby villages.

In Brazil the social and ethnic criteria for considering someone "white" or "black" are complex and fluid. There are several classifications and categories within these groups, and they reflect important social differences. Referring to terms such as "white", "black", "European", "Indian", or "Asian" (among others) in Brazilian culture, Lesser points to the fact that "as different people and groups flowed in and out of these ever-shifting categories, Brazilian national identity was often simultaneously rigid (whiteness was consistently prized) and flexible (the designation of whiteness was malleable)".[51]

This Brazilian ethnic ambiguity seemed to be clearly established, too, within the mining sphere. In my sample of requests for professional licences, which included a racial identification, there are several ways of designating non-whites, by categorizing them as *negro*, *preto*, *pardo*,

51. Jeffrey Lesser, "A Better Brazil", *História, Ciências, Saúde-Manguinhos*, 21 (2014), pp. 181–194, 185.

moreno, or *mulato*. These different classifications are by no means synonymous and meant more than just "non-white". *Pardo* and *moreno* seem to be the terms whose meaning was closest to "white", while the terms *negro* and *preto* were located at the other end of the racial scale. Being "white" thus implied a higher status in Brazilian society, in almost binary opposition to all other groups, whereas within the latter differentiations between *negro* (black), *mulato* (mulatto), and *moreno* (light brown) were of paramount importance.[52] This diversity in racial classification reflected an organized structure in which the perceived closeness to "white" was directly proportional to the possibilities of social ascension. On the other hand, there is no mention of "Indian" or "indigenous", demonstrating the absence, or perhaps social invisibility, of this ethnic group among miners ("mixed" Indians immediately ceased to be understood as such).

Figure 3 overleaf shows photographs of eight coalminers appended to forms requesting professional licences in 1933. The first three in the bottom row (left to right) were born in Brazil and were all classified as *morenos* (a glance at the pictures gives an idea of how little relation attributions such as *moreno* actually had to skin complexion). The first on the top row (left to right) came from Spain, but he curiously appears as *moreno* too. The others, also from Europe (Russia, Portugal, and Spain), were termed *brancos* (white). Interestingly, the *moreno* Spanish wore a scarf around his neck, like the Brazilians. This is a traditional custom of the region (dating back to the Federalist Revolution). The Spaniard and one of the Brazilian men are wearing a red scarf, a sign of regional political partisanship associated with the *maragatos* faction (opposed to the white-scarfed *chimangos* faction).[53]

In a series of interviews given by retired miners, Afro-descendants denounced racism only in relation to leisure, referring to their inability to enter "white" clubs. Retired miner Frontino Rodrigues Oliveira, aged seventy-three, said that he was not going to the white clubs "because I was of the black race, like they say". His colleague Cerílio Soares, aged

---

52. See Hebe Mattos, "'Pretos' and 'Pardos' between the Cross and the Sword: Racial Categories in Seventeenth Century Brazil", *Revista Europea de Estudios Latinoamericanos y del Caribe*, 80 (2006), pp. 43–55.
53. These two factions were on opposite sides during the 1923 Revolution, an eleven-month insurgency in Rio Grande do Sul. The supporters of the state president, Borges de Medeiros, fought against the allies of the farmer João Francisco de Assis Brasil, leader of the Federalist Party. The revolt followed an election to the state presidency that awarded victory to Borges de Medeiros for a second term. The opposition between the two factions had its origins in the Federalist Revolution of 1823. Borges' supporters wore white scarves and were called *chimangos*. Assis Brasil's allies were termed *maragatos*, and were identified by their red scarves. Some authors claim that the origins of the expression *maragatos* go back to a certain region in Spain (which might explain the use of the red scarf by Yugueiros). See Love, *Rio Grande do Sul*; and also Gunter Axt, "Coronelismo indomável: o sistema de relações de poder", in Tau Golin and Nelson Boeira (eds), *História Geral do Rio Grande do Sul – República – República Velha (1889–1930)*, III (1) (Passo Fundo, 2007).

Figure 3. Miners' photographs, identification data from professional licences, 1933–1943. Top row, left to right: Alexandre Yugueiros, Spanish (born 1896, arrived in Brazil 1917); Andre Kopaef, Russian (born 1901, arrived in Brazil 1922); João Pires, Portuguese (born 1890, arrived in Brazil 1913), Avelino Franso, Spanish (born 1885, arrived in Brazil 1914). Bottom row, left to right: Edemar Firmo da Rocha, Brazilian (born 1913); Laudelino Marques dos Santos, Brazilian (born 1890); Osmar Strada, Brazilian (born 1906); Ramão Peres, Spanish (born 1900, arrived in Brazil 1908). *Archive DRT-NDH/UFPel. Used with permission.*

seventy-two, reported that "the balls started at 10 or 11 p.m. and would go on until 5 in the morning. I went more often to the Tesouras Club. It was the ball of the blacks. Now, it must be all mixed up, but in the old days, whites and blacks did not mingle."[54]

Although they worked side by side in the mines, were members of the same union, and stood alongside each other during strikes and in protest movements, European descendants did not admit the descendants of slaves to their leisure clubs. Although exploited together with the descendants of slaves by corporate control and forced to accept poor working conditions, immigrants had a better position in mining society, and acted to maintain this differentiation.

CLOSING REMARKS

In many parts of Brazil, in particular in Rio Grande do Sul, the concentration of immigrants from certain ethnic groups favored the

---

54. The two testimonies were given to the Oral History Centre (CHO) of Rio Grande do Sul, 21 June 2002. Interviewer: Ulysses B. dos Santos; Archive of Museu Estadual do Carvão (State Coal Museum), Arroio dos Ratos (Rio Grande do Sul).

formation of communities with relatively isolated cultures and practices. During the Estado Novo, these groups were repressed; the teaching of foreign languages was forbidden, and several ethnic associations were abolished.[55] However, immigrant isolation seems not to have been a feature of the coalmining areas of Rio Grande do Sul. Although a large number of European immigrants arrived in the region, their varied origins hindered the formation of closed ethnic groups. This was partly the result of a conscious policy by mine operators and authorities. The prevalence of Spaniards in the mines may also have contributed to a low degree of segregation – here the linguistic similarities might have helped immigrants to "blend" into Brazilian culture.[56]

The diverse ethnic groups – both "nationals" and "foreigners" – in the Rio Grande do Sul coalmines are today often regarded as the founders of an alleged mining "race",[57] or "a class founded on virtues that had permeated generations, reaching a race-like condition".[58] Their sense of belonging to the same craft supposedly gave them a uniform identity as "miners", based on an amalgam of all the ethnic groups involved. The statue of the miner at the entrance to Arroio dos Ratos is a clear indication of this point.

This idea of the miners as a distinct group – also in terms of "class" – dated from when production at the mines peaked in the 1930s and 1940s, and coincided with the populist appreciation of the "national" worker as a key element in the progress of the nation. The populist ideology viewed "work" as a core value in a country with a heritage of slavery. At the same time, it enabled miners to shape their collective struggles in their own way. However, the construction of a distinct mining identity, often forged in terms of "class" but sometimes (and tellingly) even in terms of a mining "race", cannot hide its contradictions. The open segregation of Afro-Brazilian miners during their leisure time shows that solidarity and cohesion among workers had its limits. The social exclusion of the descendants of the slaves endured long after slavery had ended, even under the pretext of constructing a single mining "race".

55. See Geraldo, "O 'perigo alienígena'", ch. 3.
56. For the special situation of Spanish immigrants in the region, see Regina Weber, "Espanhóis no sul do Brasil: diversidade e identidade", *História: Questões e Debates*, 56 (2012), pp. 137–157.
57. See, for example, Benedito Veit, *Mineiros: uma raça* (São Jerônimo, 1992).
58. Juarez Adão Lima, "Mineiros" (unpublished manuscript, 1999). Lima was a former miner, Partido Trabalhista Brasileiro (PTB) politician, and local historian. He kindly gave me access to his writings after an interview at his home in 2008.

IRSH 60 (2015), Special Issue, pp. 185–205 doi:10.1017/S0020859015000462
© 2015 Internationaal Instituut voor Sociale Geschiedenis

Specialists, Spies, "Special Settlers", and Prisoners of War: Social Frictions in the Kuzbass (USSR), 1920–1950

JULIA LANDAU

Buchenwald Memorial
99427 Weimar-Buchenwald, Germany

E-mail: jlandau@buchenwald.de

ABSTRACT: The Kuzbass coalmining region in western Siberia (Kuznetsk Basin) was explored, populated, and exploited under Stalin's rule. Struggling to offset a high labour turnover, the local state-run coal company enrolled deportees from other regions of Russia and Siberia, who were controlled by the secret police (OGPU). These workers shared a common experience in having been forcibly separated from their place of origin. At the same time, foreigners were recruited from abroad as experts and offered a privileged position. In the years of the Great Terror (1936–1938) both groups were persecuted, as they were regarded by the state as disloyal and suspicious. After the war, foreigners were recruited in large numbers as prisoners of war. Thus, migrants, foreigners, and deportees from other regions and countries constituted a significant part of the workforce in the Kuzbass, while their status constantly shifted due to economic needs and repressive politics.

From the beginning of the twentieth century, after the building of the Trans-Siberian Railway, the economic resources of Siberia became the subject of political consideration and planning efforts by the Russian and later the Soviet state. The Kuzbass region in western Siberia amazed Soviet planners with its vast supply of very high-quality coal – the layers of coal measuring from 1.5 to 20 metres.[1] The content of ash (about 10 per cent) and sulphur (between 0.4 and 0.7 per cent) was comparatively low. This enabled the production of coking coal, which in turn is indispensable for steel production. However, the climatic, infrastructural, and socio-geographic

---

1. The term Kuzbass – an abbreviation for Kuznetskii Bassein – describes a geographical depression of 26,000 sq. km north of the Altay mountains in the middle of the Eurasian continent and south-east of Novosibirsk and the Trans-Siberian Railway, at a distance of 4,000 km from Moscow.

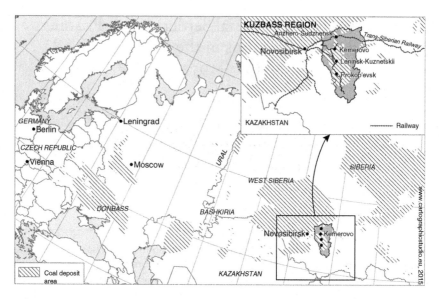

Figure 1. The Kuzbass coalmining region in western Siberia and other coalfields in Russia and Ukraine.

conditions in the Kuzbass are extremely difficult. During the long winter months, lasting from the end of September until April, the climate is harsh, with extremely low temperatures. As the region was only sparsely populated, workers and technical experts had to be attracted from other regions as well as from other countries, while an infrastructure, including housing and technical facilities, had to be built at the same time.

In the years between the two world wars the Kuzbass region, with its coal, ore, and chemical resources, was intensively developed as part of Stalin's policy of forced industrialization. Huge numbers of workers were recruited, mobilized, and deported to provide the workforce needed to construct one of the biggest Soviet centres of coal production and heavy industry, deemed crucial for fuelling economic development under Stalin.[2] The Kuzbass, located in an isolated place of strategic importance,

2. In recent years several regional and local studies have broadened our understanding of economic development under Stalin. The Kuzbass can be compared with other regions that were subject to Stalinist forced industrialization. See, for example, Stephen Kotkin, *Magnetic Mountain: Stalinism as a Civilization* (Berkeley, CA, 1995); Tanja Penter, *Kohle für Stalin und Hitler. Arbeiten und Leben im Donbass 1929 bis 1953* (Essen, 2010); Anne D. Rassweiler, *The Generation of Power: The History of Dneprostroi* (New York [etc.], 1998); and Klaus Gestwa, *Die Stalinschen Großbauten des Kommunismus. Sowjetische Technik- und Umweltgeschichte, 1948–1967* (Munich, 2010). On the Kuzbass, see Kaleriia A. Zabolotskaia, *Ugol'naia promyshlennost'* [Coal Industry] (Kemerovo, 1996); Liubov I. Gvozdkova, *Stalinskie lageria na territorii Kuzbassa (30–40-e gg.)* [Stalinist Camps in the Kuzbass in the 1930s and 1940s] (Kemerovo, 1994).

became one of the two most important sites of heavy industry in the Soviet Union.[3] During World War II, the Kuzbass was one of the main centres to which industries and workers from western parts of the Soviet Union were evacuated; after the war, requisitioned and deconstructed industries were brought to the Kuzbass, along with deportees and prisoners of war.

This article analyses the changing status and the perception of migrants of all kinds in the Stalinist economy of the Kuzbass before, during, and after World War II: new workers from the countryside, foreign experts ("specialists"), forced settlers, convicted forced labourers deported by the state's secret police and the People's Commissariat of the Interior (NKVD),[4] as well as prisoners of war. During the decade before World War II – often labelled as the "war before the war" – complex mechanisms of segregation and disintegration were at work. Social, cultural, and ethnic distinctions became increasingly important and conflicts rose to unforeseeable levels. "Foreigners" and "migrants", originally hired as "foreign specialists", and young peasants, who were intended to form a new collective of workers, were suddenly identified as "foreign spies", "enemies of the people", and potentially disloyal *kulaky* (wealthy peasants and farmers who resisted forced collectivization). In the 1940s, during the war with Germany and its allies, prisoners of war were employed coercively. In this article I will ask how policies of repression on the one hand, and the specific conditions facing developing heavy industry on the other, created differences that were connected to ethnic and cultural ascriptions, and affected everyday life in local society.

SETTLING A WORKFORCE

The first attempts to develop and exploit the vast stocks of Kuzbass coal date from the early 1920s, so before the First Five-Year Plan (1928–1932). Under the guidance of the Dutch communist Sebald Rutgers, British and

---

3. The other was Ukraine's Donetsk basin (Donbass). Some fundamental references on the latter can be found in Zoja G. Likholobova, "Der Bergmann in der Historiographie (1920–2000)", in Tanja Penter (ed.), *Sowjetische Bergleute und Industriearbeiter – Neue Forschungen* (Bochum, 2007), pp. 15–29, 15. On the industrialization of the Urals and Siberia, see Sergei A. Papkov and K. Teraiama (eds), *Ural i Sibir' v stalinskoi politike* [The Urals and Siberia in Stalinist Politics] (Novosibirsk, 2002).

4. On convict labour as a system of labour control in general, see Christian G. De Vito and Alex Lichtenstein, "Writing a Global History of Convict Labour", *International Review of Social History*, 58 (2013), pp. 285–325. In the Soviet case, administrative and penal control was exerted by the NKVD, which took over economic and social functions, and had its own economic substructure. A range of different kinds of coerced labourers are described by the Soviet administrative term *spetskontingent* – a special contingent of coerced workforce at the disposal of the NKVD and forming a social stratum of its own. See Andrei B. Suslov, *Spetskontingent v Permskoi oblasti: 1929–1953 gg.* [Special Contingent in the Perm Region: 1929–1953] (Moscow, 2010).

American communists, among them many "Wobblies" (International Workers of the World, IWW), founded a so-called Avtonomnaia Industrialnaia Kolonia [Autonomous Industry Colony, AIK], which tried to run mines, wood processing plants, and chemical industries in a unified organization.[5] Workers were recruited from the USA, Germany, and the Netherlands. In contrast to the egalitarian idea originally planned, foreigners held leading positions in production and enjoyed far better living and housing conditions. For the majority of the workers, living conditions were miserable. In the 1920s, when the Kuzbass's urban population quintupled,[6] workers lived in self-built *zemlyanki*, huts made of wood and clay, located partly in earth-holes. Sanitary conditions were appalling, with cesspits near water lines, a situation that caused endemic typhoid fever.[7] Due to these difficult living conditions, only one-fifth of the foreign specialists originally attracted to the Kuzbass could be convinced to stay.

Many of the local workers successively recruited soon left their new workplace. As many as 61 per cent of workers did not return to work in February, most likely because of difficult climatic conditions, the lack of working garments, and the long distances from their huts to the workplace.[8] The regional party committee believed miners often regarded their underground work as providing an auxiliary income to supplement their subsistence economy. Antagonisms between foreigners and local workers were frequently recorded during party meetings. The foreign leadership of the colony was perceived as a hostile takeover: "Why did you come, we got along well without you!", or: "Sir, when will you give us a caning?" Antagonisms were widespread also among the foreigners themselves: "Americans don't like the Dutch, the Dutch don't like the Germans, the latter don't like the Dutch – and we don't like any of them!"[9]

The colony was also not very successful in economic terms. Because of the lack of infrastructure, in particular railway lines, it was impossible to

5. For detailed studies on the "autonomous industry colony" experiment in Soviet Russia, see E. Krivosheeva, *Bol'shoi Bill v Kuzbasse. Stranitsy internatsional'nykh sviazei* [Big Bill in the Kuzbass: Aspects of International Relations] (Kemerovo, 1990); and William T. Smith, *The Kuzbas Colony, Soviet Russia, 1921–1926* (Ann Arbor, MI, 1979).

6. In 1920, 2,000 inhabitants lived in Prokop'evsk; by 1926 that figure had risen to almost 11,000; Julia Landau, *Wir bauen den großen Kuzbass! Bergarbeiteralltag im Stalinismus 1921–1941* (Stuttgart, 2012), p. 63.

7. Doklad o sanitarnom sostoianii Sibirskogo kraia [Report on the Sanitary Conditions in the Siberian Region], 1928, Gosudarstvennii Arkhiv Novosibirskoi Oblasti [Novosibirsk Region State Archive] [hereafter, GANO], R-47, op. 1, d. 268, l. 12–25.

8. Stenogramma zasedaniia biuro Sibkraikoma VKP (b) 5.6.1926 goda. [Minutes of the Meeting of the Siberian Branch of the Russian Communist Party, 5 June 1926], Rossiiskii Gosudarstvennyi Arkhiv Sotsialno-politicheskoi istorii [Russian State Archive of Socio-Political History] [hereafter, RGASPI], f. 17, op. 67, d. 367, l. 84.

9. Doklad Kuznetskii okrugkom 8.11.1926 [Report of the Kuznetsk Regional Party Committee, 8 November 1926], RGASPI, f. 17, op. 67, d. 367, l. 85.

transport the coal. With the monopolist state control of heavy industry established by the First Five-Year Plan in 1928, the "autonomous industry colony" experiment in the Kuzbass was closed down and transformed into the state-run monopolist Kuzbasugol' company. Foreign expertise, however, continued to play an important role into the 1930s.

The First Five-Year Plan envisaged an enormous increase in annual coal production, from 2.4 million tons in 1928 to 10.5 million tons in 1932. This plan was nearly fulfilled: in fact, almost 10 million tons were extracted in 1932. Production figures continued to rise rapidly, to 17 million tons in 1937 and 21 million tons in 1940. In summary, coal production increased tenfold between 1928 and 1940. This development was far more rapid than in the Donbass, where overall coal output, having already reached 26 million tons in 1927, rose to 83 million tons in 1940.[10] These achievements were enthusiastically used for propaganda purposes. "We build the big Kuzbass!", the title of a propaganda brochure by the head of the west Siberian party committee, was the main slogan of that time. With this propagandistic slogan, party officials hoped to promote a new local industrial identity in a sparsely populated, mostly agrarian region, trying to attract and integrate various migrants from other regions.[11]

The rapid increase in coal production was possible only because of the extensive exploitation of predominantly high layers of coal. The steep and unstable stratification of deeper layers, connected with the formation of gas, was much more challenging. Extensive exploitation was connected to extremely difficult working conditions. Living conditions remained poor as well, and did not improve with the successes in production. As a consequence, many of the newly recruited miners left after only one month. Most of the new miners came from the surrounding rural Siberian region; about 20 per cent were hired in the rural Volga region. As the newcomers could not be provided with housing space, working garments, or shoes, only a few of them could be deployed in the pits. Many of them returned home very soon, earning them the sobriquet "birds of passage".

Altogether, 40 per cent of all workers stayed for less than six months.[12] In 1932 about 60,000 new workers were registered by Kuzbasugol', while at the same time 60,000 workers left the company. The overall total number of

10. In Donbass, 83.2 million tons of coal were produced in 1940, about 52 per cent of total Soviet output; Kuzbass produced 18.5 per cent of Soviet coal output; Likholobova, "Der Bergmann in der Historiographie", p. 15; Landau, *Wir bauen den großen Kuzbass!*, pp. 74–75.
11. For a similar development in the Donbass at that time, including propagandistic athletic competitions between the regions, see Tanja Penter, "Der 'neue sozialistische Donbass' und der Aufstieg des Bergmanns zur kulturellen Leitfigur", in *idem, Sowjetische Bergleute und Industriearbeiter*, pp. 79–95, 80.
12. A.S. Moskovskii, *Rabochii klass Zapadnoi Sibiri v gody pervoi piatiletki* [The Working Class in Western Siberia in the Years of the First Five-Year Plan] (Novosibirsk, 1964), p. 51.

workers in any one month was about 32,000. Most migrants were peasants from rural western Siberia and Kazakhstan, who fled the 1932–1933 hunger crisis there, a consequence of collectivization and the state's requisitioning of entire grain harvests in agricultural areas.[13] A workplace in the mining industry meant permission to reside in the town, as well as the allotment of ration cards, necessary for survival. The allotment of bread for miners was higher than for other workers, but it differed between regions of heavy industry. The Donbass was better off than other mining regions.[14] In the Kuzbass, however, as the living conditions in the settlements around pits were extremely poor and working conditions very hard, many of the former farmers left their new workplace, searching for other opportunities in the European part of the Soviet Union.

THE LOWEST RANK OF SOCIETY: DEPORTED *KULAKY*

As the workforce of the pits changed every month, the fulfilment of production plans was constantly in danger. In this situation, the management of the pit took advantage of a contingent of forced labourers, provided by the secret police (OGPU),[15] later reorganized as the Commissariat for Internal Affairs (NKVD).[16] The leading party officials in western Siberia argued that with a deficit of 23,000 workers in the Kuzbass, it was necessary to engage detainees from the Siberian labour camps to be able to fulfil at least some of the economic plans.[17] The plea was successful, but instead of labour camp detainees large numbers of people – so-called *spetspereselentsy* ("special settlers") – were deported directly from their place of origin to work in the mines. As early as spring 1930 the OGPU had started to provide forced labourers for the most difficult and work-intensive locations.[18]

The families were deported to their new place of work in chaotic circumstances. Neither the company nor the OGPU regarded themselves as

13. In contrast to the massive famine in Ukraine in 1932–1933 (which, in the notion of *holodomor*, is widely, though not undisputedly, characterized as a deliberate attempt at genocide), the famine in Russia and Kazakhstan has been investigated only marginally and is not part of the official record. According to newer accounts, more than 1 million people left the Kazakh ASSR in 1930–1932; only 500,000 of them returned. See Rudolf A. Mark, "Die Hungersnot in Kazakhstan. Historiographische Aufarbeitung im Wandel", *Osteuropa*, 54 (2004), pp. 112–130, 116.

14. Penter, "Der 'neue sozialistische Donbass'", p. 80.

15. Obedinennoe Gosudarstvennoe Politicheskoe Upravlenie, State Political Directorate; name of the Soviet secret police from 1922 to 1934.

16. Narodnyi Komissariat (Ministerstvo) Vnutrennikh Del, People's Commissariat (Ministry from 1946) for Internal Affairs.

17. Griadinskii, Chairman of the Western Siberian Party Committee, to the Council of People's Commissars (SNK) RSFSR, 2 October 1930, GANO R-47, op. 1, d. 749, l. 160.

18. Postanovlenie SNK RSFSR 10.4.1930 [Resolution of the SNK, 10 April 1930], in Viktor P. Danilov and Sergei A. Krasil'nikov (eds), *Spetspereselentsy Zapadnoi Sibiri 1930–vesna 1931 g.* [Special Settlers in Western Siberia 1930 to Spring 1931] (Novosibirsk, 1992), pp. 28–29.

responsible for providing housing. The solution was to have the deportees build houses themselves, and in order to give them enough time before winter it was decided to start the deportations earlier in the following year, 1931. It was not until July 1931 that conditions for the special settlers were regulated at a state level. Under the resolution passed at that time, the OGPU and the companies had to agree on the financing of the settlements: the companies were to pay 25 per cent of the wages directly to the OGPU for the costs of custody and administration. Special settlers and their families were not allowed to leave the settlements, which were guarded by the OGPU. Exceptions were made to allow children aged sixteen to be sent to other workplaces. Offences were punished by fines and detention of up to one month.[19]

Altogether, from 1930 to 1932 about 23,630 *kulak* families, about 61,000 people, were brought to the Kuzbass from different regions of the Soviet Union.[20] This forced relocation was part of the larger persecution of presumed wealthier farmers, the so-called *kulaks*, who resisted grain requisitioning and the collectivization of agriculture. Strikingly, about 40,000 families from western Siberia were sent, not to the nearby Kuzbass, but to camps in the Narymsk region of northern Siberia. At the same time, more than 50,000 special settlers were sent from the Moscow region and Bashkiria to the Kuzbass.[21] Such relocations seem irrational, but we have to bear in mind that they were not primarily driven by economic motives; they were essentially political and punitive. While most male heads of the so-called *kulak* families were executed or interned in labour camps, the rest of the families were deported to special settlements, where they were meant to live and work in custody, but often without the working-age male members.[22]

19. Postanovlenie SNK ob ustroistve spetspereselentsev [Resolution of the SNK on the Settlement of Special Settlers], 1 July 1931, in Viktor P. Danilov and Sergei A. Krasil'nikov (eds), *Spetspereselentsy v Zapadnoi Sibiri, Vesna 1931–nachalo 1933g.* [Special Settlers in Western Siberia, from Spring 1931 to the beginning of 1933] (Novosibirsk, 1994), pp. 14–15. Therefore, the special settlers received – according to their ability to work – a nominal 75 per cent of their wages. The part of their wage paid directly to the OGPU was later reduced to 5 per cent; Landau, *Wir bauen den großen Kuzbass!*, p. 139; Afanas'ev et al. (eds), *Istoriia Stalinskogo Gulaga. Spetspereselentsy v SSSR*, vol. 5 [History of the Stalinist Gulag: Special Settlers in the SSSR, V] (Moscow, 2004), *vvedenie* [introduction], pp. 32–35.
20. *Dokladnaya zapiska sekretarya Kemerovskogo obkoma KPSS M.I. Guseva L.P. Berija* [Note from the Secretary of the Kemerovo Party Committee to L.P. Beria], 20 May 1953, in Gosudarstvennyi arkhiv Kemerovskoi oblasti [State Archive of Kemerovo Region] (ed.), *Neizvestnyi Kuzbass* [Unknown Kuzbass], vyp. 1 (Kemerovo, 1993), pp. 29–30.
21. Sergei A. Krasil'nikov and V.V. Sarnova, "Deportatsia", *Entsiklopediia Sibiri* ["Deportation", Encyclopaedia of Siberia], http://russiasib.ru/deportaciya/, last accessed 29 July 2015.
22. This "archipelago" of special settlers was almost unknown for a long time and their history was less developed than that of the Gulag detainees. Large-scale experience with special settlers working in difficult and distant workplaces preceded the exploitation of Gulag detainees for all branches of industry. See Lynne Viola, *The Unknown Gulag: The Lost World of Stalin's Special*

In terms of economic aims, to exact labour from those who had newly arrived was thus highly inefficient – though the work norm was set in some places twice as high as for the free workers.[23] Also, due to neglect during and after deportation, many of the special settlers were unable to work at all. In August 1931, only 26 per cent of the special settlers in Prokop'evsk were deemed fit enough to work – the others were fit only for repairing shoes, weaving baskets, or repairing tools.[24] Because of insufficient food, housing and medical support, 8-12 per cent of the children under three years of age died.[25]

Kuzbasugol' intervened in the repressive policies of the OGPU, demanding deportations of young males only, and implementing economic stimuli, including offering release from forced settlement and a partial rehabilitation in exchange for fulfilling the high work targets. Although in most cases these promises were not fulfilled, many of the younger special settlers were among the most productive, even affiliating themselves with the Stalinist values of social hierarchy. Also, the regime offered these younger detainees certain opportunities for advancement. The Central Party Committee decided in December 1935 that young special settlers would be allowed to graduate in polytechnic institutes, though only at a medium level.[26] For educational purposes they were allowed to leave their forced settlements for a short time. As Gulag officials noted approvingly, this part-time separation alienated them from their mostly "anti-Sovietic" parents.[27]

In addition to the Gulag prisoners and the special settlers mentioned above, further contingents of forced labourers arrived in the following

Settlements (Oxford, 2007); and Sergei A. Krasil'nikov, *Serp i Molokh. Krest'ianskaia ssylka v Zapadnoi Sibiri v 1930-e gody* [Sickle and Moloch: Deportation of Peasants in Western Siberia in the 1930s] (Moscow, 2003).

23. The OGPU criticized the irregular high-work norms and appealed to local OGPU representatives to equal them. See Tsirkularnoe pis'mo OGPU, 21.7.1931 [OGPU circular], 21 July 1931, in Danilov and Krasil'nikov, *Spetspereselentsy v Zapadnoi Sibiri, Vesna 1931–nachalo 1933g.* pp. 53–56, 54.

24. In fact, only 16 per cent of the special settlers in Prokop'evsk were actually sent to work, as the OGPU noticed. See Spetssvodka PP OGPU v Krajispolkom, 21.8.1931 [Special OGPU report to the West Siberian Central Executive Committee], 21 August 1931, in Danilov and Krasil'nikov, *Spetspereselentsy v Zapadnoi Sibiri, Vesna 1931–nachalo 1933g.* pp. 146–151, 146–147. See also note 20 on pp. 314–315.

25. Informatsia OGPU v TsKK VKP (b), Janvar' 1932 [OGPU report to the Central Control Commission of the Soviet Communist Party], January 1932, in Danilov and Krasil'nikov, *Spetspereselentsy v Zapadnoi Sibiri, Vesna 1931–nachalo 1933g.* pp. 76–84, 81.

26. Postanovlenie SNK i TsK VKP (b) no. 2663, 15.12.1935 [Resolution of the SNK and the Central Comittee of the Soviet Communist Party], 15 December 1935, cited in Afanas'ev *et al.*, *Istoriia Stalinskogo Gulaga. Spetspereselentsy*, p. 741, n. 86. See Landau, *Wir bauen den großen Kuzbass!*, p. 339.

27. Doklad nachalnika GULaga I.I. Plinera narkomu vnutrennykh del SSSR N.I. Ezhovu o sostoianii trudovykh poselkov NKVD na 1 sentiabria 1936g. [Report by the Director of the Gulag I.I. Pliner to Commissar N.I. Ezhov], 31 October 1936, in Afanas'ev *et al.*, *Istoriia Stalinskogo Gulaga. Spetspereselentsy*, pp. 227–235, 234.

years: those deported after 1939 because of their "suspect" nationality (ethnic Germans, for example), and in the late 1940s prisoners of war and internees from Germany and Japan. Being subordinated to the NKVD as well, these groups are included in the contemporary term *spetskontingent*. They were constricted and discriminated against in various ways. At several Kuzbasugol' mines they comprised between 25 and 40 per cent of the workforce.[28] Repressive measures were taken to dissolve any familiar or ethnic boundaries and loyalties, thereby creating, by administrative means, a new and dependent social group.

THE HIGHER RANKS OF SOCIETY: FOREIGN SPECIALISTS IN THE 1930s

In the early 1930s, foreign mining and engineering specialists were again recruited from abroad, but with decisive differences compared with the recruitment of foreign specialists for the "autonomous industry colony" in the 1920s. Now the focus of the recruitments changed: foreigners – mostly German, Austrian, and Czech engineers and miners – were recruited, not because of their communist background and their willingness to support the construction of the Soviet Union, but strictly because of their expertise. Foreign specialists were deployed to operate special, newly imported machines. Contrary to their professional ethics and habits, a miner was engaged not as a general specialist for complex and different challenges in underground mining, but as an isolated specialist for complex machinery, for example the newly imported coal-cutting machine. This nexus was advantageous on the one hand, as it allowed these foreign specialists to negotiate higher wages in accordance with their "special" profession. On the other hand, it exposed the specialists and made them vulnerable, as they could be made responsible for the functioning – or non-functioning – of these imported and costly machines.

Campaigns organized by newly established offices in the Soviet trade missions in Berlin and Vienna promised high wages to mining engineers, including payments in foreign currency, while ordinary foreign workers received just one-fifth of their wages and were provided only with single rooms in residential accommodation instead of apartments.[29] Many skilled workers therefore tried to get acknowledged as "specialists" in order to

---

28. Doklad o peredache khoziaistvennoi deiatel'nosti UNKVD [Report on the Economic Activity of the UNKVD], 8 February 1938, Gosudarstvennyi Arkhiv Rossiiskoi Federatsii [Russian Federation State Archive] [hereafter, GARF], f. 9414, op. 1, d. 5, l. 8–9, 31.

29. Osnovnye usloviia priglasheniia v SSSR inostrannykh rabochikh [Conditions of Invitation of Foreign Workers to the SSSR], 16 February 1931, Gosudarstvennyi Arkhiv Kemerovskoi Oblasti [Kemerovo Region State Archive] [hereafter, GAKO], f. R-177, op. 3, d. 9, l. 87. I am grateful to Dr Elena Kuznetsova, Kemerovo, for introducing me to this collection of documents in the Kemerovo Region State Archive.

negotiate better contracts.[30] As a result of these recruitment policies abroad, about 1,500 foreign specialists and workers moved to the Kuzbass between 1931 and 1938. As Kuzbasugol' was unable to guarantee the terms and conditions of the contracts, many of these workers left after a short time, a matter of major concern to the local trade-union administrations, as well as to the Politburo in Moscow. Disillusioned returnees posed enormous problems for foreign propaganda. While the narrative of Soviet propaganda was one of economic expansion in line with the First Five-Year Plan as a counterstatement to the world economic crisis, the returnees told a different story. "At home in Germany even the unemployed live in better conditions than workers here in the Soviet Union", a German coal hewer was cited as reporting.[31]

Local trade unions worried especially about the wives of foreigners. Foreign women, not knowing any Russian and selling eggs on the black market, were perceived as loafers who demoralized their husbands.[32] In reality, however, they acclimatized very quickly to the omnipresent deficits and managed to supply themselves and their families with food during the famine.

Most of the foreign workers returned home. In 1937, there were only 126 foreigners left in the Kuzbass, among them communists and Jewish workers seeking refuge from National Socialist persecution. The returning workers and engineers were closely interviewed by the German Political Police (Gestapo) in order to extract first-hand material for anti-communist propaganda. Given their original purpose, these interviews have to be treated critically, but they nevertheless give valuable insights into the conditions of local society in the Kuzbass. The dwellings of the Russian workers were "fumy and damp", one German hewer recorded after his return:

> There were no separate spaces; the whole family lived in one room, which was bedroom, living room, and kitchen in one. No German worker would have lived in such a room for one day, let alone for the long Siberian winter. The Russian worker was as primitive as his accommodation. There was no light and water for these self-constructed dwellings.[33]

30. Walter Szevera, "Österreichische Facharbeiteremigration in den 30er Jahren in die Sowjetunion", in Barry McLoughlin, Hans Schafranek, and Walter Szevera, *Aufbruch, Hoffnung, Endstation. Österreicherinnen und Österreicher in der Sowjetunion 1925–1945* (Vienna, 1997), pp. 71–158, 96, and 98.

31. Kharakteristika Lidtke Ernst (= Ernst Lüdtke), GARF, f. 5451, op. 13a, d. 465, l. 9. "Kharakteristika" was a personnel assessment of a member of the union, written by other members and without his or her approval. These assessments could serve as evidence for presumed political misconduct.

32. Stenogramma soveshchaniia inorabochikh i spetsialistov pri TsK Soiuza ugol'shchikov [Minutes of the Meeting of Foreign Workers and Specialists at the Central Committee of the Miners' Union], GARF, f. 7416, op. 1, d. 150, l. 114.

33. Vernehmung August Dreyer, 5 November 1937, Politisches Archiv des Auswärtigen Amtes [hereafter, PA AA] R 104553A.

On the one hand, these statements show the influence of National Socialist propaganda, deducing habits and living conditions from an essentially "national" character. On the other hand, these observations can complement official Soviet documents, which speak of barrack rooms allotted to foreign workers but scarcely mention that special settlers were left on their own to build simple earthen caves instead of houses: "In the coalmine areas, where I was working, the workers lived in primitive earthen caves and simple wooden barracks. One can see these earthen caves along each road; they even form quarters in the town. They consist of dirt and mud."[34]

Inadequate infrastructure and housing caused a distinct hierarchy among the poor. The allocation of living space was an exclusive process, in which only a few were privileged enough to live in houses, even fewer in houses built of stone, while many had to live on their own, in self-dug earthen caves.

ACCIDENTS AND GROWING DISCONTENT

The "hierarchy of the poor", constitutive for local society in the Kuzbass in the 1930s, was apparent in many ways: differential forms of housing and different access to goods marked one's position in local society.[35] The common experience of omnipresent deficits and shortages, together with the openly visible privilege of a few, was dangerous and caused a potentially unstable situation. But open conflicts began to surface only against the background of the extremely dangerous underground working conditions. Different rock formations and steeply sloping layers of gaseous coal tending to self-ignition represented enormous problems for engineers and workers in the Kuzbass pits. In summer 1931 a gas explosion in Kemerovo and an underground fire in Prokopyevsk left six people dead and nine badly injured.[36]

Success in increasing coal production could not be achieved without cost, and it was the workers who paid the price. Leading engineers were aware of this and discussed the problem of how to increase production in line with economic plans without endangering the workers, a problem that they were

34. Vernehmung Wilhelm Bednarz [Interrogation Wilhelm Bednarz], 3 November 1937, PA AA R 1045564.

35. Elena Osokina, *Za fasadom "Stalinskogo izobiliia". Raspredelenie i rynok v snabzhenii naseleniia v gody industrializatsii, 1927–1941* [Behind the Face of "Stalinist Abundance": The Role of Distribution and Markets for the Supply of Soviet Public during Industrialization, 1927–1941] (Moscow, 1998), p. 126; [edited English version: *Our Daily Bread: Socialist Distribution and the Art of Survival in Stalin's Russia, 1927–1941* (New York [etc.], 2001)].

36. Protokol zasedaniia komissii ZapSibKraiispolkoma ot 17.6.1931 po obsledovaniiu proisshedshego vzryva [Protocol of the Meeting of the Commission of the Western Siberian Executive Committee Investigating the Gas Explosion, 17 June 1931], GARF, f. 7416, op. 1, d. 70, l. 54–56.

ultimately unable to resolve. Until 1931 coal was extracted in higher beds and extracted cavities could be worked using the block-caving method. At deeper layers and for thicker seams, it was necessary to use backfilling technologies. As only 40 per cent of the wood necessary was to hand, the existing wood often being wet and difficult to work, pillars of coal were left in the field. Apart from the economic loss this represented, since it entailed leaving up to between 40 and 60 per cent of the coal in the goaf (that part of a mine from which the coal has been partially removed), this method was dangerous as it caused the evolution and spontaneous ignition of gas.[37]

As early as 1933, the leading engineers had to cope with an increasing number of underground fires. A special ministerial commission investigated the situation in the Kuzbass mines and demanded that the mines use only backfill, for which clay should be used since it was a cheaper building material. But in spite of this explicit order, a separate decision was made for some shafts in Prokopyevsk containing high-quality coking coal. During a "transitional period" the miners were required to use the block-caving method, as coking coal was urgently needed for steel production in the Urals.[38] Not surprisingly, the number of accidents sharply increased during pre-war years. In 1931 almost 6,000 accidents were reported, in 1936 more than 20,000. Most of these accidents occurred because of falling rocks, coal, and fragments. The death rate was almost constant over the years (2.5 per 1,000 workers from 1932 to 1936), but the increasing number of accidents was alarming.[39]

Contemporaries held the Stakhanov movement, which began in 1935, responsible for the increasing number of accidents and the damage to machines. After Aleksei Stakhanov, who was well prepared and supported by the local party committee, had set a record in extracting coal, the campaign was rolled out across the USSR, with individual production records being rewarded in all branches. The campaign promoted the *Stakhanovtsy* workers as the new elite among workers. They prided themselves on having accomplished a complete personal transformation. Having been illiterate shepherds or small farmers in the past, these workers had managed to train themselves to the level of skilled miners and were now able to work with

---

37. *Zhavoronkova, Istoriya sistem razrabotki moshchnykh krutopadayushchikh ugol'nykh plastov Prokop'evsko-Kiselevskogo mestorozhdeniya Kuzbassa (1917–1948)* [The History of Working on Steep Seams in the Prokop'evsk-Kiselevsk Seam in the Kuzbass (1917–1948)], Trudy po istorii Tekhniki. Materialy pervogo soveshchaniya po istorii tekhniki [Works on the History of Technology: Proceedings of the First Convention on History of Technology] (Moscow, 1954), pp. 17–47, 29.
38. Protokol zasedaniia komissii NKTP po sistemam razrabotok [Protocol of the Meeting of the Commission in the People's Commissariat of Heavy Industry on Caving Systems], 6 March 1933. Rossiiskii gosudarstvennyi Arkhiv Ekonomiki [Russian State Archive of the Economy] [hereafter, RGAE], f. 7566, d. 125, l. 6–9.
39. GARF, f. 7416, op. 1, d. 187, S. 75; RGAE, f. 7566, op. 1, d. 1981, l. 59.

new and difficult machines. They were privileged in many ways. They got better accommodation, clothing, and medical care, and ate their meals in special canteens. Within the company, however, neither the authorities nor the co-workers liked the Stakhanov workers, as they challenged the fragile relationship and unexpressed agreement between workers and directors: to keep production at a level that would not evoke increasing demands from the central authorities. They thus faced open hostility. For instance, as the local trade union recorded, one Stakhanov worker was screamed at, pilloried, and robbed at the market.[40]

At the same time, antagonisms between leading personnel and individual workers increased in general. Several sources tell us about the growing discontent among workers. Party records, for instance, include a report about workers who, after repeating the official slogans of "critique and self-critique", went on to criticize low safety levels at work, the lack of garments for workers, and defective machines. This criticism was voiced despite worker awareness that they could be punished for openly questioning government measures. As German returnees reported, not only was discontent growing, fear was pervasive.[41]

CHANGING PERCEPTIONS: "FOREIGN SPIES" AND "ENEMIES OF THE PEOPLE"

On 22 September 1936 a build up of methane gas exploded in Kemerovo's Central Mine. Ten miners died and fifteen were severely injured. Although the accident was nothing new after an increasing number of explosions and fires in the previous two years, local and central officials used it to start a campaign to have the alleged culprits tried and convicted, thus shifting the blame to a number of exposed persons in order to direct possible discontent in directions less perilous for the regime. Although the social dimensions of Stalinist society have been studied very thoroughly,[42] few attempts have been made to analyse the impact of mass repressions in their interdependence with specific environmental and labour conditions.[43] The impact of the Stalinist terror on mining seems to have been of

---

40. Stenogramma zasedaniya Zapsibkraikoma [Minutes of the Western Siberian Party Committee], GANO, f. R-1115, op. 2, d. 7, l. 27.
41. See Landau, *Wir bauen den großen Kuzbass!*, pp. 313–317, for further references.
42. See, among others, the work of Sheila Fitzpatrick, Anne D. Rassweiler, David R. Shearer, Moshe Lewin, Melanie Ilich, Wendy Z. Goldman, Roberta Manning, Arch Getty/Oleg Naumov, Viktor I. Isaev, Sergei A. Krasil'nikov, Sergei A. Papkov, Oleg Khlevniuk, and Gabór T. Rittersporn.
43. See, for the years 1948–1967, Klaus Gestwa, *Die Stalinschen Großbauten des Kommunismus. Sowjetische Technik- und Umweltgeschichte 1948–1967* (Munich, 2010). Rittersporn's assessment from the early 1990s remains, in my view, valid even today: Gabór T. Rittersporn, "The Omnipresent Conspiracy: On Soviet Imagery of Politics and Social Relations in the 1930s", in

particular importance, as the mining industry played a key role in Stalinist industrialization propaganda. The miner was a propagandistic hero and it was therefore no coincidence that the hewer Stakhanov became the figurehead of the movement named after him.

Directly after the explosion in Kemerovo, local party and NKVD officials established an investigative commission. However, it was deemed less important to find the reasons for the accidents than to allocate blame. Before the investigation had even been completed, the NKVD arrested leading engineers and the head of the mine administration.[44] The Kemerovo explosion coincided with another important turn in the politics of Soviet repression. Four days later, on 26 September 1936, the People's Commissar of the Interior, Genrikh Jagoda, was arrested and replaced by Nikolai Ezhov. The following show trials investigating the Kemerovo accidents marked the beginning of the "Great Terror" of 1936–1938.

A show trial in Novosibirsk was prepared, taking place in November 1936. Among the leading engineers arrested and convicted was the German engineer Emil Stickling, who was accused of preparing a fascist coup d'état together with Russian engineers. Other engineers arrested were to be heard as "witnesses", after being manipulated into giving evidence under torture. One of them was Mikhail S. Stroilov, who had been involved in the recruitment of foreign specialists in the Ruhr and had only recently, in 1935, been awarded the Orden Lenina for his mining inventions. The accusations of "contacts with foreigners" and "foreign expertise" played an important role during the trial in Novosibirsk and in the following trial in Moscow in January 1937.

In Novosibirsk, the process was held partly in secret. Stickling was interrogated in a secret session, where he admitted the accusations against him after being threatened that his Russian wife would be executed. Finally, in the Novosibirsk trial the nine defendants were found guilty and sentenced to death. The sentence was proclaimed before a selected public audience and the event already had all the hallmarks of the show trials to come. Later, three of the defendants, among them Stickling, were amnestied and the death penalty was commuted to imprisonment.

The Novosibirsk trial was followed by another, larger show trial in Moscow, which adjudicated on several problems in all branches of heavy industry. The main accused were Georgy Pyatakov – the Deputy People's Commissar for Heavy Industry – and Karl Radek, former leader of the KPSU's international bureau. From the Kuzbass, the local leading engineers

Arch Getty and Roberta Manning (eds), *Stalinist Terror: New Perspectives* (Cambridge, 1993), pp. 99–115, 100.
44. On these events see Sergei Papkov, *Stalinskii Terror v Sibiri, 1928–1941* [Stalinist Terror in Siberia, 1928–1941] (Novosibirsk, 1997), p. 162.

were on trial. According to the accusations, a group of alleged conspirators in the Kuzbass had been instructed by Trotsky, together with German and Japanese spies, to induce fires and explosions in the mines. The local Kuzbass newspaper reported extensively on the trials. In addition to the trial documentation, the newspapers printed letters to the editor in which "the workers" allegedly demanded a thorough investigation of what they saw as the murder of ten miners in Kemerovo and "merciless punishment" for the "villains".[45] These letters – though collectively written by workers under the watchful eye of the party committee at their place of work – produced a direct connection between the process in the capital and the events in the Kuzbass.

The accused were sentenced to death or to long prison sentences (though those sent to prison were also later shot).[46] The trials were documented in propaganda brochures and longer accounts in Russian and other languages. In these propagandistic accounts, "spies" and "agents" played a central role, being directed by foreign powers to fight against the Soviet Union from within. Indeed, during the pre-war years, the Soviet Union was on a per-manent state of military alert – which was not completely unjustified given Hitler's accession to power, the civil war in Spain, Italy's invasion of Ethiopia, and the German remilitarization of the Rhineland. The explosions and fires in the mines seemed to prove specifically, and onsite, the existence of a "Fifth Column".[47] At the same time, this intimidation enabled the mining society to retain its own, distinct rules and to keep the potential for unrest and solidarity under control.

The resonance of the Kemerovo trial on mining "wreckers" and its importance for Soviet international propaganda is illustrated by a brochure written by the émigré Austrian communist and author Ernst Fischer and published by Workers' Library Publishers in New York in 1937. The author, working as a journalist for the Communist International (Comintern), depicted the international "Trotskyite wreckers" in the Kuzbass (Figure 2). A year later he emigrated to Moscow, where his wife, Ruth von Mayenburg, claimed that he was himself in danger.[48]

In the following years, the repressions against leading personnel and foreigners in the mines continued. After 1938, over 70 per cent of leading personnel were either arrested or executed.[49] By 1937, only 43 of the 1,000

---

45. *Kuzbass* [local daily newspaper], 22 January 1937.
46. Kaleriia A. Zabolotskaia, "Oni zhili v Kemerovo i sozdavali bol'shoi Kuzbass" [They Lived in Kemerovo and Built the Big Kuzbass] (Kemerovo, 1998), pp. 70–73, 72.
47. Roberta T. Manning, "The Soviet Economic Crisis of 1936–1940 and the Great Purges", in Getty and Manning, *Stalinist Terror*, pp. 116–141, 136.
48. Ruth von Mayenburg, *Hotel Lux, Das Absteigequartier der Weltrevolution* (Munich, 1991 [1978]), p. 202.
49. Kaleriia A. Zabolockaia, *Ugol'naia promyshlennost'* [Coal Industry] (Kemerovo, 1996), p. 158.

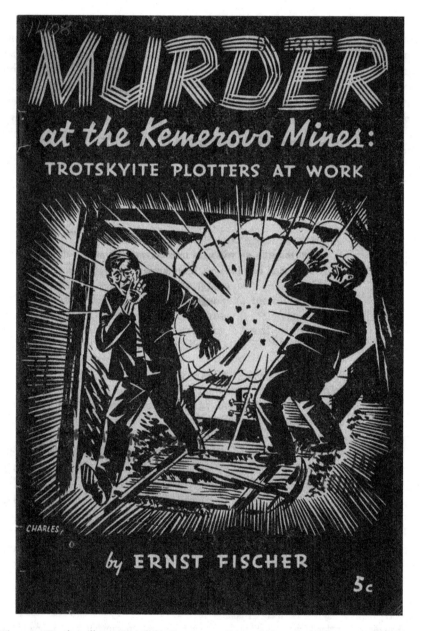

Figure 2. Woodcut illustration of the Kemerovo mining accident, September 1936. The miner on the left represents the elder "Trotskyite" spy, getting himself out of danger, while the worker on the right is caught by the explosion.
Cover of the brochure Murder at the Kemerovo Mines: Trotskyite Plotters at Work, _by Ernst Fischer (New York, 1937). A digital copy is available at Florida Atlantic University Digital Library: http://fau.digital.flvc.org/islandora/object/fau%3A4432; last accessed 20 August 2015._

foreigners working in the Kuzbass in 1932 were left. However, these years saw not only the complete replacement of the elite workers in the mines, but also significant technological advances. Now, backfilling technologies and safety protection facilities, such as iron plates, became more important.[50] The catastrophes of the early 1930s seemed to have been overcome, and the number of accidents decreased until the beginning of the 1940s.

A second wave of Stalinist repression in the Kuzbass was directed against the special settlers. Starting in summer 1937 and continuing until 1938, the NKVD arrested thousands of special settlers – who were still highly marginalized despite the restricted freedoms they had been given in exchange for good production results (concessions that did not, of course, include freedom of movement). But even after submitting to the goals of the authorities, the special settlers continued to be seen as potentially disloyal. In June 1937 the local head of the party committee, Robert I. Ejche, reported to the CPSU's Central Committee concerning the successful arrest of a group of over 20,000 alleged conspirators accused of acting on behalf of German and Japanese agents.[51]

This formed part of the major campaigns during the years of the "Great Terror", in which thousands of people were arrested and executed on NKVD orders directed against former *kulaky* and "anti-Soviet elements" (in summer 1937) as well as against "national minorities" (during 1938). In these orders, quotas defined the number of people in every region who had to be deported or executed; local NKVD officials asked the central authorities for permission to raise these quotas and were given approval to do so. *Kulaky* of Soviet-German origin were seen as especially dangerous, as they were alleged to have contacts with German specialists. Thus, the Soviet-German special settlers were accused of forming the rank and file of a fascist movement in Russia, with the German specialists cast as their leaders.

PRISONERS OF WAR

After the German attack on the Soviet Union, the system of different camps and colonies expanded, organized by the POW administration of the Commissariat of the Interior (Glavnoe Upravlenie Voennykh i Internirovannykh) [GUPVI]). Kuzbasugol' called for new camps near the mines to keep the workforce at the necessary level, as young men had been

---

50. Landau, *Wir bauen den großen Kuzbass!*, p. 299.
51. Tezisy doklada N.I. Yezhova na iiunskom plenume TsK VKP (b), 22.6.1937 [Theses of the Speech by N.I. Yezhov at the June Plenum of the Central Committee of the All-Russian Communist Party, 22 June 1937], in Viktor Danilov et al. (eds), *Tragediia sovetskoi derevni. Kollektivizatsiia i raskulachivanie. 1927–1939: Dokumenty i materialy*, Vol. 5, *1934–36* [The Tragedy of the Soviet Village: Collectivization and "De-Kulakization", 1927–1939] (Moscow, 2002), pp. 306–308.

recruited for the Red Army. The first group to be interned in the camps were "mobilized soldiers of the workers' army", men and women of Soviet-German origin, who were supposed to be collectively disloyal to the Soviet state. In 1942 special camps were built around the pits and extended the following year. Later, once the war had finally ended, leaving a country totally devastated and depopulated, more than 26,000 prisoners of war and internees, men and women, among them Germans, Polish, Japanese, Chinese, Austrian, Slovakians, and Ukrainians, were sent to the Kuzbass. About 60 per cent of them were assigned to work in the mines.[52]

After their arrival in the Kuzbass, the prisoners of war and internees were divided into different groups, according to their health status. As it turned out, many were unable to work due to malnutrition and the epidemic diseases that had spread during their long journeys. Also, the camps were not prepared for the high number of new internees and were therefore unable to provide food, housing, clothes, and shoes. For example, only 60 per cent of the internees in Camp No. 525 near Kemerovo could be put to work – even after the Deputy Commissar of Mining, Egor T. Abakumov, had announced to the director of the Kemerovo coalmines in 1944: "We have to exploit the workers that the state is giving to us maximally and to the full".[53] But as most POWs were increasingly failing to meet their work targets, with rates dropping from 50 per cent to only 10 per cent, the managers knew that they had to give POW workers some time to recover in order to meet production plans. In the devastated country, the food supply was catastrophic, decreasing dramatically in winter 1945 and becoming even worse in 1946. Only one-half of the POWs were able to work in 1946. As their food ration depended on work targets being met, those unable to work were in a desperate situation. In the face of this, and constantly decreasing supplies by the state, the camp administration at last deployed some prisoners to procure food, by fishing or collecting mushrooms and herbs for example.

As the number of prisoners and internees able to work in the pits remained low, they were replaced by internees from the so-called special camps in Germany, where people had been interned because of their prior role in the Nazi administration or propaganda apparatus, or simply because they were assumed to be potentially dangerous. Contrary to official announcements,

---

52. Nina M. Markdorf-Sergeeva and Rashid S. Bikmetov, "Soderzhanie i trudovoe ispol'zovanie inostrannykh voennoplennykh v Kuzbasse" [Position of Foreign Prisoners of War and their Exploitation to Work in the Kuzbass], in Nina M. Markdorf-Sergeeva and Rashid S. Bikmetov (eds), *Inostrannye voennoplennye v Kuzbasse v 1940-e gody. Dokumenty i materialy* [Foreign Prisoners of War in the Kuzbass in the 1940s: Documents and Materials] (Kemerovo, 2002), pp. 11–63, 18.
53. GAKO, f. P-75, op. 1, d. 151, l. 7–8, cited by Markdorf-Sergeeva and Bikmetov, *Soderzhanie i trudovoe ispol'zovanie*, p. 16.

which spoke of 8,500 internees to be sent to the Kuzbass, actually only 5,332 were sent to the Kuzbass and the Karaganda basin in Kazakhstan in 1947. Food supplies had been catastrophic also in the Soviet occupation zone in Germany, especially in winter 1946–1947. The internees in the Soviet special camps were to receive only 300 grams of bread per day, the food ration of a "non-working" person, and one-third of the internees died in the special camps in Germany's Soviet zone. It is thus not surprising that the commission in charge of choosing possible workers in the camps found that only a small proportion were healthy enough to be sent to the Soviet Union for work.[54]

After 1947, the situation improved. As many workers in poor health were repatriated, Kuzbasugol' helped the remaining workers with higher food rations and improved dwellings – but only to those deployed in the coal industry, and always strictly according to profession, workplace, and nationality. Under the new regulations, a hewer would receive one kilo of bread per day, other underground miners only 900 grams. However, a Japanese hewer was allotted only 750 grams of bread per day.[55] Due to better food provisions and health care, the situation further improved in 1948. Now almost 90 per cent of prisoners were designated "able to work".

Also, the status of a prisoner of war improved fundamentally. They were now employed according to their professions, which enabled them to earn a premium. However, wages were not paid in cash. After a deduction of 35 per cent to pay for the maintenance of the camp, their wages were credited to personal accounts at special stores in the camps, where they were able to buy tobacco, clothes, and other products. These "luxury goods" – and in the context of the postwar misery in Soviet Russia these products were indeed luxurious – were an indication of their improved social status. Also, their confinement was eased, not least because guards, usually former soldiers, increasingly refused to accept the authority of the camp administration and did not leave their barracks, which were far away from the POW camps. Guards now consisted of other POWs, who were equipped with whistles and white armlets. At some camps, the gate was left open during the day. Around it, the locals often traded with the POWs, who sold self-made pocket knives, lighters, pencils, and medals. While control was thus shifted to the POWs themselves, denunciations were rewarded by the

---

54. Beschluss des Ministerrates Nr. 2728–1124ss "Zum Abtransport von in Gefängnissen und Lagern inhaftierten Deutschen aus Deutschland" [Decision of the Council of Ministers No. 2728–1124ss "On the Deportation of Interned Germans from Prisons and Camps in Germany"], in Sergej Mironenko, Lutz Niethammer, and Alexander von Plato (eds), *Sowjetische Speziallager in Deutschland 1945–1950, Bd. II: Sowjetische Dokumente zur Lagerpolitik* (Berlin, 1998), pp. 268–269, and Dok. 64, pp. 276–277; Ralf Possekel, "Einleitung", in *ibid.*, p. 76.
55. Prikaz ministerstva ugol'noi promyshlennosti vostochnykh raionov SSSR, 1.2.1947 [Order of the Ministry for the Coal Industry of the Eastern Regions of the USSR], GAKO, f. R-456, op. 4, d. 43, l.40, in Markdorf-Sergeeva and Bikmetov, *Inostrannye voennoplennye*, pp. 101–102.

authorities. In particular, a POW who failed to report an escape attempt would be putting himself in danger.[56]

The relationship to the surrounding population was fraught and multi-layered. On the one hand, every family had its own victims of the war to bemoan. Those who had been evacuated from the European part of Russia to Siberia, or even from besieged Leningrad, faced the Germans with open hatred. On the other hand, postwar Soviet propaganda depicted the German people generally as having suffered under Nazism and thus having been victims of "financial capitalism". Although marriages between Soviet citizens and foreigners were forbidden by state law in 1947, there were secret affectionate relationships and extramarital affairs between POWs and Soviet women. Having a child born out of such a relationship could result in being relocated elsewhere and in social isolation, as one female miner remembers:

> In the shaft worked a young and handsome guy, Johann. We made friends. He spoke Russian very badly, but we understood each other anyway. He tried to help me. One day he asked me to marry him. I was frightened and refused. If you had a relationship with a prisoner of war, no one would hug you. If one of us women had an affair with a German, she would hide it. There were rumours that one worker had a child with a POW. It was spoken about secretly, even the name was mentioned and after the birth of the child she did not return to the mine. No one knew what had happened to her; maybe she moved somewhere else or ended up in the places "not so far away" [i.e. the Gulag camps].[57]

Incidents against POWs could be reported and charges were heard in a military court. These processes reveal the improved status of the foreign POWs and internees. For example, an electric welder at the Anzherougol mines was convicted for taking the work gloves from an interned German female worker, another for beating a German POW.[58] While most of the German and Japanese POWs were repatriated between 1948 and 1949, convicted POWs and many, often very young persons, who had been arrested and convicted in the Soviet Occupation Zone were held in Gulag-administered penal camps for many years to come.

CONCLUSION

In spite of the official egalitarian propaganda, the Kuzbass before World War II was a strictly hierarchic society. One's position in this hierarchy was marked by access to scarce goods. "Foreign specialists" were privileged and

---

56. Markdorf-Sergeeva and Bikmetov, *Soderzhanie i trudovoe ispol'zovanie*, p. 48.
57. Valentina Ivanova Petrova [family name changed], "Vospominaniia" [Memories], in Markdorf-Sergeeva and Bikmetov, *Inostrannye voennoplennye*, p. 137.
58. Markdorf-Sergeeva and Bikmetov, *Soderzhanie i trudovoe ispol'zovanie*, p. 52.

supplied with better housing and alimentation, while "special settlers" – forced labourers mostly from European parts of the Soviet Union – were malnourished, left on their own, and discriminated against by the secret police.

This situation caused growing unrest. Extremely dangerous working conditions underground and a sudden rise in the number of accidents intensified these smouldering latent conflicts – which were seemingly "relieved" through the repressive campaigns of the authorities. With arbitrary arrests and executions of tens of thousands of people, always in the context of a presumed Fifth Column, society was kept in a state of permanent mobilization.

While the war itself saw the arrival of POWs in the Kuzbass coalfield, it was most notably after the war that the former enemy was put to work in the Kuzbass mines. About 30,000 POWs and internees from Germany, Japan, Austria, Hungary, and Romania were forced to work in the Kuzbass mines and on nearby construction sites. In the devastated country, especially during the hunger crisis of 1946–1947, the POWs were poorly provided for, and soon only one-half of them were able to work any longer. As the economy needed a steady supply of coal, which necessitated a more efficient use of the labour force available, living conditions improved and POWs – especially those working underground in the mines – were given higher food rations and rewarded for meeting production targets. Although the POWs were supposed to work and live away from the local population, contacts and relationships at work or in the surroundings of the camps were frequent.

There is thus a long history of foreigners working in the Kuzbass coalfields, from the 1920s until 1950. This created both shared experiences and fraught relationships with other workers – who themselves had migrated or been forced to migrate from other, often faraway parts of Russia. Social hierarchies and ethnic attributions were subject to constant shifts and resulted in a series of peculiar constellations: whereas foreign specialists were comparatively privileged, both they and forced internal migrants (often with nationalities considered equally "foreign") were seen as possibly disloyal and suspicious once the Great Terror had begun. After the war, foreigners were recruited as prisoners of war and had to endure many hardships. In a country devastated and depopulated after the German assault, however, this workforce was desperately needed, and so, in the end, their status improved substantially.

IRSH 60 (2015), Special Issue, pp. 207–226 doi:10.1017/S0020859015000425
© 2015 Internationaal Instituut voor Sociale Geschiedenis

Migration, Ethnicity, and Divisions of Labour in the Zonguldak Coalfield, Turkey

E R O L K A H V E C İ

Department of Sociology, Faculty of Arts & Sciences,
Izmir University of Economics
35330, Balçova, Izmir, Turkey

E-mail: erol.kahveci@ieu.edu.tr

ABSTRACT: This article examines labour relations and labour conditions in the Zonguldak coalfield on the Black Sea coast in Turkey. From 1867, peasants from surrounding villages were obliged to work in the mines on a rotational basis. Peasants continued to work part-time in the mines after the end of this forced-labour regime in 1921, and after its reintroduction between 1940 and 1947. The article explores the significance of the recruitment of local villagers for the division of labour in the mines. Underground work was performed by low-skilled rotational peasant-miners, while migrants became skilled, full-time surface workers. Different ethnic origins added to the division of labour between these two groups. Attention is then turned to trade unionism in Zonguldak. The miners' trade union was controlled by permanent workers, mostly migrants of Laz origin, to the detriment of underground peasant-workers. Ethnographic fieldwork reveals that these divisions have persisted over many years.

At Zonguldak, located on the western Black Sea coast of Turkey, coal has been mined since the 1840s. It was the largest coalmining area in Turkey, and the sole source of the hard coal that fuelled the Ottoman navy, transport, government installations, and utilities. In fact, Zonguldak was the engine of Turkey's industrialization. Its workforce, reaching over 60,000 at its peak in the late 1950s, was the largest in the country, with the longest history. During the 1980s and 1990s coal became strategically less important, and by late 2014 the number of miners at Zonguldak had fallen to around 9,000. The Zonguldak coalfield covers an area of 13,350 square kilometres, of which 2,250 square kilometres lie under the sea. All production involved underground mining. The coal stocks at Zonguldak have officially been estimated at 1.34 billion (US) tons in 52 different seams of variable thickness, of which only 37 are workable. The inclination of these seams varies between 0 and 90 degrees and in thickness from 70 centimetres to 10 metres.[1]

---

1. Information about the Zonguldak coal reserves, markets, production, and labour force has been taken from the Statistical Yearbooks of Ereğli Kömür İşletmeleri [hereafter, EKI] and of the

Although the area surrounding Zonguldak, including Ereğli and Amasra, has an ancient history, the history of the city of Zonguldak itself goes back only 170 years. The city owes its existence to the mining industry. Until 1896 Zonguldak was a sub-district of the village of Elvan, in the Ereğli district. In 1896 Zonguldak was given the status of a district itself; in 1924 it became a province. That year the population of the city was 29,000; the population of Zonguldak province as a whole was 240,000. Early coal production was located at the centre of the city and in its immediate vicinity. Looking at the city's relatively short history and rapid population growth, it can be stated that the vast majority of its inhabitants in these years were migrants.[2] As more mines and the port opened, businessmen and workers filtered in from across the empire and beyond.

The Zonguldak coalmines were not privately owned, but contracted by the state to various foreign and native investors. At the start of operations, skilled migrant workers from Croatia, Montenegro, Britain, and France were brought in by contracted companies. Later, other workers migrated from the northern Black Sea area (these migrants were ethnically referred to as Laz) and eastern Turkey (Kurds). Donald Quataert, one of the foremost specialists in Ottoman labour history in general and of the early Zonguldak coalfield in particular, reproduces some first-hand accounts from the recollections of two expatriates from Zonguldak: "You could find people of all nationalities here: Greeks, Armenians, French, Turks, Italian, Kurds"; and "In the past Zonguldak was insignificant [...]. Everybody, Turks as well as Greeks, came from somewhere else. There was no native population. There were no indigenous Zonguldaklis. Whoever settled there was a foreigner."[3] Almost all miners in the city of Zonguldak were migrants. Some came from surrounding villages, others from further afield. Migration brought an ethnically diverse people together. Throughout the years, migration and ethnic divisions in the labour force had a significant impact on the lives of Zonguldak miners.

Mine operators, whether they are working with state or private capital, can deploy a host of strategies to overcome the lack of labour or the

Turkish Hardcoal Company [hereafter, TTK]; EKİ was renamed TTK in 1983. These Statistical Yearbooks have been published annually since 1940. They can be found in the library of the TTK in Zonguldak. The archival sources consulted for this article are housed in two locations in the city of Zonguldak. Most are in the reading room at Karaelmas University and in the Education Bureau of the TTK headquarters. The author accessed these materials between 1992 and 1996. These materials were also consulted by Donald Quataert in 1997, 1998, and 2004. For a complete inventory of all holdings see Donald Quataert and Nadir Özbek, "The Ereğli-Zonguldak Coal Mines: A Catalog of Archival Documents", *Turkish Studies Association Bulletin*, 23 (1999), pp. 55–67.

2. See Erol Kahveci, "The Political Economy of the Zonguldak Coalbasin and its Labour Force: 1848–1995" (Ph.D. dissertation, University of Bristol, 1997), pp. 202–208.

3. Quoted from Donald Quataert, *Miners and the State in the Ottoman Empire: The Zonguldak Coalfield 1822–1920* (New York, 2006), p. 34.

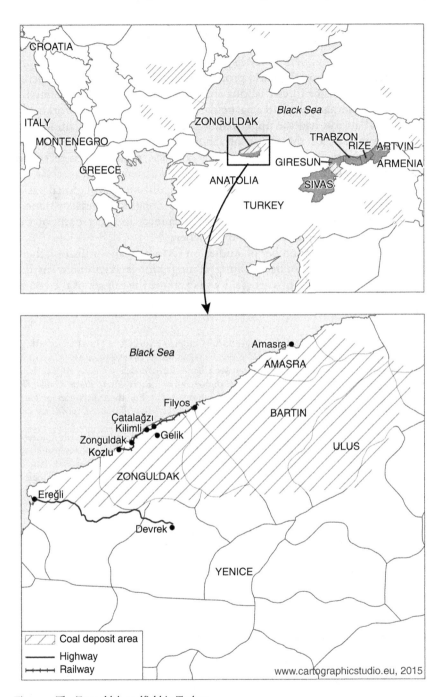

Figure 1. The Zonguldak coalfield in Turkey.

unwillingness of a local population to endure the unsafe and harsh working conditions in coalmining. In some cases, scarcity of labour resulted in advantages for the miners in terms of better wages and social provision. But shortage of labour could also prompt extraordinary measures to coerce workers into forms of forced-labour and slave-like conditions. The highly centralized Ottoman state had a particular impact on the lives of workers in general, and always had the upper hand in the recruitment, retention, and the determination of the rights of labour.[4] In the case of Zonguldak, unskilled underground, and particularly coalface, miners were recruited from its surrounding villages by extra-economic coercion. Peasants were forced by the state to work in the mines of Zonguldak on a rotational basis. In this respect, some of the experiences of the Zonguldak peasant-miners show a remarkable resemblance to those of miners in other parts of the world, in Africa, Latin America, and elsewhere.[5]

Among the growing number of studies on Ottoman labour history, there are no contemporary studies looking at migration and ethnicity in the Zonguldak coalfield.[6] In this article, I will examine the impact of the ethnic divisions in the Zonguldak mining labour force in terms of the labour

4. Huri İslamoğlu and Çağlar Keyder, "Agenda for Ottoman History", in Huri İslamoğlu-İnan (ed.), *The Ottoman Empire and the World-Economy* (Cambridge, 1987), pp. 42–62.
5. For the experiences of African mine labour see Charles van Onselen, *Chibaro: African Mine Labour in Southern Rhodesia, 1900–1933* (London, 1973); Ruth First, *Black Gold: The Mozambican Miner, Proletarian and Peasant* (Brighton, 1983). For the experiences of Latin American miners see June Nash, *We Eat the Mines and the Mines Eat Us: Dependency and Exploitation in Bolivian Tin Mines* (New York, 1979).
6. In his book on Zonguldak, *Miners and the State in the Ottoman Empire*, Donald Quataert concentrated on the Ottoman period, and migration and ethnicity were not his main pre-occupations. There is agreement among Ottoman labour historians that there is a lack of documentary sources relating to workers. See Suraiya Faroqhi, "Labor Recruitment and Control in the Ottoman Empire (Sixteenth and Seventeenth Centuries)", in Donald Quataert (ed.), *Manufacturing in the Ottoman Empire and Turkey, 1500–1950* (New York, 1994), pp. 13–58; I. Bulbul, "The Workers of the Balya-Karaaydin Mining Company (1901–1922)", *Balıkesir Üniversitesi Sosyal Bilimler Enstitüsü Dergisi*, 13 (2010), pp. 227–240. Apart from the lack of documentary sources, historical labour studies in Ottoman Turkey have had to come to terms with the limited scope of industrialization. Even as late as the early twentieth century, workers in manufacturing industry comprised only a tiny segment of the population, not exceeding 14,000 in 1915. Some recent publications which have attempted to overcome these challenges are: Akın Sefer, "From Class Solidarity to Revolution: The Radicalization of Arsenal Workers in the Late Ottoman Empire", *International Review of Social History*, 58 (2013), pp. 395–428; M. Erdem Kabadayı and Kate Elizabeth Creasey, "Working in the Ottoman Empire and in Turkey: Ottoman and Turkish Labour History within a Global Perspective", *International Labor and Working-Class History*, 82 (2012), pp. 187–200; Touraj Atabaki and Gavin Brockett (eds), *Ottoman and Republican Turkish Labour History* (Cambridge, 2010); Donald Quataert, "Labor History and the Ottoman Empire, c.1700–1922", *International Labor and Working-Class History*, 60 (2001), pp. 93–109; idem, *Workers, Peasants and Economic Change in the Ottoman Empire, 1730–1914* (Istanbul, 2010); Suraiya Faroqhi, *Artisans of Empire: Crafts and Craftspeople under the Ottomans* (New York, 2009).

process, different types of labour relations, working conditions, and company provisions. The article highlights the existence of two historical regimes of forced labour, each with its impact on subsequent forms of labour relations.

PEASANT-MINERS AND THE FIRST FORCED-LABOUR REGIME, 1867–1921

At the beginning of the Crimean War (1853–1856), primitive conditions characterized the small amount of mining carried out in the Zonguldak area. Only about 500 people were reported to be employed in the mines. Those cutting the coal and boring the galleries were mainly Croats; there were also some British miners. Increased coal production was needed to meet the extra demand from the Ottoman navy, transport, and other government installations and utilities.[7] To provide more coal, the state began to develop the coalfield more systematically in the 1850s, by opening up a new shaft to exploit the more deeply concealed seams, constructing a basic railway network between the mines and the harbour, and adopting more efficient mining methods. This development encouraged Laz migrants from the eastern Black Sea area to work in the mines, in addition to a small number of Greeks and Armenians, as well as local peasants. Nevertheless, during this period, mine labour continued to be in short supply. Indeed, the government assigned soldiers from the local army barracks around Zonguldak to work as coalminers during their military service.[8]

Until 1867, the state's efforts to develop the mines met with little success, mainly because there were few experienced miners.[9] In May 1867, however, the government established guidelines for the exploitation of the mines that would have a decisive influence on the fortunes of coalmining in the area, and which would affect operations also later on in the era of republican Turkey. It was Rear Admiral Dilaver Paşa,[10] mine director and

---

7. According to Sefer, as late as 1905 lack of coal impeded the operations of the workshops in the Imperial Naval Arsenal; see Sefer, "From Class Solidarity to Revolution", p. 420.
8. Ahmet Naim, *Zonguldak Havzası Uzun Mehmet'ten Bugüne Kadar* [The Zonguldak Coal Basin since Uzun Mehmet] (Istanbul, 1934), p. 24.
9. When mining activities began in the Ottoman mines in Anatolia, labour was "recruited" from the Rumelia region, which had a long mining history. See P. De Wijkerslooth, "Elazığ İli Ergani Maden Bakir Yataklari Hakkindaki Bilgiye Yeni bir İlave" [Additional Information on the Ergani Copper Mines in Elazığ], *MTA Enstitüsü Mecmuasi* [Bulletin of the Mineral Research and Exploration Institute], 1 (1945), pp. 76–90, 76; Hasan Yuksel, *Osmanli Döneminde Keban-Ergani Madenleri* [The Mines of Ergani and Keban during the Ottoman Era] (Sivas, 1997).
10. In 1865 the Naval Ministry had become responsible for the mines. Between 1865 and 1882, the Naval Ministry took all the coal at a fixed price and, as a result, limited the foreign investment at Zonguldak. However, a European-controlled organization, the Ottoman Public Debt Administration, was set up in 1881 to collect payments on the loans. This subsequently acted as an intermediary with European companies seeking investment opportunities in Turkey and in this

chief official (*kaymakam*) of Ereğli (Zonguldak), who issued this set of mining regulations, laying down the rights and duties of mine operators and standards for the boring and reinforcement of the galleries. The regulations consisted of 100 articles, many of them seeking to regulate labour in the mines.[11]

According to the new regulations, villagers in the fourteen districts of Ereğli (Zonguldak) were obliged to fulfil certain tasks at the mines. Each village was assigned to provide labour for a particular mine, a service that was to be compensated in wages. Healthy, able-bodied men between thirteen and fifty years old were registered in a book kept by the *muhtar* (the village headman). He assigned workers at each pit to one of two groups, each of which would work twelve days rotationally, until the other group arrived. The miners were expected to spend the next twelve days cultivating the land in their village before returning to work. The regulations recognized four categories of worker: *kazmacıyan* (hewers), *küfeciyan* (basketmen), *kiracıyan* (who provided animals to transport coal), and *sütünkeş* (who supplied, transported, and erected pit props). *Kiracıyan* were to work in the mines with their animals on fifteen-day rotations. No *kiracıyan* was allowed to disrupt transport in the mines, so they had to provide their animals on time. If a *kiracıyan* gave up coal transport for other work, he would be punished.[12]

In the regulations, *kazmacı* (hewers) were sharply distinguished from the other groups. They could not be forced to work in a particular pit and were permitted to negotiate with the pit operator over their wages and to leave their work for better wages. Hewers' ability and experience were to be taken into account in wage negotiations.[13] So, the regulations accorded hewers the partial status of wage labourers. They were free to work for a mine operator of their choice, but they were not free to give up minework.

Some historians consider the 1867 regulations an improvement for the Zonguldak peasants. However, to a very high degree they were powerless vis-à-vis the mine operators, and abuses were numerous.[14] Although articles on wage arrangements required cash payments, these were made for the first time by the Gurci Company only in 1885, seventeen years after the regulations had been passed. Payment was often given in merchandise,

---

way was instrumental in facilitating the further penetration of European capital into the Ottoman economy, including mining.

11. For details of the regulations see Cevat Ülkekul, *Taş Kömürü Havzasında Bahriye Nezareti Yönetimi (1865–1908) ve Dilaver Paşa Nizamnamesi* [The Naval Ministry Era in the Coal Basin (1865–1908): Dilaver Paşa Regulations] (Istanbul, 2007), pp. 67–93.

12. *Ibid.*, p. 80, articles 32 and 34.

13. *Ibid.*, p. 78, articles 22 and 23.

14. Naim, *Zonguldak Havzasi*, pp. 112–113.

valued at 50 to 75 per cent above the standard price. As the miners needed cash for basic commodities, they were forced to sell the merchandise at reduced prices.[15]

Since the peasant coalminers considered themselves primarily farmers gaining supplementary income in the mines, they retained their village orientation, failing to develop a group identity based on job function or, as a result, any sense of a working-class consciousness or a desire to organize. This largely explains both the wage stagnation and the docile obedience of the workers, which was so highly prized and favourably commented on by company officials and other Europeans.[16] Indeed, an 1893 company report noted that "these populations appear to us gentle, docile, robust, they have a great respect for authority".[17]

While the company profited from the fact that its workforce considered itself to be peasants as well as miners, the workers' self-identification as peasants also posed a challenge, since they were not completely at the mercy of the firm for their livelihood, and remained independent. In 1901, for example, when the company suspended operations because of low coal prices, full-time miners would have been deprived of their income by a disastrous lengthy shutdown, but peasant-miners could survive because, not being employed full-time, they could live on the food grown in the villages when they were not working in the mines. Conversely, in the event of a crop failure, which would have meant real hardship in a purely agricultural society, those who worked in the mines had an alternative means of support. Because of the poor harvest in 1904, for example, the company found itself with more abundant manpower than usual.[18]

MIGRANT LABOUR

In a provision of long-reaching and crucial importance, the government in its 1867 regulations had restricted the obligation to work in the mines to villagers from the surrounding fourteen districts. By blocking the entry of outsiders, it sought to assure the local population of sole access to these jobs. The state also made sure that the income would be supplementary, that is, work in the mines was to be carried out on a part-time basis, in order to ensure that the villagers remained cultivators. The 1867 regulations initially assumed that more demanding and skilled tasks such as boring the galleries could also be carried out by villagers.

15. Sina Ciladir, *Zonguldak Havzasinda İşçi Hareketlerinin Tarihi, 1848–1940* [History of the Workers' Movement in the Zonguldak Coal Basin, 1848–1940] (Ankara, 1977), p. 31.
16. Kahveci, "Political Economy of the Zonguldak Coalbasin", p. 102.
17. Quoted from Donald Quataert, *Social Disintegration and Popular Resistance in the Ottoman Empire, 1881–1908: Reactions to European Economic Penetration* (London, 1983), p. 58.
18. *Ibid.*, pp. 58–60.

The primitive mining methods prevalent at the beginning of the industry perhaps limited the need for skilled labour. However, the development of mining and the increasing demand and production of coal required a wider range of more skilled labour, including drift developers to work within the rock strata to reach a coal seam, workers to pump out water, air, and gas, a foreman, and repair shop mechanics. Fifteen years after the regulations, the state stopped running the mines directly and licensed operations to a third party. In April 1882, a mining concession was granted to Serkis Bey, chief engineer of the Ottoman Empire and architect to the Sultan. Under the terms of the concession, the foreman and workers in the repair shops at the new mines would be foreigners. Miners would be hired locally; since the countryside was poor, it was said, they were readily available at a low price.[19]

In 1891 the Ereğli Coal Company (or Société Anonyme Ottomane d'Héraclée) was formed with French capital. Within a short period it would dominate the coal basin, extracting 60 per cent of its total production.[20] In 1893, two of the company's engineers filed an internal report on the mines, noting the earlier efforts made by the state to assure manpower. They described the practice of attaching a certain number of nearby villages to each mine, the part-time and rotational labour provided by the villagers, and the exemption from military service as compensation. The report, and a briefer one submitted to the authorities earlier, in 1877, indicated that Ottoman subjects from the Balkans, and even some foreigners, had also been hired to work in the mines. The earlier report noted the hiring of Bulgars and Croats, recruited by immigration agencies in Istanbul.[21] The later report also mentioned a small number of Italian and Montenegrin workers, residing permanently at the mines.

At the beginning of the twentieth century, as many as 10,000 people were employed in the coal basin, on either a full-time or part-time basis. Nearly all were Muslims. An estimated three-quarters of coalfield workers were rotational, being recruited from the farming communities of the surrounding districts; these underground and coalface workers remained at the mines for two to three weeks at a time. The remaining one-quarter was more permanent, and consisted of Kurd and Laz surface workers. After 1882, when the mine operators were first permitted to sell a portion of their coal on the open market, these permanent workers migrated from the more densely populated districts of Trabzon, Artvin, and Rize (all located in the

---

19. Quoted from *ibid.*, p. 57.
20. Later it formed a joint venture with a Turkish state-owned bank. To secure coal supplies, the Ereğli Company was nationalized in 1937, and in 1940 the remaining private coal companies were also nationalized. All Zonguldak's coal operations were carried out under the auspices of the state-owned Ereğli Kömür İşletmeleri (EKI).
21. Both reports are cited in Quataert, *Social Disintegration*, p. 57.

north-eastern Black Sea area of today's Turkey) and remained for periods from four months to several years. The Laz coming from these areas were highly regarded by the companies and received better medical care, pay, and housing than the rotational workers.[22]

In the early twentieth century migrant labour began to have an impact on industrial relations. In the months following the July 1908 revolution, for instance, the Ereğli Company was wracked by labour unrest.[23] A June 1909 report to the stockholders noted four strikes during the previous year. Foreign workers, the company claimed, prevented local labourers from operating the trains and working in the mines. The company reported its decision "to release [newly hired] miners from the Sivas and Trabzon provinces gradually and to seek to develop manpower among the local inhabitants", these migrant workers having been a disappointment.[24] As full-time professionals, the migrant miners were well aware of the value of their skills and organized themselves readily, becoming "foreign agitators" and stirring up the remaining 90 per cent of the labour force, whom the company claimed were willing to work.[25]

However, the mining engineers also reported that Montenegrin, Croat, and Kurdish workers were particularly appreciated for their energy and robustness in comparison to local labourers. In the interests of the company, and to preserve this labour force, the company offered benefits, according to the status of employees. Two primary schools, one for boys and the other for girls, were built by the company for the children of foreign personnel. In 1907 the school called Santa Barbara was attended by 53 pupils in 2 classes, with 4 Roman Catholic brothers as teachers. In 1914 there were 116 pupils, 4 classes, and 7 teachers. These paternalistic company policies did not apply to the local underground labour force.[26] The only elementary school in Zonguldak for Muslims held just 20 pupils in 1905.[27]

The company also spent at least 1 million francs on new housing, mainly for foreign and salaried employees.[28] The Ottoman subjects were lodged in collective buildings made of stone and wood; European

22. Delwin A. Roy, "Labour and Trade Unionism in Turkey: The Eregli Coalminers", *Middle Eastern Studies*, 12:3 (1976), pp. 125–172; Theo Nichols and Erol Kahveci, "The Condition of Mine Labour in Turkey: Injuries to Miners in Zonguldak 1942–90", *Middle Eastern Studies*, 31:2 (1995), pp. 197–228.
23. See Delwin A. Roy, "The Zonguldak Strike: A Case Study of Industrial Conflict in Turkey" (Ph.D. dissertation, Purdue University, 1968), pp. 165–170; Naim, *Zonguldak Havzası*, pp. 60–70; Quataert, *Social Disintegration*, pp. 64–66.
24. Naim, *Zonguldak Havzası*, p. 63.
25. *Ibid.*, p. 64.
26. Jacques Thobie, *Intérêts et Impérialisme Français dans l'Empire Ottoman 1895–1914* (Paris, 1977), p. 410.
27. *Yurt Ansiklopedisi* [National Encyclopedia] (Istanbul, 1982), p. 7730.
28. Thobie, *Intérêts et Impérialisme Français*, p. 411.

employees (sixty of them French) resided in individual houses, while the upper management's and engineers' houses were located on the hillside (the "French quarter") that overlooked the Black Sea and the town. These houses were offered at very moderate prices. In its 1912 report, the company noted that lodging for European workers and supervisors was sufficient, but that the quarters for local workers were not.[29]

An analysis of the 1913 Ereğli Coalbasin Administration Reports shows that in comparison with a surface miner an underground miner was twenty-two times more likely to be injured fatally, and ten times non-fatally.[30] Despite the lack of health and safety precautions and lack of compensation, no demand was made during the strikes to improve conditions for underground workers.

Although the government had already, in 1906, announced the abolition of the restriction on underground minework to the Zonguldak villagers, and opened employment to all Ottoman subjects, this did not alter the forced-labour regime for the Zonguldak villagers. It remained in effect until it was formally abolished with the introduction of the 1921 Labour Law.[31]

PEASANT-MINERS AFTER THE FIRST
FORCED-LABOUR REGIME

Agriculture and animal farming remained important for the Zonguldak villagers, because the extremely mountainous geographical conditions limited the area of cultivation in general and mechanized farming in particular; about 50 per cent of the land was steeply sloping (20 degrees and over). In addition, the land in Zonguldak is not very fertile, and farms were smaller than the average in what in 1923 had become Turkey.[32] Therefore, peasant-miners had never been entirely self-sufficient. The development of the mining industry enabled the villagers to participate in the commercial market.

Although no longer forced to work in the mines by law, they continued to do so after the abolition of the forced-labour regime in 1921 in order to supplement their incomes and pay off debts to the village usurer (*tefeci*). The Zonguldak mines thus remained an important source of cash for many peasant-miners. They were located within walking distance of the peasant communities (although in some cases the journey took two days). Work opportunities at the mines would almost be guaranteed for the peasants. The construction of the Filyos–Zonguldak railway in 1935 further extended

29. *Ibid.*
30. For the archival location of these reports see n. 1.
31. The official documents on the recruitment of mine labour by force in Zonguldak between 1867 and 1921 were published in Erol Çatma, *Asker İşçiler* [Soldier Miners] (Istanbul, 1988).
32. M. Çınar and O. Silier, *Türkiye Tarımında İşletmeler Arası Farklılaşma* [Differences between Turkish Agricultural Enterprises] (Istanbul, 1979), pp. 1–336, 206.

the labour market throughout the neighbouring regions of Zonguldak (i.e. Bartın, Ulus, Amasra, Tefen, and Yenice), while the opening of the Devrek–Ereğli highway in the 1930s also contributed to labour mobility. Both transport infrastructures enlarged the range of villages connected to Zonguldak, with the distance between the villages and the Zonguldak mines now varying between 25 and 110 kilometres.

The peasant-miners worked in rotations of 15 to 20 days. These workers usually went to a particular pit in groups; sometimes whole villages worked in the same pit. The reputation of the section boss and the recommendations of the village usurer were central in the villagers' choice of a particular pit. In the 1920s and 1930s companies commissioned village usurers for mass labour recruitment, a practice that guaranteed the usurer that his loan would be returned, as well as bringing him commission from mine operators. Among the mine operators, in turn, these usurers enjoyed considerable popularity and appreciation for their ability to recruit the maximum number of workers.[33]

Relatively wealthy labourers took their own beds to the mines, others slept on a piece of wood covered with a sack. Relatives and close friends shared the same "bed" rotationally on their shift turn. The dormitories had earthen floors, leaking roofs, and no windows, with only one fireplace for up to 100 workers. One miner said: "It was nice to sleep all together in the winter months, you could hardly feel the cold. During hot summer nights we slept under the bushes in the open air."[34] The old miners still speak about the lice, fleas, bedbugs, and ticks they were infested with.

The miners brought their basic foodstuffs (i.e. bread, olives, halva, and cheese) with them from the villages. After finishing their supplies in their first week in the mines, the miners used to buy food on credit from the *ekonoma* (mine store). This foods was expensive and its cost was deducted from workers' wages. The usurers or their representatives came to the mines on payday to collect their money. Since the miners' main source of livelihood was their agricultural produce, the companies were able to set their wages very low. Moreover, a large portion of the wages paid to the miners was deducted by the usurers and by the company store.

DIVISIONS IN THE LABOUR FORCE: "GREEKS", "KIVIRCIK", "LAZ", AND "KURDS"

The regional and cultural characteristics of the Zonguldak miners presented themselves in every sphere of the mining community. The traditional

---

33. On the importance of village usurers in the recruitment process, see Kadri Yersel, *Madencilikte bir Ömür* [A Life in Mining] (Istanbul, 1989), p. 14.
34. Kahveci, "Political Economy of the Zonguldak Coalbasin", p. 136. In this study 300 mineworkers in various jobs and groups were interviewed between 1992 and 1994. All translations from Turkish are mine.

Ottoman social system reinforced the interpretation that the Zonguldak villagers were *kul* (servants of the Sultan), while Croats, Montenegrins, Greeks, and other minority groups were considered to have the higher status of subjects. The Pontic Greeks were called Laz by other Greeks, just as Black Sea Turks were called Laz by other Turks.[35] During the Greco-Turkish war of 1919 and 1922, most of the Greek population left Turkey, and in 1923 the Turkish and Greek governments agreed upon a compulsory population exchange of Greeks and Turks (defined by religious adherence) between the national territories. The exchange also had an impact on the ethnic make up of the Zonguldak coalfield, as the number of skilled Greek miners dramatically declined.

Further developments during the early republican period included the Sheikh Said Rebellion in eastern Anatolia, leading to the resettlement of an estimated 1 million Kurds across the country.[36] Some moved to Zonguldak, where they settled in approximately ten new villages, increasing the number of Kurds employed in the mines. Large numbers of the Kurdish population and migrants from the eastern Black Sea region subsequently became full-time mine labourers. These permanent workers were employed on the surface in washeries and repair shops, and underground in maintenance, drift developing, transport, and other skilled work. Separated from their communities and fields, full-time miners could not rely on agricultural production for any substantial portion of their livelihoods and were entirely dependent on selling their labour power to the coal operators.

After the 1932 Law on Work and Occupation for Turkish Citizens had banned foreigners from working in Zonguldak, ethnic groups in the mines came to consist only of groups mobilized from within the Turkish nation-state. This development further helped the eastern Black Sea and eastern Anatolian migrants to fill permanent and skilled jobs. Miners were identified as Kurd, Laz, or *Kıvırcık* (peasant-miners from the Zonguldak villages), and each group was attributed a certain identity, creating an environment of ethnic division. This division also manifested itself in the distinction between skilled and unskilled labour, the permanent or rotational nature of labour, the paternalistic (or discriminatory) policies of the coal company, the emergence of trade unionism, and the provision of welfare. All these aspects influenced the complex entanglement of work and ethnicity in the Zonguldak mines. Within these relations, the peasant-miners of Zonguldak were disadvantaged, which they themselves interpreted through the lens of ethnicity.

35. Michael E. Meeker, "The Black Sea Turks: Some Aspects of their Ethnic and Cultural Background", *International Journal of Middle East Studies*, 2 (1971), pp. 318–345, 332.
36. Kendal, "The Kurds Under the Ottoman Empire", in Gérard Chaliand (ed.), *A People Without a Country: The Kurds and Kurdistan* (London, 1993), pp. 11–37.

As the percentage of full-time migrant labour increased, the segmentation within the Zonguldak miners deepened in terms of skill, tasks, wage scales, rotational or permanent work patterns, and company provisions such as housing. From the 1930s onwards, the segregation between peasant-miners and migrant labourers became even more noticeable. Apart from their social differences, both groups held deeply prejudiced views about each other. Migrants called local miners *Kıvırcık* (a kind of sheep), because of their cramped sleeping conditions and what they perceived as their docile and obedient behaviour. In return locals called the migrants, particularly the Laz, *Çakal* (jackal), because they were considered opportunist, lazy, and parasitical on the coalface miners.[37] This division also found voice in the literature: one of the best known novels on the Zonguldak miners is titled *Kıvırcık*, inspired by real-life stories of the Zonguldak peasant-miners in the 1930s, i.e. the period before a second forced-labour regime was installed in 1940.[38]

THE SECOND FORCED-LABOUR REGIME, 1940–1947

As coal became a vital element in the government's industrialization policy, in 1937, when the Second Five-Year Development Plan was launched and the French Ereğli Coal Company nationalized, the Ministry of Justice and the newly formed Türk-İş Coal Company (successor to the French company) signed an agreement to gain access to a new labour supply, allowing the company to use convict labour.[39] First, 50 prisoners were set to work constructing workers' dormitories; in May 1937 they were joined by another 100 prisoners. A new mine prison was established at Zonguldak and within a short period the number of prisoner-miners reached 1,600. These prisoners worked in coal extraction, construction, in repair shops, and on the transport of coal and tools. They wore different clothes from the rest of the labour force. One day of work in the mines cut two days from their sentences. Their nominal wages were held in a bank account until their release. This practice seems to have lasted until the mid-1940s.[40]

---

37. This ethnic division among Zonguldak miners was also the subject of a number of literary works, including: İrfan Yalçın, *Ölümün Ağzı* [In the Mouth of Death] (Istanbul, 1980); Behçet Kalaycı, *Kıvırcık: Genç Bir Madencinin Öyküsü* [Kıvırcık: Story of a Young Miner] (Ankara, 1992); M. Seyda, *Yanartaş* [Burning Stone] (1970).
38. See Kalaycı, *Kıvırcık*.
39. For an understanding of convict labour from a global and long-term perspective, see Christian G. De Vito and Alex Lichtenstein, "Writing a Global History of Convict Labour", *International Review of Social History*, 58 (2013), pp. 285–325.
40. Kahveci, "Political Economy of the Zonguldak Coalbasin"; Gerhard Kessler, "Zonguldak ve Karabük'teki Çalışma Şartları" [Working Conditions in Zonguldak and Karabük], *İstanbul Üniversitesi İktisat Fakültesi Mecmuası* [Journal of the Faculty of Economics, University of Istanbul], 9 (1948), pp. 173–196, 180–181.

Deployment of convict labour in the mines had already revealed the lack of labour there. This, however, was not enough to tackle the labour-shortage problem. A solution emerged in the shape of the National Protection Law (NPL, Milli Korunma Kanunu), promulgated on 18 January 1940. Justified by World War II, this law implemented a very repressive labour regime and reintroduced forms of paid forced labour. A co-ordination committee was established in Ankara, which issued over 600 different regulations throughout its existence.[41] One month after the law was promulgated, specific regulations were introduced for Zonguldak. These imposed a legal requirement that labour be rendered by males over the age of sixteen who were from mining families and were familiar with the work. The unemployed were similarly assigned to work in the mines. In 1940, an agency to organize this re-established form of forced labour was opened at Zonguldak, with offices in the surrounding area. Chief engineers in the coal districts gave details of labour requirements to the company's Production Department, which passed them on to the agency. The surrounding offices then obtained the labour through the *muhtars*. An armed body was formed to escort villagers to work and prevent escape.

These new forced labourers in the coalmines were required to work 3 hours longer per day than those in Ottoman times, and were prohibited from changing their work location. In this way, the Zonguldak coal basin was able to draw upon 58,000 workers in 1942. Of these, 46,000 came from the immediate vicinity, 40,000 of them working for periods of 45 days on a rotational basis. The remaining miners were allowed only occasional rest days. A further 12,000 forced labourers from the Black Sea region were also put to work on a rotational basis, forced to work 2 months on, 2 months off. The management's production requirements or bad weather could add to the time spent at the mine.[42]

AFTER THE SECOND FORCED-LABOUR REGIME: A PATERNALISTIC APPROACH

After 1947, forced labour was abolished again, making it impossible for the mining company to maintain the 58,000 workers who had been drawn upon under the NPL. It was no wonder then that its director, concerned by the shortage of labour and the decline in coal production, strongly opposed the removal of the forced-labour regime.[43] After eight years of a forced-labour regime, mining in Zonguldak was considered an unfavourable workplace,

41. M. Şehmus Güzel, *Türkiye'de İşçi Hareketi (Yazılar-Belgeler)* [Workers' Movements in Turkey] (Istanbul, 1993), p. 156.
42. A.A. Özeken, "Türkiye'de Sanayi İşçileri" [Industrial Workers in Turkey], *İstanbul Üniversitesi İktisat Fakültesi Mecmuasi*, 11 (1949), pp. 56–81.
43. Yersel, *Madencilikte bir Ömür*, pp. 28–29.

with no prospect of immediate improvement. Because of low wages, harsh working conditions, including long working hours and high industrial injury rates, many workers abandoned the mines as soon as the forced-labour regime ended. Some of the retired miners who had experienced the forced-labour regime said in interviews that they were reluctant to work in the mines after 1947, unless they were particularly in need of money. In 1948, the average working period for a miner was only two months.[44]

Alarmed by the shortage of labour, the company started to adopt a more paternalistic approach.[45] From the late 1940s onwards, the company built 1,900 houses in the Üzülmez, Karadon, and Kilimli regions for permanent workers, who paid nominal rents, and provided bus services between their homes and work stations. In 1960 the company employed around 39,000 workers; 6,000 non-married workers and 19,000 rotational workers lived in company dormitories, the latter returning to their villages after completing their rotations. Around 1,900 workers lived in company houses, 8,600 lived in *gecekondu* (shanty towns), and the rest stayed in their villages, travelling daily to their workplaces.[46] Although illegal, the company tolerated its workers building their own *gecekondu* on state-owned lands around Çatalağzı, Gelik, and Kozlu.

It also opened 9 private elementary schools and 1 secondary school. By 1960 the number of students attending the company schools was around 7,000, taught by 150 school teachers employed by the company. In all the company booklets published in the 1950s and 1960s there was a particular emphasis on the commitment to the provision of houses for workers and education for their children. A retired miner who lived in a company house in the Üzülmez region said that in the 1950s and 1960s the company security forces regularly patrolled the houses in order to prevent miners keeping farm animals in their gardens.[47] The company also opened 13 cinemas, 22 co-operatives, 1 summer camping area, and 3 private beaches for its workers.

---

44. See the interviews cited in Güzel, *Türkiye'de İşçi Hareketi*, p. 195.

45. A group of German professors of sociology and social policy (especially Gerhard Kessler and Helmut Arndt) who had escaped the Nazi regime worked at the University of Istanbul. The coal company approached them in order to solve its problems with labour recruitment and retention. Together with their Turkish colleagues (including Mehmet Ali Özeken and Orhan Tuna) they visited Zonguldak and made their recommendations to the management and to the miners' union. They also published a series of articles on labour costs, productivity, absenteeism, labour turnover, made suggestions about company policies, and wrote about how to attract workers and on the significance of spare-time activities in the *İstanbul Üniversitesi İktisat Fakültesi Mecmuası* (*Journal of the Faculty of Economics*). For further details see Kahveci, "Political Economy of the Zonguldak Coalbasin", pp. 177–182.

46. EKI, *Ereğli Kömür İşletmeleri Kitapçığı* [Handbook of the Ereğli Coal Mining Institute] (Zonguldak, 1961).

47. A retired miner was interviewed by the author in February 1993 in Zonguldak.

CONTINUATION OF ROTATIONAL LABOUR

From 1935 onwards the more traditional types of mining at Zonguldak, *oda-topuk* (pillar and stall) and *baca* (rising cut), progressively gave way to the *uzun-ayak* (longwall) method. However, unlike Europe, where the introduction of longwall mining was associated with heavy mechanization,[48] at Zonguldak the longwall method did not provide a break from the reliance on labour-intensive work. Although some new technologies were introduced, investment in Zonguldak coalfields remained notoriously low. Throughout the period reviewed, mining consisted of pick and shovel work, miners lying on their sides and crouching in the seams to cut and shovel the coal. Miners were still burrowing upwards with ropes tied round their bodies in order to pull up pit props and tools when new faces were opened and when mining took place in severely sloped conditions, as was often the case. Hewers, prop men, and many other miners still had to provide their own tools – pickaxes, shovels, hatchets, and mattocks.[49]

Systematic mechanization in the mines would necessarily have meant a sharp reduction in the number of temporary, unskilled workers. To drive up productivity by mechanization, the mines would have had to steer the miners away from the old model of semi-peasant, semi-industrial worker. However, because the government never provided sufficient investment to modernize the Zonguldak mines, the underground mining methods did not require a new composition of the labour force. As a consequence, after 1948, underground workers, recruited from the peasantry, continued to work on a monthly basis, dividing their time between mining and agriculture, while surface workers were employed on a permanent basis. Even in the 1990s, over 50 per cent of the underground labour force continued to work rotationally. The policies of the mining company resulted in certain sections of the labour force becoming full-time industrial workers,[50] but it was impossible to overcome the divisions within the labour force. Labour continued to be divided in terms of locality, work patterns, and ethnicity, and such divisions were further deepened by the favouritism shown by the company to permanent workers.

The ethnic divisions of labour, already introduced in the nineteenth century, thus survive to the present day. The rotational workers perform the

---

48. In Europe the longwall method has come to be associated with mechanization: a 600- to 800-foot-long coalface is cut by a machine and the coal is carried away by conveyor belt. The hanging wall is supported by hydraulic jacks, and the entire operation is performed by as few as half a dozen miners. See E.L. Trist and K.W. Bamforth, "Some Social and Psychological Consequences of the Longwall Method of Coal-Getting", *Human Relations*, 4 (1951), pp. 3–38; M.N. Yarrow, "How Good Strong Union Men Line it Out: Explorations of the Structure and Dynamics of Coal Miners' Class Consciousness" (Ph.D. dissertation, State University of New Jersey, 1982).
49. Nichols and Kahveci, "The Condition of Mine Labour", pp. 199–200.
50. M.D. Rivkin, *Area Development for National Growth: The Turkish Precedent* (London, 1965), p. 168.

less skilled and more labour-intensive underground work.[51] The permanent workers generally hold more skilled underground and surface jobs; thus, there are no rotational surface workers. Hewers have always been predominantly rotational labourers, so that as late as 1972 95 per cent of them fell into this category, as did 60 per cent of all underground workers. Non-rotational work was performed mainly by foremen, maintenance workers, surface, and shop-floor workers. Even by the 1980s and 1990s, when economic decline in the wages of miners forced the rotational miners to transfer to permanent status, 7 out of 10 hewers were still employed on a rotational basis, as were nearly 50 per cent of all underground workers. Those employed rotationally received no wages for the time they were not at work.

In the early 1990s, a surprisingly large number of Zonguldak miners still saw the composition of the population, not only in Zonguldak, but in Turkey in general, in terms of their own experiences as being made up of Laz, *Kıvırcık*, and Kurds.[52] Workers also made reference to the divided nature of the labour force. Some told stories about their early experiences in the mines, when they were unaware that the labour force had traditionally drawn people of an ethnic and geographical origin different from their own, and how this had been an awkward situation for them. Their accounts also highlighted the locality-based division of labour and group identity. One testified: "My village is a *taramacı* [gallery opener into the coal seam] village. But when I first started, I was assigned as a transport worker. There were many Laz workers in my work group. We had nothing in common, so I became a *taramacı*." And another:

> When I first started to work in the mines I was a *lağımcı* [gallery opener into stone strata]. I'm not a Laz, but here all the *lağımcı* are from Trabzon and Giresun. They are Laz. We didn't get on well. Soon after, I became a construction worker, where all my *hemşehri* [people from the same area] work.[53]

TRADE UNIONISM

The same divisions were reflected in trade unionism. The Zonguldak Mineworkers' Trade Union (ZMTU) had come into existence in 1947. It had started in 1946 as a Mine Workers' Society. Significantly, it was

---

51. The concept of unskilled labour with reference to underground miners must be used here with some reservations. Zonguldak miners themselves emphasized the importance of knowing where to start digging the coal. They had a pit sense and were able to read the signs of rock falls, methane gas explosions, faulty seams, and old workings or water deposits behind the seam. In other words they had an intimate knowledge of the coalface and surrounding strata. For a further discussion of this issue see Quataert, *Miners and the State in the Ottoman Empire*, pp. 56–57; Kahveci, "Political Economy of the Zonguldak Coalbasin", pp. 285–286.
52. Quoted from Kahveci, "Political Economy of the Zonguldak Coal Basin", p. 413.
53. Quoted from *ibid.*, p. 276.

formed by 11 foremen and section bosses, all permanent workers, mainly from the eastern Black Sea region, 7 of whom lived in company houses. The society managed to register 4,148 miners, a substantial majority of the permanent workers. To solve problems in collecting the monthly membership fee, the company offered help by deducting the fee from their pay slips.[54] This event marked the beginning of a long-standing collaboration between the company and the union. At the end of 1947, the number of union members reached 19,373, making it the largest trade union in Turkey. The check-off system of dues collection and the large membership permitted the union to operate from a position of relative financial stability.

From 1947 to 1963, the year in which, successively, laws regulating unions and collective bargaining, strikes, and lockouts became effective, the union's main activities were confined to mutual aid and assistance. In this period, it was impossible to carry out "normal" union activities, such as protecting workers' rights, wage negotiations, involvement in disputes between company and workers, and engaging in political activities. The union was, in fact, primarily a mutual aid society. As a company union, the ZMTU organized workers in only one company, and while as such it took a collaborative stand towards management, as a trade union it was, all in all, powerless and ineffective.

The original founders of the union continued to lead it until 1960. Almost all were Laz coming from the eastern Black Sea region (Trabzon, Rize); all were permanent workers.[55] This domination by permanent workers could be seen in all positions within the union leadership and in all positions of control. Less than 10 per cent of the delegates to the General Assembly were from the ranks of rotational workers. Until well after the 1960s miners' leaders were recruited exclusively from surface workers. They were insulated from the ordinary membership by their permanent positions, and adopted a collaborative stance towards the state-appointed management. In spite of some militancy, the position of the Zonguldak miners was one of powerlessness. Although the union leadership changed radically in 1989, the dominance of permanent workers continues to the present day.

CONCLUSION

Zonguldak as a city came into existence with the opening of the mines. It developed through and with them into the most important industrial site of the Ottoman era and later of the Turkish republic, until the beginning of its demographic and economic decline in the 1980s. From the start, skilled

54. Ömer Karahasan, *Türkiye Sendikacılık Hareketi İçinde Zonguldak Maden İşçisi ve Sendikasi* [The Zonguldak Miners and their Trade Union within the Turkish Trade Union Movement] (Zonguldak, 1978), pp. 283–284.
55. Roy, "The Zonguldak Strike", p. 250.

labour recruited by contracted companies was imported from other areas within the Ottoman Empire and beyond, while unskilled labour was recruited from the surrounding villages. From the 1860s until 1920, a first forced-labour regime in the coalfield gave specific tasks to Zonguldak villagers, assigning them solely to underground work, such as hewing coal and supplying as well as putting up pit props. Over the years, local villagers became familiar with coalmining practices and techniques. With the development of the mines and increased production, Zonguldak attracted quarry workers, iron miners, and others with experience in mining, and also other skilled workers such as blacksmiths, mechanics, and drivers. Migrant workers concentrated on skilled underground and surface work. This marked the beginning of a division of mine labour based on migration and ethnicity. Over the years this pattern became reinforced, fed by generations of migrant miners and Zonguldak villagers.

Over 150 years, the state has structured the lives of Zonguldak miners in multiple ways, by regulating and determining labour relations, as well as by its macroeconomic policies. Miners were affected, inter alia, by the state-backed influx of European finance capital into the Zonguldak coalfields in the late nineteenth and early twentieth centuries, through the introduction of 5-year industrial development plans in 1933, and through further liberalization and coal import policies since the mid-1970s. In addition, since 1940 the state has had a more direct relationship with the Zonguldak miners as employer.

In the 1860s, the government imposed a regime of forced labour on the mines in order to balance its desire for coal with that for domestic stability and continuation of the prevailing agricultural system. In a provision of far-reaching and crucial importance, it restricted labour in the mines to villagers from the fourteen surrounding districts. The state ruled that the income should be supplemental, that is, work in the mines was to be carried out on a rotational basis. This first forced-labour regime at Zonguldak was formally abolished in 1921. However, one of the major aims of the new republic throughout the 1930s and 1940s was to maintain a docile labour force in order to reach the level of production needed for the 5-year industrial development plan. Zonguldak was used by the state to subsidize the developing industries through the provision of low-priced coal, and the state was reluctant to incur increased costs by investing in mechanization and technology. A second forced-labour regime, introduced in 1940, once again served to supply the cheap manual labour on which Zonguldak coal production heavily relied.

Throughout the period reviewed in this article, the analysis of state–capital–labour relations in the Zonguldak coal basin reveals a lack of investment, a relatively low level of technology, and an accumulation policy that has remained steadfastly labour-driven. The Zonguldak mines have continued to subsidize the developing industries, without adequate investment.

The powerlessness of the miners in relation to the state has been aggravated by their ambiguous position as wage labourers and continuing divisions among themselves. This is perhaps why Zonguldak mine operators chose not to introduce a viable alternative to the system of peasant-miners, unlike their counterparts in Britain, Chile, Peru, and Rhodesia.

IRSH 60 (2015), Special Issue, pp. 227–251 doi:10.1017/S0020859015000474
© 2015 Internationaal Instituut voor Sociale Geschiedenis

Dissimilarity Breeds Contempt: Ethnic Paternalism, Foreigners, and the State in Pas-de-Calais Coalmining, France, 1920s*

P H I L I P H . S L A B Y

Department of History, Guilford College
Archdale Hall 201, Greensboro, NC 27410, USA

E-mail: pslaby@guilford.edu

ABSTRACT: Recently, historians have begun to illuminate further the role that ethnicity played in integrating immigrants into mining societies. Ethnicity, they show, shaped foreign–native relations in complex ways. Migrant culture and local norms both affected the assimilation process. This essay, focusing on France's premiere coalfield of Pas-de-Calais during the 1920s, a period of mass influx of Polish laborers, explores employers' often underappreciated influence over inter-ethnic relations, and it reveals the far-reaching effects of managerial policies. Management's ethnic paternalism influenced, though often unintentionally, relations between Poles and French miners and officials. Employer strategies to manage Poles led natives to see themselves as distinct from and even superior to immigrants. Beyond the workplace, employers used ethnic notions to attract and control Poles, yet in doing so they highlighted the dissimilarities between Poles and Frenchmen. Ultimately, coal companies reinforced foreigners' isolation from local society and roused the suspicions of officials, who strictly policed the Polish community.

The decade after World War I was one of uncertainty for coal companies, for miners, and for government officials in the French department of Pas-de-Calais, the site of France's most important coalfield. Heavy fighting and a destructive German invasion had devastated the region's mines, infrastructure, and communities. For much of the 1920s, mining firms faced unsettling prospects: could they re-establish and expand production in a postwar economy hobbled by labor shortages? Pas-de-Calais miners also

* I would like to thank Ad Knotter, David Mayer, and the participants of the workshop "Migration and Ethnicity in Coalfield History" held at the Netherlands Institute for Advanced Study in November 2014 for their comments and input on this essay.

grappled with thorny questions: could they or would they return to the jobs and communities many had fled during the war? And if so, what economic and social future awaited them? Further specific concerns weighed on local government officials: how could they restore and ensure political stability and national security in a border region once victim to foreign occupation?

For the coal industry, a solution to labor scarcity and a means to revival appeared in the arrival of tens of thousands of workers from eastern Europe, especially Poland. This immigration, however, raised new questions of how to attract, train, retain, and manage foreigners. Firms developed policies to address these issues, strategies that created a large Polish workforce in the mines and that contributed to a vibrant Polish community in the coalfields. By doing so, however, management amplified the postwar anxieties of French miners and authorities in Pas-de-Calais.

The challenges that coal companies, mining communities, and officials faced in the postwar Pas-de-Calais were not wholly unique. Indeed, mines worldwide and across time have relied upon workers migrating from within and without national borders to staff their facilities. They have thus helped to create in mining regions a host of multi-ethnic workforces and societies. Various forces shaped the acceptance of newcomers in mines, in coalfield communities, and in nations. In the past decade, scholars have increasingly illuminated the powerful influence that ethnicity and local, regional, and national identities exerted over the occupational and social position of migrant miners. They show that ethnic and other identities, varying by place and evolving over time, have shaped the attitudes and actions of foreigners and natives alike. Coalfield historians have particularly highlighted how the views and values of indigenous miners affected immigrant–native interaction in the workplace and beyond. Further, recent scholarship has suggested that native ethnic identities also influenced the valuations and actions of state authorities and of coal company leaders as they policed and managed immigrants.[1]

This essay builds on recent scholarly insights to examine the complex ways in which ethnicity and local, regional, religious, and national identities shaped the treatment that Poles received from the Pas-de-Calais miners who toiled with them, the local officials who governed and policed them, and the executives and managers who supervised them. It focuses on the decade after World War I, a period significant for various reasons. First, in these years, the number of Poles in the Pas-de-Calais coal basin and mines rapidly grew and then stabilized. Second, the period held managerial significance as one in which firms devised and then institutionalized policies

---

1. For a view of how these concerns, among other questions, have shaped scholarship, see Stefan Berger, Andy Croll, and Norman LaPorte (eds), *Towards a Comparative History of Coalfield Societies* (Burlington, VT, 2005).

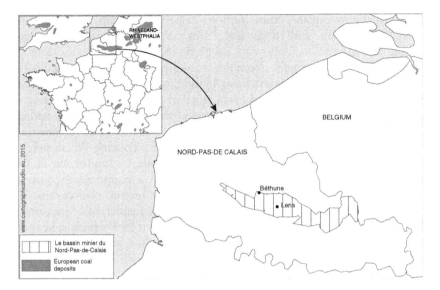

Figure 1. The department of the Pas-de-Calais occupies the western portion of the Nord-Pas-de-Calais region figured here. The Pas-de-Calais coalfields comprise the western half of the Nord-Pas-de-Calais coal basin.

toward Polish personnel. Third, it was a decade in which Pas-de-Calais natives completed, as best they could, the transition from war, destruction, and dislocation to a new postwar situation. Yet it remained a period in which native attitudes remained clouded by the experience of war and the burdens of rebuilding. Lastly, the 1920s proved a formative period for Polish–French relations in Pas-de-Calais. Indeed, the occupational and social position that Poles came to inhabit and the patterns of interaction between the immigrants and local French employers, miners, and officials that developed in that time largely characterized those of the larger interwar period.

This essay seeks to deepen scholarly understanding of the power of ethnicity and identity to shape immigrant integration into mining societies, by exploring the often underappreciated influence of coal companies and their policies over inter-ethnic relations. It reveals the far-reaching effects that managerial policies carried for French–Polish interaction and the complex influences that ethnic and national identities exerted over group perceptions. Managerial policies inside and outside the mines greatly influenced, though often unintentionally, relations between immigrants and coalfield natives and local French officials. In the workplace, employer strategies to assign, to train, and to manage Polish workers led French miners to see themselves as distinct from and even superior to immigrants, a view that impeded workplace ties between natives and newcomers.

Beyond the workplace, ethnic notions helped guide employer efforts to attract, to maintain, and to control Poles, as firms revamped company housing and paternalist support for religious and voluntary associations to accommodate and benefit from the immigrants' particular cultural preferences. Such ethnic paternalism highlighted the ethnic and national dissimilarities between Poles and Frenchmen in the coalfields. Ultimately, it reinforced the foreigners' isolation from local working-class society and its institutions. Company ethnic paternalism also influenced the relationship between immigrant Poles and the French state. By creating Polish neighborhoods, by fostering Polish clubs and associations, by supporting Polish clergy and religious institutions, and by taking a cooperative position toward representatives of the Polish state in the region, coal companies fostered an immigrant community that aroused the suspicions of local state officials. And from suspicion discrimination grew, as local officials, keen to protect the security and power of the French republic, strictly policed and harshly punished members of the Polish community.

LABOR SCARCITY AND THE CHALLENGES AND OPPORTUNITIES OF POLISH IMMIGRATION

After World War I, the Pas-de-Calais mines faced a dearth of workers that threatened the coal industry's postwar recovery and future productivity. Before 1914, executives managed their operations confidently, relying on abundant and stable local labor. The war swept away such certainties. German occupation and heavy fighting transformed the coalfields into a battle zone. Materially, the war devastated the region's mines, cities, and infrastructure, and reconstruction demanded a great mass of workers. At the same time, the war restricted labor supply. Military service cost the mines thousands of workers, as an estimated 22 per cent of all Pas-de-Calais miners mobilized never returned from the war.[2] Population displacement wrested away still more workers. Thousands fled the German invasion and combat in the region; migrating elsewhere in France, many never came back. Civilian flight also sapped labor supply by arresting apprenticeships. Indeed, during four years of war, no young apprentices trained as miners in Pas-de-Calais.[3]

2. Paul Georges, "Rapport de M. L'Ingénieur en Chef des Mines sur la Situation de l'Industrie minérale dans l'Arrondissement minéralogique d'Arras pendant l'Année 1922", in *Département du Pas-de-Calais Conseil Général, deuxième session de 1923, Troisième Partie Rapports des Chefs de Service et Renseignements divers* (Arras, 1923), pp. 311–349, 320–321; "La main-d'œuvre dans les Mines du Pas-de-Calais, I", *Nord Industriel*, (1923), p. 1460. Unless indicated otherwise, articles from the *Nord Industriel* – a fortnightly journal about and for the north's industries – did not specify any author.
3. Georges, "Rapport de M. L'Ingénieur en Chef des Mines [...] 1922", pp. 318 and 320.

Beyond demographic change, shifting postwar social and cultural attitudes among Pas-de-Calais workers contributed to postwar labor shortages. Indeed, wartime upheavals aroused new ambitions among coal basin natives. In fact, immediately after the armistice, industry observers reported significant transformations in the "aspirations of workers".[4] One mining engineer noted that after the war miners wished "to live in a more bourgeois manner". This shift in the outlook of miners was reflected in their evaluations of work. Miners no longer venerated physical brawn and adeptness. On the contrary, the greater "intelligence" a position demanded, the more they valued it. They increasingly esteemed office personnel as "intellectual workers", and they admired tradesmen such as pipe fitters, electricians, and machinists.[5] Miners aspiring to less taxing and more lucrative positions indeed found jobs both inside and outside the postwar coal industry. Rebuilding and modernizing the mines produced much service and maintenance work.[6] Such attractive positions remained plentiful for much of the 1920s, providing miners with alternatives to toiling underground.[7] Other Pas-de-Calais workers avoided mining altogether. Instead, they found positions restoring war-damaged buildings and infrastructure, jobs employing thousands in Pas-de-Calais until the mid-1920s.[8]

4. "La Raréfaction de la Main-d'œuvre et les Méthodes d'Exploitations des Mines: Développement probable des Machinisme dans les Mines, I", *Nord Industriel*, (1921), p. 329.
5. See the following contemporary analysis: John Condeveaux, *Le Mineur du Nord et du Pas-de-Calais: sa Psychologie, ses Rapports avec le Patronat* (Lille, 1928), pp. 14–16.
6. "La Raréfaction de la Main-d'œuvre [...], I", p. 329.
7. Georges, "Rapport de M. L'Ingénieur en Chef des Mines [...] 1922", p. 318; *idem*, "Rapport de M. L'Ingénieur en Chef des Mines sur la Situation de l'Industrie minérale dans l'Arrondissement minéralogique d'Arras pendant l'Année 1925", in *Département du Pas-de-Calais Conseil Général, Troisième Partie Rapports des Chefs de Service et Renseignements divers* (Arras, 1926), pp. 97–111, 104.
8. Archives départementales of Pas-de-Calais, Dainville [hereafter, ADPdC], Series 1Z Subprefecture 1Z209, 25 March 1924, Prefecture du Pas-de-Calais to Ministère du Travail, 25 March 1924. The archival sources for this essay are drawn from two institutions. First, the departmental archives of the Pas-de-Calais in Dainville provide official information, observations, and opinions regarding immigrants in the Pas-de-Calais coalfields. In particular, the analysis employs documents held in the M series devoted to general prefectoral administration in the department. Important here are files M3229 *Groupements de main-d'œuvre étrangère dans le Pas-de-Calais, 1925*, M3231 *Rapports général sur Immigrés polonais*, and M6857 *Immigrants polonais: renseignements généraux*. It also uses documents in the 1Z series comprised of documents from the subprefecture of Béthune. Important here are files 1Z209 *Étrangers: Divers, 1919–1925*, 1Z277 *Syndicat des mineurs, 1924–1926*, and 1Z501 *Polonais, 1924–1935*. The second archival institution central to this essay is the Archives Nationales du Monde du Travail [hereafter, ANMT] in Roubaix. These archives permit an appreciation of the place of immigrant labor in the coal industry. This study makes particular use of the papers and publications of the coalmine employer association held in the 40 AS series *Comité Central des Houillères de France* [hereafter, CCHF], especially files 40 AS1 and 40 AS7. It also uses the papers of the individual coal companies held in the series 1994 *Houillères du Bassin du Nord et du Pas-de-Calais*. The essay draws on the files in 1994 050 *Houillères du Bassin du Nord et du Pas-de-Calais, Compagnie des Mines de Bruay*, and most extensively on the documents in 1994 048 *Houillères du Bassin du Nord et du Pas-de-Calais, Mines de Marles*.

Indeed, reflecting displeasure with mining, turnover among French workers remained high in the mines.[9]

Facing a limited and unreliable pool of native labor, firms turned to immigrants to fill gaps in the workforce. And it was workers from Poland which the Pas-de-Calais mines were most successful in contracting. By hiring tens of thousands of them, they overcame postwar personnel shortages. The arrival of immigrants was massive, sudden, and altered the composition of the mining labor force. Before the war, foreign manpower played no significant role in Pas-de-Calais mines. Beginning in 1919, the arrival of Poles and other immigrants dramatically increased the foreign presence. By 1922, the number of immigrant workers topped 21,500, or 26 per cent of the entire mining staff.[10] By 1924, some 50,000 foreigners comprised more than 40 per cent of the labor force.[11] Though immigrant recruitment ebbed and flowed from 1925 to 1931, foreign manpower remained significant. In fact, in this period French workers seldom formed more than 60 per cent of the Pas-de-Calais mining workforce.[12]

Surging immigration also altered the traditional demographic and ethnic composition of Pas-de-Calais. Before the war, non-French residents of Pas-de-Calais, most of them from nearby Belgium, represented approximately 3 per cent of the department's inhabitants. By 1926, however, the number of non-native residents had grown sharply to over 153,000, or fully 13 per cent of the Pas-de-Calais population.[13] Polish immigration contributed mightily to this larger increase. From under 3,400 in 1921, the Polish population rose to 91,000 in 1926, constituting 8 per cent of all Pas-de-Calais residents and the department's largest single immigrant group.[14]

For Pas-de-Calais coal firms seeking to make foreigners a productive component of their postwar workforce, attracting, incorporating, and maintaining immigrant staff presented a host of challenges. Enticing Poles to the mines was the first hurdle. Would-be Polish emigrants had options. They could choose to leave Poland for the mines or for other employers in France.

9. Pierre Galand, *Les Mines du Nord et du Pas-de-Calais depuis la Guerre* (Paris, 1936), p. 97.

10. Paul Georges, "Rapport de M. l'Ingénieur en chef des Mines sur la Situation de l'Industrie minérale dans l'Arrondissement minéralogique d'Arras pendant l'année 1923", in *Département du Pas-de-Calais Conseil Général deuxième Session ordinaire de 1924: Rapports des Chefs de service et Renseignements divers, troisième partie* (Arras, 1924), pp. 113–136, 128.

11. *Idem*, "Rapport de M. l'Ingénieur en chef des Mines sur la Situation de l'Industrie minérale dans l'Arrondissement minéralogique d'Arras pendant l'année 1924", in *Département du Pas-de-Calais Conseil Général deuxième Session ordinaire de 1925: Rapports des Chefs de service et Renseignements divers, troisième partie* (Arras, 1925), pp. 107–124, 117–118.

12. Galand, *Les Mines du Nord*, pp. 77 and 135.

13. Michel Huber, *La Population de la France pendant la Guerre* (New Haven, CT, 1931), p. 861.

14. Georges Mauco, *Les Étrangers en France: Étude géographique sur leur rôle dans l'activité économique* (Paris, 1932), p. 166.

They could select another country, or they could simply remain in Poland. Further, communication between immigrants and families and friends in Poland permitted emigrants to evaluate employment prospects abroad. Additionally, the Polish state influenced the flow of emigrants. If it discerned that certain foreign employers offered its citizens poor pay or treatment, it could forbid them to recruit in Poland. Thus, to attract Poles, the Pas-de-Calais mines endeavored to ascertain the predilections of immigrant Poles and of their government. For instance, they noted that Polish workers welcomed, and that the Polish state approved of, opportunities to emigrate with their spouses and children.[15] They registered that immigrants much valued company housing, particularly single-family dwellings.[16] Further, executives observed that Poles aspired to maintain ties with their native language, culture, and religion while abroad.[17] Meeting such preferences would, they postulated, boost Polish labor recruitment.

Incorporating immigrants into the mines, ensuring their productivity as well as their continuance, created still other difficulties for managers. One of the issues was that many incoming Poles challenged job placements. While firms needed manpower underground above all, many immigrants pressed for jobs on the surface instead.[18] Problems of productivity created still more complications. Newly contracted Poles often entered the mines without relevant skills.[19] Even Poles with expertise – usually gained in German mines – initially extracted coal at rates below those of seasoned French workers.[20] Additionally, a high turnover among non-native staff sapped production. Foreigners often abandoned their posts soon after their hiring. For instance, over one-third of the Poles entering French mines in 1921 abandoned the coal industry before the expiration of their one-year contracts.[21] Mining executives, thus, regularly decried the impermanence of Poles, which left work teams shorthanded, disorganized, and unproductive.[22]

Though Polish workers created appreciable challenges for coal companies, they saw in the immigrants not only a source of much-needed labor but also opportunities to reshape the character of the workforce. Calculatingly,

---

15. ANMT, 1994 050/0064, 8 January 1921, CCHF circular 615.
16. ANMT, 40AS7, 18 September 1920, Secretary of the CCHF, letter to mine directors.
17. André Pairault, *L'Immigration organisée et l'Emploi de la Main-d'œuvre étrangère en France* (Paris, 1927), p. 257.
18. ANMT, 1994 048/0031, Directions des Services techniques, Procès-Verbal de la Conférence 24 February 1921: Personnel du jour des sièges.
19. Auguste Pawlowski, "Un gros problème pour l'industrie du Nord: l'Assimilation des ouvriers étrangers", *Nord Industriel*, (1925), p. 919.
20. "Aux mines d'Ostricourt", *Nord Industriel*, (1924), p. 1950.
21. ANMT, 40AS1, CCHF Assemblée Générale 1924, p. 14. It is noteworthy that such figures on immigrant worker movement did not include the number of Poles who abandoned one mine for another.
22. Pairault, *L'Immigration organisée*, pp. 144–145.

managers approved of the Poles' preference for family immigration and their tendency to have large families. Such traits appeared to be a means to stabilize the current labor force and to cultivate a future one.[23] Additionally, the Poles' widespread devotion to Catholicism suggested that these immigrants shared management's preference for order, probity, and faith.[24] The idea that the immigrants' cultural differences could be exploited for the mines' benefit tantalized the executives. If management could maintain the Poles' outlook and habits, it might isolate the immigrants from the trade unionism, political activism, secularism, and family planning that managers found troublesome among French miners.[25]

MANAGING IMMIGRANTS AT THE COALFACE AND BEYOND

To meet the challenges in recruiting, in job placement, in productivity, and in worker retention that immigrant labor posed, and to maximize the managerial advantages Polish miners presented, companies developed new supervisory policies in the workplace, a brand of ethnic paternalism outside it, and they took a cooperative stance toward Polish officials.

To address some of these difficulties, companies reshaped managerial strategies in the mines. First, firms developed placement procedures for immigrants to assure that they went to where they were most needed. The tactic was simple: companies such as the Mines de Marles deliberately withheld surface positions from non-natives. In fact, the company's general director ordered his engineers to "accord [Poles] no employment [on the surface] and to dismiss them if they refused to go down into [the pits]".[26] Such policies at the Mines de Marles and across the coal basin overwhelmingly concentrated immigrants at the coalface. Second, to prepare foreigners who were ignorant of the miners' trade, companies developed training practices by which inexperienced immigrants, under the tutelage of experienced French miners, learned mining skills while on the job.[27] Third, managers had to ensure that newly trained foreigners maintained high productivity. In response, a policy of *encadrement* was developed,

23. *Ibid.*, p. 190.
24. ANMT, 1994 048/0004, Procès-Verbaux de la Réunion du Conseil d'Administration de Mines de Marles, 29 Juillet 1920: Situation générale; ANMT, 1994 048/0003, Notes pour le Rapport à l'Assemblée Générale: Exercice 1920–1921.
25. Pawlowski, "Un gros problème pour l'industrie du Nord", p. 919.
26. ANMT, 1994 048/0030, Directions des Services techniques, Procès-Verbal de la Conférence 1 July 1920: Ouvriers polonais. All translations from French are mine.
27. ANMT, 1994 048/0030, Directions des Services techniques, Procès-Verbal de la Conférence 11 December 1919 2ème partie: Ouvriers polonaise; Georges, "Rapport de M. L'Ingénieur en Chef des Mines [...] 1922", p. 319.

procedures by which French supervisory staff monitored intensely the work of all non-native miners.[28]

These placement, training, and supervisory policies proved successful for Pas-de-Calais mines. Firms effectively funneled immigrants to vacancies underground and away from support positions on the surface. Indeed, by 1924, in Pas-de-Calais mines the ratio of French to foreign workers in surface positions was 8 to 1. Yet, at the coalface, the proportion differed considerably with a ratio of 1 to 1.[29] Similarly, on-the-job training permitted inexperienced foreigners to achieve output similar to that of experienced French staff within six months of their arrival.[30] Lastly, close supervision by French managers through *encadrement* maintained non-native efficiency. At the Mines de Marles, for example, the percentage of French workers and managers to Polish miners became a standard variable in productivity. Indeed, to preserve production, the company often temporarily suspended assigning Poles to pits with elevated immigrant staff levels.[31]

While they focused on procedures in the workplace to tackle immigrant placement and productivity, mining companies developed policies outside the mines to recruit and retain Poles and to reinforce Polish customs presumed advantageous to employers. Two notions shaped management's approach to the tasks of attracting and keeping Polish workers. First, executives recognized the Poles' appreciation of comfortable company housing and their desire to maintain their cultural and religious customs while in France. Second, executives assumed that foreigners' rootlessness in France greatly contributed to their unsteadiness at work. They surmised that the immigrants' unfamiliarity with the French language, customs, and work habits often deeply frustrated them. Non-native dissatisfaction, in turn, expressed itself in the desire to seek other employment.[32] In this way, firms concluded that attention to immigrant lodgings and ethnic communities could boost the hiring and maintaining of Polish staff. Companies thus committed themselves to creating a Polish *milieu national* in the coalfields, a culturally familiar atmosphere that would, as one industry authority stated, "keep workers in contact with their former national moral and intellectual life".[33]

To construct it, mines refocused longstanding elements of employer paternalism – company housing, the funding of voluntary associations for

28. ANMT, 1994 048/0033, Directions des Services techniques, Procès-Verbal de la Conférence 4 January 1923: Production; *ibid.*, 25 January 1923: Production; *ibid.*, 12 July 1923: Production.

29. Georges, "Rapport de M. L'Ingénieur en Chef des Mines [...] 1924", p. 118.

30. *Idem*, "Rapport de M. L'Ingénieur en Chef des Mines [...] 1922", p. 319.

31. ANMT, 1994 048/0031, Directions des Services techniques, Procès-Verbal de la Conférence 15 September 1921: Ouvriers polonais; ANMT, 1994 048/0032, Directions des Services techniques, Procès-Verbal de la Conference 15 December 1922: Ouvriers polonais.

32. Pairault, *L'Immigration organisée*, p. 193.

33. ANMT, 40AS7, 26 November 1920, Secretary of CCHF Circular 608.

staff, and support for religious institutions for workers – to cater to and profit from the Poles' ethnic preferences and character. This ethnic paternalism guided executives as they allocated the choicest housing to Poles, fearing that poor accommodation would discourage further migration.[34] In assigning lodging, managers also frequently concentrated Poles into particular tracts of company housing, hoping such moves would boost the immigrants' contentment. Beyond this, companies often constructed entire *cités polonaises*, or communities devoted exclusively to Polish workers and their families.[35]

Ethnic paternalism also shaped managerial approaches to backing voluntary associations to stabilize immigrant personnel. For example, the companies helped to bankroll athletic, musical, and artistic clubs for their Polish staff, expecting that this would acclimatize them to local living conditions. Support for Polish associations mirrored those available to the larger mining workforce but with one important difference. For French staff, executives favored inclusive organizations with membership open to workers and supervisors alike. Such clubs would, they surmised, build understanding between groups as supervisors and laborers met in common cause and amusement.[36] Also, these clubs, at least in principle, did not ban non-French members. In the case of Polish associations, however, companies subsidized organizations open exclusively to Poles.[37] Lastly, ethnic paternalism influenced company support for Polish religious particularism. Indeed, coal firms contributed financially to Polish religious and prayer groups, paid Polish priests to minister in the coal basin, and constructed chapels specifically for Polish worshippers.[38]

Pas-de-Calais mines also maintained a cooperative attitude toward Polish consular and other officials active in the region. This approach served company efforts to ensure access to Polish manpower, as the Polish authorities could influence the flow of emigrants to the mines. Therefore, companies permitted consular staff to tour facilities, to interview Polish employees, and to monitor the immigrants' treatment in the mines.[39]

34. *Ibid.*

35. "Aux Mines d'Ostricourt: Inauguration de la cité polonaise", *Nord Industriel*, (1922), p. 2043.

36. "Les Œuvres Sociales dans les Houillères du Nord et du Pas-de-Calais: III", *Nord Industriel*, (1923), pp. 2288–2289.

37. *Ibid.*, "II", pp. 2244–2245; *ibid.*, "I", pp. 2152–2153; Pairault, *L'Immigration organisée*, p. 193.

38. For examples of this support see "Aux Mines d'Ostricourt", *Nord Industriel*, (1922), p. 751; ANMT, 40AS7, 26 November 1920, Secretary CCHF Circular 608; Pairault, *L'Immigration organisée*, pp. 252–263.

39. This cooperation is evidenced in, for instance, Archiwum Akt Nowych [Archive of New Records], Warsaw, Ministerstwo Spraw Zagranicznych [Ministry of Foreign Affairs], Series MSZ, MSZ 11139, 27 March 1929, Letter from Consul of Poland, Lille, to Director General of Mines de Marles.

Moreover, they allowed Polish parliamentarians to visit and address Poles residing in company-owned facilities.[40]

Coal executives doubtless approved of the apparent influence that ethnic paternalism and cordial relations with the Polish officials had on the Polish workforce. The policies enhanced the recruitment of Polish staff. Indeed, Poles swiftly filled Pas-de-Calais miners' ranks. Companies in the western portion of the coal basin, for instance, employed just 2 Poles in January 1919; this number grew to 6,000 by the end of 1921, more than 10 per cent of the labor force there.[41] As the hiring of Poles spread across the coal basin, Polish personnel increased still further, from 16,000 in 1922 to 32,500 in 1923, and 38,528 in 1924. Thus, Poles represented nearly one-third of the total mining labor force.[42]

From 1925 onward, as coal companies had amassed an adequate work-force, extensive contracting of foreign labor gave way to recruitment to suit market conditions. In periods of slack coal demand, firms neither recruited Polish workers nor sought to retain those whose contracts had expired. In the recessionary year of 1925, for example, total Polish staff fell by 1,900, about 5 per cent. Economically promising periods reversed the situation, and companies hired immigrants. For instance, in the boom year of 1929 firms added nearly 6,400 Polish workers.[43] Further, Pas-de-Calais mines successfully enticed married Poles with families to their employment. Of Polish males entering the French coal industry in 1922 and 1923, over one-third arrived with their wives and children.[44] Among the remainder, many subsequently sent for their spouses and progeny. Pas-de-Calais mines such as Bruay could, therefore, boast that married workers with children constituted 61 per cent of their immigrant staff.[45]

Ethnic paternalism also yielded dividends in enhancing managerial con-trol over non-natives, in reducing turnover among Polish staff, and in ensuring that immigrant children grew up in surroundings which made

---

40. ADPdC, 1Z501, 29 June 1924, Rapport No. 528: *Union des Travailleurs Polonais en France*, Special Commissar Lens; and ADPdC, 1Z501, 26 February 1924, Commissariat of Police, Bruay-en-Artois to Subprefect Béthune re *Réunion en Bruay*. Special commissars were officials who monitored groups and individuals whose actions were considered potentially subversive and threatening to the French political order and national security. The organizations and actions of foreigners attracted much of the attention of the special commissars. The special commissars reported both to departmental prefects and to security officials of the central government.
41. Paul Georges, "Rapport de M. l'Ingénieur en chef des Mines sur la Situation de l'Industrie minérale dans l'Arrondissement minéralogique d'Arras pendant l'année 1921", in *Département du Pas-de-Calais Conseil Général deuxième Session ordinaire de 1921: Rapports des Chefs de service et Renseignements divers, troisième partie* (Arras, 1922), pp. 333–349, 345.
42. *Idem*, "Rapport de M. l'Ingénieur en Chef des Mines [...] 1922", pp. 318–319, and "Rapport de M. L'Ingénieur en Chef des Mines [...] 1924", pp. 117–118.
43. Galand, *Les Mines du Nord*, p. 135.
44. ANMT, 40AS1, CCHF Assemblée Générale 1924, p. 14.
45. Pairault, *L'Immigration organisée*, p. 192.

them likely future miners. Company housing strategies helped to create a patchwork of Polish communities within Pas-de-Calais. By 1924, in twelve of the twenty-three mining-district communes Poles constituted one-half or more of the French population. Further, in six of these communes Poles outnumbered French residents.[46] Concentrating immigrants into specific communities permitted greater levels of surveillance. Companies, in fact, posted special guards and inspectors in foreign-worker areas, where they served as the employers' eyes and ears.[47] Management's policies also successfully promoted worker stability. The proportion of Poles leaving the coal industry within a year of their arrival shrank from 35 per cent in 1921 to 16 per cent in 1922, and then to just 2 per cent in 1923.[48] Further, firms benefitted from family immigration as Polish youths increasingly took up work in the mines.[49]

Ethnic paternalism and other strategies, however, did more than simply advance managerial agendas; they also significantly helped to shape the Polish community that emerged in postwar Pas-de-Calais. At the same time, coal firms did not create it alone. Like French executives, the Polish state, the Polish church, and immigrant Poles also pursued a Polish *milieu national* in the coalfields. The Polish government, through consular officials, defended the emigrants and advised many ethnic organizations. Polish priests and nuns attended to Polish believers, upholding the Poles' Catholic faith and religious traditions. Moreover, the ambitions and preferences of the immigrants themselves molded the Polish community. Employer efforts thus combined with those of Polish authorities, clergy, and immigrants to create a community enjoying a wealth of social, cultural, religious, and economic institutions. Indeed, no other immigrant group in interwar France possessed an ethnic support network comparable to that of Pas-de-Calais Poles.[50]

The Poles operated, often with financial assistance from employers, a dizzying variety of voluntary associations. A religious orientation underpinned many groups, such as rosary associations, the Society of Saint Vincent-de-Paul, and the Association of Saint Barbara. Other organizations focused on art and culture, staging theatrical and musical performances. Poles also pursued sport, gymnastic training, and outdoor activities in Polish soccer leagues, in athletic clubs, and in Polish boy scout troops.[51]

---

46. ADPdC, M3231, 19 December 1924, Prefect to Direction de la Sureté Générale, Paris.
47. ADPdC, 1Z501, 25 March 1925, Report of Special Commissar Lens to Subprefect Béthune.
48. ANMT, 40AS1, CCHF Assemblée Générale 1924, p. 14.
49. Georges, "Rapport de M. L'Ingénieur en Chef des Mines [...] 1923", pp. 128–129.
50. Mauco, *Les Étrangers en France*, pp. 313–349.
51. *Ibid.*, p. 330. For a discussion of this array of associations see, for instance, ADPdC, 1Z501, 25 March 1925, Special Commissar Lens to Subprefect Béthune; and ADPdC, M6857, 23 September 1929, Subprefect Béthune to Prefect Pas-de-Calais. On Polish sports associations, particularly soccer clubs, in both the Nord-Pas-de-Calais region and the Ruhr, see also the contributions by Marion Fontaine and Diethelm Blecking to this Special Issue.

Individual communities of Polish miners were awash with ethnic clubs. For example, the Poles in the commune of Bruay alone maintained forty-two separate groups.[52]

Poles also established businesses. In the coalfields a Polish merchant class arose, serving an immigrant clientele. The city of Lens, for instance, became an important site of Polish commerce. The smaller town of Sallaumines also boasted many Polish businesses. In 1924, just five years after the entry of the first contingent of Polish immigrants, Sallaumines counted nineteen different Polish-owned small businesses and Lens hosted forty.[53] These enterprises met various immigrant needs and wants. Polish-operated banks stored the immigrants' savings and money-transfer services transmitted their funds to Poland. Stores carrying Polish newspapers, magazines, and books catered to the Polish reading public. Additionally, Polish cafés and restaurants flourished, providing immigrant workers and their families with familiar foods and venues for socializing. Most numerous among Polish businesses were small groceries, butcher shops, and bakeries. Their proprietors' understanding of Polish culinary preferences permitted them to serve a market of which French establishments remained largely unaware.[54]

COMPANY POLICIES, NATIVE ANXIETIES, AND IMMIGRANT SOCIAL ISOLATION

Company efforts to attract, to retain, and to manage immigrants also profoundly shaped Polish–French relations within the multi-ethnic workforce and society emerging in postwar Pas-de-Calais. Overall, the newcomers remained isolated from the wider coalfield society in the 1920s. Scholars generally trace the social distance separating the immigrants from natives to the Poles' strong ethnic institutions. These built support among the migrants but left them without meaningful connections to their working-class French neighbors. Further, researchers point out that companies, the Polish state, the Polish church, and the immigrants together constructed the ethnic institutions that cultivated both the Poles' ethnic solidarity and also their social segregation.[55] Such views, however, overlook

52. Mauco, *Les Étrangers en France*, pp. 330–331; ADPdC 1Z209, 5 November 1924, Special Commissar Lens to Subprefect Béthune.

53. ADPdC, 1Z501, 4 November 1924, Special Commissar Lens to Subprefect Béthune; and ADPdC, 1Z501, 4 January 1925, Special Commissar Lens to Subprefect Béthune.

54. Mauco, *Les Étrangers en France*, pp. 339–340. For descriptions of the Polish businesses see, for instance, ADPdC, 1Z501, 4 November 1924, Special Commissar Lens to Subprefect Béthune; ADPdC, 1Z501, 4 January 1925, Special Commissar Lens to Subprefect Béthune; ADPdC, M3229, 22 September 1925, Special Commissar Béthune to Subprefect Béthune.

55. Such interpretations can be found, for instance, in Janine Ponty, *Polonais Méconnus: Histoire des Travailleurs immigrés en France dans l'Entre-deux-guerres* (Paris, 1990), pp. 113–142 and 147–172; Gary S. Cross, *Immigrant Workers in Industrial France* (Philadelphia, PA, 1983), pp. 71–98.

another group that powerfully shaped the immigrants' social position: Pas-de-Calais natives. Further, they fail to appreciate the complex influence that managerial policies toward Poles exerted over ethnic relations.

Ultimately, cool social interactions between non-natives and natives owed much to the cultural and socio-economic anxieties that colored local perceptions of Poles. Coal company policies, for their part, magnified the natives' misgivings and fostered their contempt for foreigners. Inside the mines, managerial procedures toward immigrants led French miners to view their Polish co-workers as occupational inferiors and to eschew workplace friendships with them. In this way, ethnic differences blunted the force of shared work experience to foster the foreigners' integration. Outside the mines, company housing for immigrants, support for Polish ethnic and religious institutions, and employer cordiality with the Polish state limited venues for Polish–French interaction, and it amplified the natives' myriad suspicions of Poles. This distance and distrust hampered the operation of working-class institutions to incorporate immigrants, as Pas-de-Calais trade unionists regarded Polish members with lack of interest or even animus.

Among coal basin natives, the immigrants' arrival sparked alarm over how it would affect the locals' economic and social position. Pas-de-Calais miners feared that foreigners would accept substandard pay and working conditions, permitting management to use them to undermine French wages and job security.[56] Further, natives worried that immigrants might rob them of opportunities for social and occupational advancement. As more and more miners aspired to abandon arduous and dangerous work underground, they coveted less demanding and high-paying service and maintenance jobs available in rebuilding postwar mines. In pursuit of these, Pas-de-Calais miners did not welcome the prospect of competition from immigrants.

The tactics that coal firms developed to assign, to train, and to supervise Polish labor in the mines helped to transform French economic and social anxieties into a sense of superiority, a sentiment that distanced natives from newcomers in the workplace. Placement procedures funneling immigrants into the most taxing and least valued jobs at the coalface and denying them access to prized surface and maintenance positions powerfully influenced Pas-de-Calais workers' views of foreigners. French miners soon perceived non-natives as their subordinates at work, as a group lacking the ability and even the intelligence to ascend from lowly occupations. On-the-job-training routines for Poles reinforced this assessment. Indeed, foreigners took up their positions only after French miners had instructed them and declared them fit for work. The system of *encadrement* similarly bolstered native

---

56. Ralph Schor, *L'Opinion Française et les Étrangers en France 1919–1939* (Paris, 1985), pp. 260–263.

miners' sense of superiority as it barred Poles from mining without French supervisors. Beyond shaping perception, these training and supervisory policies elevated the actual status of many French miners who took up positions of authority as the trainers and supervisors of Poles.

Native workers relished their elevated position and loathed challenges to it. As one contemporary observer reported, French miners chafed when non-natives received pay and job assignments similar to their own.[57] Further, they resented Poles who left lowly mining positions to open shops, cafés, and bars.[58] In their view, the Poles' place was underground, subordinated to the will of French managers, and not clawing their way into the petty bourgeoisie. Thus, managerial policies widened the gap between natives and foreigners in the mines. Indeed, as the Pas-de-Calais prefect related, in the workplace Frenchmen and Poles remained separated by an "invisible wall" across which members of one group offered the other "a brief hello" at best.[59]

Mass Polish immigration to the coalfields also proved disconcerting to the cultural sensibilities and outlook of Pas-de-Calais miners. Many coal-basin natives shared a regional identity in which they took great pride and comfort. Most traced their ancestry back to migrants from the countryside of the Pas-de-Calais and neighboring department of the Nord.[60] And they continued to speak local patois and to delight in regional folklore and customs. In fact, postwar observers remarked that Pas-de-Calais miners felt completely at ease only with other coalfield natives.[61] Such insularity even affected the local workers' movement. Despite strong trade unionism among Pas-de-Calais miners, they seldom focused on concerns beyond those of local interest. Thus, appeals to worker internationalism motivated only a minority.[62]

Beyond regional loyalties, secularism and anti-clericalism united coal basin locals. Indeed, Pas-de-Calais mining communities represented the least religious and most anti-clerical region in all of France.[63] Wartime invasion, dislocation, and destruction created still other common sentiments among Pas-de-Calais miners. They emerged from World War I deeply suspicious of foreigners, of Germans in particular, and assured in their patriotism.[64] Polish immigration troubled all these aspects of local

57. Condeveaux, *Le Mineur du Nord*, p. 15.

58. See ADPdC, 1Z501, 4 January 1925, Special Commissar Lens to Subprefect of Béthune.

59. ADPdC, M6857, 11 October 1929, Prefect Pas-de-Calais report to Interior Ministry.

60. Philippe Ariès, *Histoire des Populations françaises et de leurs Attitudes devant la Vie depuis le XVIIe siècle* (Paris, 1948), pp. 226–254.

61. On postwar local culture in general see Condeveaux, *Le Mineur du Nord*, pp. 5–16.

62. Ponty, *Polonais Méconnus*, p. 180.

63. *Ibid.*, pp. 153–154. See also Serge Laury, "Aspects de la pratique religieuse dans le diocèse d'Arras (1919–1945)", *Revue du Nord*, (1971), pp. 123–134, 123–124.

64. Ponty, *Polonais Méconnus*, p. 180.

culture and mindset as it placed a very alien group in their midst. The Poles' language, customs, and origin differed greatly from those uniting the natives. Their religiosity and reverence for the Catholic Church clashed with local attitudes. Further, the immigrants' allegiance to a nation other than France offended the miners' nationalism. Pas-de-Calais natives thus confronted a group very dissimilar to them.

Company efforts to attract and to root Poles in the coal basin through a Polish *milieu national* outside the workplace intensified the natives' cultural misgivings toward Poles. These policies thus furthered ethnic separation between the French and Poles in the Pas-de-Calais coalfields. In addition, certain managerial tactics – such as company housing practices concentrating Poles in particular neighborhoods or constructing completely Polish worker *cités* – much reinforced ethnic divisions. As Leen Beyers has revealed in analyzing immigrant–Belgian interaction in the Belgian mines, segregated housing not only inhibited positive interactions between natives and newcomers, it also fostered indigenous prejudice. By the presence of their surrounding countrymen in Belgian neighborhoods, Belgians felt reassured of the importance of their own ethnic identity, leading them to avoid and disdain immigrants, whom they deemed inferior.[65]

Company accommodations operated similarly in the Pas-de-Calais. Housing assignment based on ethnicity meant that neighborly bonds nurtured by contact, communication, and reciprocity were not likely to develop between the Poles and the French. While companies calculated that residential segregation would strengthen ethnic ties among Polish employees and their families, it worked likewise for Pas-de-Calais natives. The presence of Polish neighborhoods allowed local miners to appreciate all the more clearly the regional culture, the secularism and anti-clericalism, the patriotism, and the suspicion of foreigners that bound them together. Additionally, by backing numerous Polish-only clubs and groups, executives actually left closed avenues for Polish–French interaction and understanding that company-supported inter-ethnic organizations might have opened.

Management's support for Polish religious institutions and courtesy to Polish officials also worked to sharpen native suspicions born of anti-clericalism and nationalism. Company funds helped to cultivate a set of cultural practices doubly foreign to Pas-de-Calais miners. Not only was the immigrants' devotion to Catholicism out of place in the profoundly secular coalfields, Polish religious customs, favoring outward and communal expressions of devotion, contrasted with the often more somber and internal forms of French reverence.[66] As French miners puzzled over Polish

---

65. Leen Beyers, "Everyone Black? Ethnic, Class and Gender Identities at Street Level in a Belgian Mining Town, 1930–50", in Berger *et al.* (eds), *Towards a Comparative History of Coalfield Societies*, pp. 146–163, 151–156.
66. Ponty, *Polonais Méconnus*, p. 148.

religious life, two questions were in the forefront in their minds. How strong was the influence of Polish priests over the immigrants? And how would Polish clergy intervene in local economic and social matters? Similar questions arose as miners watched Polish officials circulate in mines and mining communities. How much power did these foreign authorities wield over their citizens and to what end might they use it?

At times, Pas-de-Calais natives gleaned troubling answers to these questions. For instance, already in the early 1920s, Polish labor leaders sought to create an ethnic-worker organization independent of the major French unions. This project earned the approval of Polish clergy and consular staff. It also electrified French miners and their unions, who rallied to oppose it. Anti-clericalism and patriotism charged their arguments against the Polish group. Union officials questioned the ability of Poles to overcome the influence of Polish priests and to see their own occupational and class interests.[67] Further, pointing to Polish church and state support for the project, Pas-de-Calais laborites decried such efforts as reactionary and dangerously nationalistic.[68]

By exacerbating cultural differences between Poles and natives, coal company policies outside the workplace contributed to a social climate of indifference and even discrimination toward foreigners. This was manifest in local working-class institutions such as trade unions. Admittedly, at the heights of union leadership, both the reformist union of the Confédération générale de travail (CGT) and the revolutionary/communist union of the Confédération générale de travail unitaire (CGTU) proclaimed common cause with foreign miners. In the fight against capital, both groups vowed to defend the interests of immigrants just as they did French workers. Union leaders, in fact, dedicated some resources to recruiting Poles. They established special sections to address Poles and founded Polish-language publications to communicate with the immigrants.[69] Yet, their efforts enjoyed limited success. In 1929, for example, the CGT had enrolled only 7,500 of some 90,000 Polish immigrant miners in France.[70]

It is clear that these official efforts did not concern, let alone mobilize, the unions' rank-and-file members, who showed scant enthusiasm for recruiting Poles. Some Pas-de-Calais trade unionists, in fact, called for discrimination against immigrants, as they argued against granting Polish miners the right to vote for mineworker delegates. They maintained that Poles would use the ballots not to serve labor interests but to please Polish priests.[71] Certain communists even advocated violently disturbing public

---

67. Schor, *L'Opinion Française*, pp. 262 and 264.
68. ADPdC, 1Z501, 29 June 1924, Special Commissar Lens, Report on Union des Travailleurs Polonais meeting.
69. Schor, *L'Opinion Française*, pp. 239–252.
70. Cross, *Immigrant Workers*, p. 144.
71. Schor, *L'Opinion Française*, p. 261.

activities such as Polish celebrations and processions, ostensibly to counter the influence of clericalism.[72] The bulk of Pas-de-Calais laborites, however, remained indifferent to Polish miners. They tolerated immigrant members, but did not push local or national unions to address immigrant concerns meaningfully. This apathy reflected local attitudes toward immigrants; it also undermined the Poles' enthusiasm for French unions.[73]

Social discrimination against Poles in the Pas-de-Calais, however, ultimately remained limited in the 1920s. Miners' unions, despite their initial unease with Polish labor organizing, rejected xenophobic policies and continued to seek, though often half-heartedly, immigrant membership.[74] This stance dampened anti-immigrant sentiment among local unionists in the long run. The immigrants' circumscribed socio-economic status also defused tension. As immigrants generally remained barred from the most lucrative and least taxing positions in the mines, French workers faced little competition from foreigners for prized jobs. In fact, the presence of immigrants in the mines often created supervisory positions for natives.[75] Further, labor scarcity in the coalfields and postwar prosperity enhanced the miners' security, well-being, and forbearance for immigrants.

Yet, tolerance of foreigners was not acceptance. One contemporary observer reported that Pas-de-Calais natives remained "extremely cool and even distrustful" of foreigners.[76] Another contemporary scholar of mining noted that in the coal basin there existed between the French and Poles "two such complete worlds, [that] interaction is not always affable".[77] For his part, the Pas-de-Calais prefect surmised that a Frenchman moved through Polish neighborhoods only as a "passer-by", between the native and the Poles arose neither "companionship" nor "friendship".[78]

COMPANY POLICIES, PAS-DE-CALAIS OFFICIALS, AND ANTI-IMMIGRANT DISCRIMINATION

Coal company policies toward immigrant staff that amplified native prejudices, suspicions, and discriminatory attitudes toward Poles in coalfield society had similar effects on the French state and its relations with non-natives in Pas-de-Calais. Scholars of interwar French immigration have

72. *Ibid.*, p. 265.
73. Cross, *Immigrant Workers*, pp. 94 and 141–165.
74. See Copy of the Reports of the Annual Congress of the Syndicat des Mineurs du Pas-de-Calais for 1923–1924, 20 April 1924, and Copy of the Reports of the Annual Congress of the Syndicat des Mineurs du Pas-de-Calais for 1924–1925, 19 April 1925, in ADPdC, 1Z277.
75. Mauco, *Les Étrangers en France*, p. 475.
76. Condevaux, *Le Mineur du Nord*, p. 7.
77. Galand, *Les Mines du Nord*, p. 46.
78. ADPdC, M6857, 11 October 1929, Prefect Pas-de-Calais report to Interior Ministry.

recently discovered that in the French government's efforts to administer and police its burgeoning immigrant population during the 1920s and 1930s, local officials possessed considerable autonomy and authority. They reveal that legislators and ministers of the central government crafted immigration regulations and directives according to their own principles and purposes. And these researchers have illuminated the way in which local contexts, conditions, and attitudes affected the implementation of immigration regulations emanating from Paris.[79] Departmental and municipal officials thus applied and enforced laws in ways shaped to a high degree by their local concerns, sentiments, and fears. Yet, by largely restricting their analytical attention to interactions between the state and immigrants, these studies have inadequately explored the considerable influence that employers exercised over the perceptions and concerns of the local officials who policed foreigners. This influence over state–immigrant interrelations, however, was considerable, even though largely unintended.

In the Pas-de-Calais, the postwar flood of immigrants to the coalfields produced a host of weighty administrative and security concerns for local authorities. Coal firms inadvertently fueled these preoccupations. By supporting Polish clergy, churches, religious associations, and ethnic organizations in the coalfields and by remaining friendly with Polish officials in the region, coal firms hoped to bolster the recruitment, retention, and managerial control of Polish staff. Watchful for any immigrant challenge to national security and the power of the French state, local officials, however, perceived the Polish *milieu national* differently.

Broadly, French officials regarded the actions and attitudes of Polish immigrants, clergy, and authorities as affronting the republican creed that guided the French Third Republic, the state they served. French republicans championed a set of universal rights, liberties, and responsibilities that would be open to all who wished to take citizenship, regardless of their origin. They expected the beneficiaries of liberty, equality, and fraternity to surrender loyalties to tradition in order to participate fully in the larger French linguistic and cultural community. Republicans thus regarded the use of the French language and secularism in public life as crucial to the unity and strength of the republic.[80] Though not citizens, immigrants

---

79. For examples see Paul Lawrence, "'Un flot d'agitateurs politiques, de fauteurs de désordre et de criminels'. Adverse Perceptions of Immigrants in France Between the Wars", *French History*, 14 (2000), pp. 201–221; Clifford Rosenberg, *Policing Paris: The Origins of Modern Immigration Control between the Wars* (Ithaca, NY, 2006); and Mary Dewhurst Lewis, *The Boundaries of the Republic: Migrant Rights and the Limits of Universalism in France, 1918–1940* (Stanford, CA, 2007).

80. Rogers Brubaker, *Citizenship and Nationhood in France and Germany* (Cambridge, MA, 1992); Edward Berenson, Vincent Duclert, and Christophe Prochasson (eds), *The French Republic: History, Values, Debates* (New York, 2011); also see Marion Fontaine's contribution to this Special Issue.

nevertheless aroused official consternation and even anxiety when they clung to their native languages and traditions and lived in tight-knit ethnic communities. To republican eyes, such tendencies could appear to threaten national unity and the political order itself.

To Pas-de-Calais officials, then, the Polish worker *cités* and the networks of ethnic and religious institutions in them did not appear to be sites and implements for employer control. Instead, they saw them as bastions and tools of foreign influence and power, sites where Polish priests and officials mobilized ethnic organizations and immigrants to serve interests separate from or contrary to those of France. Local officialdom, thus, came to view Poles as a suspect group, one warranting enhanced surveillance and harsh treatment.

The rapidly growing immigrant population after World War I created manifold responsibilities for departmental and municipal officials in the Pas-de-Calais. The central government in Paris called on its subalterns across France to administer and police immigrants in the nation's economic, public safety, and security interests. Paris sought to ensure employers' access to needed foreign labor, while protecting the French workforce from unfair competition. Thus, it tasked local administrators with regulating the labor contracts and residency requirements governing the immigrants' occupation in France. Further, the central government worked to shield citizens from any threats to public safety and property that immigrants might pose – a potential that was regarded at the time as real and rather acute. And, it pledged to defend French political institutions, sovereignty, and national unity from what was perceived as the possible machinations of alien political extremists and of governments seeking undue influence over their emigrants in France. To serve public safety and national security, Paris called on local officials to exert particular vigilance in policing the immigrants in their jurisdictions.[81]

To meet the administrative and law enforcement challenges associated with the presence of the foreign population, the central government placed arbitrary powers in the hands of departmental and local officials. For instance, they could put a suspect immigrant on *refoulement*, an action placing the migrant's right to remain in France on probation. Beyond this, local authorities could recommend that a foreigner be expelled outright. Law enforcement could issue *refoulement* and expulsion orders largely as it pleased. Transgressions warranting these punishments were not codified, and foreigners lacked the right to appeal such decisions against them in court.[82]

---

81. For further details about the security-dominated policies of the French state vis-à-vis immigrants, see Philip H. Slaby, "Industry, the State, and Immigrant Poles in Industrial France, 1919–1939" (Ph.D. dissertation, Brandeis University, 2005), pp. 205–213.

82. Jean-Charles Bonnet, *Les pouvoirs publics français et l'immigration dans l'entre-deux-guerres* (Lyon, 1976), pp. 106–107; Schor, *L'Opinion Française*, p. 281; Cross, *Immigrant Workers*, pp. 181–182.

Some of the varied administrative and law enforcement tasks associated with immigration frustrated the Pas-de-Calais authorities. Regulating the immigrants' position in the workforce created considerable administrative burdens for local officials. For instance, enforcing the labor contracts of Poles who broke agreements and drifted from employer to employer proved exasperating. Tracking down job-hoppers alone consumed great effort, as wayward immigrants often simply departed for new prospects without leaving a clue about their destinations.[83] While regulating the foreigners' place in the workforce represented administrative drudgery, Pas-de-Calais officials eagerly responded to calls to safeguard national political institutions, sovereignty, and unity from any immigrant menace. In fact, Pas-de-Calais officials pursued immigrants they deemed dangerous to the French political order and national security with such ardor that they clashed with their superiors. At times, ministries in Paris reprimanded Pas-de-Calais administrators and police for their high-handedness toward suspect foreigners. For their part, local officials, convinced of the gravity of immigrant threats, often dismissed and defied calls from Paris for restraint and evenhandedness.[84]

For Pas-de-Calais officials, the Polish mining community became a focus for much suspicion. And coal company policies toward Polish staff certainly shaped the features of the community that local authorities found disquieting. As explained above, management residentially segregated Poles, funded organizations to reinforce Polish cultural habits, built Polish churches and salaried Polish clergy, and maintained good relations with figures from the Polish state. Given Pas-de-Calais officialdom's pre-occupation with upholding the strength and authority of the French republic, it is no surprise that they had doubts. To what entities and to whom did socially isolated Poles owe loyalty? For what political or other purposes did ethnic institutions operate? What leadership did Polish priests and officials exert, and for what goals?

One of the major issues was that immigrant Poles, in the estimation of local authorities, were politicized and nationalistic. The special commissar of Lens clearly expressed these views. Poles were in his estimation "extremists of the left or of the right", and seven Poles in ten were "thoroughly nationalist", by his reckoning. Further, he had "no illusion regarding Franco-Polish friend-ship". True, he noted, Poles publicly pronounced "good intentions" toward France, but he judged such declarations "superficial", existing "only in

---

83. See the lamentations voiced in the following letter: ADPdC, M3213, 25 October 1929, Commissar of Police, City of Sallaumines, to Prefect Pas-de-Calais.

84. On tensions between central government officials, local officials, and immigrants, see Philip H. Slaby, "Violating the 'Rules of Hospitality': The Protests of Jobless Immigrants in Depression-Era France", in Matthias Reiss and Matt Perry (eds), *Unemployment and Protest: New Perspectives on Two Centuries of Contention* (London [etc.], 2011), pp. 175–198.

speeches and writings". Poles, he concluded, cared little for the future of the country.[85] Further, in Polish ethnic organizations, local officers saw institutions utterly devoted to advancing the interests of Poles. Beyond this, immigrant associations eroded national unity, as Poles flocked to them and not to French associations, where foreigners could grow to understand their French hosts.[86] Meanwhile, Pas-de-Calais officialdom's greatest misgivings surrounded Polish priests and consular staff active in the coalfields, in whom they saw leaders who exploited Polish national and religious sentiment to organize and direct immigrants. For instance, one official asserted that the Polish state, through consular authorities and priests, "dragooned" immigrants into ethnic institutions where the "love of Poland and religion" was the central tenet.[87]

Charged to protect national security and possessing discretionary powers, local authorities often acted upon the supposed political dangers posed by the Polish mining community. Public meetings of all types organized by Poles attracted police surveillance. Further, any event at which Polish consular staff or visiting Polish officials appeared drew particular police attention. When such Polish notables toured the Pas-de-Calais coal basin, they did so shadowed by French officials.[88] The police also went beyond surveillance. Local law enforcement regularly expelled foreign communists, and they brandished the threat of removal to force immigrants of all political orientations into compliance.[89] Thus, the Poles became both a community under suspicion and one facing official discrimination.

Still, a variety of factors checked state discrimination against Pas-de-Calais Poles during the 1920s. This became apparent when local administrators relished and hoped to expand their powers to police the Polish community. For instance, the special commissar of Arras lobbied for the creation of "social laws" to thwart "the excessive chauvinism of some Polish leaders".[90] However, two factors hindered such efforts. First, the

---

85. ADPdC, 1Z501, 10 October 1924, Special Commissar Lens to Subprefect Béthune.

86. ADPdC, M6857, 11 October 1929, Prefect Pas-de-Calais report to Interior Ministry; ADPdC, M6857, 30 September 1929, Special Commissar Arras to Prefect Pas-de-Calais; ADPdC, 1Z501, 25 March 1925, Special Commissar Lens to Subprefect Béthune; ADPdC, M3229, 22 September 1925, Special Commissar Béthune to Subprefect Béthune.

87. ADPdC, 1Z501, 10 October 1924, Special Commissar Lens to Subprefect Béthune. See also ADPdC, 1Z501, 25 March 1925, Special Commissar Lens to Subprefect Béthune; and ADPdC, M3229, 22 September 1925, Special Commissar Béthune to Subprefect Béthune.

88. ADPdC, 1Z501, 29 June 1924, Rapport: *Union des Travailleurs polonais* meeting, Special Commissar Lens; and ADPdC, 1Z501, 26 February 1924, Commissariat of Police, Bruay-en-Artois, to Subprefect Béthune re: *Réunion en Bruay*.

89. ADPdC, 1Z501, 14 October 1924, Subprefect report on immigrant workers to cabinet official. See also ADPdC, 1Z501, 20 December 1924, Special Commissar Lens to Subprefect Béthune; and ADPdC, 1Z501, 4 January 1925, Special Commissar Lens to Subprefect of Béthune.

90. ADPdC, M6857, 30 September 1929, Special Commissar Arras to Prefect Pas-de-Calais.

central government gave them no real credence. Though many lawmakers denounced isolated immigrant communities and resented foreign diplomats exercising authority over their nationals in France, they offered nothing to combat these. Ultimately, the French government could establish no practical procedures to force open ethnic communities and to halt foreign consulates. The Polish state stood as both a friend of France and as an ally against Germany. To bar contact between the Polish government and its citizens abroad would have sparked unwanted antagonism between the two states. Further, the Polish government could respond to such a move by restricting immigration to France, thereby cutting France off from an important source of necessary labor. For similar reasons, the government could not outlaw the immigrants' freedom to assemble in ethnic organizations or in religious congregations.

A second factor limiting efforts to break the apparent influence of Polish officials and clergy and thus diminish the social isolation of Poles were local attitudes toward coal company policies. Local officials never took aim at the pivotal role that coal companies' efforts played in segregating Poles. While company housing policies actually produced a Polish majority population in certain tracts of housing, managerial responsibility in encouraging ethnic segregation received no official condemnation. Likewise, company support for Polish cultural and religious particularism earned little mention in official exchanges. The Pas-de-Calais authorities seldom pointed out that mining companies had joined the Polish state and clergy in efforts to hinder the Poles' incorporation into the broader society.[91] Implicating powerful and prominent coal executives in creating foreign enclaves and thereby allegedly threatening national unity and the republican order appears to have been an unattractive prospect to local authorities. Holding a foreign state and church principally responsible for obstructing Polish assimilation proved a more comfortable case to make.

CONCLUSION

In the decade after World War I, Pas-de-Calais coal firms faced the challenges and opportunities of establishing and managing a multi-ethnic workforce. Polish workers offered them the chance to remedy labor shortages and to re-establish a productive and reliable labor force in the war-torn mines. Yet, to realize the potential that immigrants offered, companies had to grapple with thorny questions of how to attract, how to maintain, and how to manage newcomers. Notions of ethnic and national identity powerfully shaped coal company responses to these issues. Indeed,

91. For a rare example of when this was actually highlighted, see ADPdC, 1Z501, 10 October 1924, Special Commissar Lens to Subprefect Béthune.

a strategy of ethnic paternalism guided much of management's approach toward Polish staff. To entice Poles to the mine, to reduce turnover among them, and to enhance managerial influence over them, companies endeavored to create a Polish *milieu national* in the coalfields. They offered Poles housing in ethnic neighborhoods; they helped fund ethnic associations for Poles; and they actively and substantively supported Polish religious life. Beyond these efforts, executives remained friendly toward Polish consular officials.

Not only did aspects of ethnicity shape coal firm policies; managerial tactics also influenced perceptions of ethnic and national difference in the region. Workplace practices that relegated Poles into low-status, demanding underground tasks and that placed them under the authority of French trainers and managers encouraged native miners to perceive themselves as dissimilar from and even superior to foreigners. Further, policies that encouraged Polish residential segregation, a separate Polish associational life, Polish Catholic practice, and the presence of Polish clergy and officials in mining towns helped to underscore ethnic and national dissimilarities between natives and newcomers. Taking pride in their regional and French identity and in secularism and anti-clericalism, Pas-de-Calais miners saw the Poles as different or even menacing. Local miners thus greeted Poles with indifference or contempt.

Management activity sustaining Polish ethnic and religious life and relations between the immigrants and their home government also fueled suspicions vis-à-vis Poles among French officials in the Pas-de-Calais. Local authorities were dedicated to maintaining French strength and to a brand of republicanism that regarded the use of the French language and assimilation into the secular French culture as fundamental to the health of the French republic. To French officials a vibrant Polish mining community demanded strict, if not high-handed, policing. To them, Polish neighborhoods and organizations promoted the influence of the Polish church and state in France, while sustaining the immigrants' linguistic, religious, and cultural particularism. The coal firm policies of fostering this particularism thus interfered with the prevalent official ideas of ethnic, regional, and national identity. In this way, employers significantly contributed to the interrelations of mines, society, and state administration in the Pas-de-Calais coalfields.

The patterns of immigrant–native interaction that emerged after World War I had legacies for the larger interwar period. For employers, managerial strategies inside the mines and outside the workplace to entice and retain Polish workers and to make them productive succeeded. Yet, as native miners came to associate dangerous and demanding underground work with immigrants, companies became increasingly dependent on Poles to fill these positions. Even during the Great Depression, mines had to maintain and at times expand their Polish workforce. For local society, the perception of Poles as separate from the wider working-class community and its institutions persisted in the 1930s. Native miners continued to regard Poles largely with indifference. For instance, early in the Depression, native miners and unions did little to protect immigrants from dismissal from the mines and expulsion from France. The worker-friendly years of the Popular Front government, however, witnessed strengthening ties between Polish and French miners, as immigrants participated in mass strikes and flocked to French unions. Yet, such attitudes did not translate into sustained respect for non-natives. Unions diluted immigrant influence within their ranks and devoted scant attention to foreigners' concerns.[92] By 1938, such deafness to Polish interests caused many immigrants to abandon French unions.[93]

For Pas-de-Calais officials, their disdain for the Polish community intensified in the 1930s. In fact, as parts of the French public and the central government called for immigrant repatriation to open jobs for Frenchmen, Pas-de-Calais officials increasingly acted upon their resentments of Poles. Indeed, for much of the Depression era local authorities, seeking the immigrants' expulsion, aggressively policed Polish labor contracts and political activity. In 1934 alone, they assisted in the deportation of some 3,250 Poles.[94] For the Poles, the postwar patterns of native–immigrant interaction had perhaps the greatest implications. While the *milieu national* continued to offer them the support of their countrymen and traditions, the ethnic differences, social isolation, and the suspicion that Polish communal life encouraged often left them to experience growing marginalization and discrimination in the 1930s. Poles would have to wait until the post-World-War-II era to experience meaningful integration into French society.

92. Cross, *Immigrant Workers*, pp. 201–208, and Schor, *L'Opinion Française*, p. 642.
93. *Ibid.*, pp. 701–704.
94. Slaby, "Violating the 'Rules of Hospitality'", p. 193.

IRSH 60 (2015), Special Issue, pp. 253–273 doi:10.1017/S0020859015000395
© 2015 Internationaal Instituut voor Sociale Geschiedenis

Football, Migration, and Coalmining in Northern France, 1920s–1980s

MARION FONTAINE

*Centre Norbert Elias, Université d'Avignon et des Pays de Vaucluse
74 rue Louis Pasteur, 84 029 Avignon, France*

E-mail: marion.fontaine@univ-avignon.fr

ABSTRACT: Football is often thought to have helped erase differences between natives and migrants in mining communities and to have helped in building a homogeneous class identity. Others have described this idea as a myth. Under closer scrutiny, however, relations between migrants and football are more complex than commonly thought. This article will elaborate on these complex relations by analysing the case of the coalfield in the French region of Nord-Pas-de-Calais during the twentieth century. Migrant workers were employed there from an early date: first, from the 1920s, Poles; later on other migrants, especially of Moroccan and Algerian descent. Migrants played an important role in the development of football in this region. This article looks at the influence of football on relations between migrants and other miners. More generally, it aims to show how sport was incorporated into the industrial mining world, both in employers' policies and in the mining community.

In April 1955 the company newspaper *Douai Mines*, published by the state-owned Houillères nationales du Bassin Nord-Pas-de-Calais and named after Douai, one of the coalfield's larger cities, printed a map localizing the mining roots of some young football celebrities, from Maryan Wisniewski to Raymond Kopaszewski (the famous Kopa)[1] and Robert Budzinski, in the localities of Calonne-Ricouart to Auchel and Noeux-les-Mines in the coalfield in the north of France. Along with the map came an article (see Figure 1), with the following statement: "Coalmining, a harsh school of life, has rough names, who together form the wealth of French football."[2] The sentence and the reference to "rough" names emphasize the connections between football, coalmining, and migrant – in this case Polish – communities.

---

1. Raymond Kopaszewski was born in 1931 in Noeux-les-Mines into a family of Polish miners. In the 1950s he became a legendary footballer with a national and international career. Today, he is seen as the first great "star" of contemporary French football.
2. "Une mine [...] de footballeurs", *Douai Mines*, April 1955. The author writes of a "rude école de la vie", and of "noms rudes". All translations are mine.

Figure 1. "Une mine de... footballeurs".
Douai Mines, *April 1955.*

This connection was an effect not only of the company's advertising strategy, which sought to highlight the overall importance of the coalfield for
France. From the 1950s onwards especially, children of Polish migrants were
indeed very present in professional and non-professional football clubs. Some
of them, like Kopa, Wisniewski, and Budzinski even played in the French
national team. Today, this type of player is collectively remembered as a
symbol (or myth) of the integrative power of football, both as a medium and
as a reflection of the integration of immigrants into the French Republic.[3] This
idea is also present in local collective memory. In the northern coalmining
area, football is thought to have helped erase the differences between natives
and migrants and to have helped in building a homogeneous class identity.
This point is most often highlighted in the case of Polish migrants, who
comprised a large part of the mining workforce in northern France. Indeed, a
recent historical overview claimed that "Football in coalmining was an ideal
place to closely integrate boys who had different origins and backgrounds.
It was a way to provide social promotion."[4]

3. This is especially true for Raymond Kopa. For an analysis of how this myth functioned in the
case of Kopa and others, see, for instance, Xavier Béal, "Football et immigration: les figures de
Kopa, Platini, Zidane dans les médias", http://www.wearefootball.org/PDF/venus-d-ailleurs.pdf;
accessed 13 December 2009.
4. Centre Historique Minier de Lewarde, *Coup Franc, Journal édité pour la Coupe du Monde de
Football par le Centre Historique Minier de Lewarde et Mémoires et Cultures de la Région
Minière* (Lewarde, 1998), p. 1.

While this kind of representation, in which myth and reality are closely intertwined, may exist in other countries as well (as in Germany), it nevertheless takes on special significance and meaning in France. Generally speaking, this vision of the integrative power of sport is very powerful in contemporary French society. It merges with a major dimension of the republican project, namely the construction of an individual and political citizenship that would erase ethnic, cultural, and religious differences.[5] France's republican tradition renders any official recognition of race or ethnic origin illegitimate. Cultural identity or "community" – the word is often derogatory in France – are seen at best as an anachronism, and at worst as a threat to the unity and the values of the French Republic. Thus, if sport can have a political function, it is only as a means to homogenize ethnic and cultural heterogeneity, and not as a way to express a particular identity in the public sphere.

Over the past few decades, however, French historians and sociologists – building on the work of other researchers from Europe and the United States – have produced critical analyses of these processes and representations. The work of Gérard Noiriel can be considered seminal in this regard.[6] He was one of the first historians to take seriously the importance of immigration in the history of the French working class. He showed that there may have been some negative consequences of the republican vision of nation and of citizenship contributing not to the integration of immigrants in French society but to their exclusion. Following Noiriel's lead, numerous studies have been published to develop these themes further, especially with regard to the successive waves of migration in France during the twentieth century.[7] More recently, a number of studies have been undertaken in a similar vein, this time extending into the world of sport.[8] They have been concerned, in particular, with the reasons why the idea of integration through sport has become such a veritable myth, linked to the French conception of the nation. At the same time, these studies have attempted to clarify, in a concrete and analytical manner, the ambivalent role that modern sport – both as practice and as spectacle – may have played in the relationships between migrant and native.

5. For recent assessments of French republicanism see, for instance, Pierre Rosanvallon, *Le modèle politique français. La société française contre le jacobinisme* (Paris, 2004); Edward Berenson, Vincent Duclert, and Christophe Prochasson (eds), *The French Republic: History, Values, Debates* (New York, 2011).
6. Gérard Noiriel, *Le creuset français: histoire de l'immigration XIXe–XXe siècle* (Paris, 1988).
7. For a summary of this research by the initiator himself, see *idem, Immigration, antisémitisme et racisme en France (XIXe–XXe siècle): discours publics, humiliations privées* (Paris, 2007).
8. See, for instance, Stéphane Beaud and Gérard Noiriel, "L'immigration dans le football", *Vingtième Siècle. Revue d'histoire*, 26 (1990), pp. 83–96; William Gasparini (ed.), "L'intégration par le sport", *Sociétés contemporaines*, 69 (2008); Laurent Dubois, *Soccer Empire: The World Cup and the Future of France* (Los Angeles, CA, 2011).

It is this context that defines the scope of the present article. Beyond an abstract tribute to the integrative power of sport, it aims to explore and explain how football could alternately strengthen and erase the boundaries inside the mining communities in Nord-Pas-de-Calais, the most important of their kind in France. Based on extensive research on the coalfield's major football club, Racing Club de Lens,[9] this article tackles this issue in two major directions.

First, I will consider not only Polish migrants from the 1920s to the 1940s, but also other migrants – especially those of Moroccan and Algerian descent – who arrived after World War II. The comparison between different migratory waves allows one to understand better the ambivalent effects of sporting activities on the mining community at different periods. It will also help to transcend the stereotypes that, as in the United States (in a slightly different form), frequently place the "old" migrants in opposition to the "new": in this case, those with European origins versus those from the former French colonies in Africa.

Secondly, the article will stress the impact of the changing situation of the French mining industry. While the industry was nationalized at the end of World War II, from the 1960s on economic difficulties led to the closure of more and more pits and the mining communities began to disintegrate. This framework is essential in understanding the sporting relations between indigenous inhabitants and immigrants of different origin arriving at different moments. More generally, this article seeks to understand how sport was incorporated into the industrial mining world, both in terms of employers' policies (including their management of the labour market and social policies) and of social change in the mining communities.

THE MINING COMMUNITIES OF NORTHERN FRANCE

Since the nineteenth century, the development of a coalmining industry in the area ranging from the towns of Béthune to Valenciennes in northern France has been a source of profound, sometimes disruptive economic, political, social, and cultural change.[10] New industrial towns emerged, whose activities were all coal-related. The population of these towns grew very fast: the number of inhabitants in a city like Lens, one the most

9. See also Marion Fontaine, *Le Racing Club de Lens et les "Gueules Noires": Essai d'histoire sociale* (Paris, 2010).
10. For a general history of the coalfield see Marcel Gillet, *Les charbonnages du Nord de la France au XIXe siècle* (Paris [etc.], 1973). A comparative study of the emerging labour movements in the coalmining industries of western Europe can be found in Joël Michel, "Le mouvement ouvrier chez les mineurs d'Europe occidentale (Grande-Bretagne, Belgique, Allemagne, France): étude comparative des années 1880–1914" (Ph.D. dissertation, Université de Lyon II, 1987).

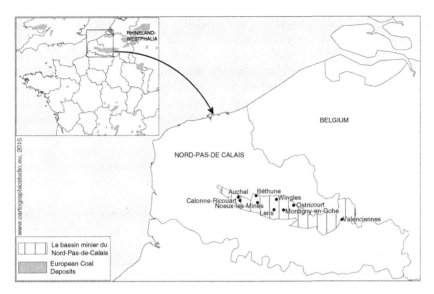

Figure 2. The northern mining region in September 1948 after the nationalization of the coal companies (which became *groupes* within the Houillères nationales du Bassin Nord-Pas-de-Calais [HBNPC]).
Centre Historique Minier de Lewarde. Used with permission.

important in the northern region, rose from 2,700 in 1851 to 31,800 in 1931. In the same period, formerly rural landscapes were transformed by the new pits and by infrastructural developments related to the coal industry. The owners of the private coal companies not only wanted to control the workforce during working hours, they also interfered in the everyday life of their workers: employers built new villages and new living quarters for their workers, and organized facilities for health, education, and leisure.[11]

This kind of employer paternalism had a pragmatic aim: it was meant to attract workers and to reduce the mobility of the mineworkers, who were frequently looking for better paid and more secure jobs. While World War I brought about the destruction of a significant number of industrial coalmining facilities in northern France, this did not result in a weakening of this paternalistic management. On the contrary, in the 1920s new industrial villages were built close to the coalmining pits and their related infrastructure. While working methods and operating procedures were partly modernized, employer control over the mining communities remained.

The mining world was neither unified and homogenous, however, nor completely under the control of the employers. On the contrary, the

11. Yves Le Maner, *Du coron à la cité. Un siècle d'habitat minier dans le Nord-Pas-de-Calais, 1850–1950* (Lewarde, 1995).

northern coalmining region was socially diverse and divided, and miners' unions were very strong, much like their British and German counterparts.[12] Political divisions were very important, especially after the French labour movement was divided into socialists and communists in 1920. Moreover, those inhabiting the mining quarters and working for the same company had different status positions, along with different duties and privileges. The size of the houses of workers, foremen, and engineers differed relative to the inhabitants' positions in the company hierarchy. This structure fuelled the rivalries, resentment, gossip, and opposition that were an integral part of life in mining communities, as well as moments of unity and collective experience, whether tragic (as after a mining disaster) or festive.[13]

A similar heterogeneity could be found in the domain of leisure. There were many leisure associations, often located in cafés,[14] ranging from amateur theatre groups and *jeu-de-boules* clubs to choral societies, to name just a few. Even in the field of leisure, interference by the employers was very strong. During the interwar period mining companies, in an attempt to monitor miners also in their leisure time, operated sports fields and other sport facilities, and many sports clubs were organized by the employers, often with a pit engineer or a teacher from the mining school serving as president.[15] These sports clubs were named after the miners' neighbourhoods, such as Saint-Pierre, Saint-Théodore, and Saint-Edouard. Their original activities had been gymnastics and military training, but in the 1920s, following a general trend in society, the nature of their physical activities changed and the older ones, like gymnastics, were replaced by new kinds of sport that were both competitive and team-based as well as rooted in mass culture – particularly football[16] and basketball.

---

12. For studies emphasizing this diversity see Philippe Ariès, "Au Pays noir, la population minière du Nord-Pas-de-Calais", in *idem, Histoire des populations françaises* (Paris, 1971), pp. 69–118; Claude Dubar, Gérard Gayot, and Jacques Hédoux, "Sociabilité minière et change-ment social à Sallaumines et à Noyelles-sous-Lens", *Revue du Nord*, 253 (1982), pp. 365–463.

13. For a study of a similar intermingling of social and local neighbourhood identities in the case of the Italian city of Turin, see Daniel Jalla and Florence Baptiste, "Le quartier comme territoire et comme représentation: les 'barrières' ouvrières de Turin au début du XXe siècle", *Le Mouvement Social*, 118 (1982), pp. 79–97.

14. Milan Vulic, "Le cabaret, le bistrot, lieu de la sociabilité populaire dans le bassin houiller du Nord-Pas-de-Calais (1750–1985)" (Ph.D. dissertation, Université de Lille III, 1990), pp. 205–312.

15. Archives Départementales du Pas-de-Calais, Dainville, France (hereafter, ADPC), archive funds T (Sports and Education) and M (General Administration): T.supp 145 (Information packs of the sports societies, 1920s–1930s); T.supp 272 (Information about sports societies, 1923–1924); M 2223 (List of sports societies, 1924).

16. About this process, see Julien Sorez, *Le football dans Paris et ses banlieues* (Rennes, 2013), pp. 71–118.

POLISH MIGRATION AFTER WORLD WAR I

Polish migrants started to arrive in the coalfield in the 1920s. They were not the first: the mining industry had attracted foreign workers, most of them from Belgium, since the nineteenth century.[17] Nevertheless, a real change could be observed in the 1920s. After World War I, the mining employers were in need of additional manpower and sought to recruit labour from abroad, first to rebuild the mining installations and related production facilities, and later to enable the growth of coal production. A minority of these immigrants came from the Rhineland-Westphalia industrial region in Germany, but most of them were Polish peasants arriving directly from Poland. Polish emigration was based on an intergovernmental agreement between France and the new state of Poland, with the support of the largest employers' union in the coalmining industry, the Comité Central des Houillères de France.[18] Women and children followed the men, and migration became massive: Polish workers had numbered only 13,000 in the north in 1921, yet reached 90,000 in 1926. They were concentrated in the coalmining area and made up a large proportion of the mining workforce. In the small town of Ostricourt, for example, the proportion of foreigners reached 70 per cent, almost all Poles.

Nearly all the immigrants were employed in the coalmining industry. Many companies employing the new miners tried to preserve them from "contamination" by trade unions or left-wing political parties. For their part, the Polish miners saw migration as a temporary affair and thought they would return to their home country after some years. Integration into French society was not their aim at that point. As a result, Polish migration at first led to the construction of segregated Polish communities within the French mining district, emerging as true *Petites Polognes*, that is to say, highly organized communities with their own shops, churches, and associations. In many villages, there were quarters or streets where everyone was Polish. These communities were rooted in national and religious values, and "identified" with Catholic Poland[19] – a phenomenon that arose with the active support of the mining companies, which contributed to the payments made to the Polish priests appointed by the Mission catholique polonaise and supported schools with Polish-language classes. A similar phenomenon could be seen in the Ruhr before 1914.[20]

17. Judith Rainhorn, "Le Nord-Pas-de-Calais, une région frontalière au cœur de l'Europe", *Hommes et migrations*, 1273 (May–June 2008), pp. 18–34, 21–25.
18. Janine Ponty, *Polonais méconnus. Histoire des travailleurs immigrés en France dans l'entre-deux-guerres* (Paris, 1988), pp. 35–81.
19. See also the article by Philip Slaby in this Special Issue.
20. Diethelm Blecking, "Sport and Immigration in Germany", *The International Journal of the History of Sport*, 25 (2008), pp. 955–973, 957–960. See, too, Diethelm Blecking's contribution to this Special Issue.

The policies of the companies and the strong national and cultural consciousness in these Polish communities engendered, at first, mutual segregation. Until the 1940s, Polish migrants were excluded from local society. Poles were seen as foreigners because of their language, their customs, and their demonstrative expression of Catholic piety (whereas French miners often kept a distance from the Catholic Church). They were disparagingly dubbed *Polaks* and often had to endure racist insults from other miners.[21] French workers, along with engineers and foremen, also called them *Boches* (a racist insult referring to the Germans in World War I), *cul-bénits*, or *curetons* ("prayboys"). In the opposition between "us" (the members of the local working class) and "them" (the others), Poles were firmly placed on the side of "them"; they were regarded as being outside the community and were seen as a threat and a source of division.

POLES AND FOOTBALL BEFORE AND AFTER WORLD WAR II

The segregation and exclusion of immigrants also held true in the arena of sports and leisure. This exclusion explains why Polish migrants created a peculiar and closed associative framework – in sports, music, and elsewhere – to assert their cultural and national identity, similar to the framework they had constructed in Germany before World War I.[22] Gymnastic events at the *Sokol* clubs,[23] cycling races, and football matches allowed migrants to get together; they could speak their own language and the sports festivities fostered a sense of community. For instance, in the mining district of Lens two *Sokol* associations were founded in the mid-1920s. After some years, in the same place, three Polish football clubs were established. The three teams were based on neighbourly relations: all team members lived in the same neighbourhood. Their establishment reflected the fact that Polish miners wanted to act on their own initiative and to play together within structures of their own creation.[24] With the same goal, they created autonomous federations such as the Fédération Polonaise de football en France, founded in 1924 (also known as the Polski Zwiarek Pitki Noznej [we Francji] – PZPN).

In addition to the individual clubs, these kinds of large social and sporting organizations offered opportunities for meetings and competitions to their members, allowing them to play without having to connect with the French sporting associations. This type of federation embodied the Polish

---

21. Janine Ponty, *Les Polonais du Nord ou la mémoire des corons* (Paris, 2008), p. 42.
22. Blecking, "Sport and Immigration in Germany".
23. These were specific gymnastic clubs that played a major role in the building of Polish/Slavic cultural and national identity: Diethelm Blecking (ed.), *Die slawische Sokolbewegung. Beiträge zur Geschichte von Sport und Nationalismus in Osteuropa* (Dortmund, 1991).
24. See ADPC, archives of the "Sous-préfecture de Béthune", 1Z 1017, report of the "sous-préfet de Béthune" to the "préfet du Pas-de-Calais" about the PZPN, autumn 1939.

community and contributed to the poor integration of these migrants into French society. These organizations were substantial in number and size: in 1937 there were 112 *Sokols*, 133 shooting clubs, and 27 football clubs in the northern coalmining region; the latter were affiliated to the PZPN.[25] As with the dynamics in the German Ruhr, the sporting networks sustained a sense of Polish identity in a foreign country. The sports associations thus strengthened the ethnic borders that divided the mining community.

But this situation did not last. In the 1930s and 1940s there was a change, initially for sport-related reasons: starting in the 1930s, football spread among miners and among the French working class in general. This new preference changed the situation for sport activities, as football and gymnastics did not play precisely the same role within the community.

Gymnastic activities were almost always organized within the framework of formalized associations, as was the case with the *Sokols*. This framework helped the *Sokols* to become an excellent medium for the promotion of Polish national identity, by means of special open-air exercises, with flags, banners, and uniforms worn by the gymnasts during the great mass festivities. In such events, Polish identity was very visible. But football had a more ambiguous side. The rules of the game were the same in the clubs in the PZPN and in the Fédération Française de Football (FFF). At the same time, the clubs in the Polish federation were often smaller and had fewer opportunities for prestigious matches. Additionally, in contrast to the *Sokols*, the PZPN clubs were less particular to the Polish community and less capable of embodying the Polish national identity. In other words, their function and their utility were less obvious. Under these circumstances, it was no wonder that many Polish children or teenagers soon preferred to play in French clubs, which had more resources and better competitive opportunities. By the 1930s, for example, children of Polish migrants comprised 30 per cent of the team of the Association Sainte-Barbe d'Oignies, an important non-professional mining club.[26]

There was another difference between gymnastics and football. Unlike gymnastics, football could be played informally, frequently in the form of street football, which was of great importance in the mining quarters, which functioned like urban villages.[27] As the British historian Richard Holt wrote:

> What seems to be clear is that such teams often sprang from a formalizing of casual street relationships, bringing a shape and a continuity to that most basic of feelings – the sense of place. [...] Organized teams provided a bridge between the childish and the adult male world, a means by which the playful enthusiasm of

25. Olivier Chovaux, "Le football, un exemple 'd'intégration de surface' dans l'entre-deux-guerres", in Marie Cegarra (ed.), *Tous gueules noires* (Lewarde, 2006), pp. 138–151, 145.
26. Archives Nationales du Monde du Travail, Roubaix, France, 1994 057 0015, Players' list of the "Association Sainte-Barbe d'Oignies" (1941–1942).
27. Grégory Frackowiak, "Théodore Szkudlapski dit Théo. Essai de biographie d'un 'galibot footballeur'", *Revue du Nord*, 355 (2004), pp. 367–389, 369.

boys was turned into the tougher style of men. Here boys learned how to drink and tell jokes as well as the language of physical aggression.[28]

This kind of learning was common for children of both French and Polish miners. They discovered football at the same time and they played together in the streets of the mining districts. This shared learning experience was undoubtedly an early way to bring young French natives and migrants' children together. The team's identity was no longer based on nationality or ethnicity, but on the neighbourhood and the local community. Football, especially, allowed the young Poles to erase the stigma of their origins: they were no longer seen as foreigners with "strange" names, language, and customs; they were now recognized as good players and sometimes as local sports heroes.[29]

This evolution became more and more pronounced after World War II, a very turbulent period for the northern coalmining region. Shortly after France had been liberated from German occupation, the mining companies were nationalized and those in the north were grouped into a new organization, the Houillères nationales du Bassin Nord-Pas-de-Calais [National Collieries of Nord-Pas-de-Calais Basin]. Nevertheless, frustration and anger among mineworkers lingered on, and the situation remained very tense until the end of the 1940s, especially during the massive wave of strikes in 1947–1948, which saw violent conflicts between strikers and non-strikers, and eventually led to harsh repression.[30] The unrest also affected the sports organizations in the mining district. On the one hand, there was much enthusiasm, thanks both to the end of the war and to nationalization, which sparked the dream of a profound, revolutionary change in society. This enthusiasm encouraged French and Polish miners to become closer. On the other hand, mining communities were now divided more than ever before. The French Communist Party continued to grow in number and influence among the miners, and denounced all representatives of the social and symbolic power of the company, including engineers, foremen, teachers, and priests.[31] The Polish migrants were divided into supporters of the new communist government of Poland and supporters of traditional, Catholic Poland.[32]

However, football grew in significance in the mining communities, and this growth became even more rapid following the disappearance of many

28. Richard Holt, "Working Class Football and the City: The Problem of Continuity", *The British Journal of Sports History*, 3 (1986), pp. 5–17, 7.
29. Beaud and Noiriel, "L'immigration dans le football", p. 92.
30. Marion Fontaine and Xavier Vigna, "La grève des mineurs de l'automne 1948 en France", *Vingtième Siècle: Revue d'histoire*, 121 (2014), pp. 21–34.
31. Dubar *et al.*, "Sociabilités minière et changement social", pp. 379–400; Augustin Viseux, *Mineur de fond: fosses de Lens, soixante ans de combat et de solidarité* (Paris, 1994), pp. 382–400.
32. Joël Michel, "La seconde guerre mondiale et l'évolution de la communauté polonaise du Nord de la France", *Revue du Nord*, 226 (1975), pp. 403–420, 410–412.

of the old gymnastics associations that had been previously controlled by the companies. In the small mining village of Wingles, for example, there was no longer just one team but four, which reflected old and new rivalries within the community: skilled versus unskilled miners, or gymnasts from the old mining association versus young and committed members of the new football clubs (which were supported by the communists). On the other hand, clubs in other small communities became more unified. Thus in the mining quarter of Saint-Pierre in Lens, a Serbian migrant, Jean Kravanja, created a new football club. His club was rooted in community life: its headquarters were located in a café, the team played on a playground in the neighbourhood, and it aimed to bring together all local residents.[33] This type of sports community was supported by a new sense of local identity: all the players and all the fans lived in the same place, often worked in the same pit, and were often affiliated with the Communist Party, the miners' union, or both. This shared identity became more important, while the difference between old inhabitants and new migrants (or their children) became increasingly weaker. Gradually, the small PZPN clubs became a thing of the past.

POLISH PLAYERS AND THEIR FANS: RACING CLUB DE LENS

This kind of development – consolidation and increasing identification by the whole local community – can also be observed in professional football, as becomes clear in the case of Racing Club de Lens ("Racing").[34] In the 1930s, this team was transformed into a professional club, controlled by the mining company in Lens. Racing's rise to prominence was part of a marketing strategy. The company directors wanted to build a successful, prestigious team to attract spectators and foster the reputation of the company. In this context, the club also attracted migrant players, but these were Hungarian or Austrian professionals who had been integrated into the international sports labour market and not Polish miners living in the neighbourhood.[35]

After World War II, the situation changed profoundly. In 1958, for instance, most of Racing's players came from Polish mining families and they had spent their childhood in the coalfield of the north.

33. ADPC, archive fund M (General Administration), M 6915 (List of new sports societies, 1939–1947). For references to this new club, see also the following local newspaper reports: *Artois-Sports*, 11 March 1947; *La Tribune des Mineurs*, 16 August 1947, 13 September 1947.
34. For a similar case, see Siegfried Gehrmann, "Football in an Industrial Region: The Example of Schalke 04 Football Club", *The International Journal of the History of Sport*, 6 (1989), pp. 335–355.
35. Olivier Chovaux, "Football minier et immigration. Les limites de l'intégration sportive dans les années trente", *STAPS*, 56 (2001), pp. 9–18, 11–14.

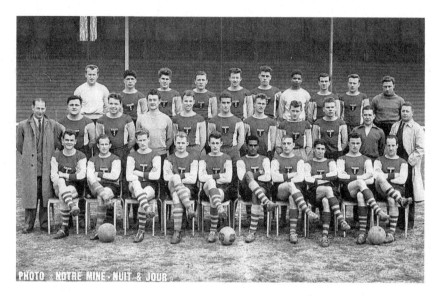

Figure 3. The RCL's team for the 1955–1956 season. Back row (left to right): Sowinski, Sarrazin, Carlier, Wattecamps, Wisniewski, Stiévenard, Dobat, Aurednik, Dumoulin, Duffuler. Middle row (left to right): Marek (coach), Klaus, Jonsson, Clément, Oswarzak, Courtin, Théo, Ziemczak, Ganczarzik, Battut, Trannin (manager). Front row (left to right): Trela, Habitzl, Kowalkowski, Polak, Demay, Louis, Marresch, Hassouna, Raspotnik, Boury. *Archives Municipales de Lens [4Fi914]. Used with permission.*

They included Kowalkowski, Ziemczak, Sowinski, Wisniewski, Placzek, and Szkudlapski.[36] A new generation of migrants was now able to penetrate professional football. This evolution can be explained by many factors, including the impact of nationalization. While the Houillères nationales continued to support local amateur sporting clubs – paternalism was not abolished by nationalization – they wanted the management of Racing to be more rational and less costly. As a consequence, Racing's leading representatives could no longer recruit players on the international market in the way they had before, and they had to turn to the human resources of the local coalfield. Moreover, following the tensions that marked the late 1940s, the managers of the Houillères nationales wanted to consolidate the unity of the mining community. They became increasingly interested in the potential role of the Racing football club, not only for marketing purposes but also as a source of social appeasement and cohesion.

These economic and social considerations led Racing's managers to change their approach to recruitment. Now they openly addressed the

36. Frackowiak, "Théodore Szkudlapski dit Théo"; Alfred Wahl and Pierre Lanfranchi, *Les footballeurs professionnels des années trente à nos jours* (Paris, 1995), pp. 134–137.

miners' children, playing in non-professional mining clubs. The directors of these clubs (often mining engineers) sent the best young players to Racing's managers. Through this deep-rooted network new promising players could be identified, such as Maryan Wisniewski (from Auchel) or the Lech brothers (Georges and Bernard Lech from Montigny-en-Gohelle). With this decidedly local model of recruitment, Racing's team became a reflection of the coalfield's population, including the Polish migrants among them. Conversely, the migrants became more conscious of the advantages of professional sports within the context of mining.

After World War II, Polish nationalism became a thing of the past and "assimilation" was the new watchword for migrants and their children. While, at that time, a career in professional football did not lead to "great" stardom, a young man who was a good player could gain better opportunities within the mining world. Racing's recruiters promised young players and their families jobs in offices or in technical services (rather than in the pits). They could earn a wage both as a player and as an employee of the Houillères nationales, and thereby hope for a better social position. As a non-professional player in Noeux-les-Mines, before he became famous, Raymond Kopa's long-cherished dream was not to become a professional footballer; rather, he saw the job of footballer as a stepping stone to a position as an electrician within the mining company.[37]

I will not dwell too much on Raymond Kopa, as his national and international career makes his case rather exceptional; the same goes for Maryan Wisniewski. For younger, less prestigious players, such as Theodore Szkudlapski, playing for Racing from 1953 to 1958,[38] or Arnold Sowinski, who played for Racing during his entire career,[39] integration into the local team provided material benefits, while allowing them to take advantage of the social rights associated with the mining profession. Those privileges came at a price, however. The mining context always prevailed, and young footballers had to be serious, modest, and respectful workers.[40] Most young Polish players thus had only a local career. They remained under the control of the Houillères nationales and were dominated by the mining managers of the club.

The relationships between these young Polish players and their fans was even more complicated. In the 1950s and 1960s, supporters became increasingly organized and came out in greater and greater numbers to support "their" team, which was considered the symbol of the local

37. Beaud and Noiriel, "L'immigration dans le football", p. 89.
38. Frackowiak, "Théodore Szkudlapski dit Théo".
39. The information about Sowinski's career is based on an interview with Arnold Sowinski, 23 January 1999.
40. For typical statements of this sort see, for instance, the interview with Eugène Hanquez (HBNPC engineer in Lens), 9 November 1998.

mining community.[41] For the fans, Racing's players had to embody the values of the ideal miner, like hard work, indomitable courage, and solidarity, and the team's offensive style of play was expected to reflect these values by privileging teamwork over the showing off of individual stars.[42] If the players succeeded, spectators would speak of them as "our boys". They were no longer seen as foreigners or as *Polaks*, but as representatives par excellence of the local community.

Yet even in this case there was a proverbial fly in the ointment. The players were admired, but also envied by their supporters, due to the special privileges they were granted by the companies: their work in the mines was a well-known fiction, yet they received higher pay than the others. In addition, the pressure from neighbours and from the local community in general could be very strong. As the footballer Stephan Ziemczak remembered:

> In Lens, we had the good and the bad fortune of being from the area. At the stadium or at home, you always saw the same thing. Your neighbour, he went to the match; the guy across the street, he went to the match; the guy who worked in the mine with my father, he went to the match. You would never leave that environment: I was my father's son, but also my neighbour's. You always had the feeling that you owed them something.[43]

If the spectacle of football thus helped to erase some of the old frontiers between native inhabitants and the children of Polish migrants – achieved in large part by turning the latter into standard-bearers of the mining community's values – it nevertheless continued to nurture all other distinctions and divisions that characterized this community.

FOOTBALL, NORTH AFRICAN MIGRANTS, AND THE CRISIS OF THE MINING MODEL

As described above, between the 1940s and the 1960s a social and sporting model rooted in the framework of mining became apparent. However, the relationship between sports, immigration, and integration cannot be told by referring to Polish immigrants alone. Indeed, the mining industry did not stop attracting migrants after 1945.[44] However, the new waves of migrants arriving in the northern coalmining area after World War II did so in a

---

41. The fans were organized in the Supporters Club Lensois (SCL), which was also supported by the HBNPC. Since the end of the 1940s SCL has published a newspaper, *Sang et Or, journal du RCL et du Supporteurs Club Lensois.*
42. There was a similar phenomenon in English working-class football; see Richard Holt, "La tradition ouvriériste du football anglais", *Actes de la Recherche en Sciences Sociales*, 103 (1994), pp. 36–40.
43. Quoted by Frackowiak, "Théodore Szkudlapski dit Théo", p. 373.
44. For an overview of post-1945 waves of immigration see Rainhorn, "Le Nord-Pas-de-Calais", pp. 27–31.

different situation, one less clearly marked by expansion. Just after the war, the mining industry needed a foreign workforce for the reconstruction of the mines and to meet growing energy needs. The Houillères nationales started to recruit new workers from Algeria. Employing this group of migrants had many advantages for the employers: the immigrant workforce was young, available, and relatively inexpensive, as Algerian migrants had fewer rights compared with other miners with respect to wages and labour conditions. Moreover, recruitment was easy because of the colonial system: until 1962, Algerian *indigènes* were theoretically considered to be French, and there were no restrictions on their mobility in metropolitan France. Under these conditions, more than 20,000 Algerians came to work in the northern pits.

From the 1960s, however, the mining industry was hit by an economic crisis that would, in the decades to come, never really abate.[45] Coal had to compete with oil, and the French coalmining industry was increasingly considered unprofitable. In 1959, the French government began to organize the closure of the pits with the *Plan Jeanneney*, followed by the *Plan Bettencourt* in 1968. The crisis successively diminished the economic and political weight of the Houillères nationales. But this process was very slow, spanning more than three decades, and it was not linear. Coal production became less and less important overall, but under certain circumstances (for instance, after the 1973 oil crisis) production did increase again slightly for a few years. In this context, the Houillères nationales still recruited migrant workers, not to enable production to grow, but to control the process of downsizing.

In the 1960s the mining company could still bring in migrant workers. During this period around 70,000 Moroccan migrants from rural areas were recruited on temporary, 18-month contracts to work in the pits in the north.[46] This arrangement provided the employers with a precarious workforce to satisfy the needs of a volatile coal production, with considerable ups and downs, while the closure of the pits was pending. Hiring Moroccan migrants was a way to maintain social peace and to close the pits without damage to the "established" miners. Generally speaking, these two generations of North African workers – arriving after the war and in the 1960s – were largely excluded from the mining community. They were often single and lived in barracks, remote from the inhabitants of the mining quarters. Their wages were low and they were considered secondary workers. They were not incorporated into existing regulations concerning mining labour or social insurance. Moroccans had to organize two major

---

45. Marion Fontaine, *Fin d'un monde ouvrier. Liévin, 1974* (Paris, 2014), ch. 1.
46. On the experience of Moroccan miners in the Nord-Pas-de-Calais, see Marie Cegarra, *La mémoire confisquée. Les mineurs marocains dans le Nord de la France* (Lille, 1999). It is noteworthy that whereas Polish migration to the Nord-Pas-de-Calais has produced a stream of academic studies, so far relatively little has been published on North African immigration to the region.

strikes, in 1980 and 1987, to obtain the rights and benefits of the *Statut du mineur* in the realms of housing, social insurance, health care, and holidays which had been acquired by the established miners after nationalization.

Polish and North African migrants shared some of the same features. In both cases, they were rural migrants who had experienced the uprooting of migration and a rupture in their traditional identities. Both migrant communities also fell victim, at least initially, to the exclusionary reactions of native inhabitants, who denounced the foreignness of their respective languages, culinary customs, and religious practices. But there were also important differences: before the 1960s, Moroccans and Algerians were not citizens but "Muslim subjects" (or *indigènes*) in the French colonial empire, and with that designation came a type of subordination and racism that the Poles had not experienced. The context of their arrival differed considerably as well. Polish workers lived through a very agitated social and political history (the crises of the 1930s, the war, nationalization, and the major strikes of 1947–1948), but in this period paternalist social policies were strongly developed and the mining communities were very much alive. The North African miners, by contrast, worked in a seemingly calm period, though in reality it saw a successive breakdown of the mining sector and of the mining communities.

These differences – both relating to the origins of the migrants and to the social dynamics of the mining community – help explain the differences between the two migrant groups. The Poles had emigrated as families, and had been able to maintain and organize their own social networks (both within and outside the world of sports) with the support of the mining companies. These social networks allowed Polish migrants to reconstitute community life, and their children eventually to integrate into the political, social, trade-union, and sporting life of the local community. In contrast, the Algerians – and even more so, the Moroccans – remained very isolated (the men were reunited very slowly with their families), with little sense of community and without the support of the Houillères nationales, which, after the mines had closed, lost interest in their fate. In this context, the older Moroccan miners lost the possibility of integrating into local workers' groups: such groups were already falling apart and losing their unionizing and political power. They did not survive much longer, except as a sense of nostalgia for an idealized mining past.

THE NEW RACING CLUB DE LENS, ITS PLAYERS, AND THE COMMUNITY

The crisis in the mining model also had an impact on local sports, as can once more be demonstrated by the case of Racing Club de Lens.[47] As the

47. The following considerations are based on Fontaine, *Le Racing Club de Lens et les "Gueules Noires"*, pp. 220–236.

Houillères nationales stopped supporting the club, it felt the full thrust of the crisis in the mining industry, to the point of near-extinction towards the end of the 1960s. However, the club managed to revive in the early 1970s thanks to support from a few local companies and also from the municipality of Lens. The city did not want to see Racing disappear, as it had become one of the rare elements of unity in a city disrupted by de-industrialization and the closure of the mines. In the 1970s, the club again enjoyed a measure of success in the national championships, and also in the new European competitions. Such success enabled Racing to develop a proper brand image, based upon its former mining background. Racing was thus described and represented as a "popular" and "modest" club, composed of local players who retained the old miners' playing style: a desire to win based on guts, courage, and solidarity, rather than on technical finesse.[48] This was the discourse not only of the media and the new club directors. The supporters, who reorganized themselves during the 1970s, adhered to it and identified with this image of the club. Although this was a destructive period for the identity of working-class communities, Racing appeared as a source of stability around which the local community could rally.

Yet, by the 1970s the Racing team had experienced a profound transformation, due in part to the changes that affected its surroundings, but also to the changing landscape of professional football.[49] Football clubs were increasingly becoming veritable entertainment companies, which recruited players through an increasingly powerful and internationalized sports market. Even if its financial means were modest, the new Racing did not escape this trend. The recruitment of players could no longer rely upon the network of mining clubs, which were disappearing along with the mines themselves. The club started to recruit footballers increasingly from the sports market, much as it had done during the 1930s. One might object that the *lensoise* team of the 1970s nevertheless still included a certain number of Polish players among its ranks: Richard Gregorczyk, Joachim Marx, and Eugenius Faber. But these "new Poles" had nothing in common with the preceding generation, nor with the immigration of the Polish workers who had established roots in the northern basin. Instead, they were purely professional athletes, who had come of age in a European sports market. The "new Poles" reinforced the image of Racing being a "mining" and "working-class club", but such designations had become no more than a convenient illusion.

Moreover, this illusion could operate as a factor of exclusion as well. With a few exceptions, such as Farès Bousdira (though he did not come from a

---

48. See, for instance, Private Archives of the Racing Club de Lens, Lens, Pas-de-Calais (France), Association des relations publiques du RCL, *Plaquette du 70e anniversaire du RCL*, 1976.
49. Anthony King, *The European Ritual: Football in the New Europe* (Aldershot, 2003), pp. 37–66.

mining background), the club of the 1970s did not tap the well of *maghrébin* immigrants who had come to the region to "close the mines". The cutting off of Racing from the last local migratory wave was primarily due to the weakening of the mining companies and the end of their informal recruitment channels, which had given the Lens-based club its local (Polish) colour. In this respect, the recruitment of players like Faber and Gregorczyk, which in theory could have served to reinforce this image, was more an indication of a loss: it signalled the irreversible rupture with the selection mechanisms belonging to the age of the Houillères, and the need to turn towards the domestic and European markets for players. Thus, the processes that had worked for the sons of Polish migrants would no longer work for the children of the Moroccans and Algerians.

This absence brought trouble. The "Polish-ization" of Racing's team had been less a cause than a result of the increasing integration of Polish-born children into the mining world and the local community. But football had also played an active role in this integration by mitigating social stigma and discrimination. Through sports (as a game and a show), those formerly known as *Polaks* had become "our boys", representing the dignity and values of courage and solidarity of the mining community. In this way, they had become symbols of the "good" migrants in local collective memory, both in terms of mining work and sports. The Moroccan and Algerian migrants, however, were excluded from this positive memory. More dangerously, even, this exclusion could contribute to a racist attitude: to some, North African migrants could not become "good" miners or "good" players, and were blamed for being "bad" migrants, in contrast with the Poles. In 1998 the mayor of Lens, André Delelis, said:

> What people like here is that footballers play like miners: effort is a quality that comes before playing technique. Poles were exceptional players in this respect, because the Pole is a hard worker, a tenacious man, who never gives up, disciplined, a little like a German. One can always count on him. That is why the Polish footballers have been more successful than the North African players. There were Algerian and Moroccan migrants here, but on the sports field they have never given the same things as the Polish migrants.[50]

As becomes clear in this statement, a situation brought about by social factors (the crisis of the mining model and the reorganization of the way footballers were recruited) could, at a certain point, perpetuate racist stereotypes.

THE PARADOX OF AHMED OUDJANI

The mayor's declaration evoked Racing's past at the time of the coal industry's golden age in the 1950s and 1960s. But he seemed to have

---

50. Interview with Andre Delelis, 9 January 1999.

forgotten that in that period the team's greatest heroes were not exclusively of Polish descent either. Indeed, from the end of the 1950s until the 1970s one of the most famous players in the team was an Algerian, Ahmed Oudjani.[51] He was recruited by the club in 1957 and played there until the beginning of the 1970s, before finding a job as football coach. To this day, he remains the best scorer in the club's history.

Yet Oudjani was the result of sports immigration and he had no connection with the Algerian miners who came to the coalfield. He began his sports career in the district of Oran (Algeria) and was recruited by the French club Vendôme (in the *département* Loire-et-Cher). He was then selected by Racing's coaches, who contracted him for their professional team. As shown above, in theory the leading representatives of the club (all of them related to mining) had to favour local players rooted in the mining community. But there were limits to this principle, and the club needed some experienced players to step up its game and to continue to attract spectators. Thus even in the post-nationalization period Racing's managers tried to recruit smaller "stars", such as the Antillean player Xercès Louis and the Algerian Ahmed Oudjani. The situation of this type of player was actually very similar to Racing's foreign players in the 1930s and, not surprisingly, it differed considerably from that of the young "Polish" players recruited by the club on the basis of the mining model. Like the other foreigners or "stars" of Racing – that is to say, the players selected within the framework of the sports labour market – Ahmed Oudjani could enjoy some specific privileges and advantages. Unlike the younger Polish-born players, he was considered a professional footballer, who had been recruited and was paid to play football only. He lived with his family in downtown Lens and not on one of the mining streets. The young Polish players were "miner-footballers" and had to follow the binding rules of the mining company and to respect the customs of the mining community, whereas Ahmed Oudjani enjoyed considerably more freedom.

Nevertheless, Ahmed Oudjani – called "Médo" by the supporters – was quickly adopted by the community and became a popular figure in the life of the mining neighbourhoods. He was a tough player and a great scorer, and he won a big audience among the miners, who made up a large part of Racing's fans. They identified with the courage of "Médo" and with his physical style of play. Ahmed Oudjani accepted the domain and customs of the neighbourhood and he was said to take part in conversations at the pub or in the street without difficulty. In short, he succeeded in embodying the rules and values of the mining community even better than many

---

51. Information about Ahmed Oudjani is based partly on an interview conducted with his widow and sons (Yacine and Chérif Oudjani), 5 and 7 November 2007. See also Marion Fontaine, "Les Oudjani et le 'club des Gueules Noires'. Parcours et représentations (années 1960–années 1980)", *Migrance*, 29 (2008), pp. 89–95.

young, Polish-born migrants or players. Over the years players such as Theodore Szkudlapski or Stephan Ziemczak, though born in the mining community and well-acquainted with its codes, often found themselves criticized by fans reproaching them for lack of discipline or for a desire to shine individually, and thus for deviating from the mining values that the team was supposed to represent.[52] In contrast, Ahmed Oudjani, who initially had no ties to the mining community, was well liked among Racing's supporters. To borrow from the racial stereotypes evoked earlier by the mayor of Lens, it might be said that Oudjani had a style that was more "Polish" than some of the Poles on the team themselves. This paradox shows the fragility of the supposed relationship between players' ethnic origins and their playing style and, more broadly, demonstrates the complexity of the relationship between sports and migration.[53]

However, Ahmed Oudjani remained an isolated symbol. In the case of the Polish migrants, the practice of playing football gained significance for the migrants' children, who from a certain moment on were likely to play in French football clubs rather than in clubs that represented a national and cultural Polish identity. Their insertion into the local sports culture was an important way for the Poles to establish roots in the local mining community, to the extent that some of them became community sports symbols in local collective memory. Ahmed Oudjani's success, however, did not testify to such a process and remained an exception. The children of Algerian or Moroccan migrants never became typical recruitees in the eyes of Racing Club de Lens. Though these children might be present today in the non-professional football clubs of the old northern coalfield,[54] they were absent from the roster of the local professional team. Currently, Racing's team no longer reflects the social composition of the local community and serves instead to reinforce, at least at a symbolic level, the exclusion of the most recent migrants. Ahmed Oudjani may have succeeded in establishing roots within the mining community, but the stigma has not changed for other North African migrants.

CONCLUSION

Several conclusions can be drawn from an analysis of the influence of sports, particularly football, on the relationship between natives and migrants in the northern mining community. For one, it should be noted that sport was not an isolated affair, but part of both the management of the mining industry and of the lives of the local community of workers.

52. For a typical example from the late 1950s of such a reproach, see *Liberté*, 5 June 1956.
53. Beaud and Noiriel, "L'immigration dans le football", pp. 94–96.
54. As Yacine Oudjani pointed out in the interview conducted on 7 November 2007.

As such, sport reflected the evolution of that industry and that community. One of the consequences of this was that mining paternalism continued to carry weight until the late twentieth century, and that the nationalization of mining companies did not alter this phenomenon. This close entanglement of the worlds of mining proper and its surrounding communities, in turn, allows one to better understand the crisis of the mining model and its consequences, which extended far beyond the closing of the mines.

The second major observation concerns the difference between the treatment of "old immigration" (that of the Poles) and "new immigration" (that of the North Africans): while the former succeeded, slowly and with some difficulty, in establishing new roots in the local community, the latter remains largely excluded from that community even today. This difference can be attributed less to ethnic and cultural causes (for example, the difference between European and postcolonial immigration) than to a difference in context. The Poles' success in taking root can be explained in large part by the social and political strength of the mining model at the moment of their arrival. In contrast, the North Africans can be seen as having "paid" the cost of the mining crisis, suffering especially from the disappearance of the social politics of the Houillères nationales and from the fragmentation of the local mining community.

All this seems to suggest that sport is not an automatic mechanism of integration nor of exclusion; instead it has ambivalent effects that can vary according to the cultural moment and the community's specific situation. The exploration of the phenomenon of sport thus invites approaches that are at once nuanced and sensitive to the particularities of mining cultures. These cultures should be observed closely – small worlds in themselves – at different levels (local, national, and international) in order to analyse the simultaneous operations of mining companies and the lives of communities that both arose and died in the vicinity of the mines.

IRSH 60 (2015), Special Issue, pp. 275–293 doi:10.1017/S0020859015000401
© 2015 Internationaal Instituut voor Sociale Geschiedenis

Integration through Sports? Polish Migrants in the Ruhr, Germany

DIETHELM BLECKING

*Institut für Sport und Sportwissenschaft,
Albert-Ludwigs-Universität Freiburg
Schwarzwaldstr. 175, 79117 Freiburg, Germany*

E-mail: blecking@aol.com

ABSTRACT: Sport, and football in particular, is described in socio-political discourse as an effective way to integrate immigrants. This thesis will be tested by means of a case study examining Polish migration to the mining areas of the Ruhr from the 1870s. It will be shown that, up until World War I, the sport participated in by Polish miners served, in contrast, as a means of nationalization, ethnicizing, and as an aid to furthering Polish ethnic identity. Only during the Weimar Republic were football clubs in the Ruhr actually used as a vehicle for integration and assimilation for males among the Polish minority. After World War II, memories of these footballers from among the Polish minority were either repressed or reduced to folklore. Based on this historical case study, sport appears in principle to be ambivalent between its ability to form "we" groups and the building of bridges between nationalities.

Following a decision by the EU Commission, almost 170 years of coalmining in Germany will come to an end in 2018 when the last five pits in the Saarland and the Ruhr cease operations.[1] In an attempt to draw up a preliminary balance sheet of its social and cultural history, a conference on "Underground Worlds" in Dortmund in May 2014 brought together a broad spectrum of studies on the cultures of mining and miners. Speakers addressed themes such as the pictorial arts, literature and film, and gender relations.[2] In their reflections on miners' cultures, however, the more "evident" topics of migration, leisure, and sport were scarcely mentioned. This is remarkable, as sports, and football in particular, have enjoyed an outstanding status in mining cultures all over the world, both for players and spectators. Also, migration processes were of paramount importance in the development of coalfields worldwide, including the Ruhr, where Polish

---

1. "EU lässt Subventionen bis 2018 zu", *Frankfurter Allgemeine Zeitung*, 8 December 2010.
2. See Arne Hordt's report on the conference "Welt unter Tage. Neue Perspektiven für die Bergbaukultur am Ende des Bergbaus", Dortmund, 23–24 May 2014, at http://hsozkult. geschichte.hu-berlin.de/tagungsberichte/id=5457; last accessed 15 July 2015.

Figure 1. Saarland and Ruhr, the two major historical coalmining regions in Germany.

migrants made up a huge part of the miners' workforce. Indeed, immigrants "from the East" comprised over 50 per cent of the workers in so-called Polish pits before World War I.[3] After the war football clubs recruited a huge number of players and spectators from among the descendants of the first generation of migrants.

All over the world, there are countless examples of football clubs in mining regions that had a special significance for regional identity, although their mining background is not always reflected in the names. They include Schalke 04 (Gelsenkirchen) and Borussia Dortmund in the Ruhr,[4] Club de

3. Christoph Kleßmann, *Polnische Bergarbeiter im Ruhrgebiet 1870–1945: Soziale Integration und nationale Subkultur einer Minderheit in der deutschen Industriegesellschaft* (Göttingen, 1978), p. 35. Here it is taken for granted that these were "Poles", even if at that time there was no Polish state.

4. Georg Röwekamp, *Der Mythos lebt. Die Geschichte des FC Schalke 04* (Göttingen, 1996); Stefan Goch and Norbert Silberbach, *Zwischen Blau und Weiß liegt Grau: Der FC Schalke 04 in der Zeit des Nationalsozialismus* (Essen, 2005); Gerd Kolbe and Dietrich Schulze-Marmeling, *Ein Jahrhundert Borussia Dortmund: 1909 bis 2009* (Göttingen, 2009). For the Ruhr in general, see Siegfried Gehrmann, *Fußball – Vereine – Politik: Zur Sportgeschichte des Reviers 1900–1940* (Essen, 1988).

Fútbol Pachuca in Mexico (founded as Pachuca Athletic Club by immigrant British miners and engineers in 1895), Shakhtar (the word means coalminer) Donetsk in Ukraine,[5] Górnik (literally, miner) Zabrze in Silesia, the *gueules noires* (black gobs) of Racing Club de Lens in northern France,[6] and Roda Kerkrade in the Netherlands. There were also a large number of amateur clubs of coalminers, from Pennsylvania to Kömürspor in northern Turkey.[7] Significantly Kömürspor is the Turkish word for "coal sport".[8]

In many cases miners working in the pits played a major role in organizing the clubs and giving them their identity. Stories about these origins live on as legends and myths in the collective memory of local inhabitants. Political discourse regularly invokes these histories, often in a populist manner, as a reference to the integrative power of sport. Such references are based on the idea that sport is able to overcome problems of ethnic heterogeneity, and to "integrate" immigrants into local society. Using history for their own particular ends, in the last few decades the standard repertoire of politicians of different colours has thus included statements on the positive historical experience of migrants in sports.[9] For the general public these statements constitute an *effet de réel*, in the sense of Roland Barthes, insofar as they give the impression that they are describing a social reality in the history of migration. William Gasparini, to whom I owe the reference to Barthes, has revealed similar mythmaking tendencies in France.[10] This article aims to deconstruct this myth in the case of Polish migrants in the Ruhr, by reconstructing the specific conditions of migration, from the starting point in the eastern provinces of the German Reich to the socio-economic and political backgrounds of their local actions in the Ruhr.

5. See the multi-award-winning documentary on the club's situation before the war in eastern Ukraine, caught between the decline of the mining industry and oligarchic policies: "The Other Chelsea – A Story from Donetsk", a documentary film by Jakob Preuss (2010), available at http://theotherchelsea.com/press.php; last accessed 15 July 2015.

6. Marion Fontaine, *Le Racing Club de Lens et les "Gueules Noires": Essai d'histoire sociale* (Paris, 2010). See also Marion Fontaine's contribution to the present volume.

7. Nicholas P. Ciotola, "Soccer in Coal Country", *Western Pennsylvania History*, 87:4 (2004), pp. 40–41, available at https://journals.psu.edu/wph/article/view/5264/5047; last accessed 15 July 2015.

8. Today the club is called Zonguldakspor, after the town of Zonguldak in the northern mining area of Turkey. See Tanil Bora, "Fußballkultur im Ruhrgebiet und am westlichen schwarzen Meer im Vergleich" (unpublished paper, p. 4). Published in part in *Der tödliche Pass*, 71 (2014), pp. 58–59.

9. For example Helmut Schmidt as Chancellor of West Germany, Wolfgang Schäuble as Minister of the Interior, and Johannes Rau as Prime Minister of North Rhine-Westphalia. See Diethelm Blecking, "Sport and Immigration in Germany", *The International Journal of the History of Sport*, 25 (2008), pp. 955–973, 956 and 967, n. 10.

10. William Gasparini, "Sport et intégration des immigrés en France. Contribution à une sociologie critique des catégories de pensée" (unpublished paper, Faculté des Sciences du Sport, Université de Strasbourg).

POLISH MIGRATION AND COMMUNITY BUILDING

Thou shalt have no other fatherland than an undivided Poland.[11]

Germany has been a land of immigration since the turn of the twentieth century. In the nineteenth century emigration had always exceeded immigration, until migrants began to arrive from countries such as Austria-Hungary, Italy, and Russia, and from the eastern provinces of Germany itself. Before World War I, internal migration, especially from the Polish areas of the German Reich,[12] created Polish-speaking minorities, mainly in the Ruhr, Berlin, and some cities in northern Germany.[13] The migration from the agrarian provinces in the east to the industrial region of the Ruhr was caused by differences in the speed and dynamics of capitalist modernization processes in various parts of the German Reich, resulting in economic underdevelopment and overpopulation in the agrarian areas of the east, the so-called Hinterland of the Reich.

Poles began arriving in the Ruhr in the early 1870s. During the economic boom between 1895 and the outbreak of World War I, successive waves of immigration reached a peak as a result of the growing demand for mine-workers. Polish-speaking people poured westwards from Upper Silesia, west Prussia, the area around Poznań, from Masuria, and the southern areas of eastern Prussia. By 1914, over 130,000 miners from the eastern provinces were working in the collieries in the Ruhr.[14] Chain migration and Polish migration networks soon destined "Westphalia" to become an "ethnoscape" of Polish migrants.[15] An estimated 300,000 to 400,000 Polish-speaking inhabitants were living in the Rhineland-Westphalian industrial region before World War I.[16] This number excludes the so-called Masurians, who were

11. From the "Ten Commandments" of Sokół athletes, quoted after Diethelm Blecking, *Polen-Türken-Sozialisten: Sport und soziale Bewegungen in Deutschland* (Münster, 2001), p. 46. All translations from German and Polish are mine.
12. For Prussia's and later Germany's policies towards the Polish areas, see Martin Broszat, *Zweihundert Jahre deutsche Polenpolitik* (Frankfurt am Main, 1972).
13. Kleßmann, *Polnische Bergarbeiter*, pp. 23–43; Anna Poniatowska, *Polacy w Berlinie 1918–1945* [Poles in Berlin 1918–1945] (Poznań, 1986); Oliver Steinert, *"Berlin – Polnischer Bahnhof!" Die Berliner Polen, Eine Untersuchung zum Verhältnis von nationaler Selbstbehauptung und sozialem Integrationsbedürfnis einer fremdsprachigen Minderheit in der Hauptstadt des Deutschen Kaiserreichs (1871–1918)* (Hamburg, 2003); Elke Hauschildt, *Polnische Arbeitsmigranten in Wilhelmsburg bei Hamburg während des Kaiserreichs und der Weimarer Republik* (Dortmund, 1986); Karl Marten Barfuss, *"Gastarbeiter" in Nordwestdeutschland 1884–1918* (Bremen, 1986).
14. Kleßmann, *Polnische Bergarbeiter*, pp. 37–43, 267.
15. On identities constructed in the process of migration see Dirk Hoerder, *Migrations and Belongings: 1870–1945* (Cambridge [etc.], 2014), p. 67.
16. Estimates range from up to 350,000 by Kleßmann, *Polnische Bergarbeiter*, p. 22, to 400,000 by Brian McCook, "Polnische industrielle Arbeitswanderer im Ruhrgebiet ('Ruhrpolen') seit dem Ende des 19. Jahrhunderts", in Klaus J. Bade *et al.* (eds), *Enzyklopädie Migration in Europa: Vom 17. Jahrhundert bis zur Gegenwart* (Munich [etc.], 2008), pp. 870–879, 871.

often confused with Poles. They were an amalgamation of the local Polish population with other groups, particularly Germans, Huguenots, Scots, and religious exiles from Salzburg (Austria). The Masurians mainly inhabited the east Prussian districts of Ortelsburg, Neidenburg, and Allenstein, and spoke an ancient Polish peasant dialect, were evangelical, and traditionally friendly towards Prussia.[17]

In this same period, the eastern parts of the Reich were the scene of bitter nationality struggles. The Prussian-German administration pursued a rigorous policy of Germanization in an anti-Polish *Kulturkampf* by repressing the Polish language, replacing Polish priests as school inspectors by Prussian civil servants, expelling Galician and Russian Poles from the province of Poznań and from Upper Silesia, and buying out Polish landowners.[18] In the end, all these attempts proved to be in vain, however. The result of anti-Polish policies was not to weaken but to strengthen the tender shoots of Polish civil society, developing under social and political pressures "from a loose conglomerate of people with an underdeveloped passive ethnic-national consciousness to a highly organized community with a broad civil, political, and cultural consciousness".[19]

The social life of the Catholic Poles, both in the Polish territories themselves and in the regions they migrated to, was organized in clubs and societies from an early date, first under the patronage of the Catholic Church. But in the process of nationalization and ethnicization other

17. Andreas Kossert, *Masuren: Ostpreußens vergessener Süden* (Berlin, 2001). Masurian immigration centred on Gelsenkirchen. See Andreas Kossert, "Kuzorra, Szepan und Kalwitzki: Polnischsprachige Masuren im Ruhrgebiet", in Dittmar Dahlmann, Albert S. Kotowski, and Zbigniew Karpus (eds), *Schimanski, Kuzorra und andere: Polnische Einwanderer im Ruhrgebiet zwischen der Reichsgründung und dem Zweiten Weltkrieg* (Essen, 2005), pp. 169–181. On the active policies of the Prussian administration to win over Masurians for its policy of Germanization, see Brian McCook, *The Borders of Integration: Polish Migrants in Germany and the United States, 1870–1924* (Athens, OH, 2012), pp. 124–125.

18. Bismarck feared a Catholic Polish–Austrian alliance. See Georg Franz, *Kulturkampf, Staat und katholische Kirche in Mitteleuropa von der Säkularisation bis zum Abschluß des preußischen Kulturkampfes* (Munich, 1954), pp. 214–215. On Germanization policies see also William W. Hagen, *Germans, Poles, and Jews: The Nationality Conflict in the Prussian East 1772–1914* (Chicago, IL [etc.], 1980); Helmut Glück, *Die preußisch-polnische Sprachenpolitik: Eine Studie über Theorie und Methodologie der Forschung über Sprachenpolitik, Sprachbewußtsein und Sozialgeschichte am Beispiel der preußisch-deutschen Politik gegenüber der polnischen Minderheit vor 1914* (Hamburg, 1979); Mark Tilse, *Transnationalism in the Prussian East: From National Conflict to Synthesis, 1871–1914* (Basingstoke [etc.], 2011); Lech Trzeciakowski, *Kulturkampf w zaborze pruskim* [*Kulturkampf* in the Prussian Part of Partitioned Poland] (Poznań, 1970); Richard Blanke, "Bismarck and the Prussian Polish Policies of 1886", *Journal of Modern History*, 45 (1973), pp. 211–239; Helmut Neubach, *Die Ausweisungen von Polen und Juden aus Preussen 1885/86: Ein Beitrag zu Bismarcks Polenpolitik und zur Geschichte des deutsch-polnischen Verhältnisses* (Wiesbaden, 1967).

19. Witold Jakóbczyk, *Studia nad dziejami Wielkopolski* [Studies in the History of Greater Poland], III (Poznań, 1967), p. 4.

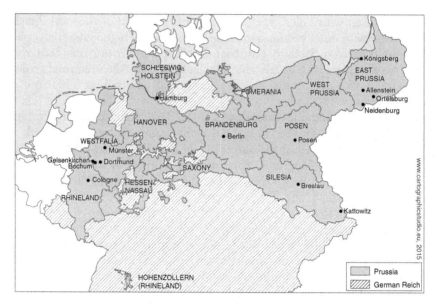

Figure 2. The German Reich, Prussia, and Prussia's western and eastern provinces before World War I.

organizations were founded that were more independent of the church (see Table 1, p. 9). The proliferation of institutions arising from this process may be characterized by the modern term "community building".[20] This phenomenon had already been described in contemporary literature on Polish migration. In 1907 Ludwig Bernhard wrote about *das polnische Gemeinwesen* (Polish community life),[21] and on the Polish side the term *społeczeństwo* (community) was used to designate Polish organizational structures within the Prussian state.[22]

Increasing ethnic tensions soon became apparent in the colonies of immigrants in the German Reich. Political and cultural repression by the Prussian-German administration led to a process of politicization among Poles, resulting in the creation of intra-ethnic networks stretching from the eastern provinces via Berlin to the Ruhr.[23] Strictly speaking, under the

20. The use of the contemporary notion of "community building" in Germany dates back to the 1980s and the debates at the time about Turkish migration. See, for instance, Jürgen Fijalkowski, "Ethnische Heterogenität und soziale Absonderung in deutschen Städten. Zu Wissensstand und Forschungsbedarf", Occasional Papers No. 13 of the research cluster "Ethnizität und Gesellschaft" at the Free University Berlin (Berlin, 1988).

21. Ludwig Bernhard, *Das polnische Gemeinwesen im preußischen Staat* (Leipzig, 1907).

22. Diethelm Blecking, *Die Geschichte der nationalpolnischen Turnorganisation "Sokół" im Deutschen Reich 1884–1939* (Münster, 1987), p. 216.

23. For an overview of recent literature on Polish migration in Germany, see Aleksander Żerelik, "Polen in Deutschland. Eine Bibliographie (1989–2011)", in Basil Kerski and Krzysztof

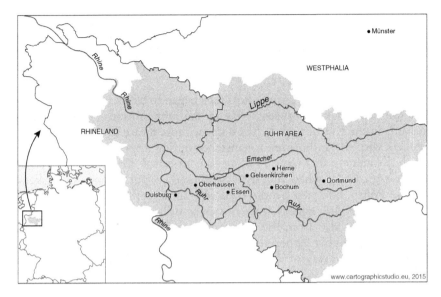

Figure 3. The Ruhr industrial region.

constitution of the German Reich, Polish migration was internal migration until the foundation of the Second Polish Republic in 1918. The majority of Polish migrants held Prussian citizenship; a more overall German citizenship only existed after 1913.[24]

Polish sporting organizations took over the watchwords of national democracy and saw themselves as a part, indeed a material surrogate, of the construction of an imaginary Polish state, connecting areas of origin and migrant communities in the west. Starting in 1884 as a reaction to the pressures of Germanization, people in and around Poznań began to set up Polish sports clubs to strengthen their social framework. Most of these were gymnastic clubs that went under the name of Sokół ("Falcon"). They were part of a movement in small towns of mostly craftsmen and small-scale entrepreneurs, who participated in the fragile and fledgling process of the modernization of Polish society. The activities of these clubs were modelled

Ruchniewicz (eds), *Polnische Einwanderung: Zur Geschichte und Gegenwart der Polen in Deutschland* (Osnabrück, 2011), pp. 299–316. See also Sylvia Haida, *Die Ruhrpolen: Nationale und konfessionelle Identität im Bewusstsein und im Alltag 1871–1918* (Bonn, 2012); Valentina Maria Stefanski, *Zum Prozess der Emanzipation und Integration von Außenseitern: Polnische Arbeitsmigranten im Ruhrgebiet* (Dortmund, 1984); Jacek Barski and Dietmar Osses (eds), *Polen in Deutschland: Geschichte und Kultur* (Essen, 2013); Peter Oliver Loew, *Wir Unsichtbaren: Geschichte der Polen in Deutschland* (Munich, 2014).
24. For the 1913 definition of German citizenship, see *Reichs- und Staatsangehörigkeitsgesetz vom 22. Juli 1913* (*Reichs-Gesetzblatt* 1913, pp. 583–593), available at http://www.documentarchiv.de/ksr/1913/reichs-staatsangehoerigkeitsgesetz.html; last accessed 15 July 2015.

on those of the German *Turnvereine* (gymnastic clubs). Polish-speaking citizens had been denied membership of the German clubs in and around Poznań. In 1893, the headquarters of the first umbrella organization of the Sokół, called the Związek Sokołów Wielkopolskich [Greater Polish Sokół League], were set up there.[25]

From 1899 onwards Polish Sokół clubs began to be set up in the Ruhr as well, the first in Oberhausen.[26] As in the area around Poznań, Polish migrants in the Ruhr diaspora had become more aware of their identity in conflicts with the authorities, for instance during a spontaneous strike by Polish coalminers in Herne in 1899, the so-called *Krawalle von Herne* ("Herne revolts"), when the army was used to put down the strikers. On the Polish side two people died and another thirty were injured.[27] The striking Polish miners were not only isolated from their Masurian workmates, but also from the German miners refusing to support them. German xenophobia rather than the supposed "rural attitudes" of the Poles stood in the way of working-class solidarity.[28] Poles working in the collieries had once emigrated from the agricultural east and lost their traditional way of living, a process that can be described as social uprooting resulting in a situation of deprived rights.[29] All this explains a yearning for a stable Polish framework, not only in their leisure activities, but also in a separate trade union, the Zjednoczenie Zawodowe Polskie [Polish Trade Union].[30]

Table 1 shows that in 1912 the total membership of the Sokół clubs in the Ruhr was only around 7,000; nonetheless, they were the second largest

25. For an overview of the early history of Polish sports clubs, see Blecking, *Die Geschichte der nationalpolnischen Turnorganisation*, pp. 70–75.
26. Anna Ryfowa, *Działalność Sokoła Polskiego w zaborze pruskim i wśród wychodźstwa w Niemczech, 1888–1914* [The Activities of the Polish Sokół in the Prussian Part of Partitioned Poland and Among Emigrants in Germany, 1888–1914] (Warsaw [etc.], 1976), and Blecking, *Geschichte der nationalpolnischen Turnorganisation*. See also Marek Szczerbiński, *Zarys działalności Sokolstwo Polskiego na obczyźnie w latach 1887–1918* [Overview of the Activities of the Polish Sokół Abroad, 1887–1918] (Katowice, 1982), and idem, "Sokolstwo Polskie w Niemczech w latach 1889–1918" [The Sokół in Germany during the Years 1889–1918], *Wychowanie fizyczne i sport* [Physical Education and Sport], 1 (1976), pp. 85–107.
27. Klaus Tenfelde, "Die 'Krawalle von Herne' im Jahre 1899", *Internationale Wissenschaftliche Korrespondenz zur Geschichte der deutschen Arbeiterbewegung*, 1 (1979), pp. 71–104.
28. For a fundamental study offering a revision of the view that the "backwardness" of Polish miners in the Ruhr acted as an obstacle to militancy and solidarity, including a detailed analysis of the 1899 strike, see John J. Kulczycki, *The Foreign Worker and the German Labour Movement: Xenophobia and Solidarity in the Coal Fields of the Ruhr, 1871–1914* (Oxford [etc.], 1994).
29. On the process of deracination, acculturation, and assimilation in the context of the confrontation between large groups and minorities, see Hoerder, *Migrations and Belongings*, pp. 56–59.
30. For a detailed history of the Zjednoczenie Zawodowe Polskie see John Kulczycki, *The Polish Coal Miners' Union and the German Labor Movement in the Ruhr, 1902–1934: National and Social Solidarity* (Oxford [etc.], 1997). On the panoply of Polish leisure activities in the Ruhr before 1918, see Haida, *Ruhrpolen*, pp. 293–306.

Table 1. *Number of organizations and their membership in the Polish community in the Ruhr (1912)*

TYPE OF CLUB OR ASSOCIATION	NUMBER	MEMBERS
Church working men's clubs	244	30,929
Rosary fraternities	68	16,297
Voter associations*	100	8,412
Sokół clubs	117	6,909
Choral societies	95	5,225
Education associations (Oswiata)	16	3,488
Straz (=guard) associations#	17	1,750
Lottery clubs	70	1,563
Youth clubs	19	1,345
Cooperatives, consumer associations	4	890
Theatre and music clubs	37	889
Trade associations	16	724
Abstinence clubs	25	695
Women's clubs	9	474
Local Polish socialist groups (PPS)	9	408
Others	29	1,534

*Polish political clubs to organize votes for Polish political interests.
#Aristocratic, nationalistic, and conservative Polish political clubs with a focus on the eastern provinces.
Source: Kleßmann, *Polnische Bergarbeiter*, p. 103.

group in the network of Polish organizations. Having said that, the number of Poles organized in Sokół clubs in relation to the number of Polish migrants in the Ruhr (1.75 per cent) was higher than the number of German members in German gymnastic clubs (1.66 per cent) in relation to the number of Germans in the Reich.[31] This is all the more remarkable when we consider that the presence of sporting organizations among industrial workers before World War I, and even up to the present day,[32] was considerably smaller than that among the middle classes. The overwhelming majority of members of the Sokół clubs in the Ruhr were mineworkers, as can be seen from a random sample of nineteen clubs in the district of Münster, administratively responsible for the north of the Ruhr: over 90 per cent of the board members were miners.[33]

31. Figures in Christiane Eisenberg, "Deutschland", in *idem* (ed.), *Fußball, soccer, calcio. Ein englischer Sport auf seinem Weg um die Welt* (Munich, 1997), pp. 94–129, 97; Hans-Ulrich Wehler, *Deutsche Gesellschaftsgeschichte. Bd. 3: Von der "Deutschen Doppelrevolution" bis zum Beginn des Ersten Weltkrieges, 1849–1914* (Munich, 1995), p. 494. See also Christiane Eisenberg, "Massensport in der Weimarer Republik: Ein statistischer Überblick", *Archiv für Sozialgeschichte*, 33 (1993), pp. 137–177.
32. Simone Becker and Sven Schneider, "Ausmaß und Korrelate sportlicher Betätigung bei bundesdeutschen Erwerbstätigen", *Sport und Gesellschaft*, 2 (2005), pp. 173–204.
33. Blecking, *Geschichte der nationalpolnischen Turnorganisation*, p. 117.

Due to a lack of data it is impossible to establish whether a significant number of Poles were members of German gymnastic clubs. This is highly implausible, however, given that Polish migrants were isolated from Prussian-German society, and that the German *Turnvereine* played a major role in the concept of German national cultural hegemony. As in the area around Poznań, German gymnastic clubs worked hand in hand with German nationalist organizations, such as the Deutscher Ostmarkenverein and the Alldeutscher Verband (All-German League), which campaigned for a hard-line policy of Germanization.[34]

The Sokół clubs' physical exercises were useful not only in creating a sense of personal identity, but also in developing a new social identity and in promoting national ideas among the Polish community in the Ruhr. Even if the exercises were based on the repertoire of German gymnastic clubs, the festive mass open-air exercises organized by Sokół clubs featured Polish red and white flags and Ulan lances.[35] In this way, the Sokół gymnastic movement presented itself as an embodiment of the Polish nation. This is clearly in contrast to the more widespread idea of "integration through sports" which is, as mentioned earlier, a hallmark of contemporary political discourses. Polish clubs can instead be described as vehicles for preventing this kind of "integration" (understood as "assimilation") of Polish migrants into German society.

If we follow the classical sociological arguments, which consider marital behaviour as a key indicator of assimilation,[36] the Polish community in the Ruhr was extremely successful in preventing such an assimilation process. Before 1914 mixed marriages were very rare.[37] This is a clear indication of mutual ethnic and social segregation. Polish clubs and associations helped people to survive in a fragmented and segmented society. Setting up their own organizations was a logical answer to exclusion.[38] Both its members and its opponents recognized the highly symbolic value of the Sokół movement for the internal fostering of the Polish *społeczeństwo*. Based on an avant-garde elite consciousness, the clubs helped to build Polish organizational structures that offered migrants opportunities to act on their own initiative and to consolidate their new identity. Polish sports clubs were thus rather part of social diversity within a segmented society than a sign of any kind of "melting pot".[39]

---

34. *Ibid.*, pp. 149–159.

35. See Diethelm Blecking, "Sokolfeste der Ruhrpolen", in Hans-Joachim Teichler (ed.), *Sportliche Festkultur in geschichtlicher Perspektive* (Clausthal-Zellerfeld, 1990), pp. 34–48.

36. See, for instance, Milton M. Gordon, *Assimilation in American Life: The Role of Race, Religion, and National Origins* (New York, 1964), p. 71.

37. Kleßmann, *Polnische Bergarbeiter*, p. 281. Members of the Sokół league were disciplined if they married a German woman; Blecking, *Polen-Türken-Sozialisten*, pp. 45–46, n. 109.

38. See also McCook, *The Borders of Integration*, pp. 144–145.

39. Richard Murphy resorted to the notion of "melting pot" when writing, in a rather euphemistic way, about the Poles in the Ruhr: "The destiny of these people is a success story of

In the Wilhelmine era (1888–1918) migrant organizations did not have the bridge-building role that has often been attributed to them. The same applies to the supposed "bridging social capital" of sport.[40] Sport did not offer opportunities for meeting and intermingling, but instead reflected the social, political, and ethnic divisions in Wilhelmine society. In addition to the nationalist German *Turnvereine* and the Polish Sokół clubs, there were also clubs associated with the socialist workers' gymnastic movement and the Jewish Zionist gymnastic movement.[41] There were no sports meetings or competitions between these organizations and their members.

Competitive modern sports, often called in the parlance of the time "English sports", mainly football, athletics, and cycling, had arrived in Germany as early as the 1870s. The centres of these sporting movements were in the sophisticated cities of Hamburg and Berlin, but industrial workers remained excluded from such sports. Originally, members of the old middle class and educated layers of society, such as students, doctors, lawyers, and professors had had the upper hand in the gymnastic clubs (until this was challenged by the workers' and ethnic-minority gymnastic movements mentioned above). In the new sports, however, it was members of the new class of white-collar employees, attaching great importance to distinguishing themselves from the working class, who dominated the disciplines of cycling, football, and athletics and comprised the largest group in the corresponding clubs (more than half).[42]

Modern sport functioned as a social medium for members of the new middle class (including those of Jewish background) who were excluded from the social elite and their caste-like rituals (like those of reserve officers).[43] At the same time, modern sport clubs also wanted to fulfil a "national mission".[44] All these characteristics combined meant that in this period football in the Ruhr was not a social or political arena for Polish working-class miners.

American dimensions"; Richard C. Murphy, *Gastarbeiter im Deutschen Reich, Polen in Bottrop 1891–1933* (Wuppertal, 1982), p. 184.

40. Andrei S. Markovits, *Sport: Motor und Impulssystem für Emanzipation und Diskriminierung* (Vienna, 2011), p. 40.

41. For overviews of the socialist and Jewish gymnastic movements in Germany, see Diethelm Blecking (ed.), *Arbeitersport in Deutschland 1893–1933: Dokumentation und Analysen* (Cologne, 1983); Lorenz Peiffer and Henry Wahlig, *Jüdischer Sport und Sport der Juden in Deutschland: Eine kommentierte Bibliografie* (Göttingen, 2009).

42. Christiane Eisenberg, *"English sports" und deutsche Bürger. Eine Gesellschaftsgeschichte, 1800–1939* (Paderborn, 1999), p. 211.

43. Wehler, *Gesellschaftsgeschichte*, pp. 1065–1066.

44. Eisenberg, *"English sports"*, pp. 178–214.

AFTER THE GREAT WAR – THE ROAD TO ASSIMILATION

During World War I internal social and political conflicts in Germany were – for the time being – eased or postponed by the so-called *Burgfrieden* between the Wilhelmine state and the workers' movement. The Ruhr also witnessed a lessening of the tensions between Poles and Germans, with many Poles loyally enlisting in the German armed forces. In February 1917 a submission by a Westphalian section of the Sokół League to the head of the police in Bochum summed up the price paid for this loyalty:

> To date 142 heroes have lost their lives and 91 Polish gymnasts in our district have been awarded the Iron Cross. All of them have fulfilled their military duties with great commitment and loyalty, as shown by the many promotions to the rank of non-commissioned officer. Gymnastic preparations in our clubs have helped them immensely to bear the stresses of war.[45]

After the re-establishment of the Polish state in 1918, the situation of the Polish inhabitants in the Ruhr changed dramatically. It is therefore hardly possible to compare the history and situation of Polish migrants in the Ruhr before and after World War I. Until January 1922 fewer than 50,000 of them opted to return to Poland,[46] and between 50,000 and 80,000 migrated further on to mining regions in Belgium, France, and the Netherlands. In 1929 the Polish consulate in Essen estimated that there were only around 150,000 Poles still living in the Ruhr.[47] This meant that the social basis of the clubs and associations had been reduced considerably. By 1924 the Sokół League in the Ruhr had only 1,227 members, of whom a mere 460 were active.[48] The steep decline in membership led to its dissolution in 1927 and its replacement by the Verband der Turn- und Sportvereine in Westfalen und im Rheinlande [League of Gymnastics and Sports Clubs in Westphalia and the Rhineland]. The League formulated a new aim for the sporting movement of the Polish minority: "[T]hat the Polish minority and German citizens who speak the Polish language should once and for all be allowed to take part in official German competitions and compete for victory with German representatives."[49]

Football had made its appearance in the Sokół movement at the end of World War I and had established itself as early as 1920. Despite the continuing resistance of traditionalists among its members, footballers increasingly expressed a wish to be able to compete against German football teams. In May 1927 the first proud reports of such competitions

45. Landesarchiv Nordrhein-Westfalen Abteilung Westfalen, Münster, Regierung Münster, Abteilung VII 34p, Bd. 1.
46. Kleßmann, *Polnische Bergarbeiter*, p. 152.
47. *Ibid.*, pp. 165–166.
48. Blecking, *Geschichte der nationalpolnischen Turnorganisation*, p. 196.
49. *Gesamtüberblick über die polnische Presse* (1927), p. 197.

were published.[50] Contrary to the situation before World War I, for those Poles who had chosen to stay there was no real alternative to engaging with German society and therefore to joining shared competitions. For a footballer a career in a "Polack and proletarian club"[51] now became an "active opportunity for assimilation".[52] This change in the aims and strategies of the Polish sporting movement in the Ruhr reflected the end of the self-referential community of Polish migrants.[53]

During World War I football had spread widely among soldiers due to its importance as a military sport.[54] After the troops were demobilized it retained its popularity as an extremely hard competitive sport, which seemed to match the experiences at the front. It is noteworthy that the first game played by Schalke 04 after the war was a match against the paramilitary Freikorps Hacketau. Other infamous paramilitary clubs like the Freikorps Pfeffer, Lützow, and the Marinebrigade Ehrhardt also played against "civilian" clubs. Attendance figures at the final games in the German league championship rose to over 50,000, and the league game between Hamburg and the Berlin club Union Oberschöneweide in 1923 attracted a crowd of 64,000. Whereas the number of members in the Deutscher Fußball Bund [German Football Association, DFB] was 161,600 in 1913, by 1921 this figure had grown fivefold to almost 780,500.[55] But here, too, white-collar workers and members of middle-class professions continued to predominate.[56]

In the Ruhr the situation looked completely different. There, football had a decidedly multi-ethnic and proletarian dimension, turning it into an ever more popular sport among the immigrant population.[57] In the vicinity

50. See the following report from a Polish-language monthly published in Germany: *Polak w Niemczech* [The Pole in Germany], no. 5:1, May 1927.
51. This was what FC Schalke 04 was called in the 1920s because of the many players from the coalmining community with Polish-sounding names; Siegfried Gehrmann, "Der F.C. Schalke 04", in Wilhelm Hopf (ed.), *Fußball: Soziologie und Sozialgeschichte einer populären Sportart* (Weinheim, 1979), pp. 117–131.
52. Hartmut Esser, *Aspekte der Wanderungssoziologie: Assimilation und Integration von Wanderern, ethnischen Gruppen und Minderheiten* (Darmstadt [etc.], 1980), p. 211.
53. But even in the years of the Weimar Republic many migrants kept up social contacts almost exclusively with other people of Polish descent; Ralf Karl Oenning, *"Du da mitti polnischen Farben ... ": Sozialisationserfahrungen von Polen im Ruhrgebiet 1918–1939* (Münster [etc.], 1991), p. 129.
54. Peter Tauber, *Vom Schützengraben auf den grünen Rasen: Der Erste Weltkrieg und die Entwicklung des Sports in Deutschland* (Berlin, 2008), pp. 239–258.
55. Eisenberg, "Deutschland", pp. 104–106.
56. Idem, "Massensport", p. 167.
57. On how this multi-ethnicity was reflected upon in the contemporary German and Polish press, see Britta Lenz, "'Gebürtige Polen' und 'deutsche Jungen': Polnischsprachige Zuwanderer im Ruhrgebietsfußball im Spiegel von deutscher und polnischer Presse der Zwischenkriegszeit", in Diethelm Blecking, Lorenz Pfeiffer, and Robert Traba (eds), *Vom Konflikt zur Konkurrenz: Deutsch-polnisch-ukrainische Fußballgeschichte* (Göttingen, 2014), pp. 100–113.

of large collieries teams were set up consisting mainly of working-class members. Indeed, there were now many players with Polish names in Ruhr teams,[58] for example in the long-established Rot-Weiss Essen. From 1919 onwards a huge number of new members with Polish-sounding names joined the club, where they also worked as officials and employees. By 1939 they made up around 10 per cent of the membership. In 1931 the club took on a groundsman by the name of Hermann Greszick, who changed his name to Kress in 1932. A change of name can generally be seen as a clear sign of assimilation, and there was a definite thrust towards this in the 1930s. Other players changed their names from Regelski to Reckmann, from Czerwinski to Rothardt, or from Zembrzyki to Zeidler. Around 240,000 people of Polish and Masurian origin in the Ruhr are estimated to have "Germanized" their names by 1937.[59] Polish names could also now be found in socialist workers' sports clubs in the Ruhr, as in the board of the Essen Arbeiter-Turn- und Sportverein Schonnebeck. Hence, it can be assumed that during the Weimar Republic people of Polish origin were not only members of Polish sporting associations but also of other sports clubs, all the way down to the small socialist workers' clubs.

Becoming an active footballer in a well-known club was one of the opportunities open to younger members of migrant families to improve their social status. Players with a Polish immigrant background were now particularly active in higher-league football in the Ruhr. Of the fifteen clubs that competed in the district championships in the Westphalia and Lower Rhine leagues in the 1937/1938 season, all without exception fielded players with Polish family names such as Rodzinski, Pawlowski, Zielinski, Sobczak, Lukasiewicz, Tomaszik, or Piontek in at least one of the matches.[60] Of all the players selected for a championship match (around 250), 68 had Polish family names. In addition, the German national team at the time featured players with names like Szepan, Kuzorra, Gellesch, Urban, Kobierski, Zielinski, and Rodzinski.

The first four players in this list were all members of FC Schalke 04 of Gelsenkirchen. The history of this very prototype of a "Polack and proletarian club", however, makes clear how ambivalent relations in the immigrant society of the Ruhr had become. Between 1934 and 1942 Schalke was German league champion on no less than six occasions. The team was full of players with Polish-sounding names, the best known of whom were the

---

58. An assessment of the multi-ethnic quality of football after World War I is complicated, however, because it is impossible to differentiate between "Poles" and "Masurians" on the basis of their names alone.

59. Werner Burghardt, "Namensänderungen slawischer Familiennamen im Ruhrgebiet", in Günter Bellmann, Günter Eifler, and Wolfgang Kleider (eds), *Festschrift für Karl Bischoff zum 70. Geburtstag* (Cologne [etc.], 1975), pp. 271–286.

60. Lenz, "'Gebürtige Polen'", p. 105.

stars who also played for the German national team, Ernst Kuzorra and Fritz Szepan. When Schalke won the championship for the first time in 1934, and the team posed for the camera with the Hitler salute, the Polish press spoke scornfully of "Poles [as] German Champions", whereupon the club management hastened to ascertain that "all our players' parents were born in present-day or former Germany and they are not Polish emigrants".[61]

In any case, the claims made in the German and Polish press were constantly at odds with the tangled realities. The majority of the parents of the Schalke players came from the southern part of eastern Prussia, and as Protestant Masurians, who had remained faithful to Prussia, did not consider themselves to be "Polish". Indeed, thirty Schalke 04 players between 1920 and 1940 can be identified as Masurians, and another three were born in Masuria.[62] In this way, the Schalke 04 championship team mirrored the complicated migration history of the Ruhr. During the Third Reich, it was players from Polish and Masurian families who ensured the strength of football in the Ruhr, in particular of Schalke 04, but also of the German national team. National-Socialist so-called *Volkstumsforschung*, i.e. pseudo-scientific studies of Germanhood based on anti-Polish, racist, and biologistic principles, managed to solve this dilemma by restricting their studies in the Ruhr to Masurians, who were declared to be "purely German in their culture and way of thinking". As to the Poles in the Ruhr, it also saw indications of what it designated successful *Umvolkung* through the Germanization of "inferior" foreign migrants.[63]

Schalke 04 was correspondingly instrumentalized to serve unconditionally the propaganda of the regime. The deputy chair of the club, a Jewish dentist, had been forced to resign as early as 1933, following pressure from the National Socialists. Kuzorra and Szepan allowed themselves to be drawn into the Nazi propaganda machine, be it more out of opportunism than of conviction. The latter even profited from the Nazis' so-called Aryanization policies, when he took over the Jewish Julius Rhode department store in Schalke's market square.

By contrast, the remainder of Polish sport was mercilessly persecuted, despite Hitler's tactical speech to the Reichstag on 17 May 1933, when he spoke out against Germanization.[64] In January 1934 the Polish newspaper *Naród* summed up the situation during 1933 as follows:

> It was a year in which Polish sporting life in Germany came to a complete standstill. We are forced to declare that the national revolution was the reason

61. Quoted by Britta Lenz, "'Polen deutsche Fußballmeister'? – Polnischsprachige Einwanderer im Ruhrgebietsfußball der Zwischenkriegszeit", in Dahlmann *et al.*, *Schimanski, Kuzorra und andere: Polnische Einwanderer*, pp. 237–250, 248.
62. *Ibid.*, p. 245.
63. Lenz, "'Gebürtige Polen'", p. 110.
64. Blecking, *Die Geschichte der nationalpolnischen Turnorganisation*, p. 203, n. 3.

behind this fact. We must openly state that it is uncertain that it will ever be able to recover. In the pursuit of opponents to the current regime our sporting sections have been dissolved and their playing fields and exercise rooms withdrawn. As a result this has led to a complete destruction of Polish sporting activities.[65]

Polish sport in the Ruhr never recovered, in spite of the astonishing fact that the five international matches between Germany and Poland between 1933 and 1938 attracted a huge number of spectators and took place in an apparently friendly and sporting atmosphere.[66] In September 1939, just a few days before the German invasion of Poland, all organizations belonging to the Polish minority in Germany were banned, and their assets confiscated.[67] By this time 249 members of the Polish minority had been interned in concentration camps.[68] In this way, after two generations, the history of Polish sport in the Ruhr came to a close.

THE POSTWAR PERIOD: THE THIRD GENERATION

The years of Nazi barbarity had a watershed effect on the collective memories of German citizens. In relation to football, memories of Jewish and Polish-born players in the German team and at club level were either wiped out, or turned into idyllic folklore tales.[69] The history of Polish clubs was completely repressed, even though the past continued to live on in family names and careers.

A player like Hans Tilkowski, for example, who played for Germany in the 1960s and made a legendary name for himself as the "man in the Wembley goal" in 1966, was the son of a collier from Dortmund, grew up on a coalmining housing estate, and began his career as a goalkeeper for Westphalia Herne. His time at Borussia Dortmund marked the high point of his career, alongside his participation in the final of the World Cup in England in 1966, where the German team were the runners-up. But the true

---

65. *Gesamtüberblick über die polnische Presse* (1934), p. 25, translation from *Naród* [Die Nation], 6 January 1934.

66. Dieter Hertz-Eichenrode, "Sportsfreunde? Die deutsch-polnischen Fußball-Länderspiele von 1933–1938", in Blecking *et al.*, *Vom Konflikt zur Konkurrenz*, pp. 114–122.

67. Verordnung über die Organisationen der polnischen Volksgruppe im Deutschen Reich, 27. Februar 1940 (*Reichsgesetzblatt*, Teil I 1940, p. 444), available at http://de.wikisource.org/wiki/Verordnung_%C3%BCber_die_Organisationen_der_polnischen_Volksgruppe_im_Deutschen_Reich; last accessed 15 July 2015.

68. Valentina Maria Stefanski, "Die polnische Minderheit zwischen 1918 und 1939/45", in Dagmar Kift and Dietmar Ossens (eds), *Polen-Ruhr: Zuwanderung zwischen 1871 und heute* (Essen, 2007), pp. 33–43.

69. The idea of "having no history" dominated the discussion on migration in Germany until well into the 1990s. See Ulrich Herbert, *Arbeit, Volkstum, Weltanschauung: Über Fremde und Deutsche im 20. Jahrhundert* (Frankfurt am Main, 1995), p. 218. The following considerations about postwar development refer to West Germany only. The development of football in the GDR and its interrelations with collective memories would need a separate analysis.

star of football from the Ruhr was Reinhard "Stan" Libuda (1943–1996), who died a tragic early death at the age of fifty-three. Libuda played for Schalke, Dortmund, and the German national team, and was vaguely aware of the similarity between his career and background and that of the legendary French footballer Raymond Kopa(szewski), who was born in 1931 in the mining area of Nord-Pas-de-Calais.[70] Although at that time this theme was generally ignored, a huge number of other players in Germany had names that rang with the history of Masurian and Polish migration.[71]

The long overdue introduction of professional football into Germany between 1963 and 1970 changed its setup profoundly, making it much more open for careers from below.[72] Anyone with enough talent could now participate, and at the start of the 1970s the proportion of working-class players in the top German leagues was, for the first time, equal to their proportion in the population as a whole. At the same time, the German market became attractive to foreign professionals, including Polish players. The first Pole to play for a German club was Waldemar Piotr Słomiany, who moved from Górnik Zabrze in the mining area of Upper Silesia – a club whose mining origins are proudly proclaimed in its name – to Gelsenkirchen to play for Schalke 04.[73]

Today, there are around 2 million Polish-speaking people living in the Federal Republic of Germany, approximately 2.5 per cent of the population. Since the 1980s the Ruhr has again become the centre of new waves of Polish migrants, who have built up fresh networks of clubs.[74] These include the League of Polish Sports Clubs set up in 2005, whose football teams take part in German leagues.[75] Players from immigrant surroundings, like Klose and Podolski, who were both born in Poland, were pillars of the German national team for many years. And history seemed to be repeating itself when the national

---

70. Thilo Thielke, *An Gott kommt keiner vorbei. Das Leben des Reinhard "Stan" Libuda* (Göttingen, 2002); Raymond Kopa, *Piłka i ja* [The Ball and Me] (Warsaw, 1975); and *idem, Kopa* (Paris, 2006). See also the article by Marion Fontaine in the present volume.

71. See the alphabetical list of German international players from Abramczyk to Zwolanowski in Dietrich Schulze-Marmeling, *Die Geschichte der Fußball-Nationalmannschaft* (Göttingen, 2008), pp. 657–664.

72. See Eisenberg, "Deutschland", pp. 115–116; Nils Havemann, *Samstags um halb 4. Die Geschichte der Fußballbundesliga* (Munich, 2013), pp. 53–68.

73. Ulrich Homann, "Die ausländischen Spieler beim FC Schalke 04", in Holger Jenrich (ed.), *Radi, Buffy und ein Sputnik. Ausländer in der Fußball-Bundesliga 1963–1995* (Essen, 1996), pp. 86–88.

74. Christoph Pallaske, "Langfristige Zuwanderungen aus Polen in die Bundesrepublik Deutschland in den 1980er Jahren", in Kerski and Ruchniewicz, *Polnische Einwanderung,* pp. 215–225.

75. Veronika Grabe and Andrzej Kaluza, "Polnischsprachige im Revier – die Ruhrpolen von heute?", in Kift and Ossens, *Polen-Ruhr,* pp. 64–73.

conservative Polish newspaper *Rzeczpospolita* described the victory of the German team at the World Cup in Brazil as "an extra satisfaction for us" (meaning Poland),[76] when it noted that the record goal scorer in the history of the world championships was the Polish-born Miroslaw Klose.

CONCLUSION

Sports clubs for Polish migrants who arrived in the Ruhr before World War I developed within the conflicted areas of nationalism, ethnicization, and new identity constructions. For this reason Sokół clubs were always more than simply sports clubs. They were the embodiment of the Polish nation, whose state had been destroyed and which continued to exist only as a cultural project. Polish transnational integration transcended the boundaries of the Prussian-German Reich and also affected Polish citizens in the Russian Empire and the Hapsburg Monarchy. The imaginary Poland was constructed from Poles in three empires.

Football clubs in the Ruhr experienced a boom in the interwar years. Some of the clubs also included miners of Polish origin and thus worked as vehicles of assimilation. After World War II a huge number of third-generation migrants pursued careers in football clubs in the Ruhr. Now memories of immigration began to fade or were degraded into folklore legends. Since the 1980s more recent waves of Polish immigrants, some of whom have become leading footballers in top clubs and the German national team, have made this history visible once again, turning it into a topic of both academia and broader society.

Research into the history of Polish sport in the Ruhr has shown that its social function can only satisfactorily be described in the context of social change. The myth of sport's (particularly football's) ability to prevail over ethnic conflicts is plausible only if the history of Ruhr Poles is restricted to the time after World War I. The outlined social and demographic changes pushed the Polish minority along the path of assimilation, but after Hitler's seizure of power the Nazis reintroduced repressive measures against the Ruhr's Poles. Accompanied by pseudo-academic attempts to "Germanize" them with the aim of making them "as invisible as possible",[77] at their most extreme these measures resorted to violently destroying Polish social organizations.

Patterns in the social dynamics of exclusion and inclusion, as well as segregation and assimilation, can also be analysed in comparison (both synchronic and diachronic). For instance, there are clear signs that in the case of Polish immigrants in northern France segregation in their own Polish clubs in the 1920s began to give way to assimilation in and through football at the end of the 1940s. This also extended to Polish players

---

76. Quoted in *Süddeutsche Zeitung* (160), 15 July 2014, p. 2.
77. Lenz, "'Polen deutsche Fußballmeister'", p. 112.

participating at the top level of football in France.[78] At the same time, diachronic comparison between Polish migration before World War I and Turkish migration into Germany since the 1960s reveals similar processes under utterly different historical conditions.[79]

While the majority of Poles were Prussian/German citizens, the Turks who came to work in the Ruhr pits in the 1960s were foreign citizens. They also set up their own independent ethnic football clubs. However, in this case it did not take long before Turkish clubs were (not without some conflict) integrated into German football leagues.[80] This was further underpinned when German policies vis-à-vis immigrants already living in the country started to change around the turn of the twenty-first century (while policies against new immigrants became stricter): diversity, equality before the law, and the possibility of naturalization were now promoted. At the same time, the German Football Association set up a talent-seeking programme aimed at youngsters, which attracted a huge proportion of players from migrant families.[81] Almost fifty years after the start of Turkish immigration, players with a Turkish background are now being selected in considerable numbers to play for German clubs and the German national team.

The interrelations of sport and migration in the history of the coalmining region of the Ruhr thus point to the basic ambivalence of sport in processes of social change: it can, on the one hand, act as a medium for setting up "we groups" and the development of ethnic, local, and regional identities; on the other hand, it can indeed help in the development of intercultural exchanges and bridges between social and ethnic groups.

78. See the article by Marion Fontaine in the present volume. For the dynamics of segregation and exclusion affecting Polish miners in the interwar period in northern France (which were induced to a high degree by both company and state policies), see the article by Philip Slaby in the present volume.

79. See Diethelm Blecking, "Polish Community before the First World War and Present-Day Turkish Community Formation – Some Thoughts on a Diachronistic Comparison", in John Belchem and Klaus Tenfelde (eds), *Irish and Polish Migration in Comparative Perspective* (Essen, 2003), pp. 183–197.

80. *Ibid.*, p. 197, and Blecking, *Polen-Türken-Sozialisten*, pp. 99–107.

81. See Diethelm Blecking, "'Ethnisch gemischte Teams funktionieren besser': Integration und Inklusion", available at http://www.bpb.de/gesellschaft/sport/bundesliga/155901/integration-und-inklusion?p=all; last accessed 15 July 2015.

Printed in the United States
by Baker & Taylor Publisher Services